D0957131

The Taste for Civilization

The Taste

Janet A. Flammang

for Civilization

Food, Politics, and Civil Society

YOLO COUNTY LIBRARY
226 BUCKEYE STREET
WOODLAND CA 95695

University of Illinois Press
Urbana and Chicago

© 2009 by the Board of Trustees
of the University of Illinois
All rights reserved
Manufactured in the United States of America
1 2 3 4 5 C P 5 4 3 2 1

∞ This book is printed on acid-free paper.

Library of Congress Cataloging-in-Publication Data
Flammang, Janet A.
The taste for civilization : food, politics, and civil society /
Janet A. Flammang.
    p.   cm.
Includes bibliographical references and index.
ISBN 978-0-252-03490-9 (cloth : alk. paper) —
ISBN 978-0-252-07673-2 (pbk. : alk. paper)
1. Food habits—United States—History.
2. United States—Social life and customs.
3. United States—Civilization.
4. Civil society—United States.
I. Title.
GT2853.U5F57   2009
394.1'20973—dc22   2009009428

For Lee Friedman

Contents

· ·

List of Illustrations

Acknowledgments

· ·

I am indebted to many people for their help and support. Santa Clara University provided sabbatical leaves enabling me to work on this project. I benefited enormously from the feedback of seminar students Shannon Allen, Mariana Barragan, Deanna Burcina, Maryanne Cafazza, Mary Chandler, Katie Garcia, Veronica Inocencio, Melissa Meek, Lindsay Myrback, Carla Vaccarezza, Maggie Wong, Lauren Wray, and Analisa Yenne. The expertise of Santa Clara University colleagues Eric Hanson, James Lai, Tim Lukes, Mike Meyer, Peter Minowitz, and Elizabeth Radcliffe helped at key junctures. Thanks to Diane Dreher for her support, and to Connie Cortez, Penelope Duckworth, Sandra Figueroa, and Nicole Sault for their helpful comments.

My gratitude to those at the book salon: Shirl Buss, Leslie Stone, Lauren Doliva, Sheryle Bolton, and Risa Nye. Laura Lawson was generous with her time and expertise. I am grateful to Alice Waters for the interview and the fascinating ideas of her delicious revolution. Lee Friedman and Glenna Matthews provided invaluable and extensive feedback and support, for which I am profoundly grateful.

Finally, my thanks to family, friends, colleagues, and editors at the University of Illinois Press for their support and encouragement.

The Taste for Civilization

Introduction

American women have historically been responsible for the civilizing functions of food—meal planning, table courtesy, the art of conversation, family
and group rituals—and in this capacity modeling the virtues of thoughtfulness and generosity. The rise of fast food and the decline of leisurely meals
mean fewer opportunities for everyday civility in speech and practice. Civil
society and democracy would benefit from a social change where foodwork,
conversation, and food rituals were seen as everyone's responsibility, and
from an economic change of a shorter workday to allow time for meals. This
book focuses on the importance of civility to American democracy and how
civility is related to everyday food practices, both at the table and in the wider
arenas of public gardens and markets.

In recent years, political writers have focused increased attention on the
study of civil society. This book makes an original contribution by examin-
ing in detail how food, meals, rituals, and sociability are integral building
blocks of civil society, and how this has been forgotten and ignored because
of the devalued nature of food and foodwork. The concept of civility remains
implicit and underdeveloped in most writings about civil society in America.
Here it will be made explicit and tied to the civic virtues of thoughtfulness and
generosity practiced in everyday life in foodwork and mealtime conversations
and rituals. Democratic speech and behavior can be practiced at the table,
and as we spend less time in common meals, we are losing an opportunity
to learn and teach the art of conversation so essential for civil society and
democratic practice.

How can we find time for food rituals in America's fast-paced, consumer,
workaholic culture? Compete with the screen culture? Resuscitate the dying
art of conversation? If foodwork and table conversation are be seen as everyone's responsibility and as integral to civil society and democracy, we need to
confront major obstacles: the unconscious association of food with women;

the mind-body dualism that privileges transcending the body, women, and foodwork; and the devaluation of taste in the hierarchy of senses. This book was inspired by Alice Waters's delicious revolution, which links a sensual approach to food with food's transformative power, not only at the table but also in forging civic ties at farmers' markets and at neighborhood, school, and jail gardens. Food and meals can give people something to talk about across ethnic, race, and class lines. This book calls for an expanded understanding of civil society and democracy by shedding light on the civility that has heretofore been confined to the shadows of women's domestic work with no public ramifications.

Civility, Civil Society, and Democracy

Most Americans think about democracy in terms of electoral politics, lawmaking, and civil rights and liberties. But these aspects of democracy rest on a foundation of civil society. Civil society is a hotly contested concept that has been dubbed *the* big idea for the twenty-first century, figuring prominently in the politics and concerns of disparate groups. Around the world, it has been a rallying call for prodemocracy advocates in former Soviet republics and in Latin America. In the United States, civil society is important for libertarians who want to reduce the scale of the federal government; for communitarians who want stronger family, neighborhood, and religious associations; and for civic-minded pundits and scholars troubled by a disengaged citizenry.[1]

These disparate groups share a common assumption that civil society is a realm of human association separate from the state and the market. Contemporary interest in civil society is in part a corrective to an exaggerated emphasis on the state and the market as optimal forms of human association. Across the globe, the state-based model loomed large between 1945 and the mid-1970s, with capitalist welfare states and socialist centralized planning. Then from the mid-1970s until the early 1990s, the market was ascendant with Reaganomics and Thatcherism, codified in Margaret Thatcher's famous dicta: "There is no alternative to the market" and "There is no such thing as society." The 1990s saw renewed interest in the relationship between the state, the economy, and civil society. Civil society is a complex puzzle, but it has three essential components: associational life, the good society, and the public sphere.[2] Writers differ in the respective weights they give to these three elements. But a common thread is the notion of civility. Civil society is not just society—it is civil.

Political writers—both empiricists and theorists—have danced around the concept of civility rather than embrace it. This is in part because they have focused on the state and the economy, and in part because of the historical baggage of civility as quaint, old-fashioned, and stifling. Michael Walzer observes that political theorists have been so focused on the state and the economy that they "have not thought enough about solidarity and trust nor planned for their future" and "have neglected the networks through which civility is produced and reproduced." He correctly points out that "most men and women have been trapped in one or another subordinate relationship, where the 'civility' they learned was deferential rather than independent and active." So it is important to reconstruct the dense associational life of civil society and its attendant norms of civility under new conditions of freedom and equality.[3]

Civility in a democracy is not the superficial glossing over of differences. Indeed, it is a virtue that is called into play precisely *when* there are differences, especially among strangers. In Stephen Carter's view, civility is "a virtue that equips us for everyday life with strangers, our daily democratic train ride with people we do not like or do not even know." It entails a generosity of spirit that assumes the best, not the worst, of the stranger. "Civility has two parts: generosity, even when it is costly, and trust, even when there is risk."[4]

The adjectives *civil* and *civilizing* are frequently used to describe activities at the table: taking turns talking, listening attentively, learning from different age groups, eating no more than one's fair share, meeting the needs of the group, showing respect for different tastes, breaking bread with companions, celebrating birthdays and anniversaries, honoring religious and ethnic traditions, meeting for coffee or tea, entertaining friends at dinner, sharing weekly meals with an extended family, experimenting with unfamiliar cuisines, and addressing differences with diplomacy. In spite of these daily experiences with the civil and the civilizing, and the universal value placed on diplomacy, table activities are usually invisible in both philosophical and empirical studies of civil society. Table activities should receive more attention in contemporary understandings of civil society insofar as they provide opportunities to practice the art of conversation and the virtues of thoughtfulness and generosity.

Political Theory: Where's the Household in Civil Society?

Most political theorists have neglected table activities because of their association with the household, a domain typically excluded from civil society. Indeed, it is the household's nonvoluntary and parochial relations that citizens

White House Dinner. Around the world, government officials value diplomatic speech at the table. Citizens need to practice addressing differences with diplomacy at the table. President George Bush sits with Vice President Dick Cheney and Secretary of State Condoleezza Rice as they host a working dinner with Afghan president Hamid Karzai (left) and Pakistani president Pervez Musharraf (right) at the White House in 2006. The meal was billed as an *iftar,* a meal that breaks the daytime fast during the Muslim holy month of Ramadan. Associated Press Photo/The White House, Eric Draper.

must jettison to form the voluntary and general-good associations of civil society. In his *Politics,* Aristotle divided the associational world into two: the domestic community (*oikos*) and the political community (*koinonia politike* or *polis*). To the ancient Romans, *civis* meant citizen, *civitas* referred to sovereign political units, and civil was distinguished from military. In medieval times civil was contrasted with ecclesiastical. By the late Middle Ages, *civil* referred to the association of citizens in distinction from the institutions of household, government, military, and church. *Civil* also became associated with *civilization,* the acquisition of manners and habits of civil persons. Its antonym was *barbarous* (i.e., foreign), whose Greek root meant "stammering," unable to speak our language. *Civil* acquired its dual usage: it applies to the status of citizen or civil society and to the manners of the civilized.[5] In spite of this dual usage in everyday life, political theorists have paid more attention to citizenship than they have to the manners and habits of civil persons.

The term *civil society* entered Western political discourse in the fifteenth century, when Leonardo Bruni, a Florentine civic humanist, used *societas civilis* to translate Aristotle's *koinonia politike*. Florentines at that time were hearkening back to the Roman Republic and the Athenian *polis* as models for the small, self-governing republics of Renaissance Europe. In the seventeenth century, social-contract theorists began to carve out new territory for civil society to reflect a new social order. The town's independence from the legal scrutiny of the manorial lord was the precondition for a public realm of equal members. As formerly household economic activities moved into town life, civil society became a commercial realm. Rousseau's entry on "Political Economy" in Diderot's *Encyclopedia* contrasted civil or political society with the household. In the *Second Treatise,* Locke said it was possible to dissolve government while leaving civil society intact. Civil society was synonymous with political society. In his 1821 *Philosophy of Right,* Hegel replaced the Aristotelian dichotomy of household and polity with the trichotomy of family, civil society, and the political state. Civil society denoted the sphere of market exchanges and the legal and social frameworks that sustained them. Karl Marx regarded civil society as a vehicle for furthering the economic interests of the capitalist class, removing its moral and pedagogical meaning as preparation for citizenship.[6]

Some political theorists have advanced conceptions of civil society that included aspects amenable to incorporating table activities and their attendant conversation, thoughtfulness, and generosity. Eighteenth-century Scottish Enlightenment theorists of moral sentiments characterized civil society as a realm of social mutuality. In his *Theory of Moral Sentiments,* Adam Smith presumed "natural affections and sociability," and Adam Ferguson's *Essay on the History of Civil Society* posited shared mutuality and trust between citizens, who acted in society "from affections of kindness and friendship." These theorists underscored the social and ethical nature of civil society and the importance of mutuality and recognition.[7]

In *Democracy in America,* Alexis de Tocqueville made a distinction between political society (relations between federal and state governments and between citizens and the state[s]) and civil society (relations of the citizens among themselves). "Political associations" were formed in part to oppose actions of the state and to preserve the independence of the citizens. "Civil associations" addressed the needs of "daily life," aimed at the preservation of civilization itself. Without such associations, citizens in a democracy would descend into "barbarism." Tocqueville expanded civil society to include associations that were not necessarily voluntary, that addressed the needs of daily life, and that were civilized.[8]

Philosophical pragmatists expanded the way we think about civil society by emphasizing political learning by doing, and in the case of John Dewey, learning through everyday food activities. Dewey saw civil society as a realm of shared political life and public improvement through debate, discussion, and persuasion. Face-to-face interactions in the family and the neighborhood were "the means by which dispositions [were] stably formed and ideas acquired which laid hold on the roots of character." The "winged words of conversation in immediate intercourse have a vital import lacking in the fixed and frozen words of written speech. . . . Vision is a spectator; hearing is a participator."[9] Dewey has been described as the philosophical tradition's only stomach-friendly thinker. In acknowledgment of humans' food-dependent condition, he established an experimental school in which the stomach took a central place. One of his obsessions was cooking.[10]

Jürgen Habermas sees in civil society both the Marxist notion of class domination and the liberal protection of individual autonomy through communicative actions and structures. Habermas has underscored the centrality of conversation to civic life, and he praises coffeehouses for the free discussions they encouraged. He and other theorists in the deliberative democracy school have elucidated a "talk-centric" democratic theory.[11]

The concept of civil society has been used by political dissidents around the world to connote a desirable social order, characterized by tolerance, nondiscrimination, nonviolence, trust and cooperation, freedom and democracy, so long as these qualities are not defined exclusively in Western terms. Examples are Poland's Solidarity, post-Franco Spain, and opposition movements in Kenya and Zambia.[12] In Latin America, dissidents' focus on civil society has reflected both a struggle against military dictatorships and a conviction that conventional political parties have failed.[13] In many repressive regimes, civil society consists of underground meetings over coffee or tea or at meals in private homes.

Social-capital theorists Pierre Bourdieu, James Coleman, and Robert Putnam have added to our understanding of civil society the importance of resources derived from durable group networks or memberships. Bourdieu emphasizes unequal access to these resources. Coleman focuses on an instrumental investment in social capital. And Putnam is interested in how trust and norms of reciprocity enhance capacity for civic engagement. According to this understanding, "bonding" social capital is within the group, while "bridging" links to outside groups.[14]

Some political theorists have included the household in civil society. Antonio Gramsci agreed with Marx that civil society was the arena of cultural and ideological hegemony, but he thought that it could also be a locus of rebellion. The family was included in civil society because it shaped the political views of citizens.[15] Michael Edwards agrees with Gramsci that we must include family life in our understanding of civil society because it plays a major role in building a society that is civil by influencing "both social norms and the political settlements that translate them into public policy." Edwards concurs with Stephen Carter that families are or should be the first civil societies, marked by sacrifice and caring for others.[16]

Jodi Dean argues that feminist theorists have been "oddly silent" on the subject of civil society.[17] In part this silence has been due to historical depictions of civil society as an arena where women were absent: "civil" was typically contrasted with "natural" (the state of nature for contract theorists) or "familial" (domestic households for most theorists). An important exception is Carole Pateman, who describes social-contract theorists' account of the origins of civil society as a story of "masculine political birth."[18] She includes the family in civil society: "The sphere of domestic life is at the heart of civil society rather than apart or separate from it. A widespread conviction that this is so is revealed by contemporary concern about the crisis, the decline, the disintegration of the nuclear family that is seen as the bulwark of civilized moral life."[19] Anne Phillips notes that while civil society has historically been "gender loaded" as masculine, to the extent that the term has come to mean intermediate associations between the individual and the state, women could be said to have an edge. Historically denied top government posts, women have practiced their politics disproportionately in voluntary and neighborhood associations.[20]

Most communitarians see the family as foundational to civil society. For example, Jean Bethke Elshtain defines civil society as "the many forms of community and association that dot the landscape of democratic culture, from families to churches to neighborhood groups to trade unions to self-help movements to voluntary assistance to the needy."[21] Alan Wolfe contends that the contemporary Left and Right rely on the state and the market to "organize their codes of moral obligation, but what they really need is civil society—families, communities, friendship networks, solidaristic workplace ties, voluntarism, spontaneous groups and movements—not to reject, but to complete the project of modernity."[22]

Empirical Studies: It's Hard to Measure the Table

If many theorists have neglected table activities because of their association with households and families, many empiricists have avoided them because they are so difficult to measure. Most empirical studies shedding light on civil society fall under the rubrics of social capital and civic engagement.[23] These studies typically focus on participation in voluntary groups and employ either survey research methodology, historical accounts of voluntary group membership, or some combination of these methods. But none of them looks at table activities. Some historical accounts of American civic life emphasize citizenship, but not the manners and habits of civil persons.[24] While the historical method lends itself to an understanding of table activities, only a few authors have linked table activities to civil society. For example, Markman Ellis's cultural history of the coffeehouse traces its association with conviviality, sociability, politeness, public opinion, and conversation.[25] More commonly, historians have studied the history of manners in general in Europe and in the United States.[26] A few political scientists, sociologists, and linguists have studied table activities, conversation, and politics. All of them have used qualitative research methods such as discourse analysis, participant observation, and personal interviews.

Political scientist Lyn Kathlene has studied legislative tables and floors. She found significant gender differences in the conversational dynamics of legislative committee hearings in a state legislature. Women chairs spoke less, took fewer turns, and interrupted less frequently. Men used their positions to control hearings, women to facilitate discussion among committee members, sponsors, and witnesses. Male witnesses interrupted female chairs, and female witnesses opposed to a bill had significantly less opportunity to participate compared to male witnesses. Female committee members waited longer before speaking in hearings, spoke less, and were interrupted more frequently.[27] When women sat next to each other and/or could see each other by sitting at a V-shaped table, they participated more actively in the committee hearings.[28]

Linguist Deborah Tannen's analysis of a dinner conversation led her to conclude that interruptions were not necessarily displays of dominance. Some cultural groups used a "high involvement style" with "cooperative overlap": a listener talks along with a speaker not to interrupt but to show enthusiastic listening and participation. This style could be off-putting to speakers who used a "high considerateness" style. This insight made her reluctant to embrace the notion that men dominate women by interrupting them. Tannen described her hermeneutic (interpretive) methodological approach as anthropologically oriented, involving a close examination of individual cases of interaction, in many of which she was a participant, and a consideration of cultural context.[29]

Dinner conversations of thirty-four families were analyzed by linguist Shoshana Blum-Kulka. She was particularly interested in politeness and power in dinner talk and the pragmatic aspects of language use. To become competent conversationalists, children had to learn how to choose and introduce topics for talk, respond appropriately, tell a story, or develop an argument. Cultural variations in providing opportunities for children to participate in dinner talk, and in monitoring their participation, resulted in differential access to adult discourse, reflected variation in perceptions of the relations between power and language, and resulted in different socialization agendas for children.[30]

Sociologist Marjorie L. DeVault conducted interviews in thirty households to understand women's invisible work caring for and feeding their families, including the "interaction work" that women do in conversations. Talk was considered an important part of family meals, and people had to work at it. In all households, children's behavior was monitored and controlled. Many parents were frustrated that they could not arrange for the kind of family meals that they remembered from their childhood, where there were real discussions. The table was also the locus of pleasure and sociability: interviewees looked forward to having people over and a pleasant dinner conversation.[31]

Group conversations in people's homes were studied by sociologist William A. Gamson to determine how people made meaning and developed a political consciousness. Participants used a combination of the media, experiential knowledge, and popular wisdom to understand political issues. Their "legendary conversational style" blended facts and interpretation. The "cynical chic" capitalized on their own ignorance and powerlessness. Gamson saw his book as an antidote to the conventional wisdom that most political issues and events do not make much sense to most working people. He was struck by the deliberative quality of his subjects' construction of meaning about complex issues and the considerable coherence of their views. People were quite capable of conducting informed and well-reasoned discussions about issues. Although most interviewees were not inclined to become politically active, the seeds of political action were present in the minds of many of them—a latent political consciousness that could be activated in the continual creation of social movements.[32]

Sociologist Nina Eliasoph used participant observation of several groups to study how citizens created contexts for political conversation in everyday life. She observed that many people had curious and open-minded private conversations but avoided political talk in wider circles. A cycle of "political evaporation" set in when citizens assumed that talking politics in a publicly minded way was out of place. The further backstage the context, the more public-spirited conversation was possible. People thought that in public they had to couch their motivations in a politics of self-interest, even though this was not necessarily true, as in the case of volunteers. Many women felt that they had to speak "for the children," engage in mandatory "public Momism," and wax nostalgic about community. The silencing of public-spirited conversations was the volunteers' way of looking out for the public good: they did not want to ruin positive feelings or alienate the common person. Each group created and enforced rules for political conversations, political manners, and etiquette. "Cultures of talk" told citizens when they needed to hide their fears and when talking helped work through fears. The democratic norms that really mattered were the unspoken norms for conversation—manners, civility, and tact—that made citizens comfortable engaging in freewheeling political conversation in an everyday-life context. Political etiquette or a sense of civility referred to citizens' companionable ways of creating and maintaining a comfortable context for talk in the public sphere.[33]

In a similar study, political scientist Katherine Cramer Walsh conducted participant observation of two groups: elderly, middle-class white men at a corner store and women in a church craft guild. The women evaded political topics for fear of disrupting the air of politeness. The men were much more likely to talk politics for several reasons: they had more shared experiences and acquaintances, interacted daily as opposed to weekly, met for social rather than instrumental purposes, and convened in the same room as "others" (blacks, women, and youth), enforcing a group solidarity of "us" versus "them." Conversation was the unit of analysis to determine how groups developed a collective perspective based on group identification, and how groups made sense of politics using their shared perspective. Walsh found that elite frames did matter, but through conversations people transformed and circumvented these frames by applying their identity-based perspectives to supplement news stories. Socially rooted perspectives were often more important than partisanship. She said that her approach showed the limits of both liberal individualism and civic republicanism. People relied on social attachments and did not act on behalf of a predetermined public good. Ideas about the common good were worked out in interaction. Public discussion was consequential for citizen action insofar as it fostered trust, clarified social identities, and reinforced exclusion of nonmembers. Walsh concluded that more interaction by itself was not the answer to a decline in civic life. Since there were tradeoffs between community and exclusion, she advocated community-wide intergroup dialogue programs.[34]

The Art of Conversation and the Civic Virtues of Thoughtfulness and Generosity

Some empiricists implicitly recognize the importance of household and table activities for civil society. Theda Skocpol recommends revitalizing American civic democracy "by mixing politics and civic activity with family life and socializing."[35] Robert Putnam has noted with concern that Americans are spending much less time breaking bread with family and friends than they did some twenty or thirty years ago. He observes that with fast-food outlets replacing conventional eating places, there are fewer conversational opportunities, but adds that this trend has to some extent been offset by the proliferation of coffee bars.[36]

Theorists have continued to grapple with the chicken-egg relationship between norms of reciprocity and trust, on the one side, and civil society, on the other. Some wonder whether voluntary associations are really so important for civil society since they account for only a few hours a week or month for a small minority of citizens. Perhaps family, school, and work have stronger effects on civil society because people spend so much more time in those settings.[37]

Wherever one draws the definitional line for civil society, table activities can be beneficial for it. They can help to form both bonding and bridging social capital. Family tables typically bring together intimates, kin, and friends. But other tables are bridges to the unfamiliar, to the strangers for whom a minimal comfort level is required for society to be civil: tables in school and workplace cafeterias, in coffeehouses, and at religious celebrations, weddings, holiday parties, picnics in the park, summer camps, and senior centers. Table activities foster the art of conversation. When people gather together for food and drink, it is customary to talk in such a way that a reservoir of goodwill is replenished, to be drawn down in times of tension and conflict. A case in point was the dry reservoir in the U.S. House of Representatives after the 1994 Republican Revolution. Congressional correspondent Juliet Eilperin attributes a decline in civility to Speaker Newt Gingrich's strategy of encouraging newly elected representatives not to move their families to

Boys at Camp Table. Tables are bridges to the unfamiliar, to the strangers for whom a minimum comfort level is required for a society to be civil. Gordon Parks took this picture of interracial activities at Camp Nathan Hale in Southfields, New York, in 1943. Campers became more acquainted around the dinner table. Library of Congress, Prints and Photographs Division, FSA-OWI Collection (LC-USW3-036802-D).

Washington. Members returned to their home districts on weekends rather than continuing past practices of dining with members of the other political party after hours. This contributed to partisan gridlock: it had been easier for representatives to compromise when they had reservoirs of goodwill replenished at dinner parties.[38]

Thoughtfulness and generosity—toward intimates, strangers, and adversaries—are two virtues given high priority during table activities. It is good to think about the food and beverage preferences of the group, about fair shares, about the common good. Selfish and rude behavior is frowned upon and makes for unpleasantness and indigestion. Conflict cannot be avoided at the table, anymore than it can be avoided in partisan politics. Critics of civility mischaracterize it as the avoidance of conflict. To the contrary, civility is necessary precisely *because* there is conflict—an expected difference between one's wants, needs, desires, impulses, views, and those of others. Civility is not needed when one is by oneself.

As classicist Margaret Visser reminds us, the words *civilized* and *civil* come from the Latin *civis,* which means a dweller in cities. Civil people are found where many people live, in an urban environment, where they become urbane. Unlike homogeneous villagers, in order to prosper city-dwellers need to learn how to deal with people from varied backgrounds: merchants, traders, travelers, borrowers and lenders, employers and employees. Civil behavior is polite: a ritual performed to please and reassure other people, especially where a rough or conflictual time is possible. Roughness needs to be smoothed by rubbing up against one another, becoming polished, to become better able to handle other people. *Polished* derives from the French *poli.* Both *politeness* and *politics* come from the Greek word for a city (*polis*). We are not naturally polite—we teach and learn the rules that grease the wheels of civilizations. Of course, if these rules become overbearing, they can stifle genuine interaction between people. "Politeness forces us to pause, to take extra time, to behave in preset, pre-structured ways, to 'fall in' with society's expectations. It is therefore the object of education. . . . But nothing about being polite is simple: the 'polish' intended to help people interact with one another can be used to prevent real contact from occurring at all. It can also become itself a barrier, keeping the 'unpolished' beyond the pale."[39]

The dynamics of civilized behavior in cities are the same as those at the table: polishing roughness, performing reassuring rituals, teaching and learning rules of proper behavior, and pausing to take the time to behave in preset ways. When they are not overbearing, civil rules and table manners create conditions for conversation, the respectful, mutual sharing of thoughts for a whole host of reasons: political, economic, social, cultural, religious, familial, and interpersonal. Learning the art of conversation at the table is good practice for the interchange of ideas in other realms.

It is one thing to be trusting and forthcoming at a table with family and friends, but how transferable is this practice to other realms? How can meaningful conversations possibly be expected to occur among strangers or self-interested political adversaries? Politics, after all, is the terrain of intrigue, deception, smooth talking, lies, self-interest, and expedient deals, to say nothing of fights to the death. In talking about politics, isn't a focus on conversation naive and overly reliant on reason to temper strong feelings? And wouldn't a conversation be distorted by whoever had the most dazzling verbal skills, leaving the less verbally aggressive party out in the cold?

The centrality of civil and persuasive speech to politics was noted centuries ago, most famously in Aristotle's *Rhetoric.* Aristotle argued that the politics of persuasion required a certain amount of dissimulation on the part of all speakers. The more one tread farther afield of trusted family and friends, the more one expected less than full candor in conversations. Persuasive and civil speech was also important in the American colonies. At the time of the Revolution, the voting qualifications in the colony of Connecticut included—in addition to being male, aged twenty-one, and a property owner—the ability to be civil in conversation.[40]

Conversations require courtesy, a respect and willingness to consider things from another conversant's position. Table manners are one form of courtesy; they are the conventions that make conversation possible. Courtesy predates liberal democracy's emphasis on freedom and equality. Courtesy, like persuasive speech, involves some holding back of what one really wants to do and say, for a larger common purpose: an enjoyable meal or a good law. Being less than forthcoming is justified for larger purposes. Thinking of a circumspect, if not entirely candid, answer to a host's question about the quality of a dish served at a dinner party is the same skill as crafting a respectful, if opposing, response to a legislative colleague.

In both cases, reason is not relied on in place of, or in opposition to, strong feelings or self-interest; rather, reason is used to deliberate about alternative courses of action, in settings with emotional import (hosts wanting to please guests) and strongly held views (political opponents having major differences of opinion). Civil relations create reservoirs of goodwill that can help people get through rough patches. Democratic human associations cannot last long without such reservoirs, given the inevitability of conflict, cruelty, and cycles of hard times.

Conversations do run the risk of leaving less verbally skilled conversants stranded. However, true conversations are democratic insofar as conversants are tuned into differences in extroversion, sophistication of vocabularies, self-confidence, and the like, and make adjustments accordingly. What better place to take such differences into account than the temporary democracy of the table, where people have the motivation and the time to hone these skills and develop this art.

Meals, Conversations, and Women

The civilizing relationships of the table have been out of the purview of most political studies because women have been in charge of them. They are presumably what women naturally do—take care of others and feed them. They are outside the bounds of the so-called real politics of waging war, nation-building, governmental decision making, interest-group lobbying, and voting. They are private, not public—peripheral to politics. The argument here is that they are constitutive of politics.

To talk about women and the politics of food in this way sounds both old and new. The traditional view of women's "proper place" puts them in the kitchen, pleasing others, and taking orders from a breadwinning husband. In this scenario, generosity and thoughtfulness mean that women should give to others and downplay their own needs. If we want more civility, women should stay home and cook and raise children. Men will do battle in the cruel, competitive world of the marketplace and seek comfort in the civilized home front. My argument is not a "proper place" argument. It is a call to redefine generosity and thoughtfulness based on democracy in the household. My argument sounds new relative to a feminist claim that women should get out of the kitchen and into the workforce. Of course, this claim has been primarily espoused by white, middle- and professional-class women who do not necessarily question the corporate fast-food and convenience-food industries and who can afford to pay others to prepare their food. Most employed women face the double duty of work for pay and responsibility for food preparation. Generosity and thoughtfulness have to be recast in terms of equitable contemporary household responsibilities.

Significant social and political costs have resulted from fast food and convenience foods, grazing and snacking instead of sitting down for leisurely meals, watching television during mealtimes instead of conversing, viewing food as fuel rather than sustenance, discarding family recipes and foodways, and denying that eating has social and political dimensions. We must be honest about these costs and devise alternatives that neither confine women to the kitchen nor pretend that the quality of our lives is improved when no one is in it.

At first glance, it may seem odd that a scholar of the U.S. women's movement is issuing a call about the importance of meals and food, since many second-wave feminists urged women to get out of the kitchen and into the workplace. Financial independence was the ticket to liberation. There were only so many hours in the day, and the less time spent on food the better. Meals were something to get out of the way, to fuel the body for the workforce, to be purchased and consumed—the faster the better. American women are having second thoughts. And whenever women question their lives, feminist scholars take note. Feminist rumblings always begin with the politics of everyday life. Feminists take women's experiences seriously and see the political ramifications of personal relationships. There are four reasons why women's experiences are at the center of concerns about food, meals, conversation, civility, community, and democracy.

First, many women feel ground between the gears of workplace and family demands on their time. Compared to their husbands, working wives put in more hours a week around the house, get less sleep, and feel run down. Even with convenience foods and reasonably priced restaurants, women need help. Most women work one shift at the workplace and a second shift in their households. Studies show that women do most of the foodwork, the often-invisible tasks of accommodating other people's food and dietary preferences, securing provisions, looking for bargains, monitoring table behavior, and juggling schedules. Since the 1970s, with their increased labor force participation, women have had less time to devote to meal preparation, the rituals of eating, festive foods, table conversation, and food sharing.

Second, women are still expected to promote the art of conversation at the table. They are the creators and keepers of mealtime rules, stories, and conventions. They encourage direct, interpersonal interactions as an important corrective to the "screen culture" of visual and auditory stimuli on television and computer screens.

Third, food is still psychodynamically and philosophically associated with women. Hunger is terrifying, and the first food is mother's milk. We cannot get everyone to do foodwork as long as it is "what women do." Household food memories are associated with women. Philosophically, we cannot advance our thinking about the centrality of food to civility until we challenge the mind-body dualism that still permeates conventional wisdom about women and food. Eating by its very nature is a simultaneous mind-body experience. We had better know about food's origins and plan carefully in its preparation, or it can kill us. Hunger is a frightening experience, so we had better do our best to plan to sate it. Food is apprehended through the senses of touch, smell, and taste, which rank lower on the hierarchy of senses than sight and hearing, which are typically thought to give rise to knowledge. In much of philosophy, religion, and literature, food is associated with body, animal, female, and appetite—things civilized men have sought to overcome with reason and knowledge.

Fourth, community and ethnic food traditions remain women's responsibility. Immigrant women's foodways forge group identity in the ongoing process of "becoming American." Food is a source of group pride, and "food travel" to a new cuisine is a way to break down barriers of race, ethnicity, and class. Americans connect with others through food at community rituals, ceremonies, and festivities. And women have been instrumental in promoting community gardens and school gardens.

One goal of this book is to draw attention to the social and political costs of the erosion of the civilizing aspects of food and meal rituals, since women have less time and energy to attend to them. A second aim is to make the case that foodwork needs to be redefined as everyone's responsibility. To this end, three major barriers need to be overcome: finding the time for food rituals in America's fast-paced, consumer, workaholic culture; competing with the screen culture; and resuscitating the dying art of conversation.

What Changes Are Needed?

With workplace and family scheduling demands, it is a challenge to arrange for common mealtimes with family and friends. Between the mid-1970s and the late 1990s, the proportion of married Americans who said that their family usually ate dinner together dropped by one-third: from about 50 to 34 percent. There was a 45 percent decline in social visiting: both going out to see friends and having them over to one's home. The number of picnics per capita plummeted nearly 60 percent.[41]

It is very difficult to take time for food in America's fast-paced culture, where people are tethered to cell phones and e-mail 24/7. Food is a commodity and fuel—not a source of pleasure and community. However, there is growing interest in the Slow Food movement, and in the wake of the September 11 attacks, many Americans vowed to spend more time with family and loved ones and to be less obsessed with work. Americans are rethinking the meanings of work, time, and caretaking in household foodwork.

Since the 1970s, America's rigid workplace norms have become more flexible to accommodate pregnancies, parental responsibilities, disabilities, eldercare, and the like; they can also bend for foodwork and food enjoyment. It is possible to be a prosperous, advanced industrial economy and still make time for meals and leisure. Europeans have the shortest workweeks and the longest holidays in the world. They value leisure, and less income, over working longer hours to acquire more material goods.[42] Until Americans' workplaces become more accommodating, they will have to reexamine how they spend their leisure hours in order to open up time for meals and conversations.

There is also growing popular fascination with the social and political importance of food. People buy more cookbooks than they can possibly use, whether for the assurance of comfort food, the nostalgia of home-cooked meals, or the adventure of learning about other cultures through their cuisines. Corporations sponsor cooking classes for their employees as team-building exercises. In many metropolitan newspapers, food sections have eclipsed society pages. The Slow Food movement is gathering momentum. Farmers markets, along with community, school, and jail gardens, are springing up all across the country. Meanwhile, farmers have dwindled to less than

2 percent of the American workforce. More is involved than nostalgia for a lost way of life or the idealization of childhood meals. Many Americans are beginning to realize that food choices have environmental, political, economic, social, and cultural consequences. But today there is little time for the joys and pleasures of the table: sparkling conversation, spontaneous sharing, sensual enjoyment, and hilarious banter. Conversation is becoming a dying art as the screen culture wins out over face-to-face encounters.

It is hard to pull oneself away from the privatizing and narcotizing screens of the television and the computer. Television is popular with stressed workers, who understandably want to relax after a hard day. It is a low-concentration activity. But it has its costs. As Robert Putnam observes, television competes for scarce time, has psychological effects that inhibit social participation, and contains programmatic content that undermines civic motivations. Average daily household viewing rose from about four and one-half hours a day in 1950 to over seven hours in 1998. Television is the only leisure activity that seems to inhibit participation in other leisure activities. Putnam writes that TV watching comes at the expense of "nearly every social activity outside the home, especially social gatherings and informal conversations." Studies show that it is habit-forming, mildly addictive, encourages lethargy and passivity, and leads to reduced contacts with relatives, friends, and neighbors. The more time viewers spend watching soap operas, game shows, and talk shows, the less active they are in the community.[43]

Computer-mediated communication has its advantages. Research cited by Putnam shows that online discussions tend to be more frank and egalitarian than face-to-face meetings. In the workplace, "computer-mediated communication is less hierarchical, more participatory, more candid, and less biased by status differences. Women, for example, are less likely to be interrupted in cyberspace discussions." Participants in computer-based groups often come up with a wider range of alternatives and a quicker intellectual understanding of their shared problems. On the down side, they find it harder to reach a consensus and generate the trust and reciprocity necessary to implement that understanding. Putnam notes that "experiments that compare face-to-face and computer-mediated communication confirm that the richer the medium of communication, the more sociable, personal, trusting, and friendly the encounter." Face-to-face conversations allow for deeper relationships than cyberspace's anonymity and fluidity. If the interpersonal going gets rough, it is easy to exit from cyberspace.[44]

American women are fighting an uphill battle against the screen culture to revitalize the dying art of conversation. Where better to hone conversational skills than in food preparation and sharing, where there is much to talk about that is pleasurable and has civic import. At the table, we connect with others—family, our cultural forebears, peers—in the making and sharing of food traditions and innovations. Meal preparation involves daily economic choices, whether to support fast-food chains, supermarkets, farmers' markets, organic producers, or new cuisines. And it involves social choices about who is responsible for foodwork, how to act at the table, and when to prepare festive and ceremonial foods. Food is a universal way to feel connected and civilized. It needs to become everyone's responsibility.

One way to degender foodwork would be to get everyone out of house-hold kitchens and reliant on fast-food restaurants, convenience food, home-delivered food, or communal cafeterias. Even though some feminist utopian writers imagined communities designed with communal eating facilities, for various reasons, this type of architecture has not taken hold in the United States, although it remains a logical possibility. Commercially produced food and home-delivered food are not realistic options for low-income households. Since most fast food is high fat and high salt, it is unethical to propose that low-income people (or anyone) live on such a diet. It is possible that middle- and upper-income households could learn the art of conversation and norms of civility over a table graced with commercially prepared and/or delivered food. Indeed, it could be argued that *more* time would be available to savor the meal leisurely without frantic meal preparation. What would be lost, of course, are the practical applications of thoughtfulness and generosity that accompany meal planning and preparation. And a class-based solution is not a satisfactory solution.

It would be preferable for everyone—men, women, and children—to go back to the kitchen, as in preindustrial days, and for the workplace to lessen its time demands on people. Many other countries have shorter workweeks and more vacation time than is the case in the United States. Over the last one hundred years, the U.S. labor movement has successfully fought to reduce the workday from twelve to ten to eight hours. In more recent years, employers have adopted flexible work schedules. As more women move into supervisory positions, they should continue with this reduction in work hours to enable all workers to spend more time preparing and sharing food.

There must also be a cultural shift in attitudes. Men and women would need to agree that women, too, deserve a nice meal at the end of a workday, and that it is a household responsibility to prepare it. Americans experienced such a seismic cultural shift once before: in the nineteenth century when men left the farms and went to work in the cities, and meal preparation became an exclusively female activity. Everyone would have to be convinced of the benefits of undergoing another change. Harried working women would probably lead this effort. They would most likely see the benefits of a rewarding family life and work life, if the demands of both could be kept to a level that was not superhuman. Children would no doubt prefer to see mothers who were less exhausted and haggard. Husbands would probably want to reduce the pressure on their wives. And the enjoyment of the pleasures of the table could also play a huge role in changing attitudes. To the extent that enjoyment at the table became more valued than additional consumer goods, people would be less motivated to work extra hours. Less income would be needed as people preferred time for food over one more "must have" gadget.

For democracy and civility to thrive, people need frequent, everyday occasions to share pleasures, fears, and opinions with others. The household table provides such a place. Children can learn about thoughtfulness and generosity, hear life stories from generations other than their own, and see how conflict can be managed without coming to blows. At the table, they can learn about their identity and what is expected of informed citizens. By becoming participants in meal preparation, they can learn that people have a responsibility to take the needs of others into account, without becoming martyrs to the needs of others. By pitching in to feed others, they can learn the importance of daily doses of gratitude for healthy social relations, and they can play an active role in creating a greater good, which is the goal of civil society and democratic politics.

The table activities that have been at the center of women's lives in the historical division of labor should now be at the center of all our lives to promote civility and democracy. In a time of widespread alienation from politics, Americans must look carefully for those places where we routinely come together for something important and pleasurable, where we put aside certain differences in order to share something in common with others, and where we afford one another the courtesy of a conversation—in short, where we practice being civil to one another. There is a connection between being cut off from food, meals, conversation, and the table, and being politically alienated, voiceless, and uncivil. Sharing a meal at a table is a temporary, yet frequent, locus of civilizing and democratic practice—people of various backgrounds and opinions agree to speak civilly to one another in order to enjoy the food. Heated arguments can wait, since the attack mode causes indigestion. People take turns, listen, and respond politely. The pleasures of the table include convivial talk about subjects worth discussing. The time has come to take a hard look at the social and political costs of America's fast-paced, convenience culture. It is important to encourage face-to-face conversations at the table, to understand why meal providers feel so pressed for time, and to examine realistic alternatives, especially in households with single parents or two breadwinners.

The following chapters elaborate on the arguments I have introduced here. To make the case for the importance of the civilizing aspects of food, meals, rituals, and sociability—integral building blocks of civil society—we will take a closer look at household foodwork, table conversations, Western philosophy, the delicious revolution of Alice Waters, and community food.

Part One

· ·

Household Foodwork

Chapter 1
. . . .
The Time Crunch

It is unrealistic to expect Americans to heed a call to spend *more* time preparing and sharing meals without acknowledging the time crunch that has threatened these civilizing activities. What exactly is "foodwork," who has time to do it, and why is it so important? What difference does it make that foodwork is gendered? What civilizing aspects of foodwork are being threatened? Household foodwork is a matter of both time and quality of life, especially as it relates to the virtues of obligation and gratitude and to groups' ongoing assimilation of becoming "American."

Household foodwork takes time and energy. Ever since the advent of industrialization, it has been "women's work," without much help from men and children. With women's increased labor-force participation, they have less time for meal planning and preparation. These activities are civilizing processes that household members need to perform. Household and family bonds are important for both children and adults. Meals are a common, frequent, safe, and pleasurable way to form the connections of civil society.

We owe it to food preparers to make their work more visible, rewarded, and universal. If foodwork continues to be regarded as invisible, unacknowledged, and female-only, then the quality of all our lives suffers. We lose out on daily civilizing dilemmas and practices. Household foodwork is loaded with a wide array of important questions relating to elitism, egalitarianism, class, race, kin, family, gender, ethnicity, identity, gratitude, and obligation. Someone answers some of these questions, consciously or subconsciously, every day in every household. Eat in or eat out? Traditional or "American" food? Elaborate or simple meal? Eat with others or alone? Eat what I want or what the group wants? Who needs to eat what at what time? Where do I procure the items? Should I try something new? What is a proper meal?

Who should pitch in? Who has the time and energy to do this work? Who should do this work?

Whether and how these questions are answered depends on who is in the household. In one-person households, fewer questions are asked, and the answers are easier in terms of daily obligations to others. The needs of others will not loom as large. In households with two or more people in them, more questions will be triggered and the answers will be more complicated. How do we divide tasks and whose food preferences and schedule will prevail? In family households, relatives depend on one another to provide meals. Gender-role expectations surface, along with gratification or resentment, depending on how much one wants to adjust the roles.

It takes "foodwork" to make a community, craft a civilization, and impart wisdom from one generation to another. We must find ways to make time for the foodwork and foodways that define who we are in relation to others in civil society.

Throughout American history, the amount of time spent on household food chores has varied dramatically. How foodwork is done explains a lot about the quality of civility, community, shared culture, and the cuisine that results. One constant feature is that it has been women's responsibility to put meals on the table. This has been the case in the households of Native Americans, colonists, slaves, slave owners, farmers, pioneers, newly arrived immigrants, migrant farm workers, urbanites, and suburbanites. However, in agrarian settings, men and children were more active participants in household food tasks than they were after industrialization.

Farm and City Foodwork

According to historian Ruth Schwartz Cowan, prior to industrialization in the United States, the word *housework* would probably have been nonsensical, since almost all people worked in or on the grounds of their house or someone else's house. In most nonplantation households before the Civil War, both males and females were bound to the house and shared in producing sustenance from it. The terms *housewife* and *husband,* which had entered the English language in the thirteenth century, referred to people whose work was focused on the house. The compound word *husband* derived from *hus,* the older spelling of our *house,* to which he was *bonded.* The status of husbands and housewives derived from home and land, the man because he had title to it, and the woman through marriage to him. Husbands and housewives formed the basis of the new middle class: they were neither aristocrats governing large households that sheltered dozens of people nor transient laborers residing under roofs that belonged to other people. They worked the land, hence the term *husbandry* for what we call *farming*. Economic security was achieved by working together and husbanding their resources. Industrialization separated home and housework from work and paid labor, and women's place from that of men, codified in the doctrine of separate spheres.[1]

In rural and preindustrial households, mothers had more assistance from husbands and children in providing and preparing food. Even though housework was socially defined as women's work, in reality the daily exigencies of agrarian life meant that relations between the sexes were reciprocal: women assisted men in the fields, and men helped women with household food-work. Husbands and children helped housewives with cooking and baking by chopping wood, shelling corn, pounding grain into meal, collecting coal, and making sausages. Most travelers' accounts of meals eaten by Americans in the eighteenth and nineteenth centuries mentioned the ubiquity of stews— meats and vegetables cooked for a long time in a liquid. Urbanization and industrialization ushered in greater choice of food products. Once industrialization introduced the cast-iron cooking stove, the automatic flour mill, and factory-produced food and clothing, housewives bore the entire burden of housework. For husbands and children, the house became a place of leisure. The kitchen became a place in which men had no useful role to play. With the advent of industrial gadgets and products came the expectation that fewer household members would pitch in and help mothers provide meals.[2]

So there is historical precedent for all members of a household to pitch in with foodwork. Indeed, it had been the norm until industrialization. It was not until the nineteenth century that most men replaced their household and farm work with wage labor; that children's household tasks (such as fetching water and coal) gradually disappeared with technological advances (such as indoor plumbing and electrical utilities); and that household chores fell increasingly on women, whose participation in the paid labor force remained lower than that of men.

Women's Labor-Force Participation and Overworked Americans

In the last half of the twentieth century, two developments had a dramatic effect on household time available to cook and share meals: mothers' entry into the paid workforce and an increase in female-headed households. Women's labor-force participation rate grew dramatically: from 30 to 55 percent. For married women with children between the ages six and seventeen, the rate grew from 28 to 68 percent; for those with children under six, from 12 to 62 percent. By century's end, half of women with children under the age of one worked outside the home, and two-thirds of all mothers were in the labor force. Both parents held jobs outside the home in 58 percent of all married couples with children. Women's increased labor-force participation was attributed to three factors. The first was an increase in the number of service jobs in the economy—clerical, sales, teaching, nursing, and the like—which were seen as appropriate for women. The second was a decline in family-wage, unionized, industrial jobs previously occupied by men with low levels of education, whose wives entered the workforce to supplement their husband's incomes. The third was the increasing number of women obtaining postsecondary education, which opened up new areas of interest and prepared them for professional jobs. In many households, women provided the sole income. Between 1970 and 2000, the percentage of families headed by women more than doubled (from about 10 percent to about 20 percent).[3]

Busy work schedules affected time for family meals. In the late 1980s, in single-earner families, only about two-thirds of mothers and about half of fathers had dinner with their children every night of the week, and only a third of households reported that both parents were always present for dinner. The comparable figures for dual-earner couples were about five percentage points lower. Only two in five single mothers were able to have dinner with their children every night. Family dinners were more common with younger children than with teenagers.[4] Nightly dinners with children were becoming the exception rather than the norm, opportunities for civilized conversations were evaporating, and mealtimes with adolescents were increasingly crowded out by other activities.

The last half of the twentieth century witnessed the rise of what economist Juliet Schor calls "the overworked American." She argues that employers have an incentive for workers to put in long hours, which will be the case absent countervailing pressure from labor unions and reformers for shorter work time. Longer work hours were the norm during the early years of the Industrial Revolution (as compared with previous work hours during the Middle Ages). In the late nineteenth and early twentieth centuries, union pressure eventually resulted in a reduction of the workday to eight hours. In the 1930s, the U.S. labor movement gave up on the shorter-hours movement, but European unions did not, and today European nations have shorter work hours than the United States does. Since 1948, the level of productivity of the U.S. worker has more than doubled. American workers have taken this "productivity dividend" in the form of income, not leisure time. They could have chosen the four-hour day or the six-month work year. Opting for income has meant that American workers own and consume more than twice what they did in 1948, but they have less free time. Compared to other industrial countries, Americans spend more hours shopping and spend a higher fraction of the money they earn, leading to an unprecedented level of material comfort. Americans' per-person annual income is sixty-five times that of half the world's population. On the other hand, the market for free time hardly exists. Employers do not offer the chance to exchange income gains for a shorter workday or the occasional sabbatical. Employees rarely have the chance to exercise an actual choice about how they will spend the productivity dividend. Consumers crowd increasingly expensive leisure spending into smaller periods of time. Schor urges Americans to break this work-and-spend cycle and to spend their productivity dividend on more leisure time instead of more goods.[5] If more Americans made this choice, there would be more time for leisurely meals and the spirited conversation of civil society and democracy.

Jerry Jacobs and Kathleen Gerson caution that not all Americans are overworked. Since 1970, variation around the average forty-hour week has increased, indicating the emergence of both longer and shorter workweeks for different groups of workers. We need to keep several "time divides" in mind. The "work-family" divide captures the fact that even though growing numbers of households rely on the income of two workers or single mothers, most jobs are based on the outmoded assumption that workers do not have household responsibilities. The growing bifurcation of the labor force has produced an "occupational divide" between jobs demanding excessively long hours (professional and managerial) and jobs that provide neither sufficient hours nor pay to meet workers' needs (contingent jobs with few benefits). There is an "aspirational divide" between the time people devote to their work and their ideal working time (one that provides a work-life balance). The "parenting divide" separates parents, who face the tightest time pressures, from other workers, who often resent the interrupted schedules and "special treatment policies" for parents. The "gender divide" leaves women paying the highest price, in terms of lower wages and responsibility for child rearing, in their attempt to reconcile family and work demands.[6]

If we are to address gender inequities in the time crunch, both the ideal worker norm and the marginalization of caregiving need to be rethought and restructured. Joan Williams notes that the ideal worker norm is male: someone who can work long, uninterrupted hours, travel frequently, and have access to a flow of family work. This norm discriminates against women, 90 percent of whom will be mothers during their work lives. Women's load of family work often interferes with their ability to perform as ideal workers. A majority of mothers remain economically marginalized: most do not work full time and roughly 80 percent work in low-paid, sex-segregated "women's work."[7]

Technology and Food Tasks

Employed women undeniably have less time to cook. But don't technological advances and convenience foods reduce the time needed to put meals on the table? There are mixed views on this subject. Historian Susan Strasser details activities made obsolete by new technologies: by 1870, most people could buy soap and candles; by 1920, they could afford to purchase most of their clothes; and by 1970, they could stop cooking. Today, most families do not get together for all their meals, and restaurants and supermarkets provide a wide range of options for buying food that somebody else has cooked. "Cooking remains the central ritual of housekeeping, but like the rest of the housekeeping routine, that ritual exists only in truncated form. The work itself, performed with gas and electric stoves, devices that do the chopping and mixing, and utensils requiring little care, bears little relation to the time-consuming, hazardous, heavy work of the colonial hearth."[8]

However, others caution that time lost on one side of the ledger is often offset by new time demands on the other. In her article in *Scientific American,* sociologist Joann Vanek notes that between the 1920s and the 1960s, time spent on food preparation decreased somewhat; however, additional time spent shopping more than made up for the decline.[9] Ruth Schwartz Cowan argues that with the advent of the automobile, women shifted from being receivers of purchased goods and services to time-consuming transporters to obtain them. During the nineteenth century, many goods and services were either delivered directly to households by peddlers, butchers, greengrocers, coffee merchants, tailors, seamstresses, and doctors, or they were a short walk away. Streets were lined with the pushcarts of vendors, knife sharpeners, and shoe repairers. Bakeries and grocery stores were nearby, so that housewives, children, and servants could run out for extra supplies whenever they were needed.[10]

Before the advent of the motor car, many transportation services were provided to the household by the husband or the servants, who hitched up the

Bread Peddlers. With the advent of the automobile, women shifted from being receivers of purchased goods and services to time-consuming transporters of them. During the nineteenth century, many goods were either delivered directly by peddlers, or they were a short walk away. Here Italian bread peddlers sell their wares on Mulberry Street in New York City around 1900. Library of Congress, Prints and Photographs Division, Detroit Publishing Company Collection (LC-D401-13585 DLC).

buggy and went into town for goods and services. As the years passed, suburbia spread, supermarkets replaced neighborhood mom-and-pop stores, and the advertising industry convinced consumers they needed a greater choice of goods; women drove cars to obtain services retailers had once offered and performed chores, such as picking up children at school, that had never existed before. The burden of providing transportation services shifted from the producer to the consumer; self-service was predicated on women's driving.[11]

Of course, other demographic factors have played a role in women's use of time in the household. There has been a dramatic increase in life expectancy and a reduced proportion of women's lives spent rearing young children—making investing in a career and going to college much more sensible, and helping to explain why women work so much more than men.

The Second Shift and the Globalization of Housework

As sociologist Arlie Hochschild observes in *The Second Shift,* there has been a "his" and "hers" history of workforce participation in the United States. When men entered the paid workforce, women, the workplace, and the culture adjusted fairly quickly. However, after fifty years of increasing numbers of female breadwinners, the revolution has stalled: neither men, nor the workplace, nor the culture has adjusted to this new reality. Major studies from the 1960s and 1970s of the time it took to do a paid job, housework, and child care showed that women worked roughly fifteen hours longer each week than men did. Most women without children spent much more time than men did on housework; with children, they devoted more time to both housework and child care. Just as there was a wage gap between men and women in the workplace, there was a leisure gap between them at home. Most women worked one shift at the office or factory and a second shift at home. Paid work was a mixed blessing. Studies showed that working mothers had higher self-esteem and were less depressed than housewives, but thanks to the second shift, working mothers were more tired and got sick more often than their husbands.[12]

A 1992 study found the same pattern: working mothers spent an average of nearly fifteen more hours doing housework and child care each week than their husbands did. Husbands married to working women did not do much more household work than husbands married to homemakers.[13] Women still did most of the cooking: only 15 percent of men married to working wives did most of the cooking, and 5 percent of men married to homemakers did. Among dual-income couples, 15 percent of men split the cooking fifty-fifty, as compared to 7 percent of men married to homemakers. Even when women contributed as much or more to family income, they still did most of the housework. Younger men did not take more responsibility than older men in cooking or shopping.[14]

The men appeared to be victorious in the "chore wars." Women's housework did decline from thirty hours a week in 1965 to seventeen and one-half hours in 1995. But they still performed about two-thirds of all household tasks; men did not pick up half the work. Barbara Ehrenreich laments that feminists no longer talked about the "politics of housework." The radical feminist demand for wages for housework had disappeared. Feminist sociologists she interviewed thought that housework had lost its former cachet. Ehrenreich suspects this was due in part to the fact that fewer sociologists—and other professionals—actually did it anymore. In the homes of the nation's opinion makers and culture producers, "the politics of housework is becoming a politics not only of gender but also of race and class, and these are subjects that the opinion-making elite, if not most Americans, generally prefer to avoid."[15]

Women from the poor countries of the south have migrated to do the "women's work" in northern countries that affluent women no longer perform. Ehrenreich and Hochschild note that a century ago, affluent women gained status through leisure; today they do so by "doing it all"—with thriving careers, children, marriages, and households. The invisible work of domestic workers and nannies is needed to preserve this illusion. The "care deficit" in prosperous economies (where women have increasingly taken on paid work) has created a demand for paid domestics and caretakers for children and the elderly. This demand has been met by a supply of women seeking to escape poverty and to gain greater personal autonomy. Migrant women do not always come from the poorest classes of their societies; they are often more affluent and better educated than male migrants. A woman may want to escape the "expectation that she care for elderly family members, relinquish her paycheck to a husband or father, or defer to an abusive husband." The "globalization of child care and housework brings the ambitious and independent women of the world together: the career-oriented upper-middle-class woman of an affluent nation and the striving woman from a crumbling Third World or postcommunist economy." This is hardly the sisterhood imagined by second-wave feminists: "mistress and maid, employer and employee, across a great divide of privilege and opportunity."[16]

Of course, most American women do not earn enough money to hire domestic workers, nor do they get much help from males in their households. Reports on household work are obtained by asking respondents to estimate the time they spend on specific tasks, such as cleaning, cooking, ironing, and taking care of children.[17] Another approach is to ask respondents to log their household activities in time diaries, and researchers then assign these activities to categories such as after-meal clean-up and marketing.[18] Even though such studies repeatedly find that women do more foodwork than men, women typically underestimate such differences.

Invisible Foodwork

Sociologist Marjorie L. DeVault calls attention to those social dynamics of meal preparation that are time consuming and invisible. Meal preparation cannot be reduced to discrete tasks of cooking. Meals are socially organized events that require "thoughtful foresight, simultaneous attention to several different aspects of the project, and a continuing openness to ongoing events and interaction." Studies limited to the performance of physical tasks miss "most of the planning and coordination involved in household work, as well as the constant juggling and strategizing behind the physical tasks."[19]

DeVault discovered this invisible foodwork in her interviews with women and men in thirty households in the Chicago area. Although meal-preparation time was bounded, strategizing for it extended throughout the day. As one woman said, "The antennas are always out." Or as explained by a mother of two-year-old twins: "As soon as I get up in the morning or before I go to bed, I'm thinking what we're going to eat tomorrow. Even though I know, but do I have this, and is this ready, and this ready?" DeVault argues that planning was largely mental work, spread over time and mixed with other activities: "Managing a meal looks like simply enjoying the companionship of one's family—and of course, is partly so—and learning about food prices can look like reading the newspaper. The work is noticeable when it is not completed (when the milk is all gone, for example, or when the meal is not ready on time), but cannot be seen when it is done well."[20]

DeVault found that none of the men who cooked did even half this coordinative work of planning; they did not share the work of feeding the family in a broader sense. The women planned; the men executed. The women referred to their husband's and children's preferences as the fixed points around which they designed the meals. One man thought that his culinary creativity was more than catering to the tastes of those he served. For another man, what was taken for granted for his wife was a planning burden for him. "We occasionally get some fresh vegetables, but we usually have frozen vegetables. Because the fresh stuff, somebody has to be there to consume it, you can't delay. Then it becomes my burden, you know, I have to be thinking, and orchestrating, how to use such a variety of food." Another man explained that he and his wife never used convenience food but then defined as a convenience the extra work his wife had put in on weekends. "One convenience that we will use sometimes is this. You know when you come home from work and you have to cook you really don't have much time. You don't have time to simmer sauces or anything like that. So sometimes on the weekend Katherine will make up something, or if she has time maybe two or three things, something that can be heated up later in the week and will actually taste better then."[21]

Women's coordinative cooking work was so obscured from view that it was not even framed as a matter for negotiation. Even the men who shared this work attributed imbalances in the division of labor to their wives' personalities: they were good planners and organizers. For nine of the couples, women took primary responsibility for feeding, with men making secondary contributions. Most of these husbands chose to do certain types of cooking, at certain times, on their own terms. More typically, husbands in these couples participated in occasional cooking defined as appropriate for fathers: summer barbecuing or preparing weekend breakfasts for the family.[22]

In single-mother households, mothers did all the feeding work, but they were somewhat more likely to recruit children to help with housework, and they experienced less pressure to elaborate their foodwork for male partners. One single mother described the difficulty of organizing shared tasks among her daughters. She tried a written schedule but found that it took too much energy to enforce: "When you work all day, and come home, it's almost easier to do it than to have to supervise other people doing something they don't want to do." The invisibility of monitoring provisions, for example, made it difficult to share the work of provisioning, because one household member never knew what others thought about what was needed. One woman gave an example. There was just a little bit of milk left in a carton, and her husband knew it because he had just handled it. But when he went to the store, he did not buy milk. Not only were the tasks of provisioning, planning, and managing the sociability of family meals invisible, but also maintaining their invisibility was part of doing the work well. So it was no wonder that people were often unable, or reluctant, to talk explicitly about these tasks.[23]

Thus even when husbands and children pitch in, it remains a mother's responsibility to prepare family meals. Women are expected to keep the big picture in mind: juggling work and school schedules, taking the preferences of children and husband into account, discovering through trial and error what people will eat, providing proper and varied meals, talking to friends about successful meal ideas, provisioning the household, and managing and educating tastes and preferences. Since much of this foodwork is invisible, it is not subject to negotiation in the household division of labor, perpetuating women's second shift and time crunch.

Solutions to the Time Crunch

The time crunch has fostered a time poverty movement, whose proponents offer analyses and solutions to ease the lives of harried American workers. To ease the burden on working mothers, and to increase nonparent workers' support for caregiving benefits, proposals include community-based and on-site child-care supports, publicly sponsored or subsidized child care for pre-schoolers, paid parental leave, after-school programs for children, increases in the minimum wage, expanded earned income tax credits, protections for workers taking time for dependent care, workplace flexibility, job security for part-time workers, a thirty-five-hour standard workweek, mandatory benefits for workers that are accrued in proportion to the amount of time worked, extension of Fair Labor Standards Act protections to professional, managerial, and other salaried workers, and medical and family-leave benefits for anyone with caretaking responsibilities.[24]

To encourage workers to value time as much as income, Juliet Schor recommends replacing overtime with comp time, prorating benefits for part-time workers, instituting job sharing, providing the option of giving up future income for time off, guaranteeing minimum vacation days, raising the minimum wage, equalizing division of labor in the family so that not only women will take advantage of shorter work hours, lessening wage discrimination on the basis of sex, and overcoming consumerism by finding other ways to create identity and self-esteem.[25]

Economist Robert Reich also takes on the unbridled consumerism of the postindustrial, new economy, what he dubs the "Age of the Terrific Deal." He eschews the personal solutions proffered by some time-movement theorists: self-awareness, time management, and voluntary simplicity. Rather, he advocates public-policy changes that would cushion people against sudden economic shocks, reduce inequalities in wealth and income, improve working conditions for caregivers, and make changes in school financing and housing policies to aid low-income Americans. To ease the time crunch on families, he recommends extending schooling to three- and four-year-olds, expanding the school day with play and study until parents get off work, and offering flexible work schedules, paid leave for child- and elder-care, and a refundable tax credit for a parent at home with a child under three. Success means more than what we can acquire—it also "depends on our spiritual grounding, the richness of our relationships, the sturdiness of our families, and the character of our communities." We need a public discussion about how best to combine economic dynamism and social tranquility.[26] Social tranquility creates the time and space for civil relations: leisurely meals, extended conversations, and the respectful give and take of democratic discourse.

Public-policy changes are also needed to address the "mommy wars" of women against women, fueled by the media. Judith Warner calls the "Mommy Mystique" the latest in a series of "motherhood religions" in times of economic anxiety. Instead of an outward-looking movement for social change,

Americans are engaged in inward-looking, moralistic mommy wars between social conservatives and feminists. Warner is impressed by the pragmatism of French policies, widely accepted and specifically conceived to enhance mothers' and families' quality of life. She recommends government-mandated standards and quality controls for child care; flexible, affordable, locally available, high-quality part-time child care; and health insurance available and affordable to part-time workers.[27]

The book *Take Back Your Time: Fighting Overwork and Time Poverty in America* describes itself as the official handbook of the national "take back your time" movement.[28] It is chock full of recommendations in addition to those already discussed above. Workplace reforms include sharing jobs with friends, "downshifting" with customized work arrangements, increasing cross-training in the workplace so that workers can take time off, sharing existing work to reduce layoffs, limiting the amount of involuntary overtime hours employers can require (Maine was the first state to do this), and limiting the workweek by law (as California does). To reduce overwork from necessity, replace the minimum wage with a living wage and expand the earned income tax credit.

Many of the book's recommendations borrow from European policies. The 1998 European Union's Working Time Directives set forty-eight hours as the weekly maximum and gave workers the right to a minimum of daily rest periods, at least one day off per week, and four weeks paid vacation a year. The workweeks in many European countries are less than 40 hours: France (35), Netherlands (36 or 38), Denmark (37), Norway (37.5), Belgium (38), and Germany (one quarter of workforce 35). European Union countries guarantee four weeks paid vacation, and several countries grant five weeks. Paid parental leave is available in Sweden, Norway, and Germany.

Some European countries provide the option of choosing shorter hours with equal conditions (individualized options). The Netherlands promotes a "1.5 jobs model" for families in which both men and women work 75 percent of their regular hours when they have young children. Some Dutch collective agreements also include multiple-choice options—giving employees the choice between additional income, days off, or periods of leave. This allows parents to buy time while caring for children. To make the shorter-hours options more attractive, a 1996 Dutch law bans discrimination between full-timers and part-timers in terms of hourly pay, benefits, and promotion opportunities. The principle of equal treatment for people who work fewer hours is now becoming law across Europe in response to the 1997 European Union Part Time Work Directive. Belgians over fifty have the right to work

80 percent or 50 percent schedules. Swedish parents can choose to work three-quarters of normal hours until children reach age eight. Norwegian parents can work shorter hours.

Several European countries allow workers to take breaks from careers for training, family reasons, and personal projects. In 1994 Denmark introduced a system of paid educational, child-care, and sabbatical leaves that allows job rotation between the employed and the unemployed and creates opportunities for career upgrading. Similar measures are found in the Netherlands, Norway, Sweden, and Germany. The employee takes up to a year off and receives unemployment benefits or paid allowance. The cost is balanced by the money saved when an unemployed person is hired as a replacement. Belgium's career-break program has evolved into a time-credit system in which employees can take a one-year leave and work a four-day week for up to five years, while receiving a paid allowance. Phased retirement programs (like that in Sweden) ease the transition for baby boom retirees, letting them work part-time and reducing the burden on the pension system.

Various sabbatical proposals have been made in the United States. In 1978 Congressmember Donald M. Fraser (from Minnesota) introduced a bill to create work sabbaticals for everyone covered by Social Security. Every worker after every ten years of work would be eligible to take one year off with full benefits. Related ideas include a sabbatical year off paid by Social Security for workers between the ages of forty-five and fifty-five in exchange for one year's delay of retirement benefits; six months or more leave without pay; and periodic sabbaticals of a week off every month or year.

Other "time off" proposals would introduce a time for rest and reflection during the workweek, designate Friday afternoons as free time, set aside seven minutes every morning and afternoon as quiet time, save one week a year as neighbor time, provide paid leave time for family and community service, and trade raises for more vacation time. Or an employee could customize a plan with an employer to combine vacation, sick days, personal leave, and unpaid time off.

The time movement has influenced the profession of urban planning. The New Urbanism calls for mixed residential, commercial, civic, and open space within walking distance; diversified housing; a town center or square; narrow, attractive, tree-lined streets with ample sidewalks to entice people to go outside; front porches; homes positioned at the front of the lot; smaller lots; and work opportunities near housing. In July 2000 the League of Slow Cities (Citta Slow) was formed in Italy as an offshoot of the Slow Food movement. The league's goal is to improve the quality of life, hospitality, and conviviality of communities. More than thirty member towns in Italy and beyond have agreed to adhere to the fifty-five pledges in Citta Slow's manifesto. One pledge is to preserve local culinary traditions.[29]

Personal solutions to the time crunch—improved time management, voluntary simplicity, and individualized arrangements with employers—are commendable. But more comprehensive changes are needed to address the issues of concern in this book: time for shared household foodwork and meals, flexibility in balancing work time and household time, time for neighborhood and community food rituals, and the leisure to savor meals and conversations. We need to rethink unbridled consumerism, the ideal worker norm, and the devaluation of caregiving and domesticity. We need the kinds of policies advocated by time-movement proponents. In the tripartite conceptual world of the economy, the state, and civil society, the state must intervene to relax the grip of the economy on people's time to create more time, and space, for civil society.

Chapter 2

Domesticity: Meals, Obligation, and Gratitude

A call for civilizing meals and conversation must not only repel the forces of workplace demands but also bolster the value of domesticity: everyday household activities that have been devalued relative to the "important" and "male" worlds of the economy and the polity and rendered invisible in writings about civil society. Domesticity will not be given the respect it deserves until it is degendered and repoliticized as essential to civil society and democracy.

Political and Gendered Domesticity

American households have always been gendered, but they have not always been devalued as apolitical and tangential to democracy. Indeed, after the American Revolution, the middle-class household was quite politicized. Mothers instilled in their children republican virtues and a commitment to the common good, and men were told to respect the domestic sphere. This "cult of domesticity" and "republican motherhood" placed moral and political value on the homes where women spent most of their time. The moral authority of the housewife gave her justification to speak out against injustices such as slavery. For example, the political impact of Harriet Beecher Stowe's *Uncle Tom's Cabin*, filled with domestic imagery, demonstrated the influence of the home on politics. Male writers also saw the home as a touchstone of values for social reform. Ralph Waldo Emerson thought that the just household was the moral foundation of a democracy. He advocated a distribution of household tasks that reflected democratic values, and he lauded the household as a fount of the virtues of charity and hospitality, which he viewed as a bridge between home and the world. The ideology of domesticity enhanced female self-confidence and empowered women both inside and outside the home, especially in the realm of civic culture. The high moral status of the home implied that those closest to it would be most capable of generosity toward the unfortunate. Denied access to male electoral politics, women made major public contributions to social-service organizations.[1]

After the Civil War, household politics began to play themselves out in a more adversarial way, as women began to attack aspects of male culture

"EAT AT YOUR OWN TABLE AS YOU WOULD AT THAT OF A KING," SAID CONFUCIUS.

Household Hospitality. The "cult of domesticity" and "republican motherhood" placed moral and political value on the home. Mothers instilled in their children a commitment to the public good and wrote about proper behavior. Mrs. E. Stevens Tilton's book, *Home Dissertations* (1890), contained this drawing, with the maxim, "'Eat at your own table as you would at that of a king,' said Confucius." Smithsonian Institution.

in the name of their higher virtue. The temperance movement harnessed women's moral authority to control male drinking behavior. Women also used "domestic housekeeping" arguments to advocate cleaning up corrupt urban politics. Jane Addams faulted the American city for lacking domesticity. In the settlement-house movement, reformers sought to carry the values of the middle-class home to the slums. All along, the valorization of the home was allied with sexual asymmetry in the minds of both men and women. Women's activism for the public good was fueled more by self-righteousness than by a desire for equality.[2]

As industrialization gained a foothold on the American economy, the home changed and domesticity declined in cultural value. Women's "moral nature" came to be trivialized. By the late nineteenth century, the middle-class home was losing its moral veneer as class tensions came to the forefront. Middle-class wives worried about the "servant problem." In the colonial period, servants were usually indentured, except in the South, which relied on slave labor. In Jacksonian America, domestics were frequently farm girls who came to cities to find work. At the end of the nineteenth century, domestics were increasingly recent immigrants from Ireland and southern and eastern Europe, who were very poor, victims of ethnic discrimination, and inexperienced in American domestic practices. As household size shrank, hired help became an increasingly intrusive presence. Around 1850, back stairs began to show up in middle-class houses to distance servants from family. The moral status of the home was also eroded by social Darwinism's reductionist and secular views of women, by domestic science's emphasis on household efficiency, and by a culture that reduced the household to a locus of consumption.[3]

By the mid-twentieth century, the household was no longer valorized for raising virtuous citizens. In classical republican thought, virtue referred to the manly pursuit of the common good in the public sphere. In the American cult of domesticity, the welfare of the republic depended on women instilling public virtues in the next generation of citizens. Virtues formerly thought to belong to civic life were relegated to private life. Virtue came to be associated with middle-class propriety rather than civic life, and selflessness applied to motherhood, not the citizen's pursuit of a common good. Current American domesticity—with women specializing in family work and men specializing in market work, framed around the assumption that ideal workers will have access to a flow of family work few mothers enjoy—still lodges selflessness in the home. But republican virtue and the common good no longer figure prominently in the home—or the polity for that matter. Nor does the polity have a major responsibility in raising the next generation of virtuous citizens. By contrast, France has demonstrated an interest in the development of its future citizens with its generous leave policies and extensive child-care systems.[4]

Gender roles continue to define domesticity, even in gay and lesbian households. Research in the 1950s and 1960s found that in gay and lesbian couples one partner took on the "masculine" role, while the other took on the "feminine" role, conforming to the classic sociological distinction between instrumental and expressive roles within the family. Studies in the 1970s and 1980s detected a more egalitarian impulse in the domestic division of labor within gay and lesbian couples. However, Christopher Carrington's study of gay and lesbian households in the 1990s revealed traditional gender roles. He noted that many of the studies with egalitarian findings relied exclusively on self-report data, in which couples, both heterosexual and homosexual, persistently made equality claims that were not supported by actual divisions of domestic labor. His research methods included questionnaires, in-depth interviews (of partners separately), and participant observation of actual household behavior. Many gay men opted for traditional masculine images of themselves. One man was embarrassed by the amount of household work he did and offended when his mother called him a housewife. He said he went to the gym quite a bit to compensate for it. Many of the women felt guilty when they opted for the masculine role and did not do much around the house. In general, Carrington was struck with how much of the caregiving that transpired in the lesbigay families he studied remained hidden and devalued; how we lack the vocabulary to capture the experiences of domesticity; and how the people he interviewed found it difficult to talk about domesticity.[5] Domesticity is a gendered institution that will remain obscure until it is degendered and repoliticized as the bedrock of civil society and democracy.

In all households, domestic roles vary depending on the nature of members' paid employment. For example, the domestic activities of wives are often strongly influenced by the demands of their husband's occupation.[6] Wealthy couples often achieve greater gender parity in their relationships by relying on the labor of poorly paid undocumented workers who clean their houses, tend their gardens, do their laundry, and make their take-out meals. Lesbigay professionals who serve lesbigay clientele, in contrast to those who serve predominately heterosexual clients, entertain in their homes more often and maintain more elaborate friend and family connections.[7] Domestic relations vary by income, race, and sexual orientation, and any democratic repoliticization of domesticity needs to take such variations into account.

Deciding on the Menu: Household Variations

Domesticity plays itself out on a daily basis in household food choices that link members to their communities and cultures. In setting up a household, most Americans begin with familiar food, with what their mothers cooked, using their mothers' oral or written recipes. For example, one of Margaret DeVault's interviewees, Theresa, a Mexican-American woman with two young children, made dinners by calling her mother, who talked her through recipes step-by-step in the early days of her marriage. And she continued to cook as her mother did.[8] Many studies show that husbands expect their wives to cook just like their mothers did, and that a husband's food preferences prevail in menu preparation.[9] A study of menu planning by Italian Americans in Philadelphia found that meals varied with the presence or absence of a husband, the stage in the family cycle, school and work schedules, social networks, and the generational cohort of the senior woman in the family.[10]

What appears on the menu depends on who is living in the household. At the beginning of the twenty-first century, households were as varied as the food choices they faced. Any discussion of household foodwork must take this variety and historical trends (in the following discussion between 1970 and 2003) into account. How many people are around to share the foodwork? Household size has changed significantly: from a majority containing three or more people to a majority comprised of just one or two people. Do most households contain families? Yes, but the proportion has dropped from 81 percent to 68 percent. (A family household has at least two members related by birth, marriage, or adoption, one of whom is the householder. Children may or may not be present.) The majority of the increase in nonfamily households is due to the growth in one-person households (up 9 percent). Women comprise more than half of one-person households. Do most households contain children? No, only about a third do, down from 45 percent. The proportion of "typical American" households comprised of married couples with children has dropped from about 40 percent to about 23 percent. What percentage of households contains single parents? The proportion of single-mother family groups has grown from 12 to 26 percent, and of single-father family groups from 1 to 6 percent. Unmarried heterosexual-partner households comprise about 4 percent.[11]

Single-person households are the most likely to rely on food prepared outside the home. In the United States, the share of food expenditures for away-from-home meals and snacks has increased rapidly, from 34 percent in 1970 to 45 percent in 1997.[12] Average per person weekly expenditures for food away from home are greatest in single-person households, somewhat less for two-person households, and still less for larger household groups.[13] For many people, a certain stigma is attached to eating alone. Out of embarrassment, some people prefer to go hungry rather than eat alone. Others approach their hunger as an empty fuel tank to be filled at the nearest acceptable eatery. Studies focusing on eating behavior have shown that when people eat alone they eat differently. They take less time to eat. Obese people will eat more when eating alone; the nonobese will eat less. Older men and women living alone prepare fewer meals at home. College women are more likely to skip a meal if they have to eat it alone.[14]

In households composed of multiple roommates, meal-preparation rules are usually quite formal, as was the case for eleven undergraduate students in Philadelphia. Each member of the household was expected to cook meals for the group three times per month. Packaged foods were frowned upon as being less healthy and more expensive. "The evening meal was an important social event which played a key role in constituting the collective identity of the household. Eating together established a strong degree of communion among the inhabitants and even articulated other 'family' characteristics. Special feasts and cakes were prepared to celebrate each resident's birthday and to mark Thanksgiving, Christmas and Passover Seder."[15] This example illustrates how even in nonfamily households, meals and food rituals create the sociability building block of civil society.

Meal preparation and sharing played a key role in constructing lesbian and gay families. One woman described her close friends as family because she and her partner ate with them and talked to them frequently. "They are people who invite us over for dinner and people with whom we spend our fun times and because of that, I think of them as family." Another woman described a close friend as family since they planned meals and celebrations together. "It feels like family to me when we talk, go shop together, and then cook the meals. I mean, it's like family when we eat the meal together, too, it's just that preparing the meal, I guess, it reminds me of working with my mother in her kitchen." Food preparers would often downplay the work involved in preparing meals, with an "Oh, it was nothing" response to a compliment, a reflection of the gendered selflessness of the food preparer.[16]

In some households, menu planning is circumscribed by dietary concerns. For people with HIV and AIDS, cooks prepare high-fat, high-protein menus to combat malnutrition and weight loss and develop recipes to address changes in taste perception due to medications such as AZT or marijuana.[17] Some households make menu choices balancing the preferences of vegetarians, vegans, meat eaters, dieters, and the like. Menus are sometimes battlegrounds between a meat-and-potatoes generation and a high-fiber, low-cholesterol, vegetarian generation.

Menu choice is also a function of household income. According to the U.S. Department of Agriculture, in 1997 Americans spent about 11 percent of their disposable personal income on food. However, low-income households ($5,000–$9,999) spent 34 percent of their income on food, and households with incomes over $70,000 spent only 9 percent of after-tax income on food.[18] People with low incomes are much more likely than the well-off to stick to a strict budget, shop for discounts, and share food among kin. DeVault notes that among the people she interviewed, those in the middle class were reluctant to talk about food costs, using vague terms such as "tight" or "comfortable," but the poorest interviewees spoke directly about money. Poor women discussed their food expenses relative to rent, utility bills, and laundry costs. On one side of their calculus was income from work, Aid to Families with Dependent Children, or food stamps, and on the other were fixed expenses, unpredictable needs, and items such as food whose cost could be reduced by careful purchasing. Most poor women talked of trying to limit their food expenses by comparing prices in the store while shopping, watching for bargains and stocking up on items on sale, and purchasing cheaper generic products rather than brand-name items.[19]

In DeVault's study, for those near the poverty level, techniques of "smart shopping" were not always appropriate or possible. Although they were aware that their neighborhood stores often charged more for many food items than stores elsewhere, few of the poorest women had transportation to other shopping areas. "One black woman, for example, knew of several stores where she could find bargains, but she had to rely on friends or her sister for transportation, or consider whether to spend extra money on a delivery service." Many poor women often chose to buy more-expensive brand-name products simply because they could not afford to experiment with cheaper items and risk wasting money on poor-quality items. "While more affluent shoppers could recite long lists of bargain items they had tried—some acceptable and some not—poor shoppers tended to report more conservative strategies for selecting foods, emphasizing the cost of a single mistake." One woman said that she went for the quality of Del Monte corn after she had bought a cheaper brand at four cans for a dollar. "And when you got it, all the husks and stuff was inside and it was just money wasted, when I could have just took that dollar and bought that one can of Del Monte. . . . To me, it really is a waste of money."[20]

In her study of poor urban blacks, anthropologist Carol Stack observed that "household" was not a meaningful unit of analysis of family life: a resident might eat in one household, sleep in another, and contribute resources to yet another—considering himself or herself a member of all three households. Durable networks of kin and nonkin interacted daily, satisfying the domestic needs of children and assuring their survival. Fluctuations in household composition did not significantly affect cooperative familial arrangements. Kin swapped hot cornbread and greens for diapers and milk.[21]

Of course, as any observer of the persistent problem of homelessness in major U.S. cities knows, not all people live in stable households. But sometimes even people in homeless shelters have a say in menu selection. At one shelter for young homeless people, residents had access to shared kitchen facilities. A staff member helped them budget and shop for food. Most meals were cooked individually, some together. The cooking sessions aimed to ensure that residents ate properly and learned food hygiene and cooking skills, since many of the residents had unstable home experiences.[22]

Gift, Obligation, and the Economy of Gratitude

The swapping of goods described by Carol Stack is a present-day example of an ancient practice: gift exchange that obligates people in relations of giving, receiving, and repaying.[23] These relations are usually between households, and they reflect a world of limited resources and credit. As a woman named Ruby described this relationship, although she did not want to beg or to be a burden on loved ones, she knew that she needed help every day and believed that people should help one another. She had given up on buying things she once wished for, such as living-room furniture and stylish clothes, because she had to provide for her kin. "Sometimes I don't have a damn dime in my pocket, not a crying penny to get a box of paper diapers, milk, a loaf of bread. But you have to have help from everybody and anybody, so don't turn no one down when they come round for help."[24]

Stack observed that people swapped things, not to try to get ahead of anyone else but because they were able to get better-quality items. Swapping provided credit where conventional bank credit was unavailable. "An object given or traded represents a possession, a pledge, a loan, a trust, a bank account—given on the condition that something will be returned, that the giver can draw on the account, and that the initiator of the trade gains prerogatives in taking what he or she needs from the receiver." Individuals who failed to reciprocate in swapping relationships were judged harshly. Over the years, gift exchanges generated feelings of both generosity and martyrdom.[25]

Generally, sharing food implied reciprocity and obligation, and it was often difficult to navigate the waters of who owed what to whom when it came to meals. A case in point was Annie, a single mother of three in DeVault's study. She cooked for her boyfriend and sometimes for his brother as well. Although the men usually brought something in exchange—some soda, perhaps—these exchange relations were delicate ones. Annie's boyfriend was embarrassed at how much his brother ate, hinting at the ambiguity of expectations that surround such relations of service and exchange.[26]

Many cooks describe the sharing of food as something they owe loved ones. Although the explicit message is one of love and caring, cooks are not always aware of the implied bargain that they are owed something—usually at least gratitude—in return. Unreciprocated gifts result in resentment or the martyrdom described by Stack. This is the crux of an important food problem faced by women, since they have the primary responsibility to come up with meals. It is culturally expected that women provide food as a sign that they care, and most women willingly do so. But women keep a subconscious tally, what Arlie Hochschild calls "the economy of gratitude": a mental balance sheet of debits and credits of gratitude. She found in her interviews that when couples struggled, it was seldom over who did what work around the house. Far more often, it was over the giving and receiving of gratitude. For one couple, a gift in the eyes of one was not a gift in the eyes of the other. Each felt taken advantage of because they differed so greatly in their expectations and gender strategies.[27]

In Hochschild's study, couples adopted traditional, egalitarian, or transitional gender strategies in dividing household tasks. In the traditional scheme, the woman identified with her activities at home (as a wife, mother, and neighborhood mom), the man identified with work, and the woman had less power than the man did. In the pure egalitarian type, both parties identified in the same way with home, work, or an agreed-upon balance between the two. Most people she interviewed fell into the transitional category: some blend of traditional and egalitarian. The typical transitional woman wanted to identify with her role at work as well as at home and believed that her husband should base his identity more on work than she did. The typical transitional man favored his wife working and expected her to take the main responsibility at home too.[28] So the gratitude balance sheet does not start out blank. It starts with the implicit assumption that a woman should be grateful for *anything* a man does around the house, and that a man does not have to express gratitude for what a woman automatically or naturally should do as a matter of course, not negotiation. Given these unbalanced expectations, it is understandable that women often felt like resentful martyrs without men having a clue.

Hochschild maintains that the gratitude balance sheet was further complicated by structural factors that contributed to some women's feeling grateful just to have a man around the house: women's lower wages, the high divorce rate, and the cultural legacy of female subordination. Many women did not want to strain their already overburdened marriages by asking for too many changes in their husbands. Carol, for example, had a string of miserable boyfriends in college whose laundry she'd washed and whose weekend dinners she'd cooked. Compared to them, Greg was wonderful. She was terrified of being a single mother whose husband did not see the kids or pay child support and grateful for the fact that Greg would never leave her. But, Hochschild notes, Greg neither feared abandonment nor pictured himself as a single father, since the supply of male commitment to share responsibility for children was far lower than the female demand for it. This fact in the wider society tipped the scales inside their marriage; it increased Carol's sense of debt to Greg. It evoked her extra thanks and inhibited her from making further household demands on Greg, who was already doing comparatively so much.[29]

In the traditional gender strategy, wives believed that husbands deserved a proper meal after a hard day at work. This view fit the pre-1950s predominantly male workforce model. But in the post–World War II era, more and more women came home from a day of work and thought that they too deserved a proper meal. In the household calculus of obligation and gratitude, didn't someone owe them a nice, relaxing dinner?

Many Americans find it difficult to talk about reciprocal obligations since such ties conflict with the dominant ethic of competitive individualism, which accompanied the rise of industrial capitalism in the West. Competitive individualism serves the needs of a market economy where it is important to cut family ties in order to move to the city for jobs and, later, to move around the country for careers. It is based on a language of contracts and rights: hours worked, pay obtained, goods delivered, and rights to certain treatment. People do not owe others anything that cannot be specified in a contract or as a right. But food and meals do not lend themselves to notions of competition, individualism, contracts, or rights. Pure competition at the table would be a disaster with everyone diving for food and elbowing others aside. Pure individualism, with everyone bringing her or his own food to the table, would not make much sense. Devising written contracts for each meal would be extraordinarily time consuming and unrealistic. And on what basis would one say one had a right to bananas for breakfast? Food and meals are precapitalist, preindustrial; as Wendell Berry puts it, eating is an agricultural act.[30] Organic, biological language and metaphors are more appropriate than mechanistic, industrial ones. The household chores that are easy to chart—take out the trash, do the dishes, vacuum the floors, clean the toilets—all involve things. Meals require attention to people: changes in their mood, diet, health, and developmental stage. The satiation of people's hunger is impossible to quantify and tabulate; it is social and psychological, as well as biological.

Psychological Memories and Social Connections

Household mealtime memories run deep and endure well into adulthood. Civil-society theorists who bracket off the household overlook the ways in which foodwork and meal rituals link the individual and the family to the larger social connections of civil society. In their memoirs, many writers see foodwork and family meals as cauldrons of connectedness and identity formation and battlegrounds of obligation and gratitude. They frequently reminisce about their mothers and grandmothers in the kitchen. The aromas and rituals of baking seem to evoke strong childhood memories. One woman recalled her childhood in the Appalachian foothills of Tennessee with the memory of her grandmother's baking—slow-paced, aromatic, pleasurable, with her grandmother welcoming her questions about farm life. She remembered her grandmother's hands ("birdlike, deeply veined, and lightly floured") kneading, patting, and rolling out biscuit dough on the old maple board, and the fragrance of raw wheat dough rising in the summer heat. Among her memories was that of "[Grandmother] in her deep southern drawl telling me of the farm 'things' I would ask about—endlessly. Days ooooozed by like molasses then."[31]

For writer Letty Cottin Pogrebin, meals were a marker for changing expectations about women's roles. She grew up in a household where her father attended meetings every night after dinner, and her mother tried to win his heart through his stomach. She begged him to stay home for their daughter's sake, to give her "a real father, a real family life." Watching him leave the house, Pogrebin lost faith in her mother's axioms for feminine success— "Freshen up for your husband," "Don't show your brains; smart girls scare men," "Always laugh at his jokes," "Act interested in his work even if you're not," and "Have a hot meal waiting when he comes home." Her mother died when Pogrebin was fifteen, and at that age, the furthest thing from her mind was the possibility that she might someday want to cook from her mother's recipes. However, when Pogrebin married in 1963, her older sister passed on to her their mother's cookbook, which Pogrebin has cooked from ever since. The cookbook was especially meaningful since it contained her mother's handwritten annotations of the recipes that she had either improved upon or simplified over the years.[32]

Many household food memories are a mixture of conviviality and social tension, especially across generational lines. Such was the case for filmmaker Caroline Babayan, whose memories of early childhood dinners in Iran were "a mixture of idyllic scenes of family members swapping news, telling jokes, and eating heartily and the silence of repressed anger and jealousy manifesting themselves into the rituals of sniffing cautiously at the contents of the plate or carefully dissecting the food into an unappetizing mound." Her aunts and uncles used food as a means to express their resentments and anger at one another and toward her grandmother. "All of a sudden, one didn't like the rice anymore, the other wouldn't eat meat. My eldest aunt would want more sophisticated continental cuisine, my uncle would demand simpler food. Even her choice of cakes could be a subject for endless squabble."[33]

In some food memoirs, daughters detect the fact that their mothers, denied aspirations outside the home, threw all their energies into cooking within it. And they rebelled against their overzealous mothers by challenging them at the table. Playwright Clare Coss says that her mother had wanted to be a nurse, but her grandfather forbade it: "No daughter of mine will nurse strange men." So the kitchen became her domain and cooking her outlet; she embellished her "traditional New Orleans recipes: from gumbos to pralines to Spanish rice (each grain separate). Mother loved to eat, relished each bite: aroma, taste, texture. Her pleasingly zaftig body was a source of incredible heat and comfort." Coss turned the dining table into territory for rebellion and challenged her mother over food. "It was the one place I could separate from her overzealous solicitation for my welfare in a noticeably dramatic way."[34] Another woman describes her grandmother as "an exuberant, almost manic cook, driven in her generosity by a complicated need to fill her own private hungers. . . . [Her] insistent generosity seemed at best self-centered and at worst downright persecutory."[35]

Sometimes meals evoke horrific memories. Writer Margaret Randall describes herself as a shameless feeder of others, who reaped joy from creating meals for herself and others. In her runaway food intake, she weighed in at two hundred pounds, and she was five feet four. She frequently dreamed about food, often in connection with scenes of violent death. After one such dream, she began a therapeutic journey, and memories began to surface of incest at the hands of her maternal grandfather. After a period during which she had to stop feeding people, she returned to cooking with great love and joy.[36]

Escape from the Household with Commercial Food

Of course, one way to escape from the tangle of emotions and relations of household food is to procure it from anonymous sellers in the marketplace—supermarkets, street vendors, diners, cafeterias, fast-food chains, casual dining chains, and restaurants. When food is a commodity, it is not entangled in the unpleasantness of intense family memories and smothering obligations. Just pay the bill and enjoy it. Fast food means freedom: more free time, no mess, no fuss, free choice, breathing room. "You deserve a break today." Food as a commodity reflects the urban, industrial values of speed and efficiency. Employers who monitor work hours have an interest in food as fuel, not sustenance. Fuel is for well-maintained, efficient work machines. Sustenance is for dawdlers who want to gossip about who knows what, wasting precious time.

According to geographer Richard Pillsbury, most colonial Americans never dined in a restaurant. Business travelers stayed at tavern inns or boardinghouses with little or no choice of food or accommodations. But by the beginning of the nineteenth century, restaurants and coffeehouses had appeared, predominantly in the larger cities, which expanded to meet the demands of the mercantile age. In the late nineteenth century, the Industrial Revolution created demand in urban centers for places to feed the multishift factory workers at all times of the day and night. The boardinghouses and taverns had inflexible times of eating, so workers turned to street vendors and "diners," wagons where patrons could sit while eating. By the 1870s, the demand for eateries was met by new restaurants for a factory age, which included lunchrooms, cafeterias, and diners, provisioned with foodstuffs delivered by the new and speedy railroads. The first quarter of the twentieth century saw the first hamburger sandwich, the rapid growth of all kinds of catering, the establishment of regional and national chains, and the development of franchising. Eating away from home became an increasingly popular leisure activity of middle- and working-class people, especially as more of them owned cars. Drive-in restaurants, which appeared in the 1920s, along with catering outlets in residential neighborhoods were associated with pleasure rather than work.[37]

Prohibition also contributed to the proliferation of commercial eating establishments in the United States. As historian Harvey Levenstein notes, when the public sale of alcoholic beverages was banned in 1920, it dealt a blow both to expensive French restaurants, which depended on wine for their cuisine, and to restaurants that had catered to men and relied on profits from alcohol sales to subsidize food provision. High-end restaurants were replaced with lunchrooms, tearooms, and cafeterias, which served low-cost food quickly, catering to the growing numbers of middle-class men and women who worked in offices and shops and ate their lunch away from home. These were respectable places for women to patronize, and the complicated French menus of hotels and restaurants gave way to American dishes and lighter fare. Between 1919 and 1929, the number of restaurants in the country tripled, accommodating a growing middle-class market that neither the old saloons nor the higher-class restaurants could tap. "Short lunch hours and expanding cities made going home for lunch impossible. Hot lunches were regarded as a necessity and lunch pails were too working-class. As a result, new kinds of restaurants tried to fill the growing gap in the middle."[38]

After World War II, the international symbol of commercial food was the McDonald's hamburger. In 1937 in a Pasadena, California, restaurant, the two McDonald brothers responded to a high demand at workers' lunchtime with a limited menu of burgers, serving large numbers at a high speed and low price. Their assembly-line procedures, with food preparation and serving broken down into simple repetitive tasks and a specialized division of labor for each stage, constituted the first fast-food factory. In 1954, the brothers moved their drive-in restaurant to San Bernardino, California, where they were visited by Ray Kroc, a devotee of scientific management, who suggested that they franchise their operation. Kroc opened the first McDonald's franchise in Des Plaines, Illinois, in 1955. The franchise package included centralized control, conformity throughout the system, uniformity of production, a standardized menu, and systematic training of staff. Customers could expect a familiar setting and food. Children could eat with abandon, without silverware and scrutiny about proper table manners.[39]

Convenience food was one answer to women's second shift. And in case they felt guilty about not providing a proper meal, they could make their children happy with toys that came with the burgers and fries. By the late twentieth century, many fast-food chains had adopted a family-oriented marketing strategy. In televised ads, McDonald's was portrayed as a hearth with family memories. This convenience was welcomed by women like Sandra, a white, suburban, middle-class mother of two who was interviewed by DeVault. Sandra cooked two dinners most evenings: one at 5:30 for her daughters and one at 10:00 for her husband. Since he put in such a long day, she did not feel that she could just tell him to get himself a sandwich. On Monday nights, she had three children to feed; on Tuesday nights just her own two. "Wednesday nights we have dancing lessons right after Jan's school, at quarter to six, and Kathy doesn't get back from hers 'til 7:30. So that's our treat. That's usually the run to McDonald's. In two shifts. Jan goes to her dancing lesson and I take Kathy to McDonald's—it's only three blocks away—then I take Kathy to her dancing lesson—because of course they're in different classes—and then I take Jan to McDonald's, come home, and another parent brings Kathy home."[40]

A 1992 survey of American households reported that 98 percent of household members had eaten out during the previous month. On average, members of a household ate out 9.42 times a week, with adult males eating out 4.68 times, adult females 3.76 times, and children and teens 4.16 times. Single people under age thirty spent the most per capita, and married couples with two incomes and at least one child spent the most per household.[41]

Commercially prepared food was another solution to the time crunch for busy people. Writer Paula Martinac describes the significance of sharing food with fellow activists in the gay and lesbian community in Manhattan. Her friend organized her life around the fast, free delivery of every ethnic food imaginable. With meetings every weekday evening, there was no time to shop or to cook. Weekends meant rest and dinners out. Take-out food did not mean diminished enjoyment of food or getting the consumption of food over with before real discussion began. Food was not an afterthought. Rather, it allowed her friend to integrate food into the activities that packed her day. Ideas from meetings would often reappear at dinner. "Food and politics have always been a good mix. People loosen up with a good meal; they share ideas and reflections brought about by the camaraderie of eating together, particularly foods that lend themselves to being passed around and shared. ('Well, I didn't want to say this in the meeting, but. . . . could you pass the dumplings? . . . I'm not really sold on What's-her-name's idea . . .')."[42]

Some convenience foods, such as commercial tortillas and frozen dinners, were obvious time-savers. For Mexican-American women, the convenience of store-bought tortillas meant they did not have to spend five hours a day kneeling at grindstones preparing the dough for the family's tortillas.[43] What was thought to be the first masa mill in the United States opened in San Antonio, Texas, in 1896. Prepared dough for tortillas was delivered around town from a wagon. By the 1920s, San Antonio had opened its first tortilla factory, competing with many other smaller producers and with housewives working in their own kitchens.[44] Frozen (TV) dinners were introduced in 1953 and became a modern staple emergency meal for American families.[45] They were especially welcomed by, and marketed to, single people.

As people flocked to fast-food restaurants and convenience food, they weighed the gains of convenience and speed against the losses of commensality and conversation. At fast-food eateries, the table is not likely to be a civilizing place for extended conversation. With uncomfortable seating, they are designed to get customers to eat quickly and leave to make room for others. Under certain circumstances, even finer restaurants could undermine civilized conversations. Sociologist Joanne Finkelstein cautioned against an uncivilized sociality that could characterize eating in trendy restaurants. To the extent that customers acted in imitation of others, according to popular images or fashion and without thought of self-scrutiny, they were relieved of the responsibility of shaping relationships with others. For Finkelstein, civility referred to exchanges between people who were equally self-conscious and attentive to one another and who avoided power and prestige differentials. Such conditions often did not exist with the artifice and pretense of supercilious waiters, power tables, and eating to be seen. Restaurants were in the business of marketing people's emotions, desires, and states of mind. By offering prepackaged formulas for relationships with others, they could prevent the development of what philosophers have called the examined life, expressed as a civilized awareness of others.[46] Scripted people were in no position to be truly civil to one another. And the advertising industry manipulated images of food and eating, subconsciously affecting Americans' food choices.

Foodwork and mealtimes open new doors to our understanding of the relationship between domesticity and civil society. The consequences for connectedness in meal planning vary by who lives in the household, school and work schedules, and generational cohorts. Food binds people to others insofar as it is a gift, an obligation, a signifier of social roles, and a conveyor of emotional memories. It is very tempting to escape from household mealtime's demands for social and civil connectedness and to flee to the comfort and convenience of anonymous, commercial fare and scripted expectations about social behavior. Of course, there are many opportunities for sociability and civil interactions at nonhousehold eating establishments. But only households offer civil challenges and rewards to people on a daily basis in relation to food: making entries into the economy of gratitude, swapping goods with kin, expressing (sometimes overbearing) generosity, and forging intergenerational bonds.

Chapter 3

. . . .

American Food

In the United States, putting food on the table raises the inevitable question: whose food? We have a colonial past, a legacy of slavery, and a history of immigration. For a while, British cookery laid claim to being "American food," in spite of the fact that American cuisine was multiethnic and regional from the start. Later on, the corporate food industry defined "American food" as the processed goods that it distributed nationally, in order to sell products to immigrant women eager to help their families "become American." Some women gravitated toward "American food" in a desire to assimilate, while others used their traditional cuisines to bolster racial and ethnic pride. In recent years, American foodways have been contested: gobbling down fast food and gulping sodas to meet the demands of a frantic workplace have been challenged by the Slow Food movement and by writers concerned with the obesity crisis and global warming. In this chapter, we will explore how definitions of and challenges to American food and food practices shed light on civility and democracy in the United States.

American Food as Multiethnic and Regional

The relations of foodways to civility and democracy were initially shaped by the colonial experience. American food bears the stamp of the indigenous population of some four million Native Americans and of the peoples who arrived here as immigrants and slaves. Colonists enthusiastically borrowed from Native American cookery. Since colonists wrote history, culinary and otherwise, American cookery was defined in terms of their practices. After the North won the Civil War, culinary history books truncated colonial cookery to mean New England cookery. So in the popular imagination, especially before the revisionist social histories of the 1960s, American food was what Yankees in Boston and New York ate.

According to food writers John L. Hess and Karen Hess and historian Donna R. Gabaccia, the myth that American food was Yankee food concealed the fact that even as early as the time of the United States' independence from Britain, almost all Americans ate a diet that blended the techniques and ingredients of two or more cultures. To prove their point, they take their readers on a culinary tour of the five major colonial areas: Virginia, New England, the Middle Atlantic (Quaker and Dutch), the South, and the Southwest. In each area, they underscore the contributions of Native Americans.

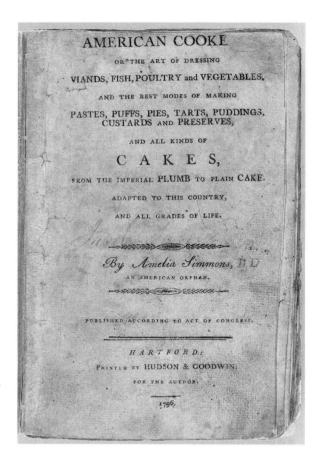

Simmons's Cookbook. From the country's earliest days, almost all Americans ate a diet that blended the techniques and ingredients of two or more cultures. The first cookbook of American authorship to be printed in the United States was Amelia Simmons's *American Cookery,* published in Hartford, Connecticut, in 1796. It contained many recipes with Native American ingredients such as cornmeal and squash. "Pompkin Pudding," baked in a crust, is the basis for pumpkin pie, a Thanksgiving favorite.
Library of Congress, Rare Book and Special Collections Division.

Colonists in Virginia incorporated with relish and appreciation the cookery of Native Americans. The Indians baked a type of bread that would later become southerners' hoecake, baked in loaves covered with leaves, warm ashes, and coals. The Indians made it with corn, wild oats, or sunflower seeds. They also roasted a great variety of corn. Colonists ate both wheat bread and "pone," made of "Indian meal" (cornmeal). Two staples of southern cookery were "homony" (Indian corn soaked, broken in a mortar, husked, and then boiled in water over a gentle fire) and barbecued meats (broiled meat laid on sticks raised on forks above the live coals). "This they, and we also, from them, call Barbacueing," said one colonist.[1] One has to wonder how many white suburbanites who fired up their grills in the 1950s knew that the quintessentially American practice of barbecuing was a Native American culinary tradition.

Virginia was seen as a veritable Garden of Eden. Native Americans cultivated peaches, strawberries, melons, pumpkins, and beans; gathered chestnuts, hickory nuts, and black walnuts; and tapped maple trees for syrup and sugar. Fish and waterfowl were plentiful, and hogs, which had been introduced by the earliest European settlers, ran wild. As early as 1622, French Huguenot refugees had experimented with vineyards, a practice that continued through midcentury, producing a "noble strong-bodied Claret, of a curious flavor." Although the Huguenots forsook their vines, they left an imprint on the cuisine of Virginia. Virginian Thomas Jefferson's passion for fine food and wine was legendary. A staggering proportion of his correspondences concerned his purchases of French wine. For his garden at Monticello, he collected seeds and cuttings from around the world. He kept a garden book from 1766 to 1824, in which he recorded some of the produce available in the market during his terms as president (1801–1809): even during winter, Washingtonians could buy at least fourteen kinds of fresh fruits and vegetables.[2]

Unlike the lush tidelands of Virginia, the stony soil of New England was hardly a Garden of Eden. Although its forests had plentiful game and its coastal waters harbored delicious seafood, the winters were long and harsh, and each spring the rocks resurfaced through the soil and had to be cleared away again. The Pilgrims had to make up by industry and husbandry for what nature did not provide. Indians taught them how to grow corn; to gather blueberries, cranberries, and other wild fruits; and to preserve them for the winter. By 1629, they were already harvesting apples. New England cookery, primarily chowders and bean dishes, never reached the elegance of Virginia's.[3]

New Englanders of English descent tried unsuccessfully to grow wheat, since wheat bread had symbolized high status in England. After 1660, they relied on native corn, supplemented by European rye and the peas and the beans of two continents. They modified England's "pease porridge" into New England's baked beans, sweetened by maple syrup or molasses. Puritan cooks added a more familiar rye grain to the coarse corn cakes of natives, producing "rye'n'injun" bread. English settlers baked pumpkin pies and hasty puddings made of maize. "Settlers of Massachusetts borrowed the French Canadian's cooking pot, the *chaudiere,* to prepare the stew of native clams, cider, cream, salt pork, and onions they called chowder." The use of ash as baking powder blended Native and European cooking techniques. "Native Americans used ash to make hominy and to flavor certain corn dishes and meat stews, but it was the European-Americans who first applied it to baking." With this new leavening, American gingerbread "soon evolved into a light, cake-like dessert, quite unlike its heavier medieval predecessor, which depended on eggs to raise the dough. Ultimately, all American breads followed gingerbread's evolution and gradually acquired the lightness associated with 'quick breads.'" Subsequent European immigrants, accustomed to the textures and long fermentation of yeast-baked breads, would note this change as a distinctive, if negative, American trait.[4]

In the Middle Atlantic region, English Quakers also adopted Indian corn. When he was in London as a colonial delegate in 1765, Quaker Benjamin Franklin responded to British claims that colonists were only bluffing when they said they would boycott British tea to protest the Stamp Act. After all, colonists had no alternative for breakfast since Indian corn was neither agreeable nor digestible. Franklin wrote a rebuttal describing Indian corn as "one of the most agreeable and wholesome grains in the world" and roasted corn as "a delicacy beyond expression." From corn Americans made "so many pleasing varieties of . . . samp, hominy, succatash, and nokehock." And "johny or hoecake, hot from the fire, is better than a Yorkshire muffin." Franklin wrote that the colonists had plenty to eat for breakfast: oatmeal, toast, ale, milk, butter, cheese, and rice. They can make tea from "sage and bawm in our gardens, the young leaves of the sweet hickery or walnut, and, above all, the buds of our pine, infinitely preferable to any tea from the Indies; while the islands yield us plenty of coffee and chocolate. Let the gentleman do us the honour of a visit in America, and I will engage to breakfast him every day in the month with a fresh variety, without offering him either tea or Indian corn."[5]

The first English Quaker cookbook in the Middle Atlantic region contained recipes for Dutch coleslaw and buckwheat cakes. Quakers also borrowed apple butter, bacon dumplings, bologna sausage, sauerkraut, and liver sausage from their German neighbors in Pennsylvania. For their part, German settlers, unlike the English, cooked on stoves instead of over the open fire and were more likely to stew rather than to roast native meats. They also devoted more attention to their kitchen gardens, cultivating a wider range of cabbages and other vegetables. The first German-language cookbook from this region reflected a cuisine of sausages, yeast baking, and hot salads, "but it also printed recipes for New England puddings and included much corn—in the form of samp, hominy, gritted bread, and dried grain. In an interesting twist, Germans even roasted corn to make it taste like their favored grain—rye." In New York's Hudson Valley, Dutch settlers had a reputation for taking pleasure in sumptuous meals and for the wealth and diversity of their larders. They made "corn an ingredient in their native dish of *hutespot,* by adding salt beef or pork, potatoes, carrots, and turnips to samp (corn) porridge."[6]

A careful reading of colonial cookbooks led John L. Hess and Karen Hess to conclude that colonists cooked lavishly, refuting the popularly held notion that the contemporary bland taste of American food could be traced back to a dour Puritan heritage that spurned sensual pleasures at the table. On the contrary, they maintain "that the various more or less Calvinist strains of our society adopted the sensual pleasures of the table as a subliminal replacement for the other joys that they abjured. It was better to eat than to burn."[7]

While the contributions of Native Americans to early American food were well documented, the written record of blacks' contribution was sketchier and based, of necessity, on oral sources, since it was illegal to teach slaves to read and write. In plantation kitchens, slave women had to learn European cooking techniques, mostly English and French. In Virginia, if the white mistress of the household did not know how to cook, she read to slaves from a cookbook. One former slave at Monticello remembered Mrs. Jefferson reading pastry recipes to the cook. Most cookbooks at the time were in English; they were very rarely in French or Spanish. Of course, slaves employed African cooking techniques whenever possible. New Orleans's cuisine absorbed more African influences than did Virginia's, in part because New Orleans's origins were not English but more aromatic Spanish and French, via Haiti. Africans had little to work with to feed themselves. "They gathered wild greens and scavenged beet tops, and cooked them with the chitterlings, the jowls, the maw, the tail, and other lowly portions of the pig that were granted them. The dish was cooked a long time and was almost a soup; they called it a 'mess o'greens' or 'pot likker' and it remains one of the favorite foods in soul cooking." Most slaves came from West Africa, and their distinct regional cuisines were lost in the intermingling of the tribes. However, the segregation of the field slaves tended to perpetuate certain uniquely African characteristics.[8]

Africans settled in the coastal regions of the Carolinas and Georgia among English, Caribbean, and French Huguenot planters. Many of the slaves of the Carolina low country came from rice-cultivating districts in western Africa. It is possible that planters imported their slaves from this region once rice cultivation became successful in the colonies. African techniques of rice cultivation continued into the nineteenth century. African cooks developed the rice kitchen cuisine of the Georgia and Carolina coasts. Slaves ate hoppin' john—a blend of cowpeas or beans and rice similar to dishes found in the African Caribbean. Some have attributed the coastal taste for hot, peppery flavors in local seafood dishes to generations of African American cooks. Gabaccia considers this a plausible interpretation, since neither English nor French settlers knew this combination of tomato, onion, and hot red peppers from their homelands.[9]

The slave trade conducted by the British and the Dutch empires brought ten million West Africans to North America over the course of two hundred years. By 1700, West African slaves had adapted their eating to New World crops: corn, cassava, peppers, sweet potatoes, pineapples, and peanuts from the Americas and rice and coconuts from Asia. These international imports had supplemented local products such as millet, beans, watermelons, palm oil, and yams. "Provisioners of slave ships in Africa often loaded foods from Central and South American origin to feed slaves en route, thus facilitating their transplantation to North America's warm southeastern colonies."[10]

The Spanish Empire also had a foothold on continental North America. The colonies of the Southwest rarely traded with the British colonies in the East, thus creating a cuisine based on a different mix of indigenous and European elements. Pueblo-dwelling Native Americans never planted wheat, which Spanish missionaries attempted to introduce. "However, they did adopt the chile peppers brought north from central Mexico by Hispanic settlers, the iron cooking pots, ovens and garbanzos from Spain, and the many domestic and herd animals introduced by the missions. Pork soon became the stuffing for tamales; pig's feet, rinds or ribs, and beef tripe found their way into stews made with *posole* (limed hominy)." They also added Spanish melons (which they called horse pumpkins) to their sweet fruits and vegetables from desert plants, and by 1700 they had even incorporated European-origin fruits into their religious rituals.[11]

Some peoples native to Arizona and New Mexico (the Zunis, the Pimas, and the Papagos [Tohono O'odham]) seem to have adopted European wheat, perhaps because they lived where corn was more difficult to cultivate. "They prepared the wheat into mush and unleavened bread baked on a stone grid-dle—the forerunner of today's flour tortillas—and eventually developed their own leavenings (mainly soured dough) for wheaten adobe breads and sweets baked in local *horno* (bee-hive-shaped) ovens." Wheat eventually became the marker that distinguished Sonoran and Southwest cuisines from that of central Mexico, where corn dominated; the wheat-flour tortilla came to symbolize the cuisine of this borderland. Of all the Native people of the Southwest, the Navajos changed their eating habits the most extensively in response to colonial change and exchange: they shifted from being seden-tary farmers and hunters to herders of European animals. "For the small southwestern farming populations of Hispanics and *mestizos* (individuals of mixed Spanish and Indian ancestry), a multi-ethnic mix of corn, wheat, frijoles, a few vegetables, and a few European fruits provided the staples for a simple, hybrid diet. . . . In California, *mestizo* settlers from Mexico brought corn, beans, chiles, and irrigation, introducing them to the migratory natives, who had depended on acorns as their staple food."[12]

As Donna Gabaccia observes, "With the possible exception of the ubiq-uitous popularity of corn and beans in all regions and among all groups, the only American eating habits of the colonial period were regional ones. No single American cuisine emerged from these exchanges. At the same time, no group's foodways survived the era completely unchanged. . . . The only way to become an American, at least as an eater, was to eat creole—the multi-ethnic cuisine of a particular region."[13]

Corporations Urge Immigrants to Eat American

The United States is a country of immigrants, and for many groups, jettison-ing traditional foods was an important way to become an American. This was especially the case during two peak periods of immigration: by Europe-ans at the turn of the twentieth century, and by Asians, Africans, and Latin Americans after the passage of the Immigration Act of 1965. Beginning in the mid-nineteenth century, "American food" began to be defined by national institutions: the federal government, when it fed its troops, and corporate food producers, whose goods were promoted by the advertising industry in national publications and transported by the transcontinental railroads. A spike in the rate of immigration at the turn of the twentieth century meant more social pressure on people to become American. During this time, a single national marketplace emerged, and its goods were defined as American: Gold Medal Flour, Coca-Cola, Van Camp's canned beans, even bananas from Central America, which were frequently mentioned in immigrants' descriptions of their first encounters with American foods on Ellis Island.[14]

The emergence of a national food marketplace coincided with a rapid increase in the number of immigrants to American shores. At the turn of the twentieth century, just over 300,000 immigrants were admitted to the United States. Within five years, the annual rate of immigration more than tripled. "And in the ten years from 1901 to 1910, close to 9 million immigrants arrived, the large majority of whom were Italians, Jews, Poles, or non-German-speaking denizens of the Hapsburg Empire." Harvey Levenstein pinpoints the origins of English food as American food in the economic differences between two strata of the working class: the relatively well-off skilled and semiskilled, mainly of British origin, and the struggling unskilled, which included the more recent immigrants from the aforementioned central and southern European ethnic groups. By the 1880s, members of the upper stratum could afford to take advantage of the new opportunities for variety in diet created by the transportation and preservation revolutions. "Ample supplies of beefsteak, fruits, and vegetables graced their tables, constituting the 'reefs of roast beef and apple pie' upon which the German sociologist Werner Sombart saw the dreams of American socialism dashed."[15]

Since the British were an earlier and relatively better-off immigrant group, their food tastes defined middle-class food habits in the United States. In a 1927 middle-class cookbook, dinner for six consisted of shrimp cocktail, vegetable soup, roast beef, Yorkshire pudding, roast potatoes, stuffed potatoes, string beans, and Peach Selma. Another typical middle-class dinner from 1923 was broiled chicken, French fries, and canned green peas. Canned goods were an expensive, high-status item in the 1880s and 1890s. As they became more affordable to native-born women, they became a symbol of Americanization.[16]

Advertisers played on the status anxieties of immigrant women, urging them to cast off the old-fashioned cookery of the home country and embrace modern American food. The American household was no longer a location for the formation of virtuous citizens; it had become a warehouse for the consumption of name-brand products. American recipes were disseminated by women's magazines with national circulation and on the women's pages of daily newspapers. Advertisements and editorials, frequently based on wire-service copy produced in a few major centers, promoted the products of national food industries. Millions of free recipe pamphlets emitted by the giant food processors were distributed nationally, "encouraging the housewife in Arkansas to cook her Armour ham or use her Del Monte canned pineapple in the same way as her counterpart in Vermont. Betty Crocker did not teach shortcuts in making hominy grits and Kraft did not encourage the use of New Mexico chiles with its cheese dishes. The result was the further nationalizing of American food habits."[17]

The federal government also defined American food when the War Department decided what to feed its troops. Before 1896, there were no standard recipes for the army or the navy. When an army manual for cooks was finally developed in 1896, there was a separate section with Spanish recipes, "which included variations on Mexican dishes such as tamales, tortillas, stuffed chiles, and *frijoles con queso*. It even called for grinding chiles in a *metate*, the traditional Mexican stone grinder." By 1916, when a new manual was issued, the Spanish section was gone. The military experience was quite a culinary shock for recent immigrants and for servicemen from areas with strong regional cuisines, such as the rural South. As Levenstein notes, "The change from a cured pork and cornmeal diet to beef, potatoes, white bread, and milk must have been as profound as that experienced by many immigrants and their children. They must have suffered from spice deprivation as well, but they were also, unwittingly, playing important roles in the process of the nationalizing of American food tastes."[18]

The standardization and homogenization of American food exerted a powerful force on menu choice in American households between the mid-nineteenth and the mid-twentieth century. The pressure on immigrant women to conform by getting rid of old-fashioned foodways was intense and often keenly felt by children facing peer pressure at school. They wanted to fit in with modern American ways. Embarrassed by what their mothers had packed in their lunches, they requested American substitutes. Hess and Hess describe one example of such pressure in Nebraska, where church suppers and cake sales had traditionally been a cornucopia of delicious goods prepared the old-fashioned way.

> The sons of one champion baker were embarrassed to take homemade bread to school and whined, "Gee, *Mor,* why can't we have store bought bread like everybody else?" She never baked bread again. Another woman made the best lemon meringue pie we ever ate—until she discovered Realemon. Recently we sat down with her son at a church-connected dinner. It was catered by Kentucky Fried Chicken, whose product has been described by no less an authority than Colonel Sanders himself as "nothing but a fried doughball wrapped around some chicken" served with gravy that was like "wallpaper paste." It was July in Nebraska, and there was not even an ear of corn on the table, not to mention real chicken and dumplings, farm pickles, or homemade pies such as would have graced the

table a generation ago. But the son insisted, "America is the best-eating country in the world."[19]

Immigrant mothers were torn between attachment to traditional foodways and a desire to have their children fit in with their peers.

Racial and Ethnic Pride in Foodways

Despite pressure on immigrants from school peers, the military, the food industry, advertisers, and the native-born to eat American, ethnic and regional foodways did not disappear. In the view of Susan Kalcik, a folklorist at the Smithsonian Institution, "clearly, for old and new ethnic groups in America, foodways—the whole pattern of what is eaten, when, how, and what it means—are very closely tied to individual and group ethnic identity."[20] Interestingly, it was during another period of a rapid increase in immigration that these older foodways were revived, and this time, the foodways of the

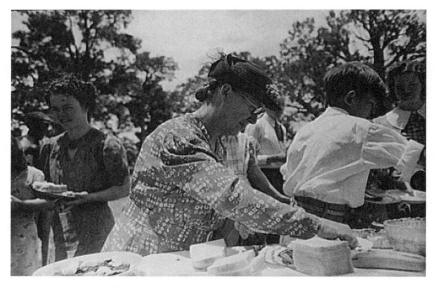

Community Picnic Table. Subject to commercial and peer pressure, some children encouraged their immigrant mothers to serve "American food" such as sliced white bread instead of the traditional fare of their country of origin. Here a farm woman arranges food on a table during an all-day community sing in Pie Town, New Mexico, in 1940. Library of Congress, Prints and Photographs Division, FSA-OWI Collection (LC-USF33-012785-MI).

new immigrants were embraced rather than scorned. Ethnic and regional cuisines were championed as a crucial part of one's identity.

A gastronomic revolution occurred in the wake of the Immigration Act of 1965, which changed the immigration laws that had ruled for almost one hundred years. National quotas had favored western and northern European countries and had severely curtailed immigration from Asia, Latin America, Africa, and Eastern Europe. According to food writer Leslie Brenner, when the act took effect in 1968, "the portals of the United States were unlocked to immigrants from around the globe, and since then millions have come from China, Hong Kong, Taiwan, Japan, Korea, Thailand, Eastern Europe, the Philippines, India, Pakistan, the Middle East, Africa, Mexico, the Caribbean, and Central and South America, bringing their foodways along with them. These new immigrants would forever change American culture."[21]

In 1968, the United States was also in the throes of the civil rights and antiwar movements. Activists criticized imperialist governmental policies and racist attitudes. They argued that people had a right to their own cultures, free of domination by the United States, by whites, or by any other privileged group. Neither the Vietnamese, nor any other Third World peoples on the international scene, nor blacks, Native Americans, and Latinos on the domestic front should be dehumanized by degrading language or assumptions about cultural inferiority. Middle-class baby boomers rebelled against fashion-magazine dictated clothing and industrially produced food and explored international and ethnic clothes and cuisines.

The revival of ethnic food in the 1960s began with African Americans. Literature professor Doris Witt describes how the black power movement contributed to the celebration of foods previously stigmatized because of their association with the slave diet: chitterlings, neck bones, maws, knuckles, pork chops, fatback, fried porgies, fried chicken, collard greens, pot likker, turnips, kale, watermelon, black-eyed peas, grits, gravy, hoppin' john, hushpuppies, hoecake, buttermilk biscuits, dumplings, and okra. She argues that members of the black middle class adopted soul food to assert their racial authenticity in response to charges from black separatists that they had assimilated into the white culture and power structure. She also notes that "the valorization of a primarily black (grand)mother-daughter practice, soul food cooking, was related to the concurrent vilification of African American women as castrating matriarchs."[22]

Descendants of white southerners and immigrants from southern and eastern Europe also expressed pride in their foodways in the 1960s. According to Gabaccia, "They mourned a different history from that of the mainstream, notably the losses—of culture, community, and identity—they had experienced by voluntarily (or in some cases involuntarily) becoming part of the national group. For these new ethnics, the task at hand was to undo the cultural effects of three generations of assimilation. Not surprisingly, food became an integral part of that effort."[23]

Susan Kalcik reports that when visitors at the Smithsonian Institution's Festival of American Folklife were interviewed, food was the most mentioned marker of ethnic identity. Furthermore, ethnic and regional foodways were often intertwined. "As with other aspects of ethnic tradition, there is often a drift from ethnic to regional identity; individuals without a strong sense of ethnicity may fill the need for a more specific identity than 'American' with regional traditions, including cooking."[24] Indeed, as we have seen, viewed historically, the cuisine of every region in the United States was a cultural hybrid.

Kalcik observes that as a general rule, an immigrant generation, especially those who were older when they emigrated, held onto their foodways longer than the second generation did, and that immigrant children often adapted first to American foodways, introducing adults in their household to American food. Sometimes the third generation took up the cooking and serving of ethnic foods skipped by the second generation. In addition to age and generation, other factors that influenced ethnic food choice were the occupation of the breadwinner, the education of the cook, the presence of young children, the affordability and convenience of food items, commercialization, and urbanization. Sometimes people dropped ethnic foodways that were considered low status or offensive to their American neighbors (as was the case with Illinois Germans who stopped eating blood sausage). Traditional foodways were often relegated to a particular meal, usually dinner, since breakfast, lunch, and snacks were more responsive to acculturation pressures.[25]

Anthropologists maintain that foodways are particularly resistant to change because, as one of the earliest formed layers of culture, they are among the hardest to alter.[26] Food habits consist of a core diet, a secondary core, and peripheral foods, with the greatest emotional resistance to changes in the core diet.[27]

For anthropologists Mary Douglas and Hortense Powdermaker, food is related to social boundaries. Douglas describes food as a code containing messages about "different degrees of hierarchy, inclusion and exclusion, boundaries and transactions across boundaries. . . . Food categories therefore encode social events." In British foodways, "drinks are for strangers, acquaintances, workmen, and family. Meals are for family, close friends, honored guests. The grand operator of the system is the line between intimacy and distance. Those we know at meals we know at drinks. The meal expresses close friendship. Those we know only at drinks we know less intimately. So long as this boundary matters to us (and there is no reason to suppose it will always matter) the boundary between drinks and meals has meaning."[28] Using the family as a unit of analysis, Douglas demarcates how boundaries are both external, that is, between family and nonfamily, and internal, among family members. Powdermaker also emphasizes both individual and group social boundaries. "The communal eating of food and customs concerning it may be said to have a double social function: (1) to maintain the cohesion of the society and groups within it; (2) to determine, in part, the relation of the individual to the society and to the smaller groups within it."[29]

Food traditions keep ethnic cultures alive. Many Americans spend considerable time and money to join family members for ritual meals for Passover, Diwali, Christmas, Easter, and Thanksgiving. People routinely send food packages to loved ones in the armed services. It is so common to send food at Christmastime that recipes for Christmas cookies often include information on how well they travel and keep. Some Mexican Americans and Vietnamese Americans leave special foods at the altars of departed family members. Italian Americans fill a child's coffin with sweets as food for the next life. For many groups, funeral ceremonies include food for the bereaved family.[30]

Often women feel a special responsibility to keep their group culture alive through food, even when they work outside the home. Many Chicanas write about keeping *la cultura* alive by teaching their children Spanish songs, stories, and religious rituals, and by teaching their daughters to cook tortillas and *chile verde*. In their effort to maintain an ethnic culture eroded by television and ignored by schools in America, Chicanas see themselves as cultural bridges between present and past. When they do not have time to be the bridges themselves, Chicana working mothers often find a "tortilla grandma" to babysit and provide *la cultura*. Many white working mothers fight similar—and often losing—battles to carry forward a domestic culture of homemade apple pie and birthday cakes.[31] Working mothers decide daily which elements of what was familiar to them as children should be passed on to their children. With limited time, they must be selective.

The Slow Food Movement

By the end of the twentieth century, many Americans had joined an international movement that called on people to slow down, savor meals, and preserve endangered food traditions. It drew attention to how contemporary foodways were inextricably linked to questions of time and quality. The Slow Food movement shunned fast food in favor of leisurely cooking and eating. It counteracted the homogenization and standardization of food with artisanally produced food and an Ark of Taste, composed of endangered food products. And it championed conviviality and commensality in the face of the abandonment of the dinner table.

The Slow Food movement started in 1986 to protest the arrival of the first McDonald's on the Spanish Steps in Rome. Its founder was Carlo Petrini, a northern Italian food journalist who lamented the erosion of civilized dining. He set up tables in front of McDonald's and invited Italy's grandmothers to serve their favorite dishes to passersby.[32] In 1989, delegates from fifteen countries met at the Opéra Comique in Paris and approved the movement's manifesto:

> Our century, which began and has developed under the insignia of industrial civilization, first invented the machine and then took it as its life model. We are enslaved by speed and have all succumbed to the same insidious virus: Fast Life, which disrupts our habits, pervades the privacy of our homes and forces us to eat Fast Foods. To be worthy of the name, Homo Sapiens should rid himself of speed before it reduces him to a species in danger of extinction. A firm defense of quiet material pleasure is the only way to oppose the universal folly of Fast Life. May suitable doses of sensual pleasure and slow, long-lasting enjoyment preserve us from the contagion of the multitude who mistake frenzy for efficiency. Our defense should begin at the table with Slow Food. Let us rediscover the flavors and savors of regional cooking and banish the degrading effects of Fast Food. In the name of productivity, Fast Life has changed our way of being and threatens our environment and our landscapes. So Slow Food is now the only truly progressive answer. That is what real culture is all about: developing taste rather than demeaning it. And what better way to set about this than an international exchange of experiences, knowledge, projects? Slow Food guarantees a better future. Slow Food is an idea that needs plenty of qualified supporters who can help turn this (slow) motion into an international movement, with the little snail as its symbol.[33]

In 2008 the movement boasted some eighty-five thousand members in 132 countries, organized into local *convivia*. The *convivium* leader organizes food and wine events, creates moments of conviviality, promotes local artisans, and educates members in matters of taste.[34]

An American Slow Food headquarters opened in New York in August 2000 to coordinate the grassroots activities of more than four thousand members, organized into forty-one *convivia*. Three hundred new members joined *convivia* each month. Northern California had the largest Slow Food membership in the United States, with nine *convivia,* including the nation's first (1996) in San Francisco and one in Berkeley headed by Chez Panisse restaurateur Alice Waters.[35]

One member of the Berkeley group was Marion Cunningham, renowned cookbook author who rewrote the famous *Fanny Farmer Cookbook.* She attended a Slow Food dinner at Chez Panisse in 1999 in honor of founder Petrini. She said, "My great concern is we're losing this community at the table, which is a far more grave loss than it seems at first glance. Slow Food is about community, about people having a lifestyle that gives them a sense of belonging, not just a Social Security number." Among the California en-dangered products inducted into the Slow Food Ark was a dry Monterey jack cheese from Vella Cheese in Sonoma. Petrini, taking delight in Vella's account of rolling up his sleeves and putting his hands in his cheeses to feel the temperature and consistency, expressed disdain for an obsession with hygiene and for computer-controlled cheese production. The founder of the San Francisco *convivium,* wine importer Lorenzo Scarpone, worked in a low-income San Francisco neighborhood to teach small groups of young teenagers how to cook. "I don't want to teach kids to be fancy. I just want them to have enough knowledge to go shopping. . . . Kids know so much about other things—music, clothes—but not about (food)."[36]

Slow Food proponents, sensitive to charges of elitism and hedonism, have distinguished themselves from their predecessors, wine and food societies, by emphasizing that they have more in mind than expensive meals and rare foods: they want to change how children relate to food and Italian foodways are a good model. Food critic Patricia Unterman wrote an account of her visit to the third biannual Slow Food Salone de Gusto (Hall of Taste) in Turin in 2000. The 120,000 attendees, including 1,000 journalists from all over the world, encountered an astonishing array of foods, all slowly, artisanally pro-duced, presented by five hundred exhibitors. Although she was overwhelmed by the embarrassment of riches, thousands of Italian schoolchildren on field trips were nonchalantly "tasting their way through the aisles. They seemed to have no problem deciding what they would or would not taste. Italian kids learn about agriculture and cooking as part of their curriculum and they are completely self-confident about food. I have never met an Italian who did not know his or her way around the kitchen and the table."[37]

The Slow Food movement has also encouraged consumers to vote with their wallets to save food items on the verge of extinction, for the larger public purposes of good taste, group tradition, and sustainable ecology. One endangered product is the native wild rice that grows along lakesides and rivers in Minnesota. It is hand harvested up to three times during a season and hand parched over a wood fire. "This laboriously prepared native wild rice is qualitatively different than either commercially cultivated, paddy grown, hybrid 'wild' rice, or machine harvested and parched lakeside wild rice. It must be rinsed more, but it cooks faster and has a nutty, delicate flavor. It sells for $8 a pound and few people outside the upper Midwest have ever tasted it. Yet the wild rice is an important part of the economy for several Native American tribes, who could actually produce more." Slow Food has linked consumers directly with such producers. It has also drawn international attention to a woman who set up a camel, cow, and goat dairy cooperative in Mauritania supplied by eight hundred nomads; a North Carolina man who protected more than one hundred rare and endangered breeds of livestock; and an Australian couple whose garden was planted with hundreds of rare fruits, trees, herbs, and medicinal plants collected over twenty years from the world's rainforests.[38]

Proponents of the Slow Food movement have taken pains to draw connections between the nexus of land, food, meals, taste, and community. However, critics have charged that the movement smacks of elitism and a romanticized view of history. Food historian Rachel Laudan has dubbed this approach to food "culinary Luddism," after the "English hand workers of the nineteenth century who abhorred machines that were destroying their traditional way of life." She argues that history should not be divided into the good sunny days of yore and the bad gray industrial present. As our ancestors had to learn the hard way, not all food found in nature was delicious, reliable, digestible, or safe. "Fresh meat was rank and tough, fresh milk warm and unmistakably a body excretion; fresh fruits (dates and grapes being rare exceptions outside the tropics) were inedibly sour, fresh vegetables bitter. . . . Fresh fish began to stink, fresh milk soured, eggs went rotten." Grains, which supplied the bulk of the calories in most societies, had to be "threshed, ground, and cooked to make them edible. Other plants, including the roots and tubers that were the life support of societies that did not eat grains, are often downright poisonous. Without careful processing, green potatoes, stinging taro, and cassava bitter with prussic acid are not just indigestible, but toxic."[39]

Although it is tempting to wax nostalgic about a time when families and friends met to relax over delicious food, Laudan maintains that it obscures the fact that historically fast food has been a mainstay of city dwellers in every society. "Deep-fried foods, expensive and dangerous to prepare at home, have always had their place on the street. . . . Bread, also expensive to bake at home, is one of the oldest convenience foods." She praises the foods of culinary modernism for being egalitarian without demanding the time and money that traditional foodstuffs did. "They allow us unparalleled choices not just of diet but of what to do with our lives." She considers it elitist to "urge the Mexican to stay at her *metate*, the farmer to stay at his olive press, the housewife to stay at her stove instead of going to McDonald's, all so that we may eat handmade tortillas, traditionally pressed olive oil, and home-cooked meals."[40]

Laudan thinks it is hypocritical to deny that the modern, global, industrial economy, and not the local resources of the wintry country around New York, Boston, or Chicago, has allowed us "to savor traditional, peasant, fresh, and natural foods. Virgin olive oil, Thai fish sauce, and *udon* noodles come to us thanks to international marketing. Fresh and natural loom so large because we can take for granted the preserved and processed staples—salt, flour, sugar, chocolate, oils, coffee, tea—produced by agribusiness and food corporations. . . . Culinary Luddism, far from escaping the modern global food economy, is parasitic upon it."[41]

American Foodways, the Obesity Crisis, and Global Warming

By the twenty-first century, Americans were reveling in the range of comestibles provided by the international economy. At the same time, they have grown more critical of the ways in which American foodways, increasingly exported around the globe, contribute to an obesity crisis and global warming. A fast-food diet, loaded with fats and sugars, has supplanted healthier fruits and vegetables. Out-of-season produce travels thousands of "food miles" to reach American tables, increasing demand for petroleum and exacerbating global warming.

Eric Schlosser has sounded the alarm that our "Fast Food Nation" is harming our landscape, economy, workforce, and popular culture. As working parents have felt increasingly guilty about spending less time with their children, they started spending more money on them, prodded by an explosion in children's advertising that began in the 1980s. McDonald's came to the rescue with high-fat Happy Meals. Fast-food franchises promote excessive soda consumption, which, coupled with an increasingly sedentary lifestyle, has resulted in an epidemic in obesity and childhood diabetes. Around the world, America has become equated with a fast food that threatens "a fundamental aspect of national identity: how, where, and what people chose to eat."[42]

Marion Nestle has documented how the food industry plays a major role in setting nutritional standards, encouraging Americans to overeat and to purchase foods high in fat, salt, and sugar, rather than the healthier plant foods. The industry markets "hyperconvenient products" that allow busy people to snack as they go about their busy lives. She encourages Americans to "vote with their forks" by purchasing locally produced, organically grown food not only for its improved taste and nutritional quality, but also because the food does not have to travel far or be stored long. Such purchases support local farmers, promote the viability of rural communities, and create diversity in agricultural production.[43]

Barbara Kingsolver "voted with her family" by moving them from Tucson, Arizona, where food arrived in refrigerated modules, to a farm in Virginia, where they could grow their own food. She is concerned that Americans' ignorance of food sources has resulted in an epidemic of diet-related diseases and an overdependence on petroleum to fly in food from around the globe, exacerbating global warming. Food marketers prey on humans' inherent weakness for fats and sugars and bombard children with a $10 billion advertising campaign. She is pleased that "better food—more local, more healthy, more sensible—is a powerful new topic of the American conversation." And she has some explanations for the French paradox: the fact that the French eat rich foods yet remain thin. They do not guzzle giant sodas, they consume many courses but in small portions, and they eat slowly and socially. "Owing to certain rules about taste and civility in their heads, their bodies seem to know when enough is enough." For the French, the paradox is how people manage to consume so much scary American food.[44]

Michael Pollan also weighs in on the French paradox, crediting their strict and stable eating rules: small portions, absence of seconds and snacks, communal meals, and leisurely pace. He remarks that the French culture of food has successfully negotiated the omnivore's dilemma, allowing the French to enjoy their meals without ruining their health. The omnivore's dilemma arises because "when one can eat just about anything nature has to offer, deciding what you *should* eat will inevitably stir anxiety, especially when some of the potential foods on offer are liable to sicken or kill you." The American food industry loves this dilemma, since the more anxious consumers are about eating, the more vulnerable they are to the seduction of the marketer and the advice of the expert. The food industry is the anti-France: encouraging us to eat large portions, go back for seconds, snack, and eat on the run.[45]

Pollan also takes food companies to task for eroding the family meal. In pursuit of new markets, they "have broken Mom's hold over the American menu by marketing to every conceivable demographic—and especially to children." When marketers at General Mills hired anthropologists to film family dinners, they found Mom eating a proper meal and salad, Dad fixing a low-carbohydrate meal, the teenager following a vegetarian diet, and the child downing pizza. Over the course of a half-hour dinner, family members roamed in and out of the kitchen, zapping single-portion entrees in the microwave, and stopped briefly at the dining-room table, where they may or may not have crossed paths with another family member for a few minutes. "Families who eat this way are among the 47 percent of Americans who report to pollsters that they still sit down to a family meal every night." Americans no longer have a cultural consensus on the subject of eating—rules and rituals that have the potential to counteract the food industry's enticing processing, packaging, and marketing. As anxious omnivores, Pollan observes that we rely less and less "on the accumulated wisdom of a cuisine, or even on the wisdom of our senses" and increasingly on "expert opinion, advertising, government food pyramids, and diet books": a state of nature in the modern supermarket or fast-food outlet. Even France is beginning to succumb to America's fast-food habits.[46]

So what does it mean in the United States to eat American food? Historically, American food began as regional fare developed through contacts between Native peoples, European colonists, and African slaves. American cuisine was democratic from the outset. Sociologically, American food was whatever was eaten by the group higher up on the social hierarchy. As a nation of immigrants, we are anxious about status and want to fit in. Politically, American food was shaped by the government feeding its troops. Soldiers returned home with a taste for items not found in regional home cooking. Economically, American food was whatever corporations marketed nationally and internationally. In practice, American foodways have always been multiethnic and democratic. Today, the rules and rituals of cuisines and ethnic traditions are a bulwark defending civil food practices—leisurely meals, healthy and flavorful food choices, communal and convivial meals—against the harmful effects of a fast-food nation.

Part Two

Table Conversation

Chapter 4
Conversation and Manners

Assuming that Americans can be convinced to value foodwork, to make flavorful and healthy food choices, and to slow down for leisurely and communal meals, then the stage is set for conviviality and conversation. Part of the civility challenge is to drive home the importance of *the courtesy of a conversation.* This chapter elaborates on the ways in which courtesy and conversation are important to civility and civil society. A vibrant civil society promotes meaningful human connections and thrives as a realm of human association independent of the economy and polity. We have seen how the rules and rituals of cuisines and ethnic traditions can join people together and stave off the encroachments of marketers telling us what to eat. Now we will explore how the rules and rituals, along with the intimacy, of conversation and courtesy can promote civic connections and model the kind of diplomatic speech that is often sorely lacking in the polity. Throughout history, conversation and manners have been so encrusted with class and gender connotations that we need to excavate these concepts to make them viable in today's world.

Conversations and Civility

The English word *conversation* has always connoted intimate connection and companionship. It derives from the Latin *conversari,* which means "to live, to keep company with." According to the *Oxford English Dictionary,* in medieval and Renaissance times, conversation meant "the action of living or having one's being in a place or among persons," "the action of consorting or having dealings with others; living together; commerce, intercourse, society, intimacy" and even "sexual intercourse or intimacy." Over time, the term was used figuratively to refer to "occupation or engagement with things, in the way of business or study; the resulting condition of acquaintance or intimacy with a matter; the manner of conducting oneself in the world or in society; and behavior, mode or course of life." Its literal meaning was "circle of acquaintance, company, society." Its contemporary meaning—the interchange of thoughts and words; familiar discourse or talk; an oral exchange of sentiments, observations, opinions, and ideas—dates back to the late 1500s.

Conversation is quintessentially a social, lively, intimate, and engaged interchange of thoughts, words, sentiments, observations, opinions, and ideas. To have a genuine conversation, all parties must be interested in the thoughts of others. Absent such interest, the conversation is a charade. Everyone must listen carefully for an intimate interchange to take place. Otherwise, the give-and-take is in bad faith. Conversants must use language that furthers rather than thwarts the conversation. Personal attacks, expressions of exasperation or impatience, know-it-all statements, and threats are conversation stoppers. Participants in genuine conversations have to be mature enough to put their own needs in the context of the needs of the group. It may be emotionally healthy to vent one's feelings, but the middle of a conversation is usually not the best time to do so. If people feel silenced, or railroaded, or put down, or insulted, then they are not likely to be forthcoming with their true sentiments.

Unless people think that they owe one another the courtesy of a conversation, there can be no civility or democracy. Conversations, civility, and democracy are all subversive of authoritarianism, whether political, social, or at the table. Authoritarian political regimes are hierarchical, with superiors giving orders to subordinates. Their survival depends on a populace willing, for whatever reasons, to accept orders. Since authoritarian regimes are always based on fear, usually of the threat of physical force from the military, the police, or the secret police, people's willingness to be ordered around warrants careful scrutiny. Some people seem to be very willing to give and receive orders. They have what philosopher Theodor Adorno and his colleagues call an authoritarian personality: they thrive on bowing to those above them and tromping on those below them. Such individuals typically come from relatively affectionless families in which parents demand strict obedience to conventional modes of conduct. They feel weak and insecure and place a high value on power and toughness, often despising weak out groups and admiring strong leaders.[1] In a less pathological sense, many people are willing to follow authoritarian rulers because they provide order. For order seekers, it is reassuring to know that everyone has his or her place in a hierarchical structure; chaos, anarchy, and equality are too unsettling. But for the most part, people throughout history have thrown off authoritarian political regimes when given the opportunity. Most people do not like being ordered around or being afraid to speak their minds.

Authoritarian social relations have been subject to upheavals worldwide. Given the opportunity, peasants and workers have become less deferential to their superiors. In the United States, many businesses have allowed employees, who used to be viewed more as subordinates than as team members, greater say in the workplace. Racial groups have defied long-held views of racial inferiority and superiority. Women have fought against notions of male superiority. Resistance to egalitarian change is expressed, for the most part, by people who want to retain a familiar, hierarchical order. For them, a world without order is too frightening, and hierarchical order is the only one imaginable.

These tensions are evident at the table. Some households have authoritarian rules, promulgated by elders, strictly enforced, and entailing severe punishments. Such rules usually deal with eating all the food on one's plate, not doing something "out of turn," or challenging the authority of the elders. Punishments include going without food, being asked to leave the table, or being forced to eat something against one's will. The vestiges of authoritarian rules remain at all tables. Elders promulgate rules to create order for the benefit of the group. But for the most part, table behavior has become less authoritarian over time in the United States.

The need for order persists, but rule making has become more democratic. When today's elders make rules, they have to provide an explanation for them. Rules are more accommodating of the needs of people of all ages at the table. Indeed, many parents are ambivalent about their role as authorities and rule makers at the table. How much say should children have about their behavior at the table? What rules harm children's self-esteem? How much participation is appropriate? What language is permissible and why? How long should they sit at the table? Whose job is it to make sure that everyone gets an equal chance to talk? What if a child is shy and dreads talking? What rules are worth enforcing? What is a good reason for a particular rule?

Table democracy and civility take constant work. Sometimes it is so exhausting that a retreat to an authoritarian "because I said so" is appealing. The dilemma is that democratic parents, in an increasingly antiauthoritarian culture, know that part of their responsibility as a parent is to be an authority, to know better. Authoritarian authorities do not have to provide reasons for what they do. By virtue of their hierarchical position, they do not owe an explanation to subordinates. Democratic parents are required to give reasons. An antiauthoritarian culture has the seductive allure of giving parents permission to abrogate their responsibility as parents—rather than take the time and energy to think of reasons for rules, they can give up on making them altogether and let their children "do their own thing." However, psychologists warn that this posture has disastrous consequences for young children, who constantly test boundaries and need adults to draw them.

Manners provide boundaries at the table, enabling us to eat in peace and to afford each other the courtesy of a conversation. Courtesy may have had courtly origins, but it remains relevant as a democratic concept. However formal and stiff courtesy may have been at court, it allowed the other due consideration. It made one person stop and consider the needs of another. It is a precapitalist notion, emphasizing obligation rather than right, reciprocity and connection rather than competitive individualism. The capitalist drive for profit, efficiency, making money, and getting ahead collides with table manners. When a meal is rushed so that everyone can get back to what really matters—work—it is a waste of time to engage others in extended conversations about their reflections or moral dilemmas. In a world where individual rights trump social obligations, why shouldn't everyone at the table have a right to say and do what suits him or her? Why would a person "owe" any particular behavior to the cook or the host? If the point is individual advancement, then what is wrong with using people for their cooking or asking for the "power table" at the "in" restaurant?

Courtesy is not individualistic; it is social. Somewhat ironically, it subverts both the feudal notion of lording over others and capitalism's competitive individualism. Without courtesy, there can be many forms of communication, but not a conversation. Courtesy is not needed to give orders, bicker, hold forth about oneself, criticize for its own sake, proselytize, or talk at. But it is necessary to converse.

In my view, conversations are the most respectful form of human communication. They are invitations for people to reveal their intimate thoughts and observations and to subject them to the scrutiny of others in a safe context. As long as agreed-upon ground rules provide a safe context, the free expression of ideas can flourish. If these rules are broken, then the conversation stops. Genuine civility and democracy depend on the free expression of ideas. Everyday table conversations give people experience in forming and expressing opinions and ideas in an intimate and safe setting. People talk because a very important part of their lives depends on it: obtaining respect as a person whose ideas matter.

Civil Society: Light Social Conversations and Heavy Political Arguments

If table conversation is so important to civility and civil society, why has it not been the focus of more scholarly attention? One reason is that political scientists and theorists tend to value "political" arguments over "social" conversations. Some theorists question the relevance of comfortable social conversation in the rough-and-tumble world of democratic practice. They are concerned about the current "cult of conversation," "the rosy glow of polite conversation that fuels liberal fantasies about social transformation," and "the romance of conversation."[2]

Michael Schudson makes a distinction between two conversational models: the sociable and the problem solving. In the sociable model, conversation is a source of pleasure and a means of cultivating sensibilities, where verbal facility, wit, and entertainment are paramount. By contrast, problem-solving exchanges are governed by reasonableness and arguments: conversational partners' formulations of and responses to views about what the world is and should be. Schudson also contrasts conversations that are homogeneous (psychologically safe, with shared values) and heterogeneous (public, with different values, and penalties for uncertainty and doubt). He argues that problem-solving and heterogeneous conversations are the kinds that promote democracy. He cautions that conversation is not necessarily egalitarian or democratic. In early modern Europe, conversation was an aristocratic practice dependent on cultivation. It may be that democracy establishes norms that affect even familial and homogeneous conversations, rather than the other way around. "Not the fact of conversation but the norms that govern it make it serviceable for democratic self-government. . . . The rules of democratic conversation can help protect the slow of speech, who are otherwise disenfranchised by the articulate and the glib."[3]

Schudson is correct in saying that problem-solving and heterogeneous conversations are the most likely types to promote democracy. However, to do justice to the complexities of civil society, we need to pay equal attention to the sociable model. One proponent of the sociable model was Michael Oakeshott, who believed that "political education is learning how to participate in a conversation," and that "conversation distinguished the human being from the animal and the civilized man from the barbarian."[4] In *Conversation: A History of a Declining Art*, Stephen Miller also defends the sociable model, arguing that spending time in "the conversible world" (David Hume's term) is likely to make people more sociable and better able to discuss political questions. He advocates conversations for their own sake, for pleasure. Raillery is his index of political health: good-humored, intelligent wit and banter. The *railleur* is an attentive listener who offers good-humored disagreement. Miller contends that most contemporary Americans have little or no interest in the art of conversation; that America's professional class does not take the art of conversation seriously; and that Americans are experiencing a proliferation of "conversation avoidance mechanisms."[5]

According to Miller, Cicero was a pivotal figure in the history of the art of conversation. *On Duties,* written as a letter to his son, was a guidebook for the Roman governing class. In it, Cicero argues that the Romans had neglected the art of conversation, which "should be found in social groups, in philosophical discussions, and among gatherings of friends—and may also attend dinners!" Cicero concedes that many guidebooks existed for oratory, but none for conversation.[6] In *The Art of Conversation,* Peter Burke maintains that the manuals on conversation that appeared in Italy, France, and Britain from the sixteenth to the eighteenth centuries were a series of footnotes on Cicero.[7] David Hume, a champion of the art of conversation, took his catalog of virtues from Cicero. Hume thought that conversations flourished in France because men and women conversed together, the monarchy promoted politeness, and Parisians spent a great deal of time in the conversible world. The main activity of the salons, which were presided over by women, was conversation.[8]

Miller found that it was primarily novelists and essayists who extolled the virtues and pleasures of conversations. Michel de Montaigne, the sixteenth-century French essayist, loved conversation: "To my taste, the most fruitful and natural exercise of our minds is conversation. I find the practice of it the most delightful activity in our lives." He invited people to attack his ideas, since agreement was boring and intellectually deadening. In his "Essay on Conversation" (1743), Henry Fielding defines conversation as "that reciprocal Interchange of Ideas, by which Truth is examined, Things are, in a manner, turned around, and sifted, and all our Knowledge communicated to each other." The narrator in Fielding's *Tom Jones* (1749) says, "A true knowledge of the world is gained only by conversation." Jonathan Swift thought of conversation as "the greatest, the most lasting, and the most innocent, as well as useful Pleasure of Life." And Samuel Johnson remarked that "there is in this world no real delight (excepting those of sensuality), but exchange of ideas in conversation."[9]

According to Miller, nineteenth-century European visitors to the United States were not very impressed with the quality of conversation they encountered. Charles Dickens said the pleasures of conversation were rare, mainly because Americans' love of trade made them narrowly self-interested. Men worried that if they talked too much they would be at a competitive disadvantage in deal making; indeed, they boasted about their distrust. Alexis de Tocqueville said that he encountered good conversation only in Boston. A slightly more positive report came from Henry James and James Bryce, who thought that conversation flourished in Washington, D.C., in the 1880s, with men specializing in business and politics, women in religion and art. Compared to Europe, women were conversational equals. Some prominent Americans disparaged conversation. Henry David Thoreau considered it a waste of time, and Herman Melville regarded the conversationalist as a con man. For Melville, America was a nation of strangers because men were so wary of the intentions of others that they reinvented themselves continually. Peter Gibian has dubbed the mid-nineteenth century America's "Age of Conversation." However, both Miller and Tocqueville considered it as more an age of oratory, lecturers, and panel discussions than an age of conversation.[10]

A conversation is only one type of democratic practice, but like all democratic practices it assumes differences of opinion among people, a point frequently ignored by its critics. Conversation certainly comes loaded with the historical baggage of class, race, and gender. But so does every other form of democratic practice: elections, use of the media, debates, group membership, and the like. Its strengths and weaknesses ought to be subject to the same scrutiny as other forms of democratic practice. Many of the things that give theorists pause about the sociable model of conversation are the very things that promote civil society. The conversible world is enjoyable, creates goodwill, enhances self- and mutual respect, helps people see one another as complex human beings rather than abstract partisans, and allows for wit and humor to ease tension. To feel good and to do good have an important place in most people's definitions of civil society.

Political arguments are certainly a mainstay of democratic politics. But as linguist Deborah Tannen has noted, an argument culture can create an adversarial stance where winning becomes more important than understanding or conflict resolution. Indeed, the very ability to formulate and engage in rational argument may depend on a social connectedness that stems from conversation and intimate talk.[11]

Neurolinguist John L. Locke writes about the biological and evolutionary importance of intimate talk. He contends that English-speaking societies are experiencing functional "de-voicing": they have been harmed by an insufficient diet of intimate talking. Many aspects of our "selves" are made public through our voices: physical, emotional, biographical, psychological, physiological, and relational. As if on cue from moral-sentiment philosophers, four-year-olds approach strange children with the query, "Do you want to be my friend?" Social talking reflects a need for companionship that leads us to say something, sometimes anything. Our impulse to congregate leads to talking followed by the justification of a topic. Talking is deeply biologic, revealing a disposition to connect with other members of the species and the group. Even impaired newborns demonstrate a biological drive to talk. We are neurologically hardwired to promote feelings of harmony. In this sense, intimate speech is more a meeting of hearts than a meeting of minds. Intimate talk alters our mood. Social bonds are in some neurochemical sense opioid addictions. When monkeys groom each other, it boosts the level of endorphins (brain opiates) in the cerebrospinal fluid of the recipient. Cathartic relief comes from social and emotional talking. With loss of intimacy comes loneliness and vulnerability to strangers who, on soap operas and the like, offer an infusion of affection. Democracy needs table conviviality. Locke recognizes a strong bond between eating or drinking and talking. "It's as though ingestion of food and expulsion of sound somehow enjoy a natural association." He cites the case of eighteenth-century Swedish rulers who, convinced that malcontents were planning revolts against them, closed down the coffeehouses. They did this by forcing medical researchers to report "scientific" evidence that coffee was harmful to health.[12]

Compared to many other forms of political practice, conversations have the advantage of sparking the imaginations of the participants. Many political interchanges falter and policies suffer from a lack of political imagination. Theodore Zeldin sees conversation as transformative: "Conversation is a meeting of minds with different memories and habits. When minds meet, they don't just exchange facts: they transform them, reshape them, draw different implications from them, engage in new trains of thought." Conversation is based on mutual respect, a private equality that can transfer to public life. He views the family as the greatest teacher of the art of conversation with strangers, but only if the family "is seen as a safe place to make discoveries about the world, and to discuss them, to digest them, without fear." Since conversations are face to face, we are forced to see individuals in all their human complexity. Zeldin argues that one's education is not complete until one has conversations with people from every continent and every civilization.[13]

Margaret Shepherd calls civilized conversation an art that transforms everyday life into something richer: engaging the mind, exciting the imagination, and expanding the view of the world. It is democratic insofar as it is a craft as well as an art, requiring a little talent and a lot of practice. The key is to listen at least as much as one talks. Etiquette and manners are generally accepted guidelines for making everyone comfortable enough to connect. Courtesy is crucial in order to connect somehow with the other person. And some of the very best talk happens when people are sitting around a table and savoring a good meal.[14]

The Lost Art of Conversation in the United States

Conversation in the United States is in danger of becoming an endangered art form. It requires skills that are in increasingly short supply: astutely observing body language, understanding the ambiguity and cultural relativity of words, listening for what is not said, and carefully choosing words to keep the conversation from devolving into other forms of verbal interaction, such as chatter, banter, insults, quarrels, posturing, scoring points, lording over others, flashing verbal pyrotechnics, and silencing with authoritative or off-putting language.

Why are our conversational skills in such short supply? The convenience of electronic communication has increased the *quantity* of our social interactions, especially outside our immediate homes and neighborhoods. However, we cannot observe body language over the telephone or through e-mail. Over the phone, at least we can detect voice inflection, levels of emotion, and silences, clues not available over the Internet or via instant messaging. The art of conversation is crafted locally: at home and in market, school, and work settings, in a native language. Increased social and geographical mobility makes it harder to decipher the ambiguity and cultural nuances of verbal expressions. We hear new languages at school, at the market, and at work; we learn the jargon of neighborhoods, academics, and pundits; and we are barraged by the catchy phrases of advertisers and the mass media. As word choice explodes, deciphering meaning becomes more daunting. Fast-paced, pragmatic Americans are impatient with pauses and silences. We do not get enough practice keeping a conversation going. We would love to, but we do not have enough time.

We all have to practice our conversational skills, since conversation is more an art than a science. We talk about "the art of conversation," not "the science of conversation." Certainly there are scientific elements of conversation: observation of patterns of behavior, hypotheses about cause and effect of word choice, and theories about human motivation. For the most part, however, conversation is experienced as a work in progress, with vigilant attention to changing cues about mood, meaning, roles, performance, attention, impact, and persuasion. A conversation is usually full of surprises: we cannot predict with great confidence its content, process, or outcome. It requires an emotional risk, which is tempting to avoid altogether. One must extend oneself and bracket one's own needs and desires, or at least translate them, in a way that makes talking sustainable.

As much as conversations are avoided for their emotional risk, they are sought for their power to connect us with others and to achieve and obtain desirable things: food, shelter, love, respect, work, power, money, prestige, identity, and meaning in life. Conversations are tailored to fit the people in the varied spheres of our lives, from the local to the global: family, friends, classmates, neighbors, coworkers, community members, and citizens of cities, states, countries, and the planet. This tailoring is largely a function of knowledge and trust. Conversations are easier the more one knows about and trusts someone: one can be more frank, let down one's guard, level with someone, say what one really means, and be more direct.

Conversations relating to food have a democratic equalizer built into them: everybody eats, enjoys delicious food, wants safe and healthy food, and shares food traditions with loved ones. Conversants can retreat to these shared experiences if the conversational going gets too rough. Safe topics provide a reprieve: time to rethink and reformulate before plunging once again into the emotionally charged terrain of extending oneself in conversation. Such thoughtfulness is often coupled with generous gestures. "Would anyone like more to eat?" allows conversants to regroup and rekindle a generosity of spirit.

Like conversations, food practices and household foodwork also cultivate thoughtfulness and generosity. They provide more reservoirs for future hard times: comfort food, family cookbooks, pleasant aromas, group collaboration on shared meals. Food memories run deep, are powerful and sensual. Meals and ritual foods make it possible for deeply felt needs and emotions (hunger, satisfaction, personal attachments, joy at weddings and birth, and sadness at loss and death) to coexist with collaborative decision making about the good of the group (meal planning and preparation), modeling democratic challenges writ larger.

Food and foodways eventually make their way to a table. Commensality is the togetherness that arises out of eating at a table. Classicist Margaret Visser describes eating around a table as "an ethnocentric way for us to express a bonding mechanism which is common to every human society: that of mealtime sharing." Manners are an essential prerequisite for commensality.

Humans need the predictability of manners in order to act in concert. "We connect, in addition, with events, dates, shared emotions, kinship and group ties, the life cycle, the world in general." Visser acknowledges that all of this is extremely complex and time consuming. But if we stop making all these customary links, we also soon cease to understand. The price for not taking the time and trouble is loss of communication and the disappearance of manners.[15]

Upper Class and Feminine: Courtesy, Civility, Politeness, and Manners

One reason for the invisibility of table activities in most writings about civil society is the historical characterization of courtesy, civility, politeness, and manners as upper class and feminine. Norbert Elias traces the modern meaning of *civility* to medieval *courtoisie* (courtesy), the behavior expected at court. Absolute monarchs in the sixteenth and seventeenth centuries enforced standards of behavior to turn warriors into courtiers: restraint, self-consciousness, affective neutrality, and heightened shame and repugnance about bodily functions. These norms required stricter childrearing, such as that outlined in Erasmus's 1530 book, *De civilitate morum puerilium* (*On Civility of Behaviour in Boys*). "Civility" soon became caught up in nationalistic and class culture wars. As the French versions of *civilité* and *civilisation* became the norm, the Germans denigrated *civilisation* as external superficiality, in contrast to German *Kultur* (culture), the inner formation of the spirit. Immanuel Kant distinguished the truly moral "culture" from "civilization's" mere semblances of morality—the love of honor and outward propriety. Throughout Europe, the rising bourgeoisie regarded courtly manners as artificial. However, they adopted their own version of civilized self-control in part to emulate the aristocracy and in part to distinguish themselves from the low manners of the peasantry and workers.[16]

Across the Atlantic, a 1595 French Jesuit manual was adapted via a 1640 English manual into a young George Washington's *Rules of Civility and Decent Behaviour in Company and Conversation*. First on the list of maxims was "Every Action done in Company, ought to be with Some Sign of Respect, to those that are Present."[17] In nineteenth-century America, etiquette advisors faced the same class pressures as Europeans. They were attacked by both Europeans and Americans with aristocratic pretensions who dismissed American society as irredeemably vulgar and viewed republicanism as incompatible with refinement, and at the same time by democratic critics who saw in civility nothing more than snobbery and class interests. As elsewhere, some Americans observed strictures of civility out of egalitarian convictions, others out of sheer self-interest in their desire to advance in social rank.[18]

Etiquette and manners could certainly be used uncivilly as exclusionary class markers. Indeed, the word *etiquette* has its origins in the French word for the "ticket," a written document that described ever-changing court formalities—a conscious attempt on the part of Louis XIV to distract nobles from political plotting. But manners also protect the powerless by requiring the powerful to restrain themselves from pushing people around.[19]

In the early days of the American republic, the founders considered etiquette a matter worthy of their deliberations. Benjamin Franklin's *Poor Richard's Almanac* mixed morals with manners, courtesy with careerism. As a youth, George Washington followed his Jesuit guidebook, and as president he

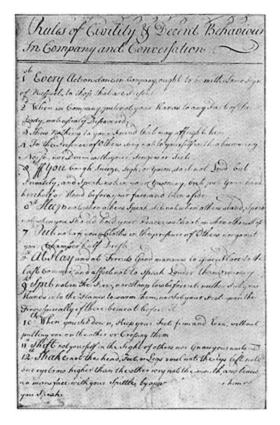

Washington's Rules of Civility. President George Washington placed a high value on civility and conversation. In his youth, he transcribed *Rules of Civility and Decent Behavior in Company and Conversation.* In conversation, one should show respect and should not flatter, turn one's back, or show delight at the misfortune of others. The fifty-fifth maxim was "Eat not in the Streets, nor in the House, out of season." George Washington Papers at the Library of Congress, 1741–1799: Series 1a.

issued his own etiquette rules, such as sitting down to dinner at the appointed hour without waiting for tardy guests. President Thomas Jefferson wanted to replace the last vestiges of imperial-appearing etiquette with an entirely republican one. He adapted boardinghouse etiquette for the White House, abolishing any sense of order in diplomatic, national, or private gatherings. As America industrialized, men left the home for factories and mills, and women became the moral guardians of the household, responsible for manners and etiquette, a subject that became increasingly trivial and feminized.[20]

The concepts of courtesy and civility are so weighted with European social-class connotations that many American thinkers are hesitant to go near them. For example, in her study of the moral dispositions of group members in American democracy, Nancy Rosenblum convincingly extols the virtues of treating people identically and with easy spontaneity and of speaking out against ordinary injustice. She posits that these moral dispositions are first learned at home. But she is reluctant to identify the democracy of everyday life with civility rules. "Across time and cultures, most forms of civility have been patently undemocratic in their attention to rank, class, office, affiliation, or social standing."[21]

Other writers worry that "civilitarians" will censor the rough-and-tumble necessary for a vibrant democracy. Randall Kennedy regards the contemporary "civility crisis" as a veiled attack on the emancipatory social movements of the 1960s. He calls proponents of civility crybabies who cannot stand the discomfort of pointed criticism.[22] Benjamin DeMott argues that incivility is an appropriate response to an elite whose behavior does not deserve the respect of the public: when you are in an argument with a thug, there are things more important than civility.[23]

Cheshire Calhoun admits that civility has three strikes against it: class-demarcating behaviors; a morally uncritical conformity to socially established rules of respect and tolerance; "an equivalent to one or more items on the familiar philosophical list of moral virtues." Nevertheless, he defends civility as a moral virtue whose function, echoing Washington's manual, is to communicate basic moral attitudes of respect, tolerance, and considerateness.[24] Along similar lines, Sarah Buss notes the importance of the expressive function of manners. She argues that courtesy is the virtue essential to good manners, and that the most important lessons in manners are lessons in how to avoid being discourteous, impolite, rude, inconsiderate, offensive, and insulting. Two of the most important objectives of manners are to encourage us to make ourselves agreeable and to prompt us to appear to be goodwilled. Buss writes that "people who are boorish or sulky or obnoxious or otherwise disagreeable are morally deficient precisely because they make so little effort to please. . . . People have a basic moral obligation to make themselves agreeable to others."[25]

For many skeptical Americans, the civic virtues of thoughtfulness and generosity, or "virtue politics" in general, conjure up images of women's quaint and naive "do-goodism" in the nineteenth and early twentieth centuries: fighting demon rum in the temperance movement and cleaning up corrupt city politics in the progressive movement. Indeed, women's role as keepers of civic virtue stretches back to colonial times. The civic republican strand of American political thought emphasized the obligation of citizens to act virtuously in pursuit of the common good. Democracy both promoted and was maintained by civic virtue. Anti-Federalists such as Patrick Henry and Mercy Warren insisted that republicanism was possible only with public-spirited or virtuous citizens who willingly put aside self-interest for the sake of the public good. Rigorous standards of civic virtue could only be maintained in small, intense communities where citizens sensed their unity with one another and where public affairs were immediately accessible and understandable.[26] Domestic life was intimately related to the commonweal: citizens had to be taught to value the public interest at home by women, what historian Linda Kerber calls "Republican Motherhood."[27] Ralph Waldo Emerson advocated democracy in the household as the moral foundation of a democratic society. The household embodied the virtues of charity and hospitality.[28]

Throughout the nineteenth century, women brought domestic moral values to bear on their civic associations: some linked their pacifism or concern for the poor with their experiences caring for children, while others vowed to clean up dirty, corrupt city politics just as they would sweep a house with a broom. Largely excluded from male political clubs, political parties, and electoral processes, they formed women's organizations with a social-feminist orientation that celebrated women's experiences and values.[29] By contrast, equality feminists, such as Charlotte Perkins Gilman, beat a quick retreat from the kitchen in the belief that home cooking was predicated on ignorance, "the habits of a dark untutored past," on people's palates instead of the latest scientific findings.[30] Feminists' divided opinions on the values of the domestic sphere resurfaced in the second wave, ranging from Simone de Beauvoir's preference for transcendent activity outside the immanence of the daily household chores to Sara Ruddick's maternal thinking.[31]

Two virtues essential for civilized relationships, and modeled by women in the historic division of household labor, are thoughtfulness and generosity. Household foodwork requires thinking daily about the sources of food, the needs of others, meal planning and timing, the sharing of tasks, and fair shares at the table. Sharing food requires trust that what we consume will not be poisonous or make us sick, that the food will taste good, that we will not go hungry, and that there will be predictability in the rituals of eating. We want food to be good for us and good for groups with which we identify—companions, families, ethnic groups, and nations. Food connects us with others and provides comfort when we feel alone. Table conversation is an art of give and take, where we think before we speak so that we do not disrupt the pleasures and sharing of the group.

Even though these responsibilities and activities are not usually seen as political, they form an invisible part of civil society and democracy. In a democracy, politics consists of people defining the good life and the common good and exercising power—either civilly or uncivilly—to bring the good life and the common good into practice. The more democratic the polity, the more people participate in both defining and bringing about what is good for everyone through civil means. Ideally, a democratic process is deliberative: people think and give reasons for what *they* think in trying to persuade *others* to agree with them. People will be more persuasive to the degree that they understand both what they think and what others think. This mutual self- and other-understanding comes primarily from conversations—reciprocal speech and listening. The table is an important place to learn the art of conversation, especially across generations. It provides an opportunity to feel connected and to develop trust in others. Civility at the table is a cornerstone of civil society and democratic processes. There is good reason to degender and repoliticize the household as a locus for the practice of the civic virtues of thoughtfulness and generosity.

The Universality of Table Manners

In every society, finding one's voice at the table develops within an elaborate framework of table manners, or rules about politeness where food and comportment are concerned. Visser claims that table manners are as old as human society itself. The fact that humans regularly share food probably gave rise to the major elements of society: "kinship systems (who belongs with whom; which people eat together), language (for discussing food past, present and future, for planning the acquisition of food, and deciding how to divide it out while preventing fights), technology (how to kill, cut, keep and carry), and morality (what is a just slice?)." The sharing of food is universally recognized as a test of moral values—everyone understands what going without food means. Good manners and polite behavior make sharing easier.[32]

In the West, words concerning etiquette, polish, and manners derive from French largely due to the influence of the French court, especially that of King Louis XIV. He and subsequent French monarchs ran a sort of school of manners at Versailles. "Courtiers lived under the despotic surveillance of the king, and upon their good behavior, their deference, and their observance of etiquette their whole careers depended. If you displeased Louis, he would simply *not see you* the following day." There was no escape; he set the stage and wrote the script. Men were expected to give up physical force as a means to get their way, and as always when "the graces" were preferred over brute strength, women began to count more. People became more equal at court and could permit themselves to respect one another.[33]

The French, of course, were not the only ones to insist on manners. Since ancient times, societies have taught manners by means of precepts, riddles, and traditional proverbs. Around 2000 BC, the Egyptian Ptah-Hotep wrote *Instructions,* apparently to his son, in the form of didactic poetry. Hesoid, some 2,700 years ago, wrote about table manners. China's three great books of ceremonial rites were compiled between the second century BC and the first century AD, all from much-older sources. Roman literature included stories of boorish behavior as object lessons. Medieval manners books contained jingles and rhyming verses that could be easily memorized since books were scarce. In the twelfth century, treatises on manners instructed novices in monasteries. Since monks came from every social class and had to live together for life, they had to learn common standards for behavior and how to behave when they suddenly found themselves dining at the local château. A fifteenth-century English manners book guided the nobility in educating their children to be pages and ladies-in-waiting. When their children reached age eight, they exchanged them with those in other aristocratic households, so that they could be disciplined outside their own homes. In sixteenth-century Germany, a whole genre of comic manners books appeared. Visser found commonalties in all these works: concern for others' opinions, ability to see oneself as others do, and fear that gaffes and lapses in physical propriety might disgust or revolt others. Although standards rose and sank and varied according to class, country, and circumstance, what remained constant was "the universal—even primordial—terror of offending 'them,' of not measuring up to what society expects of competence, awareness, and the desire not to offend."[34]

Visser maintains that one work "stood out from the doggerel verse that preceded and followed his contribution to the genre": Erasmus of Rotterdam's *De civilitate morum puerilium*. Erasmus maintained that manners were important in winning goodwill and as external signs of virtue. He thought that all boys, not just noble ones, should learn them. "No one can choose his own parents or nationality, but each man can mould his own talents and character for himself," he wrote. *De civilitate* was the standard text on manners for four centuries. Educators killed two birds with one stone by teaching children how to read Latin through construing Erasmus on manners. Over time, some of his frank examples involving loss of control over bodily orifices were censored as impolite. But his main message endured: that manners were more about generosity of spirit and companionship than about status or humiliating others.[35]

Norbert Elias writes in *The Civilizing Process* that Erasmus's *De civilitate* marked a transition in the history of manners: from courtly "courtesy" to citizens' "civility." Prior to 1530, the medieval concept of manners prevailed. It was called courtesy because noblemen at court practiced it. *Civility* was a term for a wholly new system of bodily propriety, applicable to all citizens, not merely the elite. Topics in *De civilitate* include body posture and facial expression, dress, behavior in church, table manners, conversation, and behavior at play. From this point on, bodily functions—such as belching, farting, excretion, and spitting—were displayed in public less and less; thresholds of embarrassment and shame developed between people. Whereas at medieval dinners, cutlery, dishes, and goblets were passed out for everyone to use, now each person had his or her own implements. As time went on, eaters did not touch their food with their hands except in specific cases, and they sat in ways that made even brushing against another person at table as unlikely as possible.[36]

Manners and the Middle Class

Just as manners could make people more humane and civil, they could also be used for inhumane purposes. Status-anxious people wore manners like armor to shield themselves from others, the polar opposite of the civility of Erasmus. An anonymous Victorian manual in 1879 called etiquette "the barrier which society draws around itself, a shield against the intrusion of the impertinent, the improper, and the vulgar." Class-based manners separated the "cool" from the "heated." Italian Renaissance treatises on aristocratic behavior emphasized the grace and innate good taste of the ideal courtier. The graces did not have to be learned. Grace was effortlessness, reflecting *sprezzatura,* a word meaning slightly contemptuous indifference. "The elect, the born 'powerful because best' (which is the original meaning of the Greek term *aristocrat),* must achieve *nonchalance,* literally, the state of 'not being heated.'"[37]

Aristocratic manners developed, somewhat ironically, from French aristocrats in the 1620s who met as a group to decry both the pomposity of Versailles and upstart boors and parvenus. They shared an ineffable *je ne sais quoi* (I don't know what). John Dryden was said to have been the first to introduce the term *good taste* to English. Aristocrats of taste preferred intimacy and small numbers at dinner, and "they were often invited together by a hostess, for women played a powerful role in this informal, exclusive world." As the bourgeoisie became wealthier, it became "increasingly difficult for the nobility to use wealth to mark the difference between themselves and the *arrivistes* or *parvenus* (literally, those 'who had finally—and only just—arrived')." One thing they already had was good taste and good manners. Taste implied "*experience,* direct acquaintance and familiarity with what is desirable—whether this be food or pictures or music or clothes. Manners are how things ought to be done: being polite in French is being *comme il faut* 'as you must be'; in English you do what you 'are supposed'—by other people—to do." With this kind of good taste, whenever the elite sensed too many intruders, it simply moved on and changed the fashion, the "in" place. Dinner manners remained the litmus test. As an etiquette writer advised in 1834, "Nothing indicates a well-bred man more than a proper mode of eating his dinner. A man may pass muster by *dressing well,* and may sustain himself tolerably in conversation; but if he is not perfectly 'au fait,' *dinner* will betray him."[38]

Manners were stricter and more internalized for the bourgeoisie than they were for the nobility. As Visser notes, the middle class had more to lose by making slips and gaffes, "so their self-inhibiting mechanisms had to be deeper rooted, less obviously the donning of an external persona than the nobility could permit themselves. The policing of emotions became internal, and finally invisible even to themselves; they were able to think that they acted, not in obedience to power and self-interest, but for purely moral reasons."[39]

Just as European manuals about refined manners trickled down from the aristocracy to the bourgeoisie to the working class, in the United States nineteenth-century etiquette books reflected class dynamics. Although they were modeled on English and French customs, their authors made an effort to put an American stamp on proper behavior. Americans were uncomfortable with what they saw as British deference to superiors and French affected exaggerations.

John Kasson, a historian of nineteenth-century American civility, notes that American etiquette advisors recognized a special need for a culture of civility and a code of manners in the fluid, pluralistic, and often aggressively egalitarian American society. They were fond of quoting Edmund Burke: "Manners are of more importance than laws. Upon these in great measure the law depends." America's republican revolution had been fueled by the idea that ordinary people should be treated decently and fairly. Members of the middle class increasingly demanded ritual expressions of mutual respect from one another. As new immigrants arrived, the middle class wanted to improve the manners of the working class as an attempt "to establish order and authority in a restless, highly mobile, rapidly urbanizing and industrializing democracy. Seeking to avoid overt conflict, they turned issues of class and social grievance back upon the individual" by redefining such problems as questions of social propriety and "good taste."[40]

Immigrants to America were a self-selected group that insisted on being treated fairly, wanted to fit into their new world, and resented the privileged who put on airs. By the 1920s, more Americans lived in urban than in rural settings for the first time. With urbanization came increasingly anonymous lives. Indeed, one manners manual advised that success depended on being "utterly indistinguishable from those about you." Probably the most influential early twentieth-century American etiquette manuals were written by Emily Post, beginning with her *Etiquette in Society, in Business, in Politics and at Home* (1922). She used snobby characters to represent polished society (the Oldnames, Mr. Stocksan Bonds) but also reminded her readers of the greater tradition of civility. "Best society is not a fellowship of the wealthy, nor does it seek to exclude those who are not of exalted birth." Rather, "it is an association of gentlefolk, of which good form in speech, charm of manner, knowledge of the social amenities, and instinctive consideration for the feelings of others, are credentials by which society the world over recognizes its chosen members."[41]

Judith Martin, author of a dozen etiquette books under the name of "Miss Manners," voices the American view that etiquette systems are needed to protect the powerless from the powerful. "Pushing people around because you are powerful enough to get away with it is, by definition, rude. Societies that condone or even institutionalize such practices do not even try to pretend these are polite. Instead, they define the victims as being not fully human, and therefore outside of society's system of etiquette protection." She contends that manners are not arcane rules about proper uses of forks at the table; they are consensus behaviors designed to make people comfortable. This view of manners challenges the absolute nature of generational power, restraining parents from exercising the kind of power over their children frequently found in other cultures.[42]

American table manners may be less formal than elsewhere, but they are as universal. Children are taught to limit the amount of food they put in their mouths at one time. Small children love to fill their mouths with food since, unlike adults, they have taste buds on their cheeks as well as on their tongues. Nursing infants are encouraged to "bubble up" after nursing, but belching becomes taboo once solid food is eaten. The growing child becomes accustomed to the food of the culture, first introduced through mothers' milk in the case of powerful substances such as chili peppers or fermented fish. Some parents insist that it is good manners for children to try a little of everything; others are more concerned that their children eat healthy foods.[43]

Many American families follow the Victorian proverb: "Every meal is a lesson learned." Children are taught to say "please" and "thank you." Spatial boundaries are preserved. It is rude to take food without asking first or to stare at the food on someone else's plate. There is a litany of traditional reproaches and commands: "Waste not, want not." "Whose eyes are bigger than their stomach?" "Think of the starving children [elsewhere]." "Eat it—it'll make your hair curl (girl) or put hair on your chest (boy)." Until children learn to behave at the table, they sometimes eat apart from adults.[44]

Just as European parvenus feared that improper dining behavior would betray their lack of breeding, many middle- and working-class Americans worry that their children's table manners outside the home will not reflect well on them. The dining table is a setting that their children need to master for life away from home. It is also a controlling device, a place where children eat under the surveillance of adults. "In families which are too poor, or who live in a space too confined, to possess a table where everyone could sit down together, mothers complain that it is impossible to control their children during meals." Parents worry about how much information their children will reveal about the family while away from home. The mature child knows how to conceal things embarrassing to the family. A well-behaved child learns that family loyalty is "prior even to commensal togetherness. No doubt part of the reason for our own law on children's silence before guests at the dinner table was the danger that a child might suddenly embarrass the family with its revelations." The dining table is the locus of family meals and represents, as no other piece of furniture can, the family as a whole: empty places are reminders of those not there and memories of dramas that have taken place around this symbol of family.[45] The table is the schoolhouse of manners, the site of power struggles, the locus of moral dilemmas, and the symbol of family and community.

The complex and time-consuming business of manners is, for the most part, women's work. Manners are associated with historically feminine characteristics: "the graces," polish, finesse, refinement, conventions, and the art of communication. Rudeness, fighting, swaggering, boorishness—typically masculine constructs—lose their place at the table. The watchful eye of the king, the paterfamilias, or the father might still be present, but it is the daily table instruction by the mother that lays the foundation for civility and civil society. Undoubtedly, mothers teach manners for a variety of reasons, some of which are undemocratic, for instance, class-based exclusion and a desire for upward mobility, and some of which are democratic, such as respectful inclusion. The democratic aspects of the feminine practice of teaching manners need to be taken seriously by theorists of civil society and democracy. By ritualizing the sharing of food, manners set the stage for sharing thoughts and feelings at the table and outside the household.

Manners make table conversation possible. The courtesy of a conversation is an essential building block of civil society. Conversations and manners have journeyed through centuries of class upheaval, but they always return to their roots in the Latin *conversari*, "to live, to keep company with." The conversible world is intimate, lively, sociable, and pleasurable—an indispensable part of civil society.

Chapter 5

. . . .

Table Rituals

Just as manners grease the wheels of table conversation, so too do the rituals of table and food. Rituals are a series of expected and correct actions that are constantly repeated. The repetition, in and of itself, is soothing—inducing what James Joyce called "those here-we-go-again gaieties."[1] Rituals promote togetherness, reinforce social bonds, and foster a sense of belonging, creating preconditions for civil exchanges in a structured context. In this chapter, we examine the human need for food rituals, both in routine situations and in new and unexpected settings, and the ritual relations between hosts and guests, when rules of hospitality apply. We consider how the ritual of sharing bread is both a civil practice (the basis of the word *companion*) and a signifier of gender and class relations in the United States. And we explore cross-cultural differences in rituals of talking and eating and lingering at the table.

Anthropologists, sociologists, and psychologists maintain that humans need rituals for reassurance and order. Sociologists have conducted extensive research about family rituals. A 1950 landmark study examined secular ritual behavior in four hundred American families, based on published autobiographies, free-associational writing by university students, and interviews with others whose experiences spanned from 1856 to 1949. It concluded that rituals were powerful and universal organizers and stabilizers of family life.[2] In 2002, psychologists reviewed fifty years of subsequent academic studies inspired by this landmark work. There was a consensus that family rituals involved both a practical component in organizing group behavior and a symbolic aspect fostering group identity and meaning making in group settings. The most frequently listed family rituals were birthdays, Christmas, family reunions, Thanksgiving, Easter, Passover, funerals, and Sunday activities, including

Sunday dinner. The positive features of family rituals were providing togetherness; strengthening family relationships, emotional exchange, and
stability; maintaining family contact; and providing opportunities to create
special times in single-parent families. The negative features included investing considerable time and work and eliciting family conflict.[3] It is interesting
to note that virtually all these family rituals involved ritual food. Why have
so many rituals developed around food and the table?

The Human Need for Food Rituals

One reason is the potential for danger at the table. If tempers flare or motivations are nefarious, the consequences can be disastrous. Manners facilitate sharing, but other table rituals are designed to protect people from
one another. The lurking fear of murder at dinner is especially horrendous
because it is so easy to achieve—everybody present is armed with knives,
and teeth are formidable human weapons. Table manners frequently forbid
belly laughs partly because uproarious mirth is expressed by the baring of
teeth. (Erasmus advised in such cases to cover one's face with a napkin or
the hand.) Many quarrels in the home take place at table, yet rituals reassure
people that a physical fight is unlikely. Knives are placed blade in; they are
never held upright nor pointed at others.[4]

Another reason involves the many layers of emotional meaning associated with the sharing of food: individual and group identity. Ritual expresses
solidarity; each group defines itself through ritual performance. Ritual can
raise the emotional tone of the proceedings—gaiety, joy, feasting, and celebration—but it can also lower it if necessary; for instance, ritual politeness
can prevent rage from boiling over into action. For example, among the Gogo
of Tanzania, eating together helps people to reconcile after fights. It ritually
expresses what is shared and enjoyed, after all, in common; it therefore signifies the dropping of hostilities.[5]

Anthropologists describe rituals among many peoples that indirectly acknowledge indebtedness to others where food is concerned. Table manners
everywhere insist on the rituals of starting: eat when served, or wait until
all are served, or wait for the signal from the hostess. In many countries,
people wait until all drinks are served before drinking. Some cultures begin
a meal with a ritual prayer, thanking God or spirits for providing the food
to be consumed.[6]

Food is often a ritual relaxation. In some workplaces, food rituals provide
a civilized break in the working day, "our chance to choose companions and

talk to them, the excuse to recreate our humanity as well as our strength, and to renew our relationships."[7] Family food rituals often accompany relaxing excursions. In her memoir *From My Mother's Kitchen,* Mimi Sheraton recalls savoring the fried egg and bacon sandwiches ("ever so gently warm and lusciously soggy and fragrant") that her mother prepared as a picnic breakfast to be eaten in the car when her family drove to and from their country house.[8]

Food rituals express order and endurance, especially in religions. A highlight of Passover, which commemorates the exodus of Jews from bondage in Egypt, is the ritual meal of the seder (*seder* means order). The Christian Eucharist (*Eucharist* means thanksgiving) was born directly from the Jewish Passover sacrifices; neither humans nor animals need to be sacrificed again. The Christian Mass, literally, is "the sending" of the congregation out into the world "after they have experienced what is undoubtedly the most significance-charged dinner ritual ever devised": those present at the table eat God directly.[9]

Table rituals can ease social transitions. When people leave close-knit stable communities for the anonymity and mobility in cities, their adjustment is eased when eating establishments have simple rituals. The advent of cafés in late seventeenth-century Europe was one of the prerequisites for the growth of modern city life. Egalitarian social roles not only made economic sense for the café owner seeking a clientele; they also provided social connections for people in need of them. Something as simple as familiar sitting rituals can make social change less difficult in a new environment. In the Western tradition, people use tables and chairs. In other cultures, people sit on the floor to dine, around a tray or trays of food, or each diner has a personal table. Anthropologists have cataloged at least 132 main ways of sitting; only about 30 of these involve a chair. Women are typically restricted to very few ways of sitting, with legs together or crossed; crossing their legs at the knee is quite recent. Western clothing is designed with chairs in mind. Chairs enabled rigid posture, a sign of decorum.[10]

Until recent times, most cultures observed the ritual of men and women eating apart, especially in public. In ancient Greece, wives did not attend symposia. A Greek dining room was called an *andron,* "a room for men." Often taboos ensured that people ate different food.[11] More recently, "proper" women were usually not expected to frequent bars and saloons, since the consumption of alcohol was associated with rowdy and lascivious behavior. Both men and women graced the more democratic settings of tearooms and cafés.

Food rituals address the need for proper household places and order. In Tamil Brahman households, women with grievances against family members may "abbreviate" a meal, direct family members to inappropriate places (for example, a teenager is seated with the children), or serve food in an order calculated to insult someone. Relatives or guests who are in disfavor can be avenged by the seating and serving order. In every culture, invited guests affronted by their seating can do little about it without disrupting the entire proceedings. A Spanish diplomatic etiquette book devised an ingenious tactic whereby guests who felt misplaced could turn their plates over to indicate silent displeasure until the host noticed.[12]

The ritual use of utensils reassures people that familiarity will be the order of the day at the table. The importance of familiar utensils is illustrated by people's historical reluctance to adopt new ones. In the West, the transition to using forks instead of fingers took centuries. Although an eleventh-century document describes (with wonder) the wife of the Venetian doge using one, the fork took eight centuries to become a utensil employed universally in the West. Forks were mentioned again in fourteenth-century Florence; thereafter, they were spoken of frequently. In 1605, the court of King Henri III of France was satirized for its fork-wielding effeminacy. Eventually, Italy and Spain led the West in the adoption of forks. As for plates, not until the seventeenth century did hard plates—prerequisites for the use of individual knives and forks—begin to be provided at every place setting. At medieval banquets, people had eaten on trenchers (from the French *trancher*, "to slice"), made of sliced bread to hold food taken from a central dish with the hand and to soak up sauces. In the fourteenth century, pewter or wooden underplates, also called trenchers, were placed under the bread slices. By 1700, flat ceramic plates were fairly common in France, and by the early nineteenth century, North Americans began to replace wooden trenchers with pewter and china dishes and to use forks.[13]

Table rituals reassure people that they can find order, safety, familiarity, and comfort both in everyday and in new and unexpected settings. They pave the way for social interchange at the table. There are also important rituals that pertain to the very particular relationship between host and guests.

Hospitality

Hospitality refers to hosts giving generous and cordial treatment to guests. Historically, hospitality implied a complicated, ambivalent, and interdependent relationship. Originally *host* and *guest* meant the same thing—both derived from the Indo-European *ghostis* (stranger), the origin of the Latin *hostis* ("stranger" and therefore "enemy") and the English "hostile." "Hospitality" seems to have referred to "the power of a citizen 'host' [*hospes*] who was benevolent enough to represent before Roman institutions someone who was not a Roman citizen. . . . Hostility might always lurk in the background. . . . Both sides accept, for the sake of peace, order, and the benefit of the whole community, to be constrained by intricate sets of obligations."[14]

These intricate obligations developed in cultures where people were apt to find themselves in the role of travelers or strangers at the mercy of hosts. Reciprocal rules were designed to prevent the host from taking advantage of the guest's vulnerability. In Homeric Greece, the personal "guest-friendship" meant that once a man had been entertained in the house of another, "not only the host and the guest but their descendents for generations remained joined by bonds resembling those of kinship. Two 'paternal guest-friends' could meet for the first time on the battlefield, on opposite sides of the combat, and refuse to fight each other."[15]

In the preindustrial, gift-exchange cultures studied by anthropologist Marcel Mauss, hospitality was the singular alternative to hostility. Upon first encounter, it was customary to approach a stranger with either exaggerated hostility or exaggerated generosity—nothing in between. There was either complete mistrust or complete trust. One either drew arms or offered one's goods. In the Trobriand Islands, the Kiriwina feared the men of neighboring Dobu, who were seen as cruel potential killers. A careful food ritual kept them at peace. When a Kiriwina man spit out ginger root, the attitude of the Dobu changed. They laid down their spears and received the Kiriwina well.[16]

Hospitality serves both the individual's and the group's interest in self-preservation, especially under conditions of an uncertain food supply or an otherwise hostile environment. This is the case among many peoples in Africa, where children divide their food, such as a single piece of fruit, with everybody present. In these cultures, sharing with others, even strangers, tops the list of rules of good behavior. "Sharing is the foundation of civilized behaviour: it is what links individuals, families, villages, and tribes together. People should know how to share even when they are hungry: hard times may come for you, too, and you may then look with some rightful expectancy to another's generosity." Cultures of food sharing are also found in industrial societies. A 1972 study of middle-class North American school children showed how they swapped lunch items as a way of surviving in a ruthless schoolyard world; extras and luxuries were used symbolically to create and cement friendships and alliances.[17]

In many ancient societies, rules of hospitality were sacred and permanent, as symbolized by salt in Greece, the eastern Mediterranean, and Japan. Among the Mesopotamians, sharing salt symbolized a bond between individuals—

from the highest court officials to the lowest farmers. "In the neo-Assyrian period, the phrase *amelu sa tabtiya* (man of my salt) denoted a friend, a person with whom one shared this hugely symbolic condiment. A refusal to share one's food was sometimes interpreted as a mark of hostility. Failure to treat a guest politely was a notorious mark of disrespect. The sharing of food mattered more than the ingredients of the meal, since they were of the most basic sort."[18] The sharing of salt conveyed the implied promise that no harm would be done to the guest. Salt was an appropriate symbol of permanence since it never spoils or goes stale. Spilled salt meant the breaking of this promise. In Leonardo da Vinci's painting of the Last Supper, there is spilled salt under Judas's elbow.[19] Once a desert Arab ate salt with a man, it was impossible thereafter to treat him as an enemy.[20]

For the most part, in contemporary industrial societies, the meaning of *hospitality* has evolved away from its origins in the fear of hostility from strangers. It most often describes relations among (expected) friends and acquaintances. Dinner parties are a common form of hospitality, an essential means of binding families to one another and knitting society in general together. Food is not that expensive to share, and the fact that it does not last encourages reciprocation and repetition of the act of sharing. "Potluck" originally meant inviting someone to a very informal family dinner, on the spur of the moment. The guest's luck lay in what was served. The term has changed to mean luck in uncertainty about what guests will bring. Such dinners exist in some form in most societies, celebrating the intimacy of the guests or at least the hope that they have a great deal in common. The informality gained is worth the price of uncertainty about what will be served. The important thing is to feel comfortable enough with others to share food and conversation. In many cultures, two people do not feel they can talk in a friendly way with each other until they first eat together; doing so is the equivalent of being "properly introduced." Food is an icebreaker among guests meeting for the first time at a host's house. As guests, people seek those with whom they are "sympathetic" (*sympathique* in French), a person they can literally "feel with." The ancient Greeks had a precise term used for dinner guests: *sympotikos*, "a person with whom we can enjoy a symposium, or dinner followed by a drinking party."[21]

Hostility did not disappear altogether, however, from the meaning of hospitality in the United States. Psychologist Marvelene Hughes describes how hospitality had a special meaning in the black community, forged in a hostile climate. "Until the mid-1960s, Black people had to pack food whenever they expected not to be home for meals, as Blacks did not have hotel and restaurant privileges in many geographical areas in America. They became accustomed to sharing with other Blacks, even if they were strangers."[22] Psyche Williams-Forson writes that fried chicken has historically been a survival food among African Americans. The metaphorical "chicken bone express" is a celebrated part of black folklore, describing "the days of segregation when travelers would carry shoeboxes full of food to sustain them on their journey because White food establishments were inhospitable to Blacks. As the saying goes,

Lunch Counter Sit-In. During the civil rights movement, one of the earliest forms of civil disobedience was integration of segregated public eating facilities. This sit-in at a Woolworth's lunch counter in Jackson, Mississippi, in 1963 shows food used uncivilly to resist those working for civil rights: from left, John Salter, Joan Trumpauer, and Anne Moody. Photo by Fred Blackwell.

you could identify the travel route of Black folks by following the trail of chicken bones along the highway or the railroad track."[23]

The guest-host relationship is reciprocal, gift giving, based in feelings of vulnerability in a potentially hostile situation, and in a desire for sympathetic companions. Rules of hospitality ease awkwardness among strangers and create occasions for greater civility among people by asking them to reflect on the needs of others. Certain food items are markers of hospitality.

Breaking Bread with Companions

In the West, bread is widely regarded as a symbol of hospitality and sharing with others. Central Europeans use bread and salt to welcome people.[24] In Western European languages, *bread* often means food in general, so basic is it to the food traditions of these cultures. It is expected that bread will be "on hand at every meal, as background, as completion, as dependable comforter and recompense for stress or disappointment the rest of the meal might occasion." Breaking bread and sharing it with friends signifies friendship, trust, pleasure, and gratitude in the sharing. "Bread as a particular symbol, and food in general, becomes, in its sharing, the actual bond which unites us. The Latin word *companion* means literally 'a person with whom we share bread'; so that every *company,* from actors' guild to Multinational Steel, shares in the significance evoked in breaking bread."[25]

Because of its size and shape, bread is designed to be shared. From the Dark Ages to the Renaissance, the trencher that held meat and its accompanying sauce often served two people, who thus became literal "companions." During the Middle Ages, the wealthier classes did not eat the trencher bread but gave it to the dogs and to the poor waiting outside their doors. Peasants would take hunks of bread into the fields with them during the day and eat a hot dinner of porridge in the evenings. Breakfast would often consist of bread soaked in wine. In rural Europe, bread was used to mark ritual acceptance "into the various different grades of society or even the right to pursue a trade. Such bread was accompanied by wine, and both might be shared with a man's master or his peers during initiation ceremonies. Sharing bread in the course of ceremonies or simply at ordinary meals forges bonds which, in principle, will never be loosened or forgotten."[26] A loaf of bread could symbolize class relations. In medieval times, the nobility sliced off the top portion; hence the phrase "upper crust" used to refer to an elite class.

More than any other food in the Western tradition, bread symbolizes both physical and spiritual nourishment. It is called "the staff of life." In the pre-Christian West, bread was offered to the dead, placed with the top of the loaf turned toward the powers of the underworld. In the Lord's Prayer, Christians ask of God: "Give us this day our daily bread." For Christians, the Eucharistic host is regarded as the bread of spiritual life. The word *Bethlehem,* where Christ was born, means "house of bread."[27] In the Christian tradition, one can incorporate others, figuratively and literally, through the sharing of bread. In the Catholic Mass, bread and wine are transformed into the body and blood of Christ, which are then ingested by the faithful. As one Christian ethicist describes the sharing of bread: "I refuse to consider my own life as the only worthwhile life. . . . [Around the table I treat others as] an extension of my body and my entire being. I incorporate my fellows at table into myself and myself into them." The sharing of food is a "sharing of life itself."[28] Bread symbolized the body for the ancient Mesopotamians, whose vocabulary included three hundred kinds of bread, "depending on the choice of flours, spices and fruit fillings, and the addition of oil, milk, beer or sweetener (fruit juice and honey). The breads ranged from 'tiny' to 'very large' and were shaped as a heart, a head, a hand, an ear and a woman's breast."[29] Bread and wine are symbols of physical and spiritual life and, more generally, of conviviality.

Bread in America

For European settlers in North America, bread was literally life saving. Native Americans made many types of bread, primarily from cornmeal, but also from sweet potatoes, chestnuts, beans, hominy, wild potatoes, carrots, molasses, and strawberries. Native American breads and cereals kept European settlers alive for two centuries, the time it took for other grains—rye, barley, oats, and wheat—to adapt to the North American climate and provide sufficient yield to be affordable to the average laborer. Cornmeal was not easy to handle at first for cooks familiar with only wheat flour. Indian women taught white settlers how to grind corn into meal, moisten it, flatten it into little cakes, and bake it on heated stones (in the case of "ashcakes") or over a fire on a paddle of green wood or a hoe blade or large flat seashell (in the case of "hoecakes"). The use of fine flour became generalized by the 1830s, but so closely associated with Indians was cornmeal that an 1828 cookbook suggested that cooks might like "a little Indian in [their] bread."[30]

In the early nineteenth century, the well-being of the working class was measured by the affordability of bread. In the 1840s, urban wage earners relied on bread as the cheapest source of energy. Wheat was still expensive in New England, where the poor used corn, rye, oat, and barley meal for bread making. In 1833 the weekly food budget of a Philadelphia family of three (mother and two children) was $1.48½, and the biggest expense was bread—$.62½—followed by meat at $.20. In an 1851 weekly food budget for a Philadelphia family of five, the chief expense was "butcher's meat" at $1.40 and $.62½ for a barrel of flour, enabling the housewife to bake her own bread for eight weeks.[31]

Once American women were able to obtain affordable wheat flour, they baked with a vengeance. Early nineteenth-century cookbooks are filled with recipes for bread, rolls, biscuits, cakes, and pastry. One begins with 134 bread recipes and instructions for making yeast. Baking was still being done on open fireplaces, without the aid of commercial yeast (introduced in 1868) or baking powder (introduced in 1856).[32]

Despite the time, energy, and fuel involved, throughout the nineteenth century most American housewives baked their own bread. They did not have to grind their own flour, but kneading the dough was hard work. Cookbooks recommended between forty-five minutes to an hour and a half of pummeling the dough without pause, lest it "injure" the bread. Catherine Beecher and Harriet Beecher Stowe wrote in their cookbook, "The true housewife makes bread the sovereign of her kitchen." Bread became the symbol of women's domestic values in battle with encroaching forces of industrialism. Food industries provided some gadgets (a tin bucket with a hand-cranked dough kneader, for example) and products (such as commercial yeast) that made women's job somewhat easier. Commercial bread manufacturers touted their products as healthier and better than homemade loaves, which "lay heavy on the stomach." The Beechers were scornful of women whose only standard for judging bread was its lightness, adding that commercial bread was so light that it had no substance or taste. In 1871, their brother Henry Ward Beecher attacked commercially baked bread for losing its nutritiousness. He criticized the new practice of bleaching flour for killing "the live germ of the wheat" so that "what had been the staff of life for countless ages had become a weak crutch." In 1900, American women were still holding out, with 95 percent of all the flour sold in the United States being bought by individuals for use in home cooking; however, by 1970 the private-use proportion of sales had plummeted to 15 percent.[33]

With palates accustomed to commercial bread, many Americans who traveled to Europe in the 1960s and 1970s were astonished at the flavor of French and Italian breads. At that time, unless they made it themselves, Americans had little opportunity to taste bread free from preservatives and chemicals. The "countercuisine" pitted small specialty bakers against huge baking firms in the contest for the future of America's bread. In the 1970s the industry claimed that fifty-two million pounds of white bread were consumed each day in the United States. Of the $13 million spent by consumers for bakery products, 80 percent went for marketing, while only 20 percent represented "farm value"—what the producers of the raw materials received. Bread became a bellwether of the awakening of a new culinary conscience and consciousness. In 1973, James Beard wrote in *Beard on Bread* that a revival of interest in making bread was in full swing. People were appreciating the satisfaction that comes from kneading their own dough, the aromas of a yeasty loaf baking in the oven, and the sense of accomplishment in offering nutritious bread at a meal.[34]

For many first-generation immigrants, bread is a potent symbol of ethnic identity. Even though her parents were eager to Americanize, writer Helen Barolini's father would bring home each night a long loaf of crusty bread from the bakery on Syracuse's Italian north side. "His allegiance was still intact to the staff of life that in his estimate was insulted by the spongy sliced stuff we disparagingly called 'American bread.'"[35] Warm cornbread is a comforting and delicious centerpiece of African American culinary tradition. Tortillas are a mainstay of Latino cultural identity. And naan and pita bread figure prominently on the tables of Indian Americans and Arab Americans, respectively.

Many women bring homemade bread or other baked goods into the office to enhance group well-being. Bread makes people comfortable; with its familiarity and commonness, it breaks down barriers. Sharing bread or other baked products from another cultural tradition is an effective entrée into learning more about that tradition. "Breaking bread" seems to give people permission for greater honesty and openness. Perhaps the commonality of the food makes it easier to find common ground. Since bread is eaten with the hands, without utensils, everyone's hands get crummy, or sticky, or buttery, or oily. Handling the same foodstuffs at the table may give people the impression that it is possible to handle any topic of conversation.

Talking and Eating

In general, talking is part of what makes sharing food convivial, as opposed to simply utilitarian. But the art of table conversation is adorned with as many rituals as other table behaviors are. Indeed, in some cultural contexts, talking at the dinner table is discouraged. The ancient Greeks would talk little during the meal itself, except to decide on the subject of conversation after dinner. The symposium, or drinking party, was the place and time for discussion, after stomachs were full. "In Homeric times, it was considered very rude to expect a stranger to speak at length to his hosts before he had eaten his fill; he was not even asked his name until he had been given dinner."[36]

In some societies, people drink and talk before dinner. In Nepal, Sherpa parties begin with hours of discussion, quarreling, and joking, all facilitated by the drinking of beer. This custom provides a safe environment to work through grudges. At an opportune time, the host serves dinner, and guests become silent—any remaining rough edges are smoothed over by the action of eating together. In China and Iran, people traditionally talk first, then eat. Cultures that opt for conversation during meals usually divide food into separate portions before eating begins. So the togetherness of a meal in common needs to be bolstered by people talking to one another. By contrast, when people share a common dish, they probably need to concentrate on the matter at hand just to ensure that everyone gets a fair share. In some cultures, eating is considered to be pleasurable enough without talking.[37]

Sometimes dining and talking take place in separate rooms. In the European Middle Ages, princely houses had a spacious hall where retainers ate dinner under the watchful eye of their lord. Important people sat with him at the high table. As time passed, lords gradually withdrew from this hall and dined in smaller quarters with chosen companions. The chamber into which the medieval lord withdrew was a forerunner of our "living," "sitting," or "(with)drawing" room, and "parlour" (from French *parler*, "to talk") or "conversation room." Parlors eventually split into two when the table moved into an "eating room," where diners faced each other, and then the "dining room," a term first found in 1601 and which attained common usage during the eighteenth century, as dining rooms in middle-class houses became the norm.[38]

At some extremely formal dinner parties in Western Europe, talking at the table was highly ritualized by gender. Men and women sat in alternating seats. Men got up after each course and moved "two male places down" so that everyone spoke to someone new—even if they didn't want to. Another custom was "the turning of the table": when the hostess turned her head from the guest to her left to the guest on her right, every couple had to interrupt their conversations and follow suit.[39]

More commonly, less-stringent rules are employed to promote the art of table conversation: no favoritism, whispering, or sharing of private jokes. Pay attention to everyone present, as equally as possible. Open out toward other people. Do not offend a guest by joking at his or her expense. A host should not speak too much, praise himself or the food, serve himself first, or speak about dinner parties he has given before. Do not ask pointed questions or questions requiring long replies. Do not hold forth for long periods of time. Do not talk shop or say anything so technical that others cannot understand. Bring others into the discussion. The table is a place for democracy, not lording over others. There are cultural differences when it comes to the rule about avoiding controversial topics such as religion and politics or anything that could result in an argument. Some cultures relish an animated exchange of ideas, but others do not want things to get heated at the table. "The art of dinner table conversation, as it evolved from the seventeenth century onward, was that of interaction, almost for its own sake. Diners displayed their social awareness, their manners and tact, and showed respect for the rules they were all keeping. . . . Manners were in part a moral code, forced 'good breeding' to include consideration for other people's rights and feelings."[40]

With the advent of coffeehouses, constraints on table conversation in public emerged. *The Rules and Orders of the Coffee House* (1674) expressed most of them: No swearing, quarreling, noisy disputes, maudlin mourning, excessive talk, discussion of sacred things, profaning Scripture, irreverence toward affairs of state, jests without reflection; plenty of brisk talk and innocent mirth. In the eighteenth century, "intimate suppers" for ten or fewer, with the expectation of scintillating conversation, became the height of fashion. Boorish behavior was frowned upon: drawing attention to oneself, and being loud, embarrassing, repetitious, or boring. The word *boor* first appeared in English in 1766. "Well-bred" people went to great lengths not to be considered boorish. They went so far as to think of subjects for conversation in advance and prepare witticisms. This had to be done with an air of complete naturalness and simplicity. Any sign of trying too hard or of not taking all the circumstances into account ruined the reputation of the speaker.[41]

In the United States and Europe, late nineteenth-century manners books were quite stringent about rituals of dinner conversation. People were supposed to memorize the names of everyone to whom they had been introduced, causing powerful persons to limit the number of people who could be introduced to them. One owed it to the host and to the whole company present to listen even to the most boring talker. Enmities were to be buried at the table. Emily Post describes how two dinner guests who despised each other, rather than carry on a conversation, alternated multiplication tables out of respect for the hostess. Polite conversationalists were to be sympathetic and animated but never flippant. Compliments had to be sincere, but flattery was vulgar; scandal and gossip were unacceptable. One did not interrupt or allude to another person who was at the table. Private or indelicate matters were not mentioned. All ostentatious displays of knowledge, such as use of foreign languages and quotations from the classics, were avoided. Women wrote most etiquette books by this time; an 1885 author urged gentlemen to pay ladies "the compliment of seeming to consider them capable of an equal understanding with gentlemen."[42]

In the nineteenth century, Europeans often criticized Americans' inability to carry on extended table conversations. Some attributed this to the speed with which they ate, even in elegant hotel dining rooms. In 1834, an English visitor to New York described a dining room seating fifty to a hundred people at tables lavished with a vast number of dishes. "The dispatch with which they are cleared is almost incredible; from five to ten minutes for breakfast, fifteen to twenty minutes for dinner, and ten minutes for supper are fully sufficient; each person as soon as satisfied leaves the table without regard to his neighbors; no social conversation follows."[43]

Visitors from Mediterranean countries often placed the blame on Americans' avoidance of controversial topics. In their cultures, people met in cafés and bistros to debate issues in politics, religion, and philosophy. One Frenchman observed how food and debate enjoyed a symbiotic relationship in his culture, in stark contrast to the United States:

> Social ideas are understood by the American mind as something too personal and controversial. And since you don't talk about them, you can't really enjoy the dinner. That's the reason it's boring to dine in America—there's nothing going on. In France they're totally inseparable, dining and talking. Why does lunch on Sunday at my parents' house go on for three hours (or even more if people are over)? Because people are talking. You need to find topics that are controversial to make the food last that long. At the same time, in order to make the topics last, you have to have good food to go with them.[44]

Staying at the Table

Sometimes conversations really take off once dessert and coffee are served. In some cultures the table is "de-served," or *desservie*—everything is removed and the cloth swept clean so that talking can continue, only raised to a higher level of intensity. In Hispanic countries, the practice of conversation after dinner is called *hacer la sobremesa,* "doing the tablecloth" or "doing dessert." Coffee is brought to the table, and guests talk together for hours. The Danes are also famous for their after-dinner conversation around the table. "The table is felt actually to aid the conversation: moving away to the 'withdrawing' room would mean a break in the togetherness achieved during dinner, and a moving apart from one another. . . . The table is something to lean on, to gesture over; it expresses what everyone has in common."[45]

The table is a symbol of conversational, and by extension, civil and political, equality. Marcel Mauss opines that, just as archaic societies had learned that it was in their self-interest to lay down their arms and come to the table to eat and to talk, classes and nations in "our so-called civilized world" must learn the same lesson. His moral analogy was that of King Arthur and his Round Table, where sixteen hundred knights could sit and move around and from which no one was excluded. No knight was able to engage in fighting, since the highest placed was on the same level as the lowliest. There was no longer a "high table" and consequently no more quarreling. Everywhere that Arthur took his table, his noble company remained happy and unconquerable. Mauss contended that people will be happy only when they have learned to sit down, like the knights, around a common table in mutual respect and reciprocating generosity.[46]

The egalitarian table is an important locus of polishing the art of conversation. Sociologist Erving Goffman observes that the family-sized dining-room table is a specially created open region where participants have the right to engage anyone present.[47] Part of its purpose is to show that diners have learned the rules. At table there is nowhere to hide, and the rule against silence means that there is no refuge from having to perform. Margaret Visser observes that in the United States, upper- and middle-class children are deliberately encouraged to talk at the table, to ask questions—even to ask why they should follow the rules of etiquette. Parents stage family meals because they feel that children need these meals to learn how to converse. "Our cultural tradition expects us to bring up children to ask why; and where people's lives are lived so separately, dinner-table conversation becomes a unique opportunity for the family to find out what all its members are thinking and doing."[48]

American parents like to share helpful hints about how to facilitate the art of conversation at the table. Best-selling books offer advice, such as businesswoman Doris Christopher's *Come to the Table*. She cautions against letting family dinners degenerate into interrogation sessions that invariably elicit sullen, one-word nonanswers. Instead, ask children specific questions and solicit their opinions, especially about everyday dilemmas such as schoolyard bullying. Encourage constructive differences of opinion. Strive for more fun and less criticism, and avoid giving orders. Prohibit endless bickering between siblings, or for each insult hurled, make the speaker come up with ten things he loves about the targeted sibling.[49]

Some parents make special rules to create time for conversation. One woman Christopher interviewed described growing up in a household where she loved to play outside with her sister. When dinner was called, they would go inside reluctantly, eat as fast as they could, and then run outside to keep playing. One night her father had had enough of the children's eat-and-run attitude, and he made a new household rule: everyone had to sit at the table for at least thirty minutes, whether she or he had finished eating or not. For the first few days, the children hated this. But by the end of the week, something amazing happened. "First, we were eating our dinner slowly enough to taste it. And second, we were staying at the table longer than the required thirty minutes! We were enjoying each other's company and talking as a family. Often, we would sit at the table for an hour or two without even wanting to go back outside."[50]

In all societies, people create rules and rituals relating to the art of conversation at the table. These structures make it possible to share ideas along with the food. The repetition of behavior creates group cohesion. Children's family food rituals are remembered and typically reproduced well into adulthood. The staying power of the "here-we-go-again gaieties" of food rituals is a testament to their permanence in the foundations of civil society, which requires togetherness, social bonds, and a sense of belonging. Humans need food rituals, rules of hospitality, comfort in shared foods, companionship, and conviviality. So does a vibrant civil society.

Chapter 6

Generations at the Table

Civil society needs people to connect across generations. In the United States, children are subject to intense peer pressure, creating a sense that older people just don't understand, or worse, are hostile to their concerns and life choices. For their part, many older people find that in their senior years, connections with children and grandchildren give meaning to their often isolated lives. Mealtime rituals and family stories are important antidotes to the generational segregation of geographically mobile Americans—illustrated by airport crowds every Thanksgiving. The phone and the Internet also connect generations. But there are civilizing benefits that come from face-to-face mealtime interactions.

One way to engage intergenerational conversants around a table is to tell stories. Stories help us to travel across a present-day rough spot in the road by moving it to a different time and place. One generation lets another know that they've been down that road and can see the journey in perspective, often with wisdom and humor.

Table Stories

At dinner, family members often expect to hear something about everybody's day. Children are encouraged to report an event that made an impression on them or that they did not know how to handle. The dilemmas of the day are often interpersonal conflicts involving friendships or romances or moral questions about schoolyard meanness or unfairness. Children feel less isolated when they hear that others have had similar experiences. Stories are a safe way for people to reveal something about themselves and to ask for guidance from the group. They are a subtle way to ask for advice. Stories connect people; they are opportunities for people to let others know that "they've been there," they understand. Stories are often moral tales, but they differ from the didactic proverbs or strict rules of Erasmus and manners manuals. They allow for nuance, context, complexity, ambiguity, and humor. They open people to heart-to-heart discussions. They are a way to really get to know a person.

Many of the working parents interviewed by sociologist Marjorie DeVault described their frustrating inability to orchestrate the kinds of dinner conversations they remembered having had as children. A married woman, who worked as a legal secretary, expressed these concerns. She recalled having had "real discussions at the dinner table," where "you can give a person a chance to let you in on their life. What they were doing all day when they weren't with you. You can find out more about that person." She complained, "That doesn't happen in our house at all. . . . It's time when you can show that you really care about the person in more than just a caretaking role."[1]

Parents have to work to get their children to talk during family meals. Some single mothers told DeVault that they were too exhausted after a full day's work to sustain family conversations with no one to provide some relief. It was simply too much to keep working during their own mealtimes. Some couples insisted that their children participate even when they were not in the mood to do so. An Asian American woman, married to a white professional man, said: "At dinner we usually talk about the kind of day that Mark and I had. . . . [You] try to relate what cute and wonderful thing the child did, and things of that nature. We try to talk at dinner. . . . My son will sometimes be very grumpy and grouchy, because 'The whole day went wrong,' and he's told that that's simply not an excuse for not talking."[2]

Some parents make talk a condition of being fed. DeVault quoted a single mother of four who made it her business to hear about everyone's day at dinner. "The meal is on the table, and I tell them if the steam leaves the bowl before they get to the table, the bowl goes right back in the stove and they don't get any supper. So they make sure they get to the table. And then that's our group discussion, this girlfriend played with that boyfriend at school, and I hear everything."[3]

Most parents adhere to the egalitarian norm described in etiquette books: everyone at the table should have equal time. One mother with five children worried that each child might not have an equal chance to participate in the dinner talk. So she tried to get each one to read a news item each day and report on it at the table. The system did not work, but the story revealed this mother's concern for her family's mealtime conversation.[4] Another woman, raised in a family with five children, said that her parents used an unusual ritual to get everyone involved. Her two brothers were quiet and never entered into family conversation unless they were asked direct questions. When her parents had a particularly difficult time getting the boys to open up, they would initiate a "taking turns" ritual. The father would start with a hearty laugh, then the mother "would do something really off-the-wall, like an operatic 'hee hee hee hee' up and down the musical scale. By the time we got around the table (each of us forced to take our turn with a laugh) we were all in fits of hysterics. In spite of our protests, the tradition facilitated great conversations."[5]

In some families, the heart-to-heart talks take place in the kitchen, and the family stories around the dinner table. As one woman remarked: "When I have the opportunity to visit my mom, she seldom spends time having long heart-to-heart talks unless I sit in the kitchen and join her in cooking. However, when there are big family gatherings, I learn a lot about my roots as I listen to accounts presented orally by all of the family members."[6]

Occasionally the stories children want to tell are about not what happens outside the home but what goes on within it. One family lingered after their Sunday dinner to clear the air about the issues that were on people's minds. The son campaigned for a later bedtime, while the daughter lobbied to watch more TV. Even if their requests were denied by their parents, the mother said that the children felt better simply for having been heard. These mild gripe sessions sometimes inspired productive discussions about the reason for rules and routines. Invariably, they got everyone talking. For slow conversation nights, some families resorted to deliberate strategies to prompt children to talk, such as using a deck of topic cards, each containing a subject the family thought would be interesting to discuss, or playing "Best and Worst," in which everyone took turns listing the best and the worst parts of his or her week. One mother said that this game was a safe way for kids to vent their unhappiness and to be reminded of something they enjoyed. It also showed children that life was not always easy for parents either.[7]

During the teenage years, stories, accompanied by familiar food, are often the only way to engage sullen and guarded youth at the table. One teenager stopped wanting to do things with her family and would not divulge anything about her schoolwork, friends, or life. Over dinner, her hostility lessened, and it was the only time the family could communicate with her. As they all ate her favorite dishes and talked about the past, she would slip back into her old pattern of opening up and sharing with the family. It was the one family ritual she seemed to respect, and her mother took advantage of it by cooking her daughter's favorite foods. "Telling stories and making references to funny things that happened during her childhood—or my own—helped to further restore our connection, and we lingered over those dinners as long as we could."[8]

Class Differences in Table Stories

In many cases, class differences influence expectations about table stories. In DeVault's study, informants in every class talked about meals as events of coming together, but middle-class and especially professional women were "more explicit about the effort they put into organizing talk. In a few working-class households, talk at the dinner table was an item of contention between taciturn husbands and their wives, who were striving to construct the meal as a particular kind of social occasion."[9]

In her study of child-rearing practices, Annette Lareau found that middle-class parents, both black and white, engaged in "concerted cultivation" in their attempt to foster their children's development through organized leisure activities and extensive reasoning. They enrolled their children in age-appropriate activities that dominated family life and created an enormous amount of work for mothers. They also stressed language, reasoning, and talking as their preferred method of discipline. Working-class and poor parents emphasized the "accomplishment of natural growth," with fewer organized activities, richer ties within extended families, and more directives and physical discipline. Middle-class parents were more likely to cultivate conversations with their children by asking them questions to draw them out and express their own points of view. Many aspects of daily life were open for negotiation. Mothers showed more willingness to engage children in prolonged discussions than did fathers. "In working class and poor homes, most parents did not focus on developing their children's opinions, judgments, and observations. When children volunteered information, parents would listen, but typically they did not follow up with questions or comments." Children in poor and working-class families benefited from deeper ties to their extended families. They saw their relatives more frequently, especially for birthdays and other celebrations. Older children voluntarily looked after younger ones.[10]

Generational Connections

For some people, kitchen tables are repositories of family memories, much like scrapbooks or photo albums. As one woman recalled:

> I see my ninety-year old grandmother in her farmhouse kitchen following a recipe that exists on no page, mixing unmeasured ingredients for the sugar cookies I'll never quite manage to duplicate. I see my mother rushing to the sink in the kitchen of my girlhood, a hissing pressure cooker in her outstretched hands. I see velvety raspberries still warm from the sun on the table of our Michigan cottage. . . . Fashions and foods change along with the faces. Mother's pot roast morphs into my lighter, healthier tenderloin, her Southern fried chicken into my low-fat boneless chicken breasts. But other things don't change with the generations. For instance, like my mother and grandmother, I still come to the table to connect with the people I love. . . . The table is where we mark milestones, divulge dreams, bury hatchets, make deals, give thanks, plan vacations, and tell jokes. It's also where children learn the lessons that families teach: manners, cooperation, communication, self-control, values. Following directions. Sitting still. Taking turns. It's where we make up and make merry. It's where we live, between bites.[11]

Sunday is frequently family meal day. The pace is leisurely, ideal for conversation. One woman recalls the sense of stability and larger purpose provided by Sunday dinners. It was her father's one day off from work at the service station. "I wasn't just 'me' anymore, not on Sunday. I was part of a family, one of 'us.' And we made the most of our big day together . . . with leisurely conversations over the dinner table during the one meal that never felt rushed. We discussed the events of the week—both in our lives and in the outside world." Even when people can no longer recall what their families talked about or even what they ate during Sunday dinners, the feeling of safety is a recurring theme.[12]

Having the time to prepare food also makes Sunday meals special: one woman had wonderful memories of her mother's homemade ravioli—"the making of it, flour all over the place, wetting your fingers and folding the little triangles." Alternatively, some women say that giving them a break from cooking can make Sunday meals special. One woman recalled her family Sunday dinners at a cafeteria buffet in Des Moines. Her grandmother used to say, "Sunday is, after all, the Lord's day. He rested on the seventh day, and so will I." After her grandmother's funeral, this woman drove out to find the old house where she had spent her childhood Sundays. She was sad to find that the house had been torn down but was consoled with the memory of the

Sunday cafeteria dinners. "To this day, and even in this moment, my eyes get moist when I see one of those brown-and-white custard cups on a cafeteria buffet."[13]

Many grown children return to their parents' home for a Sunday meal. In Ang Lee's film *Eat Drink Man Woman,* three grown daughters grudgingly join their father, Chu, a widower and retired chef, for an elaborate Sunday meal. The film's title derives from a Chinese proverb dealing with the basic necessities for continuing life and is used ironically to reflect how the simplest things have become very complicated. Each daughter represents outside cultural influences seeping into Chu's traditional culture: Western religion, international travel, and fast food. "We communicate through food," notes one daughter at dinner, even as the traditional cuisine increasingly fails to bridge generation and cultural gaps. A total breakdown in family communication ensues, with meals becoming occasions where family members drop bombshell revelations about themselves.

Some parents attempt to engage disaffected teens by giving them their own night to cook, a much more creative task than doing dishes, which most children get stuck with as a family chore. Teenagers love to be reminded that they will soon be on their own, so they can approach the meal as gaining practical skills without having to admit that sharing and pitching in are also worthwhile.[14]

Of course, some children are raised in households where older generations are not interested in engaging with children at the table, in part because their own relations are so conflictual. One woman remembers the dining-room table as the site of tension between her parents. Her father was distant, powerful, and opinionated, and he subjected her mother's cooking to intense scrutiny and criticism: the onions fried a bit too brown, or too many dark burned spots on the roasted *papads.* The emotional turmoil soured the taste of the meals and prevented communication across the generations. As a child, she concluded that cooking was not worth the trouble: "hours of chopping, grinding spices, stirring, sautéing, frying, boiling, and all consumed so quickly and without any appreciation or acknowledgement of the hard work." Cooking did not give her mother any authority in the family, so she identified solely with her father. "The conflicts that seeped into our meals around the dining table filled me as a child with unexpressed rage against my father. At that age, I did not have the vocabulary or the intellectual tools to speak up for my mother."[15]

Many generational food lessons are taught by grandmothers, who were newly arrived immigrants when the Americanization of food was in full force. Helen Barolini describes her parents, children of Italian immigrants, as "eager to be melted down in the common pot." The Anglo-American society of her youth demeaned Italian American women as silent, submissive, old-fashioned—"stuck in the kitchens stirring sauce"—and sent her the message that if she wanted to be anyone, she had "to get out of that kitchen, not be [her] mother, not be a cook, feign disinterest—even scorn—in food and eating, look on appetite as something nongenteel." At her grandmother's house, she ate foods that seemed foreign: "braciola, ravioli, Italian vegetables from her backyard garden like pole beans, escarole, broccoli, and zucchini that were not known then in American homes." Her grandmother herself seemed foreign, "dressed in black with her hair in an old-fashioned knob, and always in the kitchen at her big, black, wood-burning stove." The aromas in her kitchen were strikingly different from those in her mother's antiseptic, modern, all-white kitchen. She hated the "un-American" experience of shopping with her mother in the Italian section of town, where she felt like a reluctant tourist in stores with pungent cheeses and ugly eels and squids. "I even hated Josie's pastry shop because Josie, who made all those un-American cookies, was fat and foreign-looking herself, with big black circles under her eyes. She was not at all the image of the woman I wanted to be, the women I watched in the movies I saw each Saturday afternoon. American women were independent, snappy talkers with nicknames like Kitty or Patsy, and above all they did not slave in the kitchen or eat much themselves."[16]

Starting in her kitchen, Barolini's mother slowly found her way back to her Italian culinary heritage. As she remembered the foods, she related surprising stories about Barolini's grandmother. It turned out that this "kitchen-slave" immigrant from Italy was a canny entrepreneur who had started a thriving family business that she eventually turned over to her sons. Her grandmother's enterprise had started in her kitchen, where she made lunches for mill workers. This business grew into a grocery store and eventually into a successful wholesale food business. Long after her corner grocery store had grown into a business housed in a huge downtown building, her grandmother continued to plant her backyard garden both for frugality and for the pleasure of fresh produce on her table. Barolini came to see the kitchen as "an embassy of cultural tradition. The kitchen is not only the center of food-making—it is the place from which emanate ritual and tradition and family history. From food—both in the making and in the partaking—not only the body, but also mind and soul are nourished."[17]

Among the many lessons taught by grandmothers, and great-grandmothers, are that cooking is an art, not a science, and that it connects people.

One woman recounted how she learned to cook as an apprentice to her great-grandmother, grandmother, and mother, whose lineages were southern Baptist, Russian Jewish, and Polish Catholic. All of them were suspicious of religious and political intolerance and taught her to cook, to study, and to be political. "I began to realize that cooking, study and being political have in common taking the risks that always go with caring and trying to do something about it. Really, there are no recipes for the arts of connecting."[18]

Gloria Wade-Gayles remembers family meals as profoundly spiritual and intellectual gatherings that bonded generations. She said of the spiritual bond:

> I'd swear Mama put some good juju in her food. Why else did it have a way of picking me up when I was feeling low, giving me confidence when I was experiencing doubt, and making me believe that all of my friends envied me because I belonged to Mama, to the family? She seemed to know without our telling her when, emotionally, we needed a certain meal—pot roast, candied yams, collard greens, and hotwater cornbread after a quarrel with a friend; peach cobbler for dessert after a quarrel with a sweetheart. How can I explain how certain meals healed me in a way that others could not except to say that for Mama, cooking was a spiritual experience. When my friends give similar testimony about their mothers, I realize there was a mystery about black women working in their own kitchens we do not and cannot understand. It is like the 'laying on of hands' we talk about and testify to and about in the black community; the healing hands touch us through the food they prepare.[19]

Family meals were also intellectual gatherings. Wade-Gayles recalled watching a television special on President John F. Kennedy that attributed his success to a family ritual of discussing ideas around the dining table. She thought that no one would believe that a black family living in a segregated housing project in the South would observe the same ritual. It was a ritual that began during slavery when her ancestors gathered to testify, to bond, to gain strength from one another, and to imagine themselves free and empowered. It continued through her mother's kitchen in the housing project, and when her mother aged and was in failing health, it was carried on by her aunt who prepared the meals that brought them together. All the while, her mother remained passionate about ideas and polemics and continued to direct the family to intellectual dialogue.

Wade-Gayles thought that it was progress for black people to be able to eat in restaurants, but only for the principle of nondiscrimination, not for the food or service. It was progress to give black women time off from "the demanding work of love-meals: the picking and washing of greens, the shelling of peas, and the kneading of dough for homemade biscuits." But she worried about the "spiritual malnutrition" of microwaves and frozen meals, of cafeteria and fast foods. Without mothers' kitchens and "the cast-iron skillets that held memory and the weight of character . . . how do we as mothers lay hands on future generations? . . . Where do we gather with them, and when, to affirm them and affirm ourselves? . . . [When do we sit] down to eat [passing] poignant questions about life along with the tender baked chicken, well-seasoned dressing, tasty cornbread, juicy pinto beans, bubbly macaroni and cheese, and earth-red candied yams?"[20]

Tamalada (Making Tamales). Food rituals and family stories bring generations together, counteract the isolation of the screen culture, and preserve cultural traditions. This painting by Carmen Lomas Garza, *Tamalada* (1987), depicts her extended family preparing tamales in south Texas, where tamales are culturally hybrid in their ingredients: combining the meat of indigenous deer with pork and beef from animals introduced after the Spanish conquest. Painting by Carmen Lomas Garza; description from Constance Cortez, *Carmen Lomas Garza*.

Julie Dash came from a "family of rice eaters, a home where Uncle Ben was never invited to dinner." A Geechee, or Gullah, descendant of African captives from the rice-cultivating Senegal-Gambia region of Africa, her slave ancestors planted and harvested South Carolina rice. On weekends there would be big family meals where everyone—men, women, and children—would cook, tell wild stories, and argue. When she was ten, she made a humiliating mistake that her family never let her forget: she stirred a pot of red rice after it had started boiling. Her aunt had taught her the proper way to prepare rice: scrub it in a bowl of water until all the water was clear. Sometimes her aunt would change the scrubbing water up to ten times, using the discarded cloudy water to starch clothes. Only if the rice was well scrubbed to a shiny translucence would each kernel absorb the special red sauce. "Today as I stand over a bowl of cold water and rice, scrubbing, I feel Aunt Gertie watching me. Checking on me. Perhaps behind her the old souls are watching all of us, checking on the seeds that they have planted."[21]

The preparation and sharing of food at the table are occasions for linking us across generations. Seeing ourselves as part of a tradition makes us feel connected and valued. Much of a culture's history and wisdom is orally transmitted and would be lost were it not for ritual meals.

Television and Dinner

It is hard to convey the richness of family stories or discuss daily ethical dilemmas at the table if television competes for our attention. One mother did not realize this until the family TV broke. The family had gotten into the habit of watching TV during dinner. When the TV suddenly died, the family began to sit down at the dining-room table as a family again. She said that the broken TV was one of the best things that had happened to her family.[22] In a study of English working-class families, mothers battled to get their children to eat properly in the kitchen while the fathers watched TV in the next room. The mothers feared that without adult scrutiny, children might never learn how to cut and chew properly, how to notice what other people needed or said, or any of the other marks of being well brought up. The English were adamant about "Sunday lunch," deliberately staging weekly, full-dress, proper meals, with courses and tablecloths, where children could learn how to behave. One of the hallmarks of a proper meal was having the radio and TV turned off.[23]

Many quarters have sounded alarm about the dangers of television eroding family mealtime conversation. A 2000 Kaiser Family Foundation study found that two-thirds of all families with children between eight and eighteen had the television on during meals.[24] In 2001, 57 percent of children under sixteen had televisions in their rooms.[25] In May 2000, the White House held the first National Conference on Teenagers. President Bill Clinton announced findings from a report he had commissioned from the Council of Economic Advisors, *Teenagers and Their Parents in the 21st Century: An Examination of Trends in Teen Behavior and the Role of Parental Involvement.* The report concluded that teenagers whose parents were engaged and involved in their lives were "more likely to excel in school and avoid risky behaviors." President Clinton cited this "stunning statistical finding": "teenagers that had dinner with their parents five nights a week are far more likely to avoid smoking, drinking, violence, suicide and drugs. This holds true for single-parent, as well as two-parent families, across all income and racial groups." A poll commissioned by the conference showed that many families were unable to eat meals together more than a few times a week and that the number of teens who ate poorly had increased. Parents rated drugs, alcohol, and violence among their top concerns. By contrast, teenagers rated not having enough time together with parents and education as their top issues. Three out of four teens wished that they had more time with their parents. The Clinton administration announced a new public education campaign to raise awareness of the importance of parent-teen time, including family mealtime.[26]

Conference participant Ben Casey, president of the YMCA of Metropolitan Dallas, oversaw 145 centers that served a quarter of all families in the greater Dallas region. In running these programs, he found that today's parents had less family time than their parents had when they were growing up. Family mealtime was quickly disappearing. The time that parents did have to spend with their teens was frequently "dominated by logistics—did you do your homework? Have you cleaned your room? Little time remain[ed] for quality conversation, to share concerns, feelings and values." To give parents more time at home, the Dallas YMCA partnered with a grocery store and a pharmacy "to allow parents to pick up their groceries, dry cleaning and pharmacy items at the YMCA, at the same time as picking up their children from [YMCA] programs. [The Dallas YMCA's] only requirement [was] that they must go home, turn off the television, have dinner together as a family. To facilitate family conversations, the YMCA distribute[d] weekly appropriate stories, with themes for discussion, for the family dinners."[27]

Laura Sessions Stepp's book *Our Last Best Shot* is based on two years of observing families with teenagers. When she began her research, she wanted to examine teenagers' relationships with people other than their parents—coaches, teachers, mentors. "The kids, themselves, kept leading me back to their families," she notes. She learned that closeness with teens is not a given; it must be earned. Parents of healthy teens "show respect for their kids' rapidly growing minds and bodies; they give their kids an increasing amount of responsibility; and they work at keeping a close relationship with them." Robert Blum from the University of Minnesota, citing findings from a national longitudinal study on adolescent health-risk behaviors, concludes that despite popular perceptions to the contrary, families continue to matter throughout the teen years. Teens' perceptions of connectedness are influenced not so much by the *amount* of talk with parents as by the interaction of caring and connectedness and clear and consistent messages. Monitoring teens or doing activities with them without connectedness has little protective effect. What makes a difference is psychological availability: giving a young person the consistent message that you're crazy about him or her.[28]

Other professionals agree that parents must make the most of the little time they have with their children. Kay Hymowitz cautions that eating dinner with teens will not by itself reduce risky behavior: adults need to use time with children to define a moral universe for them. Just because parents are eating with their kids does not mean that they have anything to say to them. Today's parents are ambivalent about parental authority; they describe feeling tentative and uncertain in matters of authority and mean and guilty when disciplining their children. Theories of self-esteem and child empowerment encourage children to make decisions about nearly everything. Hymowitz suggests that such ideas clash with what has been the most important task of parents in any society: to shape their children's character and make them responsible members of a wider community. A survey released at the White House Conference reported that 61 percent of parents said that they frequently talked to their children about values and beliefs, but only 41 percent of teenagers reported having had such conversations. Hymowitz writes that the poll's findings about family togetherness have to be viewed with caution: more than 40 percent of the fifteen- and sixteen-year-olds who did not eat dinner regularly with their parents had been involved in serious fights, but so had close to 30 percent of those who did eat with their parents. Though 38 percent of the fifteen- and sixteen-year-olds who did not have close relationships with their parents had been suspended from school, so had over a quarter of teens who did report close relationships. Much has been made of the finding that teenagers want to spend more time with their mothers and fathers. But Hymowitz cautions that unless parents are willing to act like parents, family dinners every night of the week will not help American adolescents find their moral bearings.[29]

Of course, we can go overboard blaming television for the decline of family togetherness. Children have always received moral guidance from sources outside the family: friends, teachers, counselors, religious officials, even the mass media. But television's encroachment on mealtime seems too high a price to pay for those who want to get to know their family members through conversations. Civil society needs all the space it can find for adults to shape children's character and make them responsible members of a wider community.

The Screen Culture and Paying Attention

Television can be a springboard for table conversation. Some families watch television news during dinner to learn more about world events and to have stimulating conversations. In most ways, this is not different from the practice of asking each child to come to the table prepared to discuss a current event. However, reading and summarizing a news article for a group discussion requires more independent thinking and is less passive than waiting for visual stimuli to respond to. Also, televised news has become "infotainment," eliciting responses that are more superficial than thoughtful.

But there are problems at a deeper level. To foster thoughtfulness and generosity at the table, we must pay attention to the thoughts, feelings, and needs of others—an attentiveness that is derailed by the constant distraction of fast-paced images on television. Philosopher Sara Ruddick describes "attentive love" as a central element in maternal thought. It combines a cognitive capacity, attention, and a virtue, love, and implies that love will not be destroyed by knowledge. Indeed, real love depends on knowledge rather than on ignorance or wishful thinking. A mother "learns to ask, 'What are you going through?' and to wait to hear the answer rather than giving it. She learns to ask again and keep listening even if she cannot make sense of what she hears or can barely tolerate the child she has understood. . . . A mother really looks at her child, tries to see him accurately rather than herself in him." In the words of Iris Murdoch, "The task of attention goes on all the time and at apparently empty and everyday moments we are 'looking,' making those little peering efforts of imagination which have such important cumulative results." Ruddick insists that there is nothing natural or automatic about a mother's attentive love. Mothers have to "train themselves in the task of attention, learning to bracket their own desires, to look, to imagine, and then to accept what is different. They can be heard doing so in any playground or coffee klatch." Attentive love means more than listening; it also entails doing whatever is required for the child's safety and growth, based on the knowledge obtained by listening. Attentive love fosters trust between mother and child; both parties become trustworthy for having attended to what is really happening. Trust assures "that the work of training will not become a battlefield but a hard, uncertain, exhausting, and also often exhilarating work of conscience."[30]

All the mothers interviewed by DeVault recognized the importance of attentiveness, but their understanding of it seemed to be more tacit than explicit. They often had trouble describing it in words. A white married mother of two elementary-school-aged children wondered what she should do about one daughter's domination of mealtime conversation. Her older daughter was a chronic complainer, and the younger one never complained. "Some nights I sit and listen to [the older one] rant and rave about her various health problems, when there are none, and other nights I just simply brush her off. I'm not doing this very well. I'm not saying what I really want to say. But I guess this is an area of concern. Because I really should pay more attention to the little one, and less to the big one. And yet it seems reversed. Because of just the way their personalities are."[31]

DeVault described the thoughtful attention of mothers as a skill developed through trial and error. It stems from genuine concern for their children and from societal pressures to bear the prime responsibility for their children's well-being and development. These mothers learned from "watching the women around them that, as they say, 'If I don't do it, then no one else will'—women pay attention. As they do so, they 'pick up on' the knowledge that supports their work. . . . Over time, thoughtful attention results in knowledge that is tailored to specific situations." A black married woman with two children in high school linked a mother's attentiveness to her concern for family survival. "I believe that a lot of mothering, and homemaking, and child-rearing, is acquired. In order to survive you have to learn to do this. And for a person who cares about a family, it'll be perfectly natural for them to pick up on certain things. And maybe not even be aware that they're picking up on things, or learning to do certain things."[32] Attentive practices at the table are usually treated as women's responsibility, whether they are mothers or not.

At the table, people need to be monitored so that everyone feels connected with the enterprise at hand. One mother of two believed that monitoring was part of a mother's responsibility. She was concerned that her teenage daughter was much too thin, possibly anorexic. When asked what she did to keep track of the situation, she replied, "Well, that's what mothers are for, isn't it? I don't know if there's that much involved, except that I ask questions and hope to get the right answers. You know. Where have you been, where are you going, what's happening, are you going to do this, are you going to do that. She says, 'Get off my back, Ma.'"[33] It is tempting for adults to abrogate their responsibility in the face of such resistance. It is hard to do the exhilarating work of conscience without turning the table into a battlefield.

The screen culture thrives on short attention spans; civilizing work at the table requires long and multilayered attention spans. One has to think about choosing words carefully to be sensitive to the needs of others. After assessing the terrain of the moods of people at the table, one might decide not to raise a certain topic for conversation. The screen culture valorizes action and image over thought and character. It almost seems old-fashioned to insist on complete sentences and reflective discussion at the table, and intrusive and unnecessary to expect people to go into any depth about how they feel about what happened to them that day. The screen culture emphasizes what people *do*; the table culture probes the *significance* of what people do. The screen culture places a premium on appearances, on how people *look*; the table culture focuses on people's *character and ethics*. The table is a place to go beyond appearances, which takes time and undistracted thought.

Childhood mealtime memories are powerful and enduring: whether negative (anger at a father's relentless criticism of a mother's cooking) or positive (connection to three hundred years of cultivating and cooking rice). These memories bind people to larger worlds of history, social forces, and politics. Human connections are deepened through the sensory details of food: aromas in an Italian grandmother's house, the translucence of a grain of rice, or the burned spots on *papads*. Favorite childhood foods can reconnect a moody teen to family at the table. Bridges between generations need daily attention, construction, and repair. The table is an important construction site for this effort. Generational connections bolster civil society and democracy. When elders treat youth as people with something important to offer the group, young people can more readily imagine themselves as citizens with something significant to contribute to the polity.

Part Three

Food for Thought

.

Chapter 7
....

The Human Psyche and Mind-Body Dualism

In this chapter we dig deeper into the psychological and philosophical underpinnings of foodwork, meals, table rituals, and the art of conversation. What difference does it make that these activities have been so profoundly associated with women? We begin with a look at human psychological development—the emotional legacy in each of us of early associations of food, and survival, with mothers. Then we consider the significance of philosophical ideas that bifurcate mind and body—devaluing food, the body, and women in favor of "higher-order activities" of the mind and men. Food has been associated with women not only because they have done most of the foodwork and conversation work. There are deeper associations—in our psyches and philosophical concepts—that warrant a closer look if we are to understand civil society in all its complexity.

Food is profoundly associated with women because our early memories include first food coming from women's bodies, the terror of hunger being placated by women's actions, and the fear of poison being replaced with trust in female food providers. Food, appetite, and women take on frightening and pleasurable significance. Pain and pleasure are intensely felt and difficult to control. Most Western philosophers have sought to control them by disembodying the presumed agent of control, the mind. Even after neurological science demonstrated that the body did not work this way, the mind-body dualism continued to pervade Western thinking. What was repressed could not be understood. What was driven underground became distorted. What was bracketed from analysis threatened to call into question the validity of that analysis.

A worldview of mind-body *interdependence* is essential if everyone is to value foodwork. The mind-body dualism, with its hierarchy of senses, devalues food preparation as mundane, routine, messy, smelly, something to get out of the way so that more important things can be attended to. Mind-body interdependence allows one to be sensual, to trust the sense of smell, to use taste to discriminate among flavors, to experiment with new aromas and tastes, and to create with approximate cooking instead of rigidly following recipes.

Mind-body dualism keeps foodwork gendered. The mind, control, and reason are so psychologically and philosophically loaded as masculine, and the body, appetite, and emotion so charged as feminine, that until this dualism is broken down, everyday foodwork will continue to be seen as women's work. Challenging this dualism could lead to the conclusion that no "body" should do foodwork, which of course is impossible. The medical community universally endorses the nutritional benefits of breast milk over infant formula or cow's milk. Even if people obtain food from communal kitchens or automated dispensers, someone still has to do the foodwork. Food preparation is a labor-intensive activity. Bodies have to do it. The question is, which bodies?

Courtesy and civility do not emerge only after food has been prepared and eaten; they are essential attributes of successful food preparation and sharing. As we shall see in the *Symposium,* if the host had waited for the tardy Socrates, dinner for his other guests would have gotten cold and soggy. French food writer Jean-Anthelme Brillat-Savarin (who famously commented, "Tell me what you eat and I will tell you what you are") said there was no excuse for unpunctual guests or hosts who did not look after the welfare of dinner guests. Cooking and dining are thoughtful practices: an embodied, not disembodied, way of taking the needs of others into account, in a balancing act with one's own needs.

An understanding of civil society requires a humanistic approach to whole bodies; the mind-body dualism creates dehumanized and divided bodies, obsessed with controlling the unruly and unwieldy. Dehumanization requires dualistic thinking: superior-inferior, civilized-uncivilized, reason-appetite, mind-body, and male-female. Food is prepared by humans using all their senses intelligently, and it is shared by humans needing nourishment, pleasure, and conviviality. Divided bodies have distorted voices. Subjugated bodies are fearful of giving voice to their thoughts; dominating bodies must exercise their power by reducing the power and voice of others. If the mind does not have to *dominate* the body, then it can be alert to bodily needs, of self and others, and to the intelligent and fair satisfaction of those needs. It is unrealistic to expect fearful and intimidated people to act in the public good.

Ice cream.

2 bottles of good cream.
6 yolks of eggs.
½ lb sugar
mix the yolks & sugar
put the cream on a fire in a casse-
-role, first putting in a stick of vanilla.
when near boiling take it off &
pour it gently into the mixture
of eggs & sugar.
stir it well.
put it on the fire again stirring
it thoroughly with a spoon to
prevent it's sticking to the casse-
-role.
when near boiling take it off and
strain it thro' a towel.
put it in the Sabottiere
then set it in ice an hour before
it is to be served. put into the
ice a handful of salt.
put ice all round the Sabottiere
i.e. a layer of ice a layer of salt
for three layers.
put salt on the coverlid of the
Sabottiere & cover the whole with
ice.
leave it still half a quarter of an
hour.
then turn the Sabottiere in the
ice 10 minutes
open it to loosen with a spatula
the ice from the inner sides of
the Sabottiere.
shut it & replace it in the ice
open it from time to time to de-
-tach the ice from the sides.
when well taken (prise) stir it
well with the Spatula.
put it in moulds, justling it
well down on the knee.
then put the mould into the
same bucket of ice.
leave it there to the moment
of serving it.
to withdraw it, immerse the
mould in warm water
turning it well till it
will come out & turn it
into a plate.

Jefferson's Ice Cream Recipe. President Thomas Jefferson, who penned the Declaration of Independence, exemplified mind-body interdependence. He appreciated fine food and wine and foodwork itself. He acquired French wines and recipes, including this one for vanilla ice cream—written by Jefferson, with his own recipe for Savoy cookies to accompany the dessert on the back. Library of Congress, Manuscript Division.

If they have little reason to trust that others will meet their basic needs, then they will have little reason to put aside selfish interests when a more general interest is at stake. The thoughtful practice of everyday food provision and sharing gives people an experience with trust, a routine for allaying fears, a reminder of common needs, and an occasion to voice ideas at a level table.

Food, Mother, and Women

That food is so profoundly, and unconsciously, associated with women is not accidental. Women feed us in those early vulnerable months when the only way to get what we need is to cry. Our psychological development begins without words, in a sea of strong emotions. Women's sense of obligation to feed others and men's expectation that women will do so probably stem from an archaic impression of being fed as an infant by a mother. This memory, felt intensely long before we have the words to understand it, could leave a lasting imprint on social expectations. Gendered feeding roles may be difficult to change because they are lodged so deeply in the human psyche. Psychologists place great significance on the fact that since most people are first fed by their mothers, they have ambivalent psychological legacies of being utterly, and frighteningly, dependent on mother and, at the same time, completely, and enjoyably, satiated by her actions. Psychologists of various persuasions agree on the importance of early mother-child relations.

A cornerstone of Sigmund Freud's theory of psychoanalysis is the pleasure principle: the assertion that an infant takes pleasure from feeding from its mother's body. The infant eats to live, but also to experience pleasure. Feelings of pleasure ensure that an infant will take the nourishment that it needs to stay alive and will bond to its mother's body and love. An infant's first relationship with another person is based on the experience of one body feeding another body. From a psychoanalytic viewpoint, humans become active subjects, able to communicate, because of and in response to the primary pleasure of eating. The infant initially feels like an extension of its mother's body, which exists only for its gratification. When it is weaned, the infant becomes a subject, separate from its mother, using speech to get what it wants.[1]

Psychologist Nancy Chodorow, drawing from Freudian analysis, takes an object-relations approach to the legacy of mothering. She emphasizes social relations and the internalization of objects: the history of object choices makes up our mental life, and these choices are socially patterned. Chodorow assumes an early infantile oneness with mother, but gender differences emerge from the differential ways in which this oneness is severed. For boys, this bond ends abruptly since Western society insists on their independence. "Mama's boy" is a pejorative term. Girls do not have to undergo such a dramatic rupture of relations, so they remain psychologically preoccupied with relational issues such as primary identification, lack of separateness, and ego boundaries. In adult life, women are more likely to identify with affective and personal relations, and men with positional attributes and categories. Women are more likely to experience diffuse obligations and ambivalence toward other women, while men are prone to prefer contractual obligations and a denial of attachments to women.

Chodorow notes that, beginning in the 1940s, studies reported that American mothers were overprotecting their children and not allowing them to separate. These mothers had been influenced by the psychological theories of the 1920s, which emphasized maternal responsibility for children's development. This led women to put more time into child care even though they had fewer children to care for. Family mobility and the beginnings of suburbanization were removing women from daily contact with their female kin, so responsibility for their children's well-being fell solely on their shoulders. Chodorow maintains that society would benefit by equal parenting by fathers and mothers. If children were dependent from the outset on both mother and father, then they would establish an individual sense of self in relation to both genders. Masculinity would no longer be tied to the denial of dependence on and the devaluation of women. "Feminine personality would be less preoccupied with individuation, and children would not develop fears of *maternal* omnipotence and expectations of *women's* unique self-sacrificing qualities. This would reduce men's needs to guard their masculinity and their control of social and cultural spheres which treat and define women as secondary and powerless, and would help women to develop the autonomy which too much embeddedness in relationship has often taken from them."[2] The relational world should be everyone's responsibility.

Of course, Freud and Chodorow focus on mother-child relations in modern, industrialized, capitalist countries. If we wish to generalize about the universality of mother-child relations in relation to food and foodwork, then we have to cast a broader net. Based on observations of contemporary nomadic foragers, anthropologists argue that child-rearing and breast-feeding practices were probably different among our hunter-gatherer forebears. Weaning was gradual, with complete severance not occurring until the next child was born, and sons did not need to individuate with abrupt weaning. The Neolithic Revolution, some eight thousand to ten thousand years ago, significantly altered infant-feeding practices. As food production replaced

foraging, foods and animal milks were added to the infant diet as a comple-
ment to breast milk. These changes in feeding were closely linked to the
population explosion that accompanied the Neolithic Revolution.[3]

This did not mean that breast-feeding was abandoned. The early civilizations of the Near East (ca. 3,000 BC) produced sculptures, paintings, and
inscriptions testifying to mothers' breast-feeding, and texts described several
months of exclusive breast-feeding of infants. Wet-nursing appears to have
been a well-accepted practice in Egypt and Mesopotamia. The writings of
the philosophers of ancient Greece seldom mention infant feeding. Infants
were breast-fed, but it is uncertain whether the mother or another woman did
this initial feeding. Wet nurses were used by the wealthy. Roman physicians
from the first and second centuries AD were the first to focus significant
attention on the health of infants. They believed that the personal qualities
of wet nurses could be transmitted via their milk to infants. Spartan nurses
were highly valued for their ability to transmit stamina and good physical and
mental health. Roman infants were weaned between ages two and three.[4]

In Europe from the Renaissance through early industrialization, breast-
feeding and wet nurses were common. Maternal breast-feeding was practiced
by most mothers well into the second year of life, and weaning was sometimes
gradual, sometimes abrupt, dictated in part by the seasons. Until the late seventeenth century, most European upper-class women employed wet nurses,
rationalizing the practice as a way to avoid feeding their infants "impure"
colostrum. But ideas about sexuality and gender roles were crucial as well.
Medical authorities encouraged sexual abstinence until weaning, since it
was believed that sexual intercourse hastened the resumption of menstrua-
tion and impaired both the quality and the quantity of breast milk. Hiring
a wet nurse meant the end of a mother's sexual abstinence. Wet nurses were
chosen and supervised carefully, since it was believed that such things as
temperament, hair color, complexion, and gender-related demeanor would
be transmitted to the infant.[5]

After the Protestant Reformation, popular sentiment turned against the
practice of wet-nursing, and sermons denounced mothers who did not
breast-feed as selfish and evil. There was concern that this upper-class behavior would spread to lower-class women. "In the American colonies, wet
nursing was deplored because of the Puritan ethic, which encouraged women
to devote themselves to motherhood and not indulge their sensual urges.
Women who placed their infants with wet nurses were criticized for being
vain and sinful."[6]

With industrialization and urbanization came overcrowding, contami-
nated water and milk supplies, and infectious diseases caused by unsanitary

conditions. Wet nurses were used less frequently, and more women entered the workforce, often leaving their infants in the care of young girls. Infants were fed paps and porridges, commonly made with bread and water flavored with a little milk and sugar and kept warm on the stove all day. Research into the chemical composition of cow's milk led to the use of artificial and formula milks. By the 1930s, infant formulas were widely accepted, and by the 1950s, most babies in the United States were bottle-fed with artificial milk. With its scientific basis and medical direction, formula was deemed to be equal or superior to breast milk. By 1970, only 25 percent of babies were breast-fed, and practices differed by race and education level: 14 percent of black mothers breast-fed, compared with 29 percent of whites and 35 percent of Hispanics. In the early 1950s, the practice was most common among less educated women, but this trend was reversed by the 1970s.[7]

The women's movement of the 1970s brought a return to breast-feeding. Scientific studies showed that it provided greater resistance to disease, prevented allergies, and enhanced mother-infant bonding. Women wanted to have more say in childbirth and child care, and they turned away from the male-dominated medical establishment and toward such groups as La Leche League, founded in 1956 to provide mothers with practical knowledge about breast-feeding. By the 1980s, over half of newborns in the United States were breast-fed.[8]

In spite of the many historical and cultural variations in infant feeding, we can safely say that women were responsible for it, whether as mothers or as wet nurses. It is probably also true that infantile memories of mothers' satiation of hunger were both widespread and deeply felt. The first food was the fulcrum as the infant vacillated between hunger and pleasure. Since infant hunger and feeding evoke both terror and pleasure, it is probable that women, as providers of early food, are also remembered in such an ambivalent way.

Hunger, Fear, and Food

Hunger is terrifying; infants scream in order to be fed. Economically comfortable people often forget this terror; poor people do not have to be reminded of it. Hunger is the most basic, compelling, and agonizing human need, experienced universally and daily. Infants and toddlers want food immediately, and caretakers decide whether and how to indulge, delay, or regulate providing it. Since delayed gratification is invariably involved at some point, children often express their frustration by complaining, yelling, crying, biting, refusing food, or throwing food. Children may also be jealous when parents feed siblings, and angry if caretakers do not give them their fair share. Eating and feeding are central to the psychosocial maturation of children since they involve the first experiences of love and autonomy, pleasure and aggression, frustration and rage.

Anthropologist Carole M. Counihan studies the psychological significance of food for young children by analyzing their fantasy stories. Drawing on the psychoanalytic literature, she argues that expressions of hunger may represent children's neediness, which is either overwhelming or controllable. Greediness may reflect their fear of loss of motherly love and perceived rejection, or sibling rivalry. Children present themselves as either the hungry, needy ones or the empowered satisfiers of hunger. Their stories are riddled with violence and aggression, often expressed in oral terms. Food, as the vehicle of satisfaction of hunger, could stand for the satisfaction of all needs, just as hunger could represent all needs. Food symbolism allows children to identify with mothers, both affirming their deep connection with them and helping them overcome fear of separation. Children can gain parental potency by taking on the mother's feeding role in stories; they can identify with characters that nurture by providing food, or they can exert arbitrary retribution by withholding it. Children can also use food gifts or refusals to share food in their stories to signify the making or breaking of relationships.[9]

In Counihan's analysis of 489 stories told by 168 middle-class European American children in the 1950s and 1990s, she found that half of all stories included references to food and food-centered activities. Both girls and boys used food themes to mark time, to sustain the plot, to introduce the child's family and central issues of parental identification and sibling rivalry, and to express aggression and fear of not getting enough to eat. But there were gender differences as well. Girls made more frequent references to meals and to foodwork (food events, tasks, and workers). They were more attuned to the social role of food, describing themselves or others as shopping, cooking, or giving food to others. They were much more likely than boys to use food as a vehicle for enacting a social role, exercising power through the ability to withhold or give food. Girls made more references to food in its eating and provisioning senses, and boys made more references to eating as devouring. Almost one-third of all boys' food references were to eating as devouring or killing, twice the frequency of girls. In stories about the fear of hunger, girls more often overcame neediness through social and alimentary activities such as feeding or baking, whereas boys more often coped with dependency frustration through hostility and violence in their stories, such as biting, chewing, or eating others. When greed was the theme, boys' stories often resulted in harm, whereas girls' usually had benign or ambiguous resolutions.[10]

Counihan cites anthropological evidence that in cultures where food is scarce, girls' closeness to their mothers enables them to satisfy their hunger more successfully than boys, and boys and men are more likely to suffer hunger anxiety coupled with lifelong dependency frustration. For example, certain personality characteristics, such as selfishness, emotional detachment, and insecurity, among the Gurage of Ethiopia are attributed to their inconsistent early childhood feeding patterns and later cycles of want and glut. Gurage children are often neglected when hungry, then fed to excess after crying for hours. Adults normally eat sparingly and occasionally are forced to eat when they are not hungry at feasts or as guests. An uncertain food supply makes low-status men particularly prone to "spirit possession," marked by loss of appetite, nausea, and intermittent attacks of severe stomach pain. The affliction is cured through a collective ritual with a special food.[11]

Childrearing practices among the Ojibwa, who live in Canada's harsh climate with persistent food shortages, exacerbate children's dependency frustration, particularly among boys, and in extreme cases result in "the *wiitiko* psychosis." Ojibwa infants are breast-fed on demand, then weaned harshly, exposed to cold and solitude, and forced to fast and endure hunger for hours at a time. Such harsh and early independence training, directed especially at boys, sometimes results in lifelong dependency cravings and an association of food with power and of hunger with weakness and rejection. Symptoms of the *wiitiko* psychosis are depression, nausea, loss of appetite, and eventual possession by a cannibalistic figure known as the *wiitiko* monster. When possessed, the victim sees family and friends as fat, luscious animals, which he desires to devour.[12] Other anthropological studies relate conditions of severe food scarcity to spirit possession and document anxiety reduction through therapeutic rituals.[13]

One of the first anthropologists to focus on the centrality food to culture was Audrey Richards, who studied the Bemba of Zambia in the 1930s. She thought that their inhospitable ecological environment gave rise to a preoccupation with food, and she emphasized the importance of nutritional institutions in shaping a group's belief systems.[14] Cultures around the world enact rituals to ward off hunger by propitiating fertility and limiting appetites. Starvation, as a primordial fear, lurks beneath a culture's beliefs, attitudes, and values. Learning about one's environment means first and foremost learning how to obtain food—mother's milk or daily bread. Screaming to be fed only works for a limited time; at some point the quest for food involves more complex cognition and the use of language.

Psychologists and anthropologists have documented the universality of human hunger, its attendant fears and pleasures, and the resulting ambiva-

lence toward women as providers of infantile food. These emotional legacies lie beneath the surface of table pleasantries and conversation, creating
powerful expectations about social food roles. These deep-seated emotions
need to be consciously acknowledged in order to degender foodwork.

The Mind-Body Dualism in Western Philosophy

Implicit assumptions about food and women are also lodged in the language
and concepts we use. Given that language itself probably evolved as a means
to communicate about hunger and food, it is ironic that a major barrier to
understanding the centrality of food to culture, and of women to food, is
the pervasiveness of a philosophical approach to knowledge that separates
the mind from the body. This mind-body dualism has been detrimental
to women, to self-understanding, and to knowledge about human culture,
society, economics, and politics. On one side are women, the body, and
foodwork; on the other are men, the mind, and "higher-order activities" that
transcend bodily needs and desires. It will be difficult to convince people
to help with foodwork if such work is assumed to be a trivial, unimportant,
even debased activity. Philosophers have not paid attention to food. It is not
a serious subject.

According to philosopher Deane W. Curtin, the philosophical neglect
of food is no accident. There are deep structural reasons why the Western
philosophical tradition *cannot* take food seriously: to do so would challenge
the very questions asked by that tradition, as well as the methods used to
answer them. Philosophers in the dominant tradition confine their attention to those aspects of thought ordered by theory—abstract, disembodied,
atemporal schemes, as opposed to concrete, embodied, and temporal aspects
of life such as food relations. Since food relations are too ordinary and bodily,
they are excluded from the pursuit of truth about important questions.[15]

Beginning with Plato, standard accounts of personhood concern au-
tonomous and disembodied minds, not breast-fed bodies with deep-seated
ambivalence toward mother-feeders. In the *Phaedo* dialogue, Plato depicts
Socrates as saying that the true philosopher despises the pleasures connected
with food, drink, and other bodily pleasures. The body just confuses the
mind in its pursuit of the absolutely true. The philosopher-kings of Plato's
Republic are intellectuals determined to escape the prison of the body. In the
allegory of the cave, they must climb out of the image world of the cave to
gain illumination from the sun, the Form of the Good. Meanwhile, back in
the cave, women, slaves, and free manual laborers must get the meal on the

table. Plato sees the world in terms of exclusive dualisms: mind-body, self-other, and reason-emotion. Ordinary life in the cave is a dangerous illusion, as opposed to the extraordinary life of the philosopher. For Plato, humans struggle with a mind in conflict with the body. The mind, reason, morality, culture, and theory are at odds with, and indeed must tame, the body, emotions, desires, others, nature, and common food practices.[16]

Plato, through the voice of Socrates in *Gorgias,* belittles cookery as not "an art at all." It is a "kind of knack gained by experience" that is "aimed at gratification and pleasure." Cookery does not employ rational calculation but simply follows routine. Plato scorns a wine retailer, a baker, and the author of a Sicilian cookbook for fattening bodies, for giving Athenians what they desire, not what serves their best interests. According to Athenaeus's *Deipnosophists (The Sophists at Dinner),* philosophers at Plato's Academy smashed a casserole to bits because it was too fancy. Diogenes the Cynic teased Plato about sailing to Syracuse in Sicily for its delicious food. In his *Seventh Letter,* Plato responded that he found "nothing whatever to please [him] in the tastes of a society devoted to Italian and Syracusan cookery, where happiness was held to consist of filling oneself full twice a day, never sleeping alone at night, and indulging in the other pursuits that go with such a way of living." In *The Republic,* Socrates maintains that food should be kept simple, unlike Sicilian cooking, since "elaborate food produces disease." Plato describes bodily appetites as insatiable; those who succumb to them are like animals. "They bend over their tables, like sheep with heads bent over their pasture and eyes on the ground, they stuff themselves and copulate, and in their greed for more they kick and butt each other with hooves and horns of steel, and kill each other because they are not satisfied, as they cannot be while they fill with unrealities a part of themselves which is itself unreal and insatiable."[17]

According to sociologist Michael Symons, in Plato's ideal state, people would feast on wine, wheaten loaves, barley cakes, salt, olive oil, cheese, vegetables from which to make various country dishes, figs, peas, beans, and myrtle berries and acorns to roast. In this vegetarian diet, fish was notably absent, since Athenians saw fish eating as synonymous with the habits of a gourmand. "Plato's warning against cooks—as mere seducers of the palate, with this-worldly preoccupations and apathetic to theoretical principles—accompanies his philosophical dualism." Dualists cannot explain how the mind might synchronize with the body. Plato's solution posits that the higher instincts ought to dominate the lower: reason rules the senses.[18]

Plato splits both the polity and humans into three parts, with the higher aspect controlling the lower through an intermediary. *The Republic* describes three social classes in the ideal state: the philosopher-kings who govern, the middle class of guardians with military powers, and the artisan class engaged in handicrafts and agriculture. They are matched by a threefold human psychology: the soul is divided into reason, spirit, and appetite. Plato emphasizes self-control, achieved by thought or reason, which, mediated by emotions, controls appetite. In *Timaeus,* even the human anatomy has three parts—the head at the top houses reason, the heart in the middle is home to courage, and the stomach below is the seat of appetite. The appetite for food and drink is found in a "kind of manger for the body's food" (the stomach), which is located "as far as possible from the seat of deliberation, and causes the least possible noise and disturbance, so leaving the highest part of us to deliberate quietly about the welfare of each and all." Fortunately, human anatomy is designed in a way that prevents the quick passage of food. Thanks to bowels wound in coils, the body is not compelled "to want more and make its appetite insatiable, so rendering our species incapable through gluttony of philosophy and culture, and unwilling to listen to the divinest element in us."[19]

Plato's hierarchical worldview, in which mind and reason control body and appetite, appears at first glance to be contradicted by symposia, after-dinner drinking parties where philosophers held extended conversations. Indeed, many of Plato's writings took the form of his jotting down what Socrates said at such gatherings. An example is *The Symposium,* a discourse in praise of love, which takes place at the house of Agathon. Friends talk on the way to his house; they describe the road to Athens as "made for conversation"; and servants lead the friends into a banquet hall where guests are reclining in anticipation of a feast. Socrates has "stayed behind in a fit of abstraction" and "retired into the portico of the neighboring house," from which he will not budge in spite of the calls from the servants. One guest advises that Socrates be left alone: "He has just a habit of stopping anywhere and losing himself without any reason; don't disturb him, as I believe he will soon appear."[20]

Agathon instructs his domestics to put on the table whatever they would like. As his guests eat, he several times expresses a wish to send for Socrates, but Socrates' companion, Aristodemus, will not allow him to do so. When the feast is half over—"for it, as usual, was not of long duration"—Socrates enters, takes his place on the couch, and eats. When the meal ends, libations are offered, and a hymn is sung to the god, followed by the usual ceremonies. As they are about to begin drinking, a guest reminds the group that most of them are still recovering from having drunk too much wine the day before. Since Socrates is "an exceptional being," he is "able either to drink or to abstain." The rest of the group agrees not to drink and, in order to start the conversation, sends away the flute girl, who is free to play by herself or to the women who are in another room.[21]

After an extended dialogue about love, a band of revelers suddenly enters and spoils the order of the banquet. Someone had left the door open, so the revelers have found their way in and made themselves at home. Great confusion ensues, and everyone is compelled to drink large quantities of wine. As the night wears on, some guests leave, and others fall asleep. At daybreak, Socrates, one other guest, and the host Agathon are drinking out of a large goblet, which they pass round, and Socrates is discoursing to them. Only after the other two have fallen asleep does Socrates depart with Aristodemus.

So the symposium included table talk, but it took place after the meal, not during it; meal decisions were left to domestics; and the banquet and conversation were out of the sight and earshot of women. For his part, Socrates could hardly be bothered with such a quotidian matter as the meal itself; he had more important questions on his mind, and the group accommodated his idiosyncratic behavior because he was exceptional. Excess and revelry ruined the exchange of ideas. Even at table, Plato retained his hierarchical and divided world: the mind and reason flourished only when the body and appetite got out of the way.

The mind-body dualism continued throughout the history of Western philosophy, most notably in the works of Augustine and Descartes. In his *Confessions,* Augustine describes the body as a prison from which his soul or mind sought to escape. Life on earth is a trial of restraint from evil, the first of which is lust of the flesh, and the second eating and drinking. "This necessity is sweet to me, and I fight against its sweetness, so that I may not become its prisoner; by fasting I carry on war every day, often bringing my body into subjection, and the pain I suffer in this way is driven out by pleasure. For hunger and thirst are pains; they burn us up and kill us like a fever, unless we are relieved by the medicine of nourishment. . . . This you have taught me, that I should have the same attitude toward food as I have toward taking medicine."[22] Augustine aligns male-female dualism with soul-body dualism. Woman is carnality, ethically dangerous to man. Femaleness as body decrees a natural subordination of female to male, as flesh must be subject to spirit in the right ordering of things. Woman is the symbol of the fall and sin, the bodily principle in revolt against its ruling spirit. Woman is thus a submissive body in the order of nature and a revolting body in the disorder of sin.[23]

The mind-body split continued with the philosopher René Descartes. His metaphysical dualism of mind versus matter, known popularly as Cartesian dualism, was derived from his famous dictum, "I think, therefore I am." As he writes in his *Discourse on Method,* "I concluded that I was a substance whose whole essence or nature was only to think, and which, to exist, has no need of space nor of any material thing. Thus it follows that this ego, this soul, by which I am what I am, is entirely distinct from the body and is easier to know than the latter, and even if the body were not, the soul would not cease to be all that it now is."[24] Cartesian "Rules for the Direction of the Mind" were rules for the transcendence of the body—"its passions, its senses, the residue of 'infantile prejudices' of judgment lingering from that earlier time when we were 'immersed' in body and bodily sensations."[25]

Repairing the Dualism: Eating with Mind and Body

Obviously, both eating and cooking simultaneously involve "mind" (reasoning, thinking, strategizing, and planning) and "body" (hunger, appetite, taste, and pleasure). Plato's hierarchical scheme is conceptually and empirically inadequate to the task of understanding food's centrality to human knowledge and culture. "Mind" cannot be lifted out of a "body" oblivious to hunger. Even Socrates had to come to the table eventually. "Mind" must plan to get food, even if all that means is planning to have servants and companions provide it for you, as was the case for Socrates. Cooking is certainly empirical, but it is more than a "kind of knack gained by experience." Without adequate provisioning and careful preparation, people will starve or get food poisoning. Experience helps in this regard, but so does intelligent experimentation with new foodstuffs. A safe, monotonous diet requires little skill, but history has shown that most people will abandon such a diet when given the choice. Although Plato disparages food as "aimed at gratification and pleasure," his solution, unrealistically, is to control and transcend gratification and pleasure rather than to acknowledge their significance in daily meals and foodwork. Plato's mind-body dualistic thinking became a cornerstone of a Western philosophical tradition pervaded by such thinking.

Imagine for a moment Agathon's house: women behind the walls, domestics in a master-servant relationship, revelers coming uninvited through the front door and disrupting order, and a preoccupied Socrates coming to the table when he felt like it. Now imagine a household where one learns about love and justice (themes of *The Symposium* and *The Republic,* respectively), thoughtfulness and generosity, from everyday dilemmas, not from insight "from above." From which vendors should we obtain food? Whom should we feed? Whose tastes and dietary preferences should be accommodated?

What is appropriate table behavior? Who has a voice at the table? What is a fair share of food? How long should women breast-feed? How often should children eat? Who should work in the kitchen? Should we continue with family recipes or try new ones? Should we pass on our culinary traditions to our children? Why didn't Plato, or the philosophers who succeeded him, ask these questions? Why haven't these been important questions?

It is possible that some adults could live, at least for a while, in a house like Agathon's. Certainly the very rich do not need to do much meal planning, chopping garlic and onions, or running to the store for a last-minute carton of milk after an exhausting workday. There are no cranky babies at their restaurants, decorum prevails at their dinner parties, and they can eat when they please. Feeding can be reasonable and orderly. Appetites can be kept in check and satiated in a measured fashion. But for most people most of the time, reason, planning, and thinking are constantly drawn into the service of solving the puzzles of hunger, appetite, and pleasure.

A more fruitful approach to understanding and appreciating meals and conversation begins with the premise of mind-body *interdependence*. Consider the Italian cookery that Plato rejected as unpleasant, elaborate, indulgent, and disease producing. Just as the Platonic mind-body dualism reappeared throughout centuries of Western history, so too did the mind-body integration of Italian culture and foodways. Anthropologist Carole Counihan studied families in Florence, Italy, between 1908 and 1984. She was struck by how Florentines celebrate the physical pleasure of eating, calling it *gola*—a love of and desire for food. Someone who really appreciates eating is called a *golosalo*. *Gola* means throat as well as desire for food. She observes that for Florentines, the throat is the passageway both for food to enter the body and for voice to exit it. The implication is that these actions are reciprocal. "The food goes in and makes the person; the voice goes out and externalizes the person. Because *gola* implies both 'desire' and 'voice,' it suggests that desire for food is a voice—a central vehicle for self-expression, an animated manifestation of life and personhood." In sharp contrast to Plato's view of the stomach as a manger and the abdomen as a locus of desire-delaying coils, the Italian word for waist is the same as that for life: *vita*. For Counihan, "this etymology further emphasizes a conception of the body as vital rather than inert, self-expressive rather than self-reflecting, and active rather than passive." In their concept of *gola*, Florentines define the self as having a legitimate right to love food but also a moral obligation to eat judiciously and avoid excess, which destroys desire and pleasure, upsetting the balance between desire and control.[26]

The French, who are known for their love of food and the joys of eating, also emphasize the difference between a healthy love of food and the excesses of overindulgence. They even petitioned the pope to have *gourmandise* ("gluttony" in English) removed from the list of the seven deadly sins. In a movement started in 2001 by baker Lionel Poilane, adherents sought to polish the image of *gourmandise*. Catherine Soulier, the president of the group De la Question Gourmande, maintains that the concept connotes not gluttony but "a warmhearted approach to the table, to receiving and giving pleasure through good company and food." Moderation is important: *gloutonnerie,* which also translates as "gluttony," is gross; *gourmandise* is life enhancing and measured. Soulier says that she is generous and gives pleasure to her guests and "would far rather be a zestful gourmand than a picky, priggish gourmet." The group's headquarters are conveniently located on a street named after Jean-Anthelme Brillat-Savarin, author of *The Physiology of Taste* (1825). He was a French judge, whose dinners were famous for their culinary excellence and witty conversations. Brillat-Savarin wrote that *gourmandise* is no sin, au contraire: "The casuists have classified gourmandise as one of the seven deadly sins, but if it is not tainted by the vice of drinking to inebriation or eating to excess, it deserves to be on par with the theological virtues." In the text he sent to the pope, Poilane made the point that the life of Jesus was marked by associations with food from the wedding at Cana through the Last Supper. His hope was to replace *gourmandise* with *gloutonnerie,* more along the lines of English *gluttony.* English, of course, has no word for *gourmandise,* which the French would take as proof of the joylessness and awful food that they associate with Protestant countries.[27] However this semantic-theological question is resolved, it serves notice that love of food is a legitimate part of the philosophical quest for the good (and measured) life.

Instead of imagining a Platonic self whose head and heart *control* the stomach, the Italian and French self *gains its voice* through food. The throat symbolizes both the desire for food entering the body and the voice of self-expression exiting the body. One need not worry about the excess of gluttony, since the pleasure principle works against it, as does self-control. Where Plato saw wisdom and insight resulting from conversations after meals and without families, the French and the Italians praise the self- and social knowledge gained at family meals. Counihan notes, "Just as commensalism—eating together—reproduced the family, it was also a primary means of forging and soldering extrafamilial relationships. Couples marked their official engagement—*fidanzamento*—by having a special meal with each other's families, and then they began the regular, lifelong habit of eating together that continually reaffirmed their connection." Where Plato saw people giving into insatiable desires like uncontrolled animals at pasture, Italians see healthy, communal outings in the countryside. "Friends got together for *scampagnate*—outings to the countryside—where they ate and drank in raucous company and had a great time together. They loved going out to eat with friends—for the simultaneous pleasures of food and conviviality—and were not willing to give them up to lose weight."[28]

Many eating and cooking words of Latinate origin suggest that food connects the mind/body with the outside world. To keep company is to share bread (*com* "with" + *panis* "bread"). Commensality derives from table talk (*com* "with" + *mensa* "table"). *Recipe* is the Latin imperative for "take." Food does not magically appear on a table; ingredients have to be procured. In all recipes, the first task is acquisition of ingredients. As Michael Symons observes, a recipe opens onto an entire culture. "It is a condensed survival guide, applicable to a set of physical and social circumstances."[29]

Safe and Delicious Recipes: Mind the Ingredients

The human practices of cookery and cuisine development are compelling illustrations of the importance of eating with the mind and the body. Since humans are omnivores, they are in constant danger of making mistakes about safe foods. Cooking provides rules about preparing the tested and approved. Recipes signal safe, proper, and delicious eating. Cooks are empiricists, developing cuisines through trial and error. They satisfy human cravings for certain tastes, especially salts and sugars.

Cooks' use of salt is a perfect example of how safety and taste are interrelated. The human need for salt came with the Neolithic Revolution. As people ate less game and more vegetables, they valued salt for reasons of both taste and health. The relatively tasteless plant products and cereals did not contain enough salt to meet human nutritional requirements. The invention of cooking pots resistant enough to be placed over a fire enabled boiling, which conveniently required little of cooks' attention. But unlike roasting, which conserved the salt content of meat, boiling leached it out. Both herbivorous animals and agrarian peoples needed additional salt, so salt became related to the history of Western civilization. The world's oldest known city, Jericho, over twelve thousand years old, probably developed as a salt-trading center along the Dead Sea. Rome's "Salt Road" (Via Salaria) crossed to the Adriatic and covered the route used by the Sabines to collect salt from marshes near the mouth of the Tiber. Around 500 BC, the saltworks at the mouth of the

LEAD.

Dissolve a handful of Epsom or glauber salts in a pint of water and give it at once; after vomiting is produced, use sweetened water. If the symptoms continue, do as directed for acids.

POWDERED GLASS.

Stuff the patient with thick rice pudding, bread, potatoes, or any other vegetable; then give five grains of tartar emetic to vomit him, after which use milk freely; injections, warm bath, fomentations, are not to be neglected.

OPIUM.

Let a tea-spoonful of Cayenne pepper, or twice the quantity of black, be steeped in about half a tea-cup of boiling water, give a tea-spoonful as often as possible until the whole be down. Immediately after give an emetic, as soon as it operates freely the patient should take a little more of the Cayenne and a table-spoonful or more of lemon juice, or strong vinegar, and kept in motion until danger is over. In an hour after taking the lemon juice, give a little broth or light nourishing food, well seasoned with Cayenne or black pepper. This simple process will always subdue the poison of opium or any other narcotic. Infants have been relieved and saved from an over dose of paragoric or laudanum, by giving a spoonful of vinegar immediately.

MUSHROOMS.

Give the patient immediately, three grains of tartar emetic; twenty-five or thirty of ipecac; and an ounce of salts, dissolved in a glass of water; one third to be taken every fifteen minutes until he vomits freely, then purge with castor oil.

TOBACCO, HEMLOCK, NIGHT-SHADE—SPURRED RYE, ETC.

An emetic, as directed for opium. If the poison has been swallowed some time, purge with castor oil. After vomiting and purging, if still drowsy, bleed and give vinegar and water.

Skilful Housewife's Book. Cooks are empiricists, developing recipes and cuisines through trial and error to determine what is both safe and delicious. The many important functions of domestic cookery are listed in the title of Lydia Green Abell's *Skilful Housewife's Book; or, Complete Guide to Domestic Cookery, Taste, Comfort and Economy* (1853). On this page, she lists household remedies for various poisons: lead, powdered glass, opium, mushrooms, tobacco, hemlock, nightshade, and spurred rye. Smithsonian Institution.

Tiber became a state monopoly. The word *salary* is derived from the Roman soldiers' salt-money. Ancient Greeks used salt as a charitable gift. Venice, a hub of the spice trade, shipped salt up the Po River. Salzburg means "salt castle." A salt tax was cited as a major cause of the French Revolution. The Russian word for hospitality is literally "bread-salt." The English word *sauce* has its origins in the Latin for "salt." Salt was so universally employed that sauces might well be explained as a means to add it. Accustomed to the taste of excessive salt through its near-universal use as a preservative, people eventually felt the need to add it. Sauces and flavors became a cuisine's stamp of approval for foods. Cuisines replaced instincts as guides for what to eat.[30]

Cooks pass along their knowledge about food safety and taste for the sake of the survival of the group. Most anthropologists agree that in hunting and gathering societies (our condition for most of human existence), insofar as men had to hone their hunting skills, women played a crucial, if not causative, role in selecting and propagating healthy plants. In their natural state, plants did not evolve because they were good to eat. To the contrary, plants with substances toxic to their predators (humans, animals, insects, and microbes) were better able than others to survive. Humans and animals ate them at their peril, sorting out those that, based on experience, could be safely added to their diet. The presence of toxins in plants was an important determinant of the dietary habits of our forebears. "Compounds toxic to humans are more likely to be encountered in foods of plant origin because they have not been subjected to toxicological screening by first having been consumed by animals. . . . Some toxins in plants are destroyed by cooking, but this method of food preparation appears to have been practiced only during the last 20 percent of human existence."[31]

To remove toxins from plants, early farmers and cooks experimented with plant breeding and modes of food preparation and processing, thereby adding many new foods to the modern mixed diet. Also, commerce in foodstuffs diluted the high concentration of toxins present in plants grown in specific localities, such as the high levels of selenium found in the soil in some areas of the western United States. To this day, cooks must watch out for preventable toxicological risks associated with the modern diet. In addition to allergens, these include "formation of microbial toxins in poorly preserved foods; overdosing or accidental poisoning with synthetic vitamins; ingestion of harmful bacteria, residual plant enzymes and antinutrients resulting from inadequate cooking; consumption of carcinogenic amino acid derivatives produced by overcooking meats; and ingestion of natural toxicants in such foods as mushrooms."[32]

We all have to trust that our cooks know what they are doing on many fronts: catering to food allergies or sensitivities; paying attention to temperatures in preserving foods; discarding spoiled foodstuffs; cooking meats long enough, without overcooking them; and choosing their wild mushrooms very knowledgeably.

The flip side of this trust is fear of poisoning. Cooks are in a position to use their knowledge for nefarious purposes. Just as primordial mothers fed, archetypal witches poisoned. In the witch-hunting craze of fourteenth-century Europe, witches were accused "not only of murdering and poisoning, sex crimes and conspiracy—but of *helping and healing.*" Village specialists in herbs were demonized as anticooks, concocting devilish brews. The very doctors who campaigned against women healers as witches were summoned as expert witnesses at their trials. The real issue was control: "Male upper class healing under the auspices of the Church was acceptable, female healing as part of a peasant subculture was not." Ironically, the female healer was the scientist of her time. "She relied on her senses rather than on faith or doctrine, she believed in trial and error, cause and effect. . . . In short, her magic was the science of her time."[33]

In folklore and mythology around the world, women bent on harm are often poisoners because they have access to food and not fighting weapons. Knives are male weapons, used to fight, wage war, and hunt. At the table, they are used to carve meat. In medieval Europe, for example, men were supposed to cut for their womenfolk at table. By contrast, poison is secretive, often liquid, and administered in food.[34]

Throughout history, powerful people had elaborate rituals to prevent their food from being poisoned. Margaret Visser describes how noble houses in medieval Europe had extraordinarily lengthy rituals whereby the food for the high table was "assayed" by officers whose job it was to die if the food was poisoned. "Tasting was called 'credence,' because of the belief or confidence which the ritual was meant to instill; side tables at feasts were known as 'credence' tables. (The term is still in use for the table standing near the altar in a church; and an Italian sideboard is known today as a *credenza.*)" Assaying often involved touching the food with substances, such as animal horns, stones, or crystals, reputed to change color if poison were present. "The fear of being poisoned appears to have haunted the medieval imagination, and indeed unintentional food poisoning, ergotism, and germ-infested water were a constant danger."[35]

Ergotism, a fungal disease affecting cereals, especially rye, was an illness that occurred across Europe throughout the Middle Ages. Cooking did not necessarily neutralize its toxic effects, and bread baked with the tainted flour was extremely dangerous. Since symptoms of ergotism included burning pains in the limbs, itching skin, and convulsions, it was called Holy Fire or St. Anthony's Fire. Its cause was not discovered until 1670, when a French country physician deduced its connection with rye bread, a staple of rural peasant families.[36]

In the court of Louis XIV in seventeenth-century France, dinners were brought to the royal table under armed guard in a procession through Versailles nearly a quarter of a mile long. Only the most important people had their food tested for poison in a ceremony that conferred enormous prestige. It was flattering to be considered important enough to be a candidate for assassination.[37]

Ordinary people have different ways of coping with their fears about food safety. They face the "omnivore's paradox": the state of being simultaneous drawn to and fearful of new foods. People experience the opposing pulls of both *neophilia* (the inclination to sample novel food items) and *neophobia* (caution when confronted with novel items, based on the possibility that they may be harmful). Eating is a profoundly ambivalent activity, and this ambivalence is resolved differently in traditional and industrial societies. In traditional societies with low rates of social change, long-established culinary customs, beliefs, and rituals provide confidence and a taken-for-granted frame of reference within which food-related anxieties can be submerged or neutralized. However, industrialization, trade, and the global food supply increase food choice and decrease people's reliance on traditional frameworks about food safety. Synthetic products do not provide obvious clues to the senses about what is safe. When scientific experts weigh in about food safety, it has the paradoxical effect of *increasing* consumer anxiety. Since by its very nature scientific knowledge is provisional and subject to refutation and replacement, it does not provide the security and reassurance of traditional knowledge. Furthermore, scientific ideas are often inaccessible to the general public. Therefore, scientific reports on food and nutrition do not necessarily produce public reassurance and confidence.[38]

Indeed, public perceptions of food-related dangers often differ from those of experts. In studies in contemporary Sweden and the United States, consumers actually reversed the rank order of risks assessed by experts: dietary fat, sugar, and salt, followed by food poisoning, natural poisons, residues, and additives. Consumers regarded poisons (mercury and heavy metals) as the greatest risk; then came pesticides, bacteria and mold poisons, with fat, sugar, and salt well down the list.[39]

Modern Americans, less than ever integrated into the supportive networks of family and community and unsure of expert advice, still need to trust that the food they eat is safe. They develop various strategies of confidence to assure themselves in the face of confusing advice. Some people choose natural foods; others develop a repertoire of trusted foods and exclude all others. Some consumers seek confidence through the reidentification of foods: more-detailed labeling of food products, elaborate listing of ingredients, and formal guarantees of purity and quality.[40] Still others find reassurance in brand loyalty or the predictability of fast food. New rituals and reassurances are needed to replace traditional folk wisdom about trust and danger.

Minding the ingredients is a social act, incorporating reason and pleasure, science and emotion. Dualistic thinking blocks our understanding of the interdependence of knowledge and trust, reason and emotion, mind and body. Every day in everyone's lives, foodwork and meals require a delicate interchange, the dynamics of connection to civilized relationships—safe, commensal, and companionate. We trust food providers to nourish us and give us voice: food goes into the throat to make the person, and voice comes out to externalize the person. A true love of food entails a moral obligation to avoid excess. The mind is interdependent with the body. Even though we experience this interdependence every day when we eat, the devaluing of food and the body in favor of higher-order activities stubbornly persists in dualistic thinking. And archaic memories and deep-seated emotions subconsciously link food to women. A full appreciation of civil society requires that we view humans with mind-body interdependence and make conscious the unconscious connection between women and food.

Chapter 8

Appetite and Taste

The household and foodways have been shoved off the civil society stage in large part because appetite is feared as a craving that needs to be controlled, and taste is trivialized as personal subjectivity rather than appreciated as an entrée to knowledge and meaning. Viewed in these ways, what could appetite and taste possibly have to do with civility? This chapter argues that appetite is not just something to be controlled so that people can be civil; rather it can create the opportunity for commensal joys, festivities, and sharing. If appetite is simply something to be feared, then its civilizing potential will escape scrutiny. A constructive alternative to "appetite control" is the notion of "thoughtful food practice." Similarly, taste is not just a matter of subjective preference. It is also a gateway, along with the more privileged sense of sight, to human knowledge, cultural understanding, and civilized behavior. This chapter illuminates neglected facets of appetite and taste so that they can figure more prominently in our understanding of civil society.

A formidable barrier to understanding the civilizing potential of gustatory appetite is its association with sexual appetite and women. Philosopher Carolyn Korsmeyer observes that appetite "connotes both sexual and gustatory craving for satisfaction, an association that appears to be more or less universal across dramatically different societies; indeed the ambiguity of words referring to gustatory and sexual appetites is found in vastly different languages." Anthropological studies detailing the prevalence of links between appetites for sex and food in different cultures include Claude Lévi-Strauss's *The Raw and the Cooked,* Jack Goody's *Cooking, Cuisine and Class,* and Peter Farb and George Armelagos's *Consuming Passions.*[1] In a similar vein, philosopher Susan Bordo writes that female hunger is a cultural metaphor for unleashed female power and desire. Cultural representations across the globe and the centuries include the blood-craving Hindu goddess Kali (who eats her own entrails), the fifteenth-century Christian work *Malleus Malificarum* (which states that for the sake of fulfilling the mouth of the womb, witches consort with the devil), and lyrics from the rock song "Maneater" (which warn, "Watch out boy, she'll chew you up").[2]

Appetite Control: Domestic Science and the Diet Industry

In the United States, the two major attempts to tame the appetites of women were the domestic science movement of the 1880s and the contemporary diet industry, which began in the 1950s. Interestingly, it was women themselves who did the taming through domestic science. The discovery of the existence of bacteria in the 1880s led to concern about germs in food. Well-meaning upper-middle-class women saw it as part of their mission to Americanize newly arrived immigrants with the latest scientific discoveries about food safety. Food writer Laura Shapiro describes the late nineteenth century as the era that made American cooking American, transforming a nation of honest appetites into an obedient market for instant mashed potatoes. Fear of germs enhanced the authority of scientists in the eyes of cooks, teachers, writers, and housekeepers who championed a scientific approach to housework. They were also intrigued with rationalizing and professionalizing housework along the lines of a well-regulated office or factory. They blamed unschooled, tradition-bound housekeepers for the failures of the American home that led directly to poverty, disease, alcoholism, and unemployment. The American housekeeper would guide the nation's homes from chaos to an ordered scientific era.[3]

Reformers attempted to change the foodways of immigrant women through cooking schools, domestic-science magazines, clubs, and lecture tours. They worked in tandem with research universities, government agencies, and the food industry to help Americans forget what they knew about food and to opt for convenience and progress. When they met with only limited success, they turned their attention to the daughters of immigrant women, through home-economics courses in the public schools. The year 1899 marked the birth of home economics as a profession, giving reformers legitimacy for their uphill battle in a world that still thought of them as housekeepers with wild ideas. Scientific cooks shared with food-industry officials the ideals of uniformity, sterility, and predictability. One domestic scientist praised the virtues of American factory cheese over foreign varieties by noting that American cheese lacked the individuality that characterized foreign cheeses. Her description reads like the antithesis of the Slow Food movement's approach to food. "Those who can remember the great diversity in taste, structure, and composition which was so noticeable in the old farmhouse cheeses can appreciate the greater uniformity in the factory product. The method is more economical of material, time, and labor; it removes this burden from our farming women; neatness and cleanliness are obligatory; the quality of the product can be gauged and assured, and the cost and trouble of marketing are greatly lessened."[4]

Industrially processed foods were uniform, sanitary, and convenient; they were also marketed as "dainty" to appeal to proper middle-class ladies. An advertisement for Heinz baked beans read, "A dainty dish for luncheons." One home economist forbade "brain-workers" (i.e., middle-class professionals) from eating noncanned baked beans even once a week, since canning made beans more digestible. A food writer praised the virtues of canned peas by saying that hands had never come into direct contact with the peas throughout the entire process from vine to table. Cleanliness was of the utmost importance for the housekeeper who struggled to keep her kitchen and its contents free from dirt, germs, and consequent disease.[5]

Home economists devised charts breaking food down into its constituent nutrients. They were convinced that industrial food was the wave of the future. Old-fashioned kitchens were reduced in size and function to kitchenettes. Home economists even conducted experiments to demonstrate that home cooking as they knew it was a thing of the past, at least for city dwellers. To prove the point, in 1900 a group of college-educated Boston women invited a Wellesley graduate to conduct an experiment to compare the cost and taste of home-cooked and ready-made foods. They hoped that by proving the superiority of the latter, they would convince conservative homemakers to accept the inevitable course of industry. But the experiment backfired. Three days' worth of meals were tested. In all cases, tasters of both products preferred the homemade meals, and they cost less.[6]

Dietary standardization was perfectly suited to mass production. One domestic scientist argued that all healthy people with the same amount of exercise needed the same quantity of food of the same composition. Only unenlightened people demanded food variety, due to their "acquired appetites" or lack of interests besides eating and drinking. She thought that when people advanced to the stage of "rational living," with outdoor exercise and work that led to physical, mental, and spiritual development, they would find that "unreasonable preferences for particular foods" disappeared. Appetite, like nutritional requirements, would be alike in everyone. The campaign to put Crisco in every kitchen was an example of this standardization. Developed and tested in a laboratory, Crisco was promoted by home economists and the advertising industry. Laura Shapiro dubs Crisco white sauce the epitome of scientific cookery: "a food substance from which virtually everything had been stripped except a certain number of nutrients and the color white."[7]

Students in cooking schools and home-economics courses were not supposed to eat the meals they made. Meals were assembled, not enjoyed. Recipes mattered more than results. Women were supposed to be dainty eaters whose appetites were curbed by science and technology. The virtues of cookery were obscured. As Shapiro notes, "The act of eating, not to mention its indelicate companion, appetite, had long been anathema to femininity, and the reigning value in the modern kitchen was convenience, not coziness, or even apple pie." Scientific cookery triumphed in 1953 with the appearance of TV dinners that blunted flavors and symbolized the dream of a nutritional democracy with all Americans eating the same way. Cooking became brief, technological, and impersonal. Food was reduced to a necessity, manipulated and brought under control "as quickly and neatly as bodily functions were handled by modern plumbing."[8]

Of course, this was the food industry's definition of democracy. In fact, it was an assault on the authority of the individual's taste and food preferences. The result was to convince millions of people to eat canned and processed food that was virtually flavorless. As food declined in tastiness, so too did the desirability of sitting around a table for a leisurely meal with lively conversation.

Beginning in the 1950s, American women increasingly curbed their appetites through dieting. This time, women were the recipients, rather than the creators, of appetite taming. According to historian Joan Jacobs Brumberg, the origins of American women's obsession with dieting can be traced to the 1920s. In part it stemmed from a legitimate concern about health. Between 1900 and 1920, the traditional association of fatness with prosperity and good health was replaced with an ideal body type that was decidedly thinner. During this time, the medical establishment and the insurance industry compiled the first medicoactuarial standards of weight and health and concluded that overweight was a serious health liability. Pediatrics also contributed to the trend of standardized weights. Public schools participated in programs weighing children. But in larger part dieting was due to the emergence in the 1920s of an American beauty culture: the fashion and cosmetics industries, beauty contests, the modeling profession, and the movies. Elite women heeded the dictates of French haute couture, and America's emerging ready-to-wear garment industry quickly followed suit. For many women, fashion became a statement about social and sexual liberation, related to the availability of birth-control devices. Women's magazines emphasized celebrity, status, and guilt if one's body did not conform to the ideal. By the 1920s, calorie counting was on the increase, as was bulimic behavior, and the use of enemas, cathartics, and iodine in the effort to reduce weight. Weight control was so important to beauty that women came to feel increasingly at odds with their appetite.[9]

During the scarcity and national emergencies of the Great Depression and World War II, dieting seemed a frivolous preoccupation. But in the postwar period, a new audience was targeted: adolescent girls. "Baby fat" became childhood obesity, and commercial interests sold to girls what they had marketed to their mothers. After a brief flirtation with curvaceous female body ideals in the 1950s, the collective taste returned to thin, childlike figures. Since the 1950s, weight has declined for fashion models, Miss America contestants, and *Playboy* centerfolds. In the 1960s and 1970s, many Americans began to change their diets for greater fitness and health. And in the mid-1970s, a new emphasis was placed on physical fitness and athleticism. In the 1980s, half of American women said that they were on a diet at any given time, and close to 80 percent of prepubescent girls restricted their eating in the interest of not getting fat. In 1985, Americans spent over $5 billion in an effort to lose weight. Diet books became fixtures on the nation's best-seller lists. Weight control became a specialty in American medicine: bariatrics.[10] By the late 1990s, diet-industry revenues were $33 billion and surveys reported that 80 percent of American women dieted on a regular basis.[11]

Pathological Appetite Control: Eating Disorders

An emphasis on health and fitness was a positive step for most women, but some took it to a dangerous extreme. Anorexia nervosa resulted from the twin behaviors of compulsive exercising and chronic dieting for body control. How much one ran and how little one ate became a moral calculus. Although its causes were largely individual and familial, cultural admiration for extremely thin women contributed to an increased number of young women at risk for anorexia nervosa. Eating disorders became rampant on college and university campuses, where women's food habits became increasingly problematic after the 1960s. In response to student pressure, campuses reduced their in loco parentis role by relaxing controls on students' social life and sexuality. One casualty was the decline in family-style meals on college campuses. Students became vagabond eaters, with indiscriminate eating habits. In this permissive and highly individualized food environment, overeating and undereating became easier, often accentuating the anorexic's emotional and physical problems. Brumberg observes that the anorexic was often more troubled than liberated by her autonomy with respect to food. In spite of the insights of the women's movement, appetite remained an important voice in her female identity: food represented fat and loss of control. She feared and hated her appetite; eating became a shameful and disgusting act; and the denial of hunger loomed as a central facet of her identity and personality.[12]

According to Susan Bordo, anorexics take to an extreme the language of mind-body dualism and its resulting need for control. Just as Plato, Augustine, and Descartes experienced the body as alien, the not-self, the not-me, anorexics speak of hunger as an alien invader. Many describe the dread of hunger, of not having control, of giving in to biological urge, to the craving, never-satisfied "thing." They are terrified of taking just one bite of food, lest they never be able to stop. Bulimic anorexics, who binge on enormous quantities of food, indeed cannot stop. They use Augustinian language of a contest between good and evil: mind and will versus appetite and body. In this battle, thinness represents the triumph of will over body. Fat means becoming all body, tainted, wanton, a state of mental stupor or decay.[13]

Some therapeutic approaches to eating disorders involve reconnecting with food. Popular self-help books provide specific exercises and self-reports, encouraging readers to allow themselves to enjoy the food they consume.[14] In the group Appetite for Change, psychologist Catherine Manton conducted group-therapy sessions, which included discussions, food journals, simulation and role-playing, homework, and preparing and sharing a common meal. The goal was not to lose or gain weight, but rather to challenge assumptions underlying cultural attitudes toward food and body size. Many women talked about food as fuel and used the machine model to describe themselves. They regularly referred to their bodies as entities separate from their minds. One homework assignment asked a member whether she could request that her spouse sit with her one night a week at the table rather than eating in front of the television. Another assignment was a joint visit to a health-food store to explore alternative food sources. In the informal discussion around the dining table, members often revealed an increased awareness of advertising and food marketing efforts that encouraged their alienation from the sensual and nurturant pleasures of food. In keeping with national findings about women with eating disorders, about two-thirds of the women in Appetite for Change had been sexually abused as children. A common theme in many women's eating experiences was their inability to nurture themselves and to feel that they had a right to food, especially given that so many of them had been put on diets by their mothers at an early age. Some mothers had even taken their young daughters to diet doctors who prescribed amphetamines to curb their appetites.[15] Like the food reformers before them, many postwar American mothers had some misguided notions of what was best for female appetites.

From Appetite Control to Thoughtful Food Practice

The mind-set of appetite control has had some very unhealthy, even self-destructive, consequences for women. An obsession with food control cuts off the sensual origins of important human knowledge about the natural world, about how to create something life sustaining for one's self and for others, and about rules for obligation and sharing. Food pleasure, if hammered into submission, cannot be a source of knowledge or a basis for human connection and civility. The pursuit of pleasure and the pursuit of truth are not necessarily at odds. Thinking is part of eating, not something done by a disembodied mind in opposition to an eating body. Sophisticated thought—the pursuit of wisdom, the exploration of complex ideas—is not something that happens only after eating is out of the way. Thought is an essential part of food making and food enjoyment, and wisdom can be derived from these activities, as happened for the women in Appetite for Change.

Foodmaking combines thought and practice. As philosopher Lisa M. Heldke notes, "Foodmaking, rather than drawing us to mark a sharp distinction between mental and manual labor, or between theoretical and practical work, tends to invite us to see itself as a 'mentally manual' activity, a 'theoretical practical' activity—a 'thoughtful practice.'" Philosophers in the Western tradition tend to value human activities to the extent that they are head work ("knowing activities" such as science, theory, and art) as opposed to hand work ("doing activities" such as cooking, farming, and cleaning). Practical activity is disparaged as getting one's hands messy. Foodwork does get one's hands messy, but it does not respect the boundaries of theory and practice. "Kneading bread dough is not a 'subservient' physical activity which 'supports' bread-making 'theory,' even while violating the separation between 'bread theorizer' and dough. Rather, kneading is an essential part of the theoretical-and-practical process of making bread—a part in which subjects' and objects' boundaries necessarily meet, touch, and overlap."[16] Historically, of course, the privileged who did the head work were often, and conveniently, oblivious to the hand work of wives, servants, slaves, and manual laborers, whose activity sustained their way of life.

Heldke derives the concept of thoughtful practice from American philosopher John Dewey, for whom the difference between theory and practice is one of degree, not kind. Theorizing is in fact a kind of practice. Thoughtful practices are intelligent, inherently and immediately enjoyable, full of meanings, wary, observant, and sensitive to slight hints and intimations. When foodmaking is approached in this way, new connections between the self and the other can emerge. Thoughtful practice also recognizes bodily knowledge derived through taste, touch, and smell. A cook must finger a ball of pie dough to tell if it needs more ice water, and smell when garlic is about to burn as it sautés in oil. "The knowing involved in making a cake is 'contained' not simply 'in my head' but in my hands, my wrists, my eyes and nose as well. The phrase 'bodily knowledge' is not a metaphor. It is an acknowledgement of the fact that I know things literally with my body, that I, 'as' my hands, know when the bread dough is sufficiently kneaded, and I 'as' my nose know when the pie is done."[17]

Thoughtful practice also means that pleasurable eating is intelligent eating. As writer Wendell Berry observes, there is more to eating than pleasure for its own sake. When eating is done with pleasure that does not depend on ignorance, it is "perhaps the profoundest enactment of our connection with the world. In this pleasure we experience and celebrate our dependence and gratitude." He contends that knowing about the health and beauty of the garden where one's vegetables are grown "relieves and frees and comforts the eater. The same goes for eating meat. The thought of the good pasture, and of the calf contentedly grazing, flavors the steak." He realizes that some think it is cruel to eat fellow creatures, but he defends eating meat as long as one understands the lives and worlds from which food comes and expresses gratitude.[18] Berry's thinking about eating animals leads him to a conclusion vastly different from that of vegetarians, but the point here is that pleasure and intelligence are twin forces at work in eating as a thoughtful practice.

Cuisines are another example of thoughtful practice. They are bodies of knowledge: distilled over time through a process of trial and error, passed down by word of mouth and hands-on learning or perhaps in written form, providing sustenance and pleasure on a daily basis. Haute cuisine feeds the elite, but nonelites have their cuisines as well. Cuisines are defined in terms of the use of major foodstuffs, especially grains and cooking fats,

Tasting Cookie Dough. Foodmaking is an example of what American philosopher John Dewey calls a thoughtful practice—intelligent and enjoyable. Knowledge is derived through taste, a sense often devalued as a gateway to knowledge. Sampling cookie dough is one way to determine if it has the right consistency. Photo by Big Ben (Gaijin Biker), Flickr Blog, uploaded May 11, 2006.

or "flavor principles," culture-specific repetitive flavor combinations. They are intelligent and pleasing guides to what to eat, a common marker of a civilization.

In satiating appetite, all the senses come into play to produce pleasurable and intelligent eating: inquiring about food sources; figuring out a way to get more of what tasted good; feeling connected with, rather than alienated from, foodways; and enjoying the aromas, textures, and sensual pleasure of preparing and eating meals. A healthy relation to, and accurate understanding of, food requires the use of all the senses. If taste, smell, and touch are devalued, then so are food, appetite, body, and hand work. One reason it has been so difficult to uncouple the dichotomies of mind-body, theory-practice, and reason-appetite is the philosophical tradition of valuing the sense of sight and devaluing the role of other senses as gateways to knowledge and understanding.

Where Is Taste in the Hierarchy of Senses?

In her philosophical investigation of the sense of taste, Carolyn Korsmeyer observes that the literal sense of taste is noted by philosophers only insofar as it provides a metaphor for aesthetic sensitivity: discrimination regarding objects of art and standards about artistic judgment. Literal taste is dismissed as unworthy of serious consideration—it is mundane, it means pleasure as opposed to rationality, and it is associated with appetite, instinct, and animal existence. Taste stands in stark contrast to vision, which receives the most attention for its delivery of important information about the world. In the hierarchy of senses, "higher" vision and hearing are at the top, and "bodily" smell, taste, and touch at the bottom. Sight and hearing are the cognitive or intellectual senses, providing more of the sensory information necessary for the exercise of the rational faculties and the development and communication of human knowledge. They are less involved with the experience of pleasure and pain and thus appear to be comparatively detached from subjective experience felt as sensations *in, not with,* the body. Taste requires intimacy with objects of perception that enter the mouth and deliver sensations experienced in the mouth, the throat, and the digestive track. Korsmeyer writes that the degree to which the body is experienced as involved in the operation of a sense contributes to the value assigned to the objects of that sense. Artifacts such as paintings and music, which are crafted for the delight of eyes and ears, can achieve the status of works of art; objects of the other senses are valued more for sensuous pleasure, such as the enjoyment of perfumes or food and drink. For this reason, she states, only vision and hearing are traditionally considered genuine aesthetic senses. By contrast, taste, touch, and smell constitute the "bodily" and "lower" senses.[19]

As we have seen, for Plato, the rational soul had to conquer the senses and emotions of the body in order to achieve wisdom and virtue. His most famous parables involved visual images, such as *The Republic*'s allegory of the cave in which the sun was equated with the Form of the Good. Plato called vision "the most sunlike of all the instruments of sense." He also acknowledged the importance of hearing to the development and exercise of language and to the perception of music. Taste remained mired in the flesh. Unlike Plato, Aristotle insisted that souls required bodies and that flesh was not simply the stuff that interfered with the operation of the rational soul. Senses were sources of pleasure, which was an important component of practical wisdom, but he too singled out sight and hearing as the highest and cognitively more-important senses. Aristotle was less squeamish than Plato about bodily pleasures, and his doctrine of "the mean of virtue" called for the mean between extremes of excess and deficiency. Temperance, or moderation, was, after all, one of the Greek cardinal virtues. But special dangers lurked in the pleasures associated with taste and touch: gluttony, drunkenness, and sexual debauchery. For both Plato and Aristotle, sight and hearing had the advantage of operating from a distance, providing more objective information relatively untainted by the subjective feelings of pleasure and pain derived from the senses of taste, touch, and smell.[20]

For subsequent thinkers, the eye continued to be the symbol for the intellect, and the lower senses caused concern. Marcus Aurelius expressed contempt for food and matters of the body. Thomas Aquinas, who disseminated Aristotelian ideas throughout the medieval Christian world, wrote, "It is clearly impossible that human happiness consist in pleasures of the body, the chief of which are pleasures of the table and of sex." Descartes opined: "The conduct of our life depends entirely on the senses, and . . . sight is the noblest and most comprehensive of the senses." Even the British empiricists, who were dedicated to showing that all knowledge derived from sense experience, devoted most of their attention to vision. Contemporary writings in the philosophy of perception almost invariably focus on visual perception—and for many of the reasons advanced by Plato and Aristotle.[21]

Korsmeyer argues that the hierarchy of senses is gendered. Implicit in Plato's view is the belief that "the ability to transcend the body, to govern the senses, to gain knowledge, is a masculine ability that when exercised well will keep one embodied as a male. There is, therefore, an implicit gendering of the use of the senses themselves, with the higher, distal senses of sight and hearing paired up with the appetites and the dangerous pleasures that are in one way or another associated with femininity." For Aristotle as well, distance senses were well suited for the activities of men, and the bodily senses for those of women. The minds of women were less able to apprehend knowledge in an abstract, universal form and more inclined to particular judgments of sense. Aristotle thought that the gaze of menstruating women clouded mirrors and other reflecting surfaces.[22]

The sense of taste is devalued as a path to knowledge even in its metaphorical usage. In many languages, taste connotes appreciative judgment. This connection can be found as early as the fifteenth century, but it was in the seventeenth century that the usage became more common. Korsmeyer writes,

"In Spanish, Italian, English, French, German, the practice spread using literal taste (*gusto, gout, Geschmack*) analogically to describe an ability to discern what eventually would be designated aesthetic qualities." Taste referred to the ability to perceive beautiful qualities, complex artistic compositions, social sensitivities, and manners. Aesthetics appeared in modern philosophy as an adaptation from the Greek term *aestheta,* or things perceived, as opposed to *noeta,* or things known, that is, the content of intellectual knowledge and objects of logic. Again, a distinction was drawn between deep, permanent, and objective truth-seeking, and superficial, transient, and subjective truth-seeking. Taste was a matter of subjective relativity resisting systematic understanding, hence the aphorisms *Chacun à son gout* (To each his own taste) and *De gustibus non est disputandum* (There's no disputing about taste). Taste was idiosyncratic, private, and resistant to standards. The philosophical prejudice against taste, both gustatory and metaphorical, rests on the notion that it is natural, direct, "intimately acquainted with incorrigible pleasure," and unmediated by rational deliberation. Taste is "a *subjective* sense that directs attention to one's bodily state rather than to the world around, that provides information only about the perceiver, and the preferences for which are not cogently debatable."[23]

The Science of Taste

Korsmeyer challenges this prejudice with evidence that there is indeed a science of taste, based on a wide array of anthropological and sociological studies, a vast international and historical literature on gastronomy and cuisine, and physiological studies of the sense of taste. Philosophers have failed to take the findings of social scientists into account: eating is an activity charged with significance beyond the pleasure it affords and the nutritional sustenance it provides. Just like works of art, food is an intimate part of hospitality, ceremony, and rituals both religious and civic. All five senses contribute to food preparation and eating experiences. A cook hears when water boils, kneads dough to the proper consistency, and creates dishes that look, smell, and taste good. Tastes convey meaning and have a cognitive dimension. Foods are employed in symbolic systems ranging from the rituals of religion to the everyday choice of meals. Eating has intense social meaning for communities large and small. A comprehensive study of taste involves perception, cognition, symbolic function, and social values.[24]

An early defense of the science of taste was Jean-Anthelme Brillat-Savarin's *Physiology of Taste* (1825). Brillat-Savarin lived at a time when taste—both aesthetic and gustatory—was of foremost intellectual and social interest. Korsmeyer maintains that his approach was "wholeheartedly scientific as well as sensuous . . . a series of aphorisms, dialogues, essays, and ruminations about the sense of taste, food, appetite, drink, sex, and pleasure. The book blends science, theory, history, and practice, and to the latter end includes some recipes and tips for food preparation."[25]

Brillat-Savarin is best known for his aphorisms, which he claimed serve "as a prologue to his work and an eternal foundation for his Science." Instead of worrying about the baseness of appetites, he focused on pursuing their satisfaction by distinguishing between nourishment and gastronomy: "Gourmandism is an act of judgment, by which we give preference to things which are agreeable to our taste over those which are not." Gastronomy distinguishes humans from animals: "Animals feed; man eats; only the man of intellect knows how to eat," and it prevents excess: "Drunkards and victims of indigestion do not know how to eat or drink." Gastronomy is a key to human, cultural, and social understanding: "Tell me what you eat: I will tell you what you are"; "The fate of nations depends on the way they eat"; and "The pleasures of the table belong to all times and all ages, to every country and every day; they go hand in hand with all our other pleasures, outlast them, and remain to console us for their loss." The table is a locus of courtesy and conviviality: "The table is the only place where the first hour is never dull"; "The discovery of a new dish does more for the happiness of mankind than the discovery of a star"; "To wait too long for an unpunctual guest is an act of discourtesy towards those who have arrived in time"; and "The man who invites his friends to his table, and fails to give his personal attention to the meal they are going to eat, is unworthy to have any friends."[26]

Brillat-Savarin asserted that taste is "a faculty so delicate that the gourmands of ancient Rome were able to distinguish in taste, a fish caught between the bridges from one caught lower down the river," and present-day gourmands "can tell the latitude in which the grapes of any given wine ripened." He maintained that gastronomy, "the reasoned comprehension of everything connected with the nourishment of man," is a civilizing force that brings people together. "It is gastronomy which makes a study of men and things, in order to transport everything that deserves to be known from one place to another, so that a well-ordained banquet seems like an epitome of the world, every part of which is duly represented." Brillat-Savarin even wrote of "political gastronomy": "Meals have become a means of government, and the fate of nations has often been sealed at a banquet. . . . Read the historians, from Herodotus down to our own day, and you will see that there has never been a great event, not even excepting conspiracies, which was not conceived, worked out, and organized over a meal."[27]

The science of taste also has a physiological and chemical basis. Taste buds, too small to be seen unmagnified, were discovered in 1867 on the wall of the observable bumps, or papillae, on the tongue. Taste buds are clusters of taste-receptor cells: globular shaped with an opening "taste pore" at the top. "Molecules of dissolved substances—'tastants'—enter the taste pore and interact with microvilli, stringy projections from interior taste cells that surround the pore. In the microvilli, chemical reactions between the tastants and receptor molecules in the taste cells cause reactions that produce further chemicals, which act as neurotransmitters and stimulate neurons that extend into the taste bud. The neurotransmitters convey information along one of several cranial nerves to the brain, and then the taste sensation itself occurs to consciousness." Sensitivity to the four basic tastes—sweet, sour, salty, and bitter—is centralized in specific areas of the tongue: sweetness at the tip, sourness along the sides, saltiness along the front and sides, and bitterness at the back, just before the throat. "It is speculated that this distribution constitutes a safety factor, for tentative licks of sweetness can detect healthful carbohydrates, and many poisons are intensely bitter. The bitter receptors thus stand guard at the last point where swallowing can be halted, and indeed very bitter substances stimulate a gag reflex." The chemistry of taste has only recently been understood, contributing to its relative mystery as compared to the fairly full scientific comprehension of sight and hearing.[28]

There is physiological evidence that taste can vary from person to person, given the tremendous variation in the numbers of papillae on the tongue and the numbers of taste receptors among papillae. By one estimate, about 20 percent of the population are "supertasters," people with densely packed papillae who are especially sensitive to flavors, especially to sweet and sour. Another 20 percent have comparatively few taste buds and dull taste perception. The remaining 60 percent fall in between. In old age, the number of taste buds steadily declines. Certain genetic factors also determine whether a person can taste certain substances at all. Thresholds for discernment can be either very high or very low for certain bitter tastants.[29]

It is important to keep these physiological differences in mind: delicious food at a common table is more likely to entice supertasters than those with dull taste perception. Corporate-processed and canned foods are not solely to blame for the dulled palate of many Americans. One might speculate whether the desire for delicious meals lessens with age, as the number of people's taste buds slowly declines. Even if this is the case, it is possible that social motivations for common foodways, such as love of family and ethnic traditions, may draw older people to the table just as strongly as their taste buds once did.

Enzymes also influence food preferences. Not all people can digest cow's milk and dairy products after infancy, and globally these products exhibit uneven consumption patterns. Since many peoples in Asia and Africa stop secreting lactase, the enzyme that digests the lactose in milk, by late childhood, their cuisines lack milk products. Eating patterns and taste preferences are also influenced by agricultural resources and animal use.[30]

But apparently there are also universal patterns of taste. People eat because they are hungry, need nutrients, and desire to taste something pleasurable. There appears to be a universal, genetically based preference for the taste of sweet things, which is functional from an evolutionary viewpoint, since in nature sweet taste means ripe fruit. A liking for sweetness does not seem to be learned. Salt, a necessary nutrient for the body, is similarly liked universally among humans and other species as well. Sour and bitter tastes are acquired. According to psychologist Elizabeth Capaldi, "In nature, poisons are bitter; sour fruit is not ripe; and a preference for salt will produce ingestion of many needed nutrients. Beyond these simple genetically mediated preferences, however, food choice is learned."[31]

Sociocultural factors also seem to play a universally important role in a person's taste and food selection. As psychologist Paul Rozin observes, the meaning of food—source of nutrition, source of pleasure, social-moral statement—is dictated by culture. He notes that if you want to know as much as possible about the foods another person likes and eats, and can ask that person only one question, it should be "What is your culture or ethnic group?" Cultures operate according to the "law of contagion," which holds that "once in contact, always in contact." Human preparers or handlers of food are linked to the eaters, loading food with interpersonal messages such as "Grandma's soup can be better because it was made by Grandma." For example, among Hindu Indians, sharing food made by a common third person has homogenizing social and moral significance; refusal to share establishes distance, or "heterogenizes." Hindu caste structure can be reconstructed from information on who can eat whose food. The order of serving and rules about eating leftovers maintain family hierarchy. The body is the temple of the soul, so eating is a moral transaction linking humans and gods.[32]

Around the world, taste is also related to social class. According to anthropologist Jack Goody, societies having both strong class hierarchies and written records, such as ancient Egypt, China, India, and Persia, and the classical Arab world, developed distinctions between high and low cuisines and produced culinary writings to pass along information about preparing, serving, and eating food. Written food traditions expanded the vocabularies used to refer to tastes. Having discriminating distinctions available in words contributed to the refinement of the experience of subtly different tastes.[33]

Taste has much to do with civility and civilization. World civilizations have devoted considerable time and treasure to the codification of high cuisine, reflecting ornate class and even cosmological orders. But every culture also has its low cuisine, transmitted by contagion to group members. By definition, group membership and foodways imply the existence of outgroup membership and foodways. How groups decide to bond and to view outsiders are, of course, crucial matters for civility. Taste creates group solidarity, whether the group in question is a world civilization, a nation-state, a class, a caste, an ethnic group, or a family. Taste is not merely subjective, private, capricious, and subject to the whims of incorrigible pleasure. Philosophical prejudice devalues taste, along with smell and touch, as base and bodily, imperfect pathways to knowledge and understanding. Western culture pays a high price for not coming to its full senses. Taste promotes practical knowledge about our connectedness to social groups, identity, and meaning. It is as much a key to civilization as are the other senses. Appetite also has a bearing on our understanding of civility. It is not just something to be controlled and feared or tamed by experts and the diet industry. An obsession with appetite control robs us of the opportunity to create something life-sustaining for ourselves and others, and to forge the rules of obligation and sharing, thoughtfulness and generosity. On a daily basis, appetite gives rise to occasions for thoughtful food practices, customary reminders of the need to channel personal gain and pleasure into a common welfare and conviviality.

Part Four

· ·

One Woman's Revolution

Chapter 9

. . . .

Alice Waters's
Delicious Revolution

Up to this point, a case has been made for an expanded understanding of civil society that encompasses household foodwork and challenges unexamined assumptions about the devaluation of foodwork because of its association with women, the body, and appetite. The location of the argument has been largely in the household and around the table, with harried workers preparing nourishing meals, ethnic groups preserving their foodways, parents perpetuating the rituals and manners that make possible the art of conversation, and generations reaching out across age differences to create commensality. For the remainder of the book, the argument about civility will be extended outside the household and into the world of restaurants, schools, jails, community gardens, and farmers' markets. In all these settings, foodwork is a surprising and exciting—and definitely understudied—source of civility and civil society.

We begin with restaurants through a case study of restaurateur Alice Waters and Chez Panisse. Her delicious revolution illustrates how one woman fused delicious food with both a political philosophy and practical applications in her community. There have been several interesting accounts of Waters and her delicious revolution, but none has analyzed her efforts from a framework of civil society and democracy.[1] Most political scientists would not think of the delicious revolution either as a revolution or as fertile ground for civil society. An extended case study is warranted here because the delicious revolution was my inspiration for writing this book, and because it represents a practical application of the book's central themes.

The Delicious Revolution

The foundational premise of the delicious revolution is that good food is a right, not a privilege. Once people are exposed to delicious food (ripe, in season, and organic), it will appeal to their senses in such a way that they will come to prefer it to unhealthy fast food and tasteless, out-of-season, canned, and processed food. Agribusiness, corporate marketers, and employers have convinced people that food is fuel and meals should be quick. Waters believes that children need to learn about delicious food by cultivating it in school gardens and sharing it with classmates. Americans need to slow down to savor meals and conviviality. She also supports jail gardens and procures produce from them for her restaurant. Her efforts remind us that the civilizing aspects of food transpire not just at the family dinner table but also in restaurants, school gardens, and even jail gardens. Indeed, given the time crunch at the family table, civilizing practices need to be fostered in as many settings as possible.

Since many families spend less time engaging in foodwork and fostering thoughtfulness and generosity at the table, Waters correctly raises the question: if these things are being done less often at family dinners, can other institutions, such as schools, pick up this work and have the same civilizing effect? Schools have been asked to step into family shoes in the past: to oversee discipline and living arrangements on campuses, to provide information on sex education, to encourage physical activity, to administer psychological counseling, and to promote physical health. It is not a stretch to ask schools to reconnect children with the land and with others through meal preparation, community foods, and civil table behavior. Waters's delicious revolution reverberates across many institutions: schools, jails, restaurants, and farms.

Probably the most unconventional aspect of the delicious revolution is its emphasis on sensuality, pleasure, and seduction. How necessary is this? Why not settle for a cognitively based food-centered philosophy: we know the medical reasons why organic food is healthier than nonorganic; we know from ecological studies why the land must be cared for; we see the need for manners at the table to keep order; for any society to survive, it must teach its children proper speech and communication skills. The problem with an instrumental depiction of food is that it tells only part of the story. In our everyday lives, food is something more than an instrument for larger, abstract purposes such as health, order, and stability. To provide a complete picture of food, we need to draw attention to its emotional impact: the terror of starvation, the fear of poison or spoilage, the force of cravings and appetites, the pull of memories evoked by aromas, the feelings of well-being after a pleasurable meal. Conviviality at the table is a pleasure, related to a satisfying meal. Needy bodies prepare and share food. Too often, civility is seen as something that transpires after "bodily" needs are met and appetites sated, something that transcends our "base" emotions. But the table is such an important locus of civility precisely because it necessarily calls into play mind and body, reason and appetite, pleasure and obligation, indulgence and sharing, ritual and cravings. Waters is right to redirect our attention to the pleasures of the table, especially if we are looking for a way to lure children away from the draw of video games and television.

Alice Waters has very clear ideas about the kind of food at the center of her worldview: it is delicious, ripe, in season, local, and organically grown. She claims that this ideal is worth upholding, even in climates less ideal than California's. Her delicious revolution reminds us that any analysis of the role of food must be seen in a social and historical context. Should we listen to her because she is a successful restaurateur? In my view, the delicious revolution is not another food fad, but rather a serious worldview applied successfully in several, and disparate, settings. How do her claims compare to our mothers' cookbooks or oral food traditions? Ethnic food traditions? Home economists? Nutritionists? Advertisements? When Waters asks us to take food choices seriously, she reminds us that they are intimately related to who we are, who we want to become, and how we relate to others.

Waters underscores the importance of the conversation that accompanies food preparation and sharing at the table. Who will be eating? When shall we eat? What shall we serve? Do we have the right ingredients? How does this taste to you? Who chops, stirs, bakes, fries? Who sets the table? Where do people sit? What are the rituals at the table? What shall we talk about? She was elated when children engaged in these civilizing activities, especially across race and class lines at tables at a local middle school. Whatever differences children, or inmates for that matter, bring to the table, people take pride in gardening and sharing the fruits of their labor in meal preparation. The conditions are ripe for respectful conversation. Waters's delicious revolution asks us to investigate why table conversation is so important and provides some practical solutions to prevent it from becoming a vanishing art in light of hurried meals in front of the television.

Waters also correctly emphasizes food's role in building communities of various kinds. Food creates and evokes family memories. It is a central feature of every ethnic, regional, and national culture. Festive and ceremonial foods become markers of people's identities. Community gardens bring people together. School gardens and farmers' markets are increasingly connecting urban dwellers with agricultural ways of life. Jail inmates are finding satisfaction in experiencing the productivity of the soil and sharing its harvest. Communities are built through shared experiences. Communities are occasions for civil discourse. Although communities can impede civility if their in-group affiliations are based on out-group exclusion, their foods can be shared with nonmembers and become ambassadors for greater cross-community understanding.

Waters claims that she wants people to come to Chez Panisse not because the food is good for them but because it tastes good. She extends the argument to children, whom she wants to entice with good food. Distressed with the fast-food eating habits of her daughter's peers, Waters was instrumental in getting a garden installed at a local middle school, where children could learn about organic farming and take pride in growing and sharing food that tastes delicious. She said that she got the idea for this school garden from a garden program at the San Francisco jail, where inmates experienced the transformative power of growing, cooking, and sharing food. When some participating inmates reported that they did not want to leave when their sentences were up, a program was instituted in which they could use their gardening skills after release. Waters figured that if inmates' lives could be given meaning through food, so could those of children and teens.

The juxtaposition of *delicious* and *revolution* is intriguing. *Revolution* usually means a radical, fundamental transformation brought about by a violent conflict between political opponents. Although it is nonviolent, Waters's revolution has radical components: the claim that good food is a right, not a privilege, and a critique of pesticide use, corporate agribusiness, and a fast-paced consumer culture that devalues eating slowly and civilly. It has transformative elements: bringing people together through the common acts of eating, conversing, and building community across race and class lines, both privately in homes and in public institutions (community gardens, jails, and schools). She maintains that people can eat organic food inexpensively from gardens and farmers' markets and that food brings people together for conversation and community. For example, the school garden curriculum involves working in the garden, cooking in the kitchen, and eating at the table. It aims to teach children about the importance of taking care of the land, nourishing themselves, offering food to family and friends, and engaging in conversation. This garden classroom is touted nationwide as a model. Waters tirelessly lobbies state and federal officials to install garden classrooms in public schools.

Responses to the Delicious Revolution

Responses to Alice Waters's delicious revolution run the gamut from praise and admiration, to interest and curiosity, to skepticism, disagreement, and ridicule from both the Right and the Left. I commend her for using her celebrity status to further public awareness about important political, economic, social, and cultural issues. She has helped the local community—schools, garden projects, organic farmers, and farmers' markets—through fundraisers and media interviews. Her message about the centrality of food, physically as well as socially, and the need for connection and community is important. She is very effective in getting her views communicated to a variety of audiences, including educators, politicians, children, parents, wealthy donors, and environmentalists. Her style is friendly, respectful, and good humored. She devotes enormous amounts of energy to put her beliefs into practice.

Waters's use of the moniker "delicious revolution" has aroused curiosity among the general public and the media. It seems slightly irreverent and playful, an invitation to probe its meaning more deeply. She does not use charts, tables, data, and dry academic terminology. Her views are accessible, related to everyday concerns, interconnected, and radical. Those who share her affinity with community and her critique of corporate capitalism's role in food production welcome a fresh approach to these issues. Some critics raise the point that she tends to downplay the fact that U.S. productivity has made it the breadbasket of the world, providing food in sufficient quantities to keep prices low, improving the health of many families. They add that organic food is still a stretch for many families' food budgets.

Skeptics question whether her noble ideals can realistically be applied outside Berkeley or California. At times her claims seem too sweeping, her embrace of agricultural over industrial modes of life too romantic, her valorization of nature too uncritical, and her critique of technology too short-sighted. Perhaps she underestimates self-interested behavior, individualism, and competitiveness. Of course, some skeptics have a hard time taking the ideas of anyone from California seriously, especially a "foodie" with an internationally known "gourmet" restaurant.

Some leftists think that economic class, not food, should remain at the center of social and political analysis. They accuse Waters of substituting aesthetics for politics, hedonism for a concern for the poor. Her emphasis on food is seen as a retreat from serious politics and philosophy into superficial and privatized aesthetics. In his review of Waters's *Chez Panisse Menu Cookbook* in the *Nation,* David Sundelson refers to Chez Panisse as a "new privatism" turned inward rather than outward to public issues and commitments. He is dismayed that "the counterculture has become a Counter Culture—the counter at the gourmet butcher, the pastry shop, the charcuterie . . . the *Cookbook* shows how we have changed. 'Aesthetics' is the ruling term in its vocabulary; life must be pretty. 'Understanding,' 'philosophy,' and 'ideology' now apply only to the kitchen." He adds that Berkeley has always been serious, "but in a braver time, that seriousness was applied to the Vietnam War and not to an apricot soufflé."[2] Some feminists are uneasy about a call to return to the kitchen. Many mainstream politicians are not convinced that what she is saying is really politically relevant or important. Most conservatives do not share her critique of corporate capitalism's consumerism and agribusiness.

Waters is also taken to task by those who say that it is easy for her to put food at the center of her life, since that is what she does for a living. She can double-dip when it comes to her family and work food activities and responsibilities. Her use of the language of seduction, pleasure, sensuality, and the goodness of nature is caricatured as California, or Berkeley, "touchy-feely," "nuts and berries." To some, her approach to food is just too precious.

My response is that Waters's delicious revolution is a provocative political philosophy, which she has tried to put into practice in fascinating ways.

Why Delicious Food?

It is not just food that is at the center of Alice Waters's revolution; it is *delicious* food. She locates her analysis in the context of the post–World War II United States, where the use of chemical fertilizers and pesticides on large farms produced food shipped across the country and around the world at low prices. However, Waters is concerned about the taste of these food products. Canned, packaged, and processed food arrives in supermarkets after long journeys, often out of season and devoid of taste. She claims that when the manufacturing model is applied to agriculture—quantity over quality, efficiency over flavor, mass production over artisan craft—it exacts hidden costs. As canned and frozen peas replace fresh ones, the palates of Americans are dulled. As tasteless out-of-season tomatoes replace in-season varieties, Americans loose touch with seasonal cycles. As canned mushroom soup is used as a quick sauce, Americans get used to the tinny taste of cans. In step with advertising that urges Americans to consume more, bigger portions are touted as better than delicious morsels of local produce.

For Waters, farming is not manufacturing; it is "a continuous relationship with nature that has to be complete on both sides to work." Humans have severed their side of this relationship: food lacks flavor and is "aesthetically dead" because it is treated as dead while it is growing. We tolerate deadened food "because our senses, our hearts, and our minds have been in some senses deadened, too." Waters writes,

> I've always felt that it was part of my job as a cook and restaurateur to try to wake people up to these things, to challenge them really to taste the food and to experience the kind of community that can happen in the kitchen and at the table. Those of us who work with food suffer from an image of being involved in an elite, frivolous pastime that has little relation to anything important or meaningful. But in fact we are in a position to cause people to make important connections between what they are eating and a host of crucial environmental, social, and health issues. Food is at the center of these issues.[3]

Waters wants Americans to pay attention to eating with all their senses. She herself did not begin to do this until her junior year in college in Paris. Like many Americans who travel to France, she was impressed with how the French put food at the center of their lives—adopting "a critical approach to food as a matter of course," thinking of good food "as an indispensable part of their lives," and punctuating each day "by food-related decisions." Each day began early with a fresh, hot baguette, and included "an hour or so in the afternoon at the café with one's friends." Her friends "ate food only when it was in season, because that was when it was the least expensive and the best tasting. Eating together was a ritual that filled life with meaning, a sacred moment of the day, when flavors and smells intermingled with ideas and feelings." She says that she had never before thought about food or pleasure so seriously. She recalls, "[I] wasn't making an intellectual effort to understand all this; I was absorbing these lessons by osmosis. I had begun to feel that there is an intimate connection between food and the quality of peoples' lives."[4] This sensual reconnection with food required delicious food. And pleasures at the table were simultaneously sensual and intellectual.

During her travels, Waters also learned that delicious food is fresh. In Corfu, she "lived for a while on practically nothing, very simply, watching the sun and the moon rising and setting over the sea. We ate fish just caught from the same sea, and picked fruit from the trees. There was a sense of immediacy and aliveness to the food." Waters comments, "I was unmistakably part of the natural rhythm of the place. Everything seemed comprehensible. Looking back, I see now that I was learning that eating in this way can keep you in harmony with the earth." She also learned that delicious food is enhanced by hospitality and generosity, qualities she sought to replicate by opening her

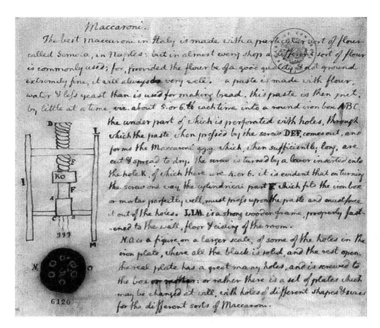

Jefferson's Pasta Machine. The French and the Italians put food at the center of their lives—valuing quality ingredients and rituals of eating together. When Thomas Jefferson served as minister to France, macaroni was a popular food in Paris. He drew this plan for a "maccaroni" machine while touring northern Italy in 1787. The accompanying recipe calls for flour of good quality, ground extremely fine. Library of Congress, Manuscript Division.

restaurant, Chez Panisse. In Turkey, she "experienced the kind of hospitality you usually only read about—the no-questions asked, totally accepting and generous sharing that only people who live close to the land seem to be able to offer to total strangers." She describes an experience to illustrate her point: "Once we were camping out in the countryside, not far from some goatherds, and when we woke up in the morning in our little tent, we found that they had silently slipped a bowl of goat's milk under our tent flap while we slept. They simply shared the best they had. This is how we were treated everywhere we went. I didn't know then that the things I was learning about food and hospitality would profoundly alter the course my life would take." Not too long afterward, she moved back to Berkeley and started her restaurant "with a small band of friends and ten thousand borrowed dollars." Waters recalls,

"I was twenty-seven years old. I was unbelievably naive, but obsessed with the desire to replicate the experience of eating I had loved over there. I didn't appreciate how out of the ordinary it would be to think about food this way in an American restaurant."[5]

Institutionalizing Delicious Food at Chez Panisse

Waters's attempt to institutionalize delicious food at Chez Panisse took years. She had a hard time replicating the flavors she remembered from Europe. "Cooking food in season, for example, seemed like a foreign concept when we were starting out. In this country, we were used to frozen food, and produce shipped from far away, available year-round. We had come so far from enjoying fruit right off the tree and only served right then, at its very best and ripest, that when we did serve fruit like that, a single perfect peach could be a revelation." Produce was not picked young enough nor delivered to markets quickly enough. Fish had not been caught that morning. "The simple recipe for roasted chicken that had been so delicious in France never tasted right, because the chickens we could get had had all the flavor bred out of them." She began by asking neighbors to grow foodstuffs such as radishes and sorrel in their backyard gardens, and she ended up with a network of over seventy-five purveyors in California and Oregon, including a farm in Sonoma that took the restaurant's compost and a little money in exchange for vegetables.[6]

She discovered a relationship between delicious ingredients and environmental responsibility. When she looked for the freshest and best-tasting ingredients, "the people who produced them were frequently the most environmentally responsible." She notes, "When we tried to find the products that were certified organic, we found that if they were fresh and ripe, they usually tasted the best." She believes "that actions have consequences, and that people acting responsibly can make a difference. . . . How you eat, and how you choose your food, is an act that combines the political, your place in the world of other people, with the most intensely personal, the way you use your mind and your senses, together, for the gratification of your soul."[7]

Waters wanted Chez Panisse to be a place where people would eat to educate their senses. "If you let your senses be deadened, and settle for food that's processed and wrapped and refrigerated, you're depriving yourself of the wealth of information that comes from sensual stimulation. Eating food is the best way to open up these pathways; it's something you do every day.

So pay attention to what you are eating. If you choose food that is aromatic, with rich colors and varied flavors, your senses will be stimulated in ways that will enhance your consciousness—and that will improve your ability to communicate, not just about food, but about everything."[8]

Before starting Chez Panisse, Waters was a Montessori teacher. Drawing from the Montessori philosophy of education, she believes that when the senses open to food, the mind opens to ideas. Maria Montessori, an early twentieth-century educator, advocated training the senses to "prepare the ordered foundation upon which the child may build up a clear and strong mentality." For Montessori, children must try things in order to learn things. Information is obtained through the senses, and if sensory pathways are blocked, all the information can't get in. Waters observes, "Eating food is the best way to educate your senses; it's something you do three times a day, and it involves all five of them. Montessori understood that if we don't fully exploit our abilities—if we haven't been educated to taste, see, hear, and feel, to the maximum of our abilities—we can't fully communicate with each other."[9]

In her vision for Chez Panisse, Waters is careful to distinguish this child-like sense of wonder and openness from hedonism. "I want people to share the excitement of good things, beautiful foodstuffs, little lettuces from our garden, herbs in bloom, a gnarly local pippin from somebody's old tree—and if I can see that people are receptive then something wonderful happens: time stops—you're a child again, but still an adult, and not just a satisfied, pleasure-seeking hedonist either, but a participant in something shared: And you know, it may not matter whether or not the soufflé turned out perfect."[10]

Waters is convinced that her revolution will take hold only if it is based on pleasurable experiences, like eating a ripe peach or wandering through a farmers' market. "Once you've eaten a ripe peach, it's very hard to go back. It is a very sensual experience, eating. It needs to be positive spirited. It can't be something that's telling people what not to eat." For Waters, the experience at a farmers' market is more than just finding good food that's in season and organically grown. It's also about being "with a lot of other people who are caring about what they're eating and helping their children. You're just getting it through osmosis, which is the very best way. You're not being lectured to." She says, "That's the way I'd like to feed people. I don't want anybody to come to food because they're told that it's healthy. I want them to come because they fall in love. And that's really what keeps them there. When it tastes good, that's when it sticks. That's when change really happens, the transformation happens."[11]

Why Revolution?

Alice Waters is very self-conscious about the revolutionary nature of her project: it is radical, transformative, and easy to digest.

> I've always thought of this as revolutionary work. But I think it is very important to know that this isn't something that's difficult. This is very revolutionary and very easy because we're asking people to buy food that is ripe and delicious tasting. And when they buy food that is ripe and delicious tasting and organically grown and in season, they support the people who care about our nourishment. So the idea just makes people receptive in a way that they might not be if you just talk about doing something radical. This is radical and good, good tasting. And because of that, it's something that stays with you.[12]

She regards her revolution as universally applicable: daily and universally people make food choices. "What I'm trying to do is seduce people into an experience that is pleasurable and fortunately has values that are at the very heart of it. And just think if you eat two or three meals a day, in a very specific way with those values associated, it begins to change your life."[13]

Her revolutionary ideas were formed in the free speech and antiwar movements in the 1960s. In 1964, she and her three Berkeley roommates became involved in the free speech movement, and two years later they campaigned for *Ramparts* editor Robert Scheer, who ran for Congress on an antiwar platform. Waters and graphic designer David Goines shared an apartment, where she began to cook for friends and fellow activists. "Seeing her role as bringing politics and food together, she tried to 'seduce' others into thinking that although dingy T-shirts, peanut-butter-and-jelly sandwiches, granola and Campbell's tomato soup were trademarks of the Berkeley Left, even French communists enjoyed good food." Waters describes why she relied on Elizabeth David's *French Country Cooking*. "Her aesthetic is about simplicity and a kind of fragrance . . . she had a great sense of the seasons and always about the life around the table—the setting, the conversation. It was always more than just food because her recipes were not very specific, to say the least. I remember being frustrated, but it made you think. She was saying something pretty profound about the recipe process—that food changes all the time. It's never, never the same. The climate, the location, all make a difference."[14]

Waters challenged her fellow leftists by drawing attention to a new location for politics: the table, where one could leisurely discuss politics and savor the opening of senses and minds. She started Chez Panisse so that she could have a place for extended political conversations. "All I cared about was a place to sit down with my friends and enjoy good food while discussing the politics of the day. And I believed that in order to experience food as good as I had had in France, I had to cook and serve it myself. The timing and the location encouraged my idealism and experimentation. This was during the late sixties, in Berkeley. We all believed in community and personal commitment and quality. Chez Panisse was born out of these ideals. Profit was always secondary." At the restaurant, Waters wants customers to try new things and to take time with the food. The format of serving only one five-course dinner each evening "often surprises people at first, but I think the appealing aromas and the roasted flavors of food cooked over the charcoal grill, and the earthiness of those lettuces, tend to seduce the hesitant. For me food is a totally painless way of awakening people and sharpening their senses. I opened a restaurant so that everybody could come and eat; remember that the final goal is to nourish and nurture those who gather at your table. It is there, within this nourishing process, that I have found the greatest satisfaction and sense of accomplishment."[15]

Table conversation creates community. Waters's home in Berkeley was "a virtual salon where politics, food and films held sway." When it came time to name her new restaurant, she chose the name of a character from a film by Marcel Pagnol, the Marseilles sail maker Panisse, a warm, fatherly, Provençal man with humor and wisdom. "The trilogy of films made by Pagnol in the early 1930s presented an ideal of friendship and community in which Alice could see herself gathering her friends around her table, nourishing them in the spirit of an earlier time. 'Pagnol is a big window into where I'm coming from,' she has always admitted. 'There's this fantastic ambiance in the films. All of these characters are such friends. They're trying to get through life together. There's such a *joie de vivre.*'"[16] The Pagnol films evoked "the sunny good feelings of another world that contained so much of what was incomplete or missing in our own—the simple wholesome good food of Provence, the atmosphere of tolerant camaraderie and great lifelong friendships, and a respect both for the old folks and their pleasures and for the young and their passions."[17]

Theory: The Connection between Land, Food, Meals, Conversation, and Community

The theory underlying the delicious revolution has five component parts— land, food, meals, conversation, and community—each of which is essential to its overall logic. It is based on a view of the land that is more ecological than profit maximizing. The land needs to be cared for in the long term, not just the short term of profitable yield. The long-term costs of environmental pollution from the use of pesticides are not justified in terms of plentiful short-term food production. The ability to serve a delicious meal depends on a healthy ecosystem. Waters insists,

> A restaurant can be no better than the ingredients it has to work with. As much as by any other factor, Chez Panisse has been defined by the search for ingredients. That search and what we have found along the way have shaped what we cook and ultimately who we are. The search has made us become part of a community—a community that has grown from markets, gardens, and suppliers and has gradually come to include farmers, ranchers and fishermen. It has also made us realize that, as a restaurant, we are utterly dependent on the health of the land, the sea, and the planet as a whole, and that this search for good ingredients is pointless without a healthy agriculture and a healthy environment.[18]

Alice Waters's view of the land, and of most things, is biological rather than mechanical. She often uses the term *osmosis* to describe how people will absorb her revolution. Osmosis is a biological process whose dictionary definition is "movement of a solvent through a semipermeable membrane (as of a living cell) into a solution of higher solute concentration that tends to equalize the concentration of solute on the two sides of the membrane."[19] This metaphor connotes inner and outer biological worlds that need to be in balance. People can be made aware of ecological imbalances not only through lectures about the horrors of ecological damage but also by eating delicious food that leaves a lasting, sensory impression of an alternative to agribusiness and processed foods. She calls into play all the senses, not just the sight and sound of written and spoken arguments and data.

Waters also challenges a mechanistic view of humans as machines fueled by food. She laments how Americans treat food "as if it were just a fuel for the furnace. We don't understand the connections between food and agriculture so we continue to destroy the land and the water, and that's where our food comes from."[20] "We don't understand the difference between fueling ourselves and eating for pleasure and eating wholesome food. We don't have the pleasure of the table that's so reflective of a quality of life and a purpose on the planet. It's just a whole misconception of what food is meant to be, and we have to turn that around."[21]

Her call for traditional, organic modes of agriculture is preindustrial, antedating railroads, giant food corporations, canning technology, and agribusiness. It is radical both in the sense of going back to earlier roots and in the sense of challenging the power of corporate food giants. She maintains that her insistence on organically grown produce "developed less out of any ideological commitment than out of the fact that this was the way almost everyone [she and her friends] knew gardened."[22] Waters contends,

> We have never been interested in being a health or natural foods restaurant; rather, organic and naturally raised ingredients happen to be consistent with both what we want for our kitchen and what we want for our community and our larger environment. Such ingredients have never been an end in themselves, but they are part of a way of life that inspired the restaurant and that we want the restaurant to inspire. Most of us have become so inured to the dogmas and self-justifications of agribusiness that we forget that, until 1940, most produce was, for all intents and purposes, organic, and, until the advent of the refrigerated boxcar, it was also of necessity fresh, seasonal, and local. There's nothing radical about organic produce: It's a return to traditional values of the most fundamental kind.[23]

Locally produced food is delivered to her restaurant through a network of farmers' markets, community gardens, foragers, and organic farmers, people who care about the land. She is convinced that everyone can have access to locally produced food and that with sufficient demand, the price of organic produce will eventually become competitive with nonorganic goods. According to Waters, eating mass-produced, fast food supports

> a network of supply and demand that is destroying local communities and traditional ways of life all over the world—a system that replaces self-sufficiency with dependence. And you are supporting a method of agriculture that is ecologically unsound—that depletes the soil and leaves harmful chemical residues in our food. But if you decide to eat fresh food in season—and only in season—that is locally grown by farmers who take care of the earth, then you are contributing to the health and stability of local agriculture and local communities. When I buy food from farmers' markets, the food is alive, and it is irresistible. If we demand fresh, nourishing food, we help ease the stigma of elitism that is attached to good food in this country. Wholesome, honest food should be an entitlement of all Americans, not just the rich.[24]

Of course, eating fresh food only in season poses problems for people in cold climates. This part of her argument is perhaps the most unrealistic, given Americans' quest for a variety of foodstuffs year round. And many low-income people cannot afford organic produce. Waters maintains that growing one's own food is the least expensive way to eat. Even if one does not have access to a community garden or a farmers' market, "something as simple as a backyard garden or a pot of fresh herbs on a windowsill can counter the alienating experience of frozen entrees, fast food, and rubbery tomatoes out of season."[25]

In the delicious revolution, securing organic food is followed by its preparation and sharing in meals, conversation, and community. Waters is particularly concerned about children who are disconnected from the experiences of food preparation and intergenerational meals.

> It's not just the food, it's what we do with it. If we are going to eat ethically, we had better start eating together with each other and our children. When you eat together, and eat a meal you cooked yourselves, you are involved with the process in a different way. You shelled the peas, you peeled the potatoes, and you want everyone to enjoy every last bite. These are the kinds of meals we should be eating with our children. To paraphrase Wendell Berry, such meals honor the materials from which they are made; they honor the art by which they are done; they honor the people who make them, and those who share them.[26]

She is concerned about the current generation of children who watch television during meals, who have never participated in the growing of food or the preparation of meals, and "who have never sat down together at a table with other generations and learned the meaning of mutual responsibility, and the caring and love that families can only express . . . by sharing nourishment."[27]

Waters believes that when families were both food-producing and food-processing units, humanistic values were "instilled, more than *anyplace else,* at the dinner table. Families eating together passed on values such as courtesy, kindness, generosity, thrift, respect, and reverence for the goodness of Nature—pretty much the whole Boy Scout package of virtues." For Waters, "the ritual of coming to the dinner table was once the *basis* of community."[28]

She agrees with the sentiments of Francine du Plessix Gray, who wrote in a *New Yorker* essay aptly titled "Starving Children," "The family meal is not only the core curriculum in the school of civilized discourse; it is also a set of protocols that curb our natural savagery and our animal greed, and cultivate a capacity for sharing and thoughtfulness. . . . The ritual of nutrition helps imbue families, and societies at large, with greater empathy and fellowship."[29] Gray, analyzing the movie *Kids,* writes that it depicted cruel, amoral teenagers who "boorishly gulped" a "feral" fast-food diet. She fears that we were witnessing the first generation in history that has not been required to participate in that primal rite of socialization, the family meal. She contends that dinner rituals have nothing to do with class, or working women's busy lives, or any particular family structure.

> I've had dinners of boiled potatoes with families in Siberia, suppers of deli cold
> cuts with single welfare mothers in Chicago, bowls of watery gruel in the Saha-
> ra—all made memorable by the grace with which they were offered and by the
> sight of youngsters learning through experience the art of human companion-
> ship. The teenagers in *Kids* are not only physically starved . . . by the junk food
> they consume. . . . Far worse, they are deprived of the main course of civilized
> life—the practice of sitting down at the dinner table and observing the attendant
> conventions.[30]

Waters admits that what Gray calls "the ritual of nutrition," like any ritual,
requires sacrifices—it takes time and effort to get dinner ready—but making those sacrifices nurtures both family and society. Cooking and eating
together teaches us compassion.[31]

Alice Waters traces the decline of family meals and conversations to three
factors: television (which obviates "the necessity for a family unit to amuse
itself with its own resources, and for its members to communicate with each
other"), commercial convenience foods, and an economic order that devalues
the role of women in the home. We have to make time for patterns of eating
based on delicious food.[32]

Acknowledging that in single-parent and two-income households, time for
family meals is hard to find, Waters nevertheless challenges people to rethink
their use of time. Since the rituals of food are disappearing in homes, she
thinks that they need to occur in the schools and in communities. "It's the
extended family experience, where you're always raised to bring people to
the table. It doesn't have to happen in the family. It can happen in the school.
It can happen in the community center. It can happen in the workplace. It
can happen in many, many places, if people want it to happen and encourage
that, because they know how important it is."[33] Whether at home, at school,
or in a community setting, civil relations start at the table. "If we lose the
connection between what we eat and the world around us, we begin to lose
our culture, our civilization. It all starts at the table. That's where we become
civilized."[34]

> At the table, children should be brought in as participants, as equal to everyone
> else there, and know they are respected and appreciated and not just there to be
> told that they have to eat all of the food on their plates. Children are trying to
> learn about their culture and become civilized. As they grow up, they need help:
> how to pass the plate, offer to other people, don't take it all. Those things are not
> happening anymore. The kids are not passing the plate and experiencing that
> ritual. They aren't having that moment in the day when they can connect with a

family that is caring and can hear about their problems and when they can learn what is expected of them.[35]

Conversations can happen at the table because food rituals typically create favorable preconditions: sharing, equality, enjoyment, and participation, a pleasant open forum with the understanding that no one will be boorish, selfish, obnoxious, or offensive. Waters says that she and her daughter had "the most fascinating conversations about everything under the sun: from resolving conflicts, to world problems, to talking about art. The table is a place where that can happen and it's about communication. Gathering at the table is about communication."[36] Conversation and conviviality are also her goals at Chez Panisse. "Communication around the dinner table and the sense of family that come with it are largely missing in our society. One of my goals at Chez Panisse is to re-establish the gastronomic excitement that inspires and encourages conversation and conviviality. Depersonalized, assembly-line fast food may be 'convenient' and 'time-saving,' but it deprives the senses and denies true nourishment."[37]

The conviviality at the table spirals into a sense of community that reaches back to the land and outward to the polity.

> Food is just put to the side as simply one of the things that we need to do in our society. But for me, it's the center of a wheel with all these spokes going out. It addresses all of the other problems that we're having: about health, education, and the environment. As soon as you find out that your food comes from nature, and that you need nature to eat, then you start taking care of nature. People who do not see eating as part of politics are certainly missing out on a way of connecting with people and seducing them to your point of view because everybody wants to eat good food. They need to eat. So it's just a mystery why politics are really not about food policy. And of course I see it as the center of politics. I think that when you make the right decisions about what you are going to eat, you make the right decisions about everything that you are doing in your life. It's a place where you can find meaning in your life. People want others to be nice and to form a community, but that just doesn't happen naturally. . . . What really brings people together are the everyday experiences of going out and buying your bread, and having somebody there at the counter who gives it to you, and you say thank you; it's nourishing for you and it supports them. And ultimately, that's what I understood after twenty-five years at the restaurant—that I just didn't have people that I bought food from; I had a group of friends. They counted on me and I count on them, and that is a community, when you feel mutual responsibility for one another and you feel connected. What better way to feel connected than around

the table and around the purchasing of food; and to know that people are growing the most beautiful things for you to eat![38]

The delicious revolution combines sensuality and politics and analyzes various types of community bonds, forged in food practices, beyond the family table. But the dynamics are the same: pleasure, nourishing relationships, interdependence, mutual responsibility, sharing, thoughtfulness, companionship, and rituals of nutrition and conviviality. These are the dynamics of civil society.

Chapter 10

· ·

Putting the Delicious Revolution into Practice

The theory of the delicious revolution is one thing—land, food, meals, conversation, and community. Putting it into practice is quite another. Waters implemented her revolution at Chez Panisse and in four other arenas: organic food and farmers' markets, the San Francisco Jail's Garden Project, the Edible Schoolyard Project, and school lunches.

Chez Panisse and Foragers, Organic Gardeners, and Farmers' Markets

Probably the best-known way that Alice Waters put her theory of a delicious revolution into practice is working with the community of food providers to Chez Panisse: a complex system of foragers, organic farmers, and farmers' markets. When Chez Panisse served its first meal in 1971, the ducks came from Chinatown in San Francisco and the other ingredients mostly from two local supermarkets. The original cooks were not professionally trained and did not even know about specialized restaurant suppliers. Waters thinks that this ignorance shaped the restaurant. "Often, we simply couldn't cook what we wanted to cook because we couldn't find the level of quality we needed in the required ingredients, or we couldn't find the ingredients at all." By necessity, the cooks foraged for ingredients. Indeed, Waters refers to the early restaurant as a "hunter-gatherer culture." "We gathered watercress from streams, picked nasturtiums and fennel from roadsides, and gathered blackberries from the Santa Fe tracks in Berkeley. We also took herbs like oregano and thyme from the gardens of friends." Produce was the main problem area, since its flavor had suffered under postwar American agriculture. "Although we've been able to have as much cosmetically perfect, out-of-season fruit and vegetables as anyone could possibly want, the flavor, freshness, variety, and wholesomeness of produce have been terribly diminished. With the notable exception of Chinese and Japanese markets that even in the early seventies emphasized flavor and quality, we really had nowhere to turn but to sympathetic gardeners who either already grew what we needed or would undertake to grow it for us."[1]

In 1977, Chez Panisse attempted an ill-fated experiment to cultivate its own produce on rural farmland. Eventually, local urban gardens were producing quite successfully. One of the cooks, Jean-Pierre Moullé, gardened on land in the Berkeley Hills owned by the restaurant's doctor and his wife. The head pastry cook, Lindsey Shere, returned from Italy with seeds for then-exotic rocket and other greens, which were cultivated in her father's garden. Jeremiah Tower, Chez Panisse's main cook from 1973 to 1977, caused a stir when he sent substandard meat back to a supplier. A friend who brought in some delicious California sea mussels he had gathered near his home became the restaurant's fish dealer.[2]

The produce supply problem continued, and the restaurant made a second attempt at farming in 1980, this time on land near Sacramento owned by a local chef. When this venture failed, Waters realized that the restaurant had two options: extend and formalize the system of urban gardeners already in place and establish direct relations with farmers who would farm on their behalf. In the early 1980s, restaurant staff established several salad gardens in Berkeley, one of which was in Waters's backyard. In 1982, a friend introduced Waters to produce grown near San Diego by the Chino family. To this day, a weekly shipment from their farm is delivered to the restaurant.[3]

In 1982, Sibella Kraus became the first official forager for the restaurant, and a year later she started the Farm-Restaurant Project. She spent her time on the road locating farmers, tasting their produce, and arranging for a schedule of deliveries to Chez Panisse. The Farm-Restaurant Project was a produce network among a number of San Francisco Bay Area restaurants and local farmers. For years, it held an annual event, Tasting of Summer Produce, at which dozens of small-scale, quality-conscious farmers displayed their produce to the food community and the general public.[4]

In 1985, Waters asked her father to find a farmer who would be willing to make a long-term agreement to grow most of the restaurant's produce according to its specifications. With help from the University of California at Davis and local organic-food organizations, he compiled a list of eighteen potential farmers, and they chose Bob Cannard, who farms twenty-five acres in the Sonoma Valley. Cannard frequently visits the Chez Panisse kitchen and pitches in, and the restaurant sends its cooks to his farm to help him. Waters explains, "He takes all the restaurant's compostable garbage each day, which he then uses to grow more food. He is also a teacher at his local college and a major force in his local farmers' market. He sees that his farm and our restaurant are part of something larger and that, whether we acknowledge it or not, they have a responsibility to the health of the communities in which they exist and of the land on which they depend."[5]

The quest for high-quality bread ended in 1983, when the restaurant helped a former employee launch Acme Bakery, which bakes for Chez Panisse and many other local restaurants and markets. As for meat, not until the late 1980s did the restaurant discover ranchers and farmers who raised beef, veal, and lamb without hormones and under humane conditions.[6] By the late 1990s, Waters was able to procure naturally fed beef, with the aim of having those animals fed organic grains. Her goal was to have everything at the restaurant sustainably raised and grown.[7]

By 2000, a total of seventy-five vendors were supplying Waters's three restaurants: downstairs Chez Panisse Restaurant (with prix fixe dinners ranging from $38.00 to $68.00 per person), the upstairs Café at Chez Panisse (which opened in 1980 with an open kitchen, a wood-burning pizza oven, and an à la carte menu), and Café Fanny (a stand-up café serving breakfast and lunch, which opened a few miles away in 1984). The downstairs restaurant is the most famous, and expensive, beyond the reach of low-income people. Critics who reduce Waters's delicious revolution efforts to this one, expensive, venue fail to take into account the many fronts on which she makes significant contributions. The downstairs restaurant seats fifty and the upstairs café seventy. Waters realizes that the number of patrons at her restaurants is limited, and that not all restaurants are able to have the kind of relationship she has with Bob Cannard. But in many public settings, she encourages both restaurants and the public to buy locally grown organic products.

Farmers' markets are an important source for these products. Waters supports them because they contribute to the local economy, promote more variety and quality in the marketplace, and create community. She hopes that when both restaurateurs and ordinary consumers meet the people who grow their food, it will lead to an interest in the future of farms, of rural communities, and of the environment. "This interest, when it helps to ensure the continuing provision of open space near cities and the diversity of food produced on it, is to everyone's benefit. Country and city can once again become a mutual support system, a web of interdependent communities. That's why fresh, locally grown, seasonal foodstuffs are more than an attractive fashion or a quaint, romantic notion: They are a fundamental part of a sustainable economy and agriculture—and they taste better too."[8]

Waters is sensitive to the criticism that it is not easy to rely on farmers' markets' local produce in all parts of the country. Indeed, even Chez Panisse gets a weekly produce delivery from the Chino farm in southern California. But she still holds to the ideal. She admits one needn't forgo all ingredients that are not locally produced but maintains that "local materials must become the basis of our cooking and our food; this is true for every region of the planet that has produced a flavorful, healthy cuisine."[9]

In support of farmers' markets and sustainable agriculture, Waters is affiliated with many civic groups: the Land Institute (Salina, Kansas); National Committee for Mothers and Others for Pesticide Limits (Washington, D.C.); Public Voice on Food Safety and Health (Washington, D.C.); San Francisco's Ferry Plaza Farmers' Market; and the National Board of Slow Food U.S.A. (New York City).[10] She has given public talks about the ethics of eating at the 1994 commencement at Mills College in Oakland, California (when she received an honorary degree); at the 1996 meeting of the Annual Ecological Farming Conference in Asilomar, California; and at a 1999 fund-raising luncheon for the Children's Garden at the Strybing Arboretum and Botanical Gardens in Golden Gate Park in San Francisco.[11] She spoke about food and community at the 1997 meeting of the U.S. Conference of Mayors in San Francisco, where Mayor Willie Brown told visiting mayors at the Ferry Plaza Farmers' Market: "More than a quarter of a million people shop here. Housewives as well as domestic partners shop here. It's a great place for a politician to shake hands."[12]

Waters is active in the San Francisco Ferry Plaza Farmers' Market "Shop with the Chef Program." As participating chefs go through the market, they fill a basket with fresh produce and offer shoppers suggestions for how to use it. At the end of the tour, the chef's market basket is raffled off as a fundraiser.[13] As a member of the San Francisco Public Market Collaborative, Waters lobbied the San Francisco Port Commission to expand the hours of operation of the farmers' market.[14] A journalist who shadowed Waters and other Bay Area food notables on their rounds at the Ferry Plaza Farmers' Market was surprised to learn that they were there not just to find the perfect peach but to visit friends in what they described as "one of the few surviving senses of community left in the city. . . . This is like a piazza . . . You run into

Waters and Petrini Toasting. Alice Waters, an activist in the Slow Food movement, toasts movement founder Carlo Petrini in May 2007. They critique fast food, encouraging people to slow down and savor fresh, local, and delicious food, accompanied by companionship and conversation. Associated Press Photo/Paul Sakuma.

people you know without having to make a plan." One of Waters's assistants noted, "I come here when it's raining, when the farmers need us. Alice taught me that." Waters mentioned that she shopped regularly at farmers' markets, both for herself and for the restaurant, adding, "Important information comes at the farmers' market through osmosis. It comes through all of your senses, so you effortlessly begin to care about seasons, freshness, ripeness, sustainability, community." When a friend mentioned to Waters that the husband of a favorite vendor was battling cancer, Waters already knew, prompting the journalist to remark, "And suddenly it clicked. I was back in Florence, watching those Italians at the market. Like them, the shoppers at farmers' markets aren't here just to buy food. This is their 'third place'—a community outside of home or work where they socialize, share ideas, relax, gossip, grow. Vendors often become friends, people you get to know by coming week after week, year after year. Before you realize it, you care as much about the person who sells you shelling beans as you do the beans."[15]

In an effort to persuade the federal government to adopt strict guidelines for the certification of organic foods, Waters testified at a public-comment hearing in 1998. For the first time, the U.S. Department of Agriculture (USDA) was crafting federal standards for the $3.5 billion organic food industry, rules that would supersede existing voluntary private codes and state laws. California's standards, adopted a decade earlier, were among the most stringent in the country. Most speakers allowed that standardized national, and even international, rules were needed. They had no problem with most USDA proposals. But Waters was among the Bay Area food notables who spoke out against proposed rules that would allow producers to stamp a "USDA Certified Organic" label on food that was irradiated, or genetically engineered, or fertilized with treated waste. She opposed genetically engineered foods and supported European-style safeguards against them.[16]

The San Francisco Jail's Horticulture and Garden Projects

A second front on which Alice Waters has implemented her delicious revolution is the San Francisco County Jail's Horticulture Project and Garden Project. The jail's counselor, Catherine Sneed, was the moving force behind both ventures. In 1982, she began the Horticulture Project at the county jail in San Bruno, working with inmates on a ten-acre organic garden within the prison grounds and teaching them how to become gardeners. Their harvests were donated to soup kitchens, homeless shelters, and AIDS hospices. But Sneed found that once these gardeners left prison, they weren't able to find jobs and often lapsed into their former pattern of crime and drug abuse. In 1992, sponsored by the San Francisco Sheriff's Department and with donations from San Francisco companies and private foundations, Sneed launched the Garden Project. She convinced the owner of a bakery in the Hunter's Point section of San Francisco to donate a half-acre of land, where she set up a garden and offered former inmates an opportunity to work as gardeners for a six-dollar-per-hour wage. In 2002, the Garden Project had about 125 employees, each of whom was required to work a minimum of sixteen hours a week and to earn a high school diploma if he or she did not already have one. Those who worked in the Garden Project had a recidivism rate of only 24 percent compared to nearly 55 percent for the average postrelease population. Their produce was sold to prominent Bay Area restaurants and at the Saturday morning Ferry Plaza Farmers' Market. Giving employees an opportunity to sell directly to customers at the market was Sneed's idea.

She wanted former inmates to have an opportunity to interact with a larger public than they would normally see in their daily lives.[17]

Waters worked with Sneed to raise funds for the Garden Project and publicized the fact that she served many of their vegetables at Chez Panisse and at fundraising events.[18] When a San Francisco society columnist reported on a lunch that Waters had prepared for Hillary Clinton, she wrote, "Alice Waters created the delicious and politically correct lunch: Dungeness crab salad with produce from the San Francisco County Jail garden project, ravioli with white truffles and an apple lemon galette. Herbs came from the Martin Luther King Jr. Middle School's Edible Schoolyard."[19]

Sneed's projects had a profound effect on Waters. Their relationship began when, out of the blue, Sneed called her at the restaurant and asked if she would be interested in organically grown produce from a local garden. Waters said yes and was impressed during her first site visit to the jail's Horticulture Project. She recalls,

> The inmates in this program—Catherine calls them her "students"—learn organic gardening at the county jail, and the fruit and vegetables they grow are taken to the homeless centers in San Francisco. The first time I went out to the garden, I was overwhelmed by the beauty of the produce, and the dedication of the students. I met a 22-year-old guy, who had been in and out of jail for seven years, who said: "I don't know if I should really be talking about this garden; this is only my first day here. But so far, this is the best day of my life." When prisoners who had been trained in the horticultural program at the jail had started to be released, many of them told Catherine that they wanted to go back to jail, just so they could keep on gardening![20]

When Waters visited the off-site Garden Project in South San Francisco, she also found it a very moving experience. "Where there had been piles of rubble and garbage, now there are flower beds and row on row of vegetables, with brick paths leading among them. For lunch they had covered a long table with checkered tablecloths, big bowls of lettuce, perfectly picked radishes, and big bouquets of fresh-cut flowers. After lunch, the students spoke about what the garden had meant to them. Catherine announced that she might run out of funding, but all the gardeners said they would keep coming and working anyway. They had found something they needed and wanted to do." Waters was struck with how the Garden Project incorporated everything that she thought was important about food: "digging in the ground, planting, husbanding, harvesting, cooking, preserving, putting it all out on the table, serving it up to your friends and family, and sharing it with them."

Feeding others should focus on nourishment, not manipulation or selling. "Food is not a commodity, it is the most important thing we can give each other. Feeding one another is the most basic, fundamental part of healthy and moral living. Offering people things that help them grow, physically and spiritually—that's what parents and teachers should be offering our children. This should be the foundation of their moral education."[21]

Waters believes that the Garden Project is a remarkable model for transformation that "gives people skills to nourish themselves physically and spiritually, and shows that even the most difficult segments of society can find hope and self-worth if they're given just a small opportunity."[22] She credits Catherine Sneed with teaching her "that it's not just working in the garden that helps these inmates. It's the offering of food to other people that changes them. That's a big part of it." She asserts, "You don't believe it, but when you see it, you know that it's true."[23]

Waters's association with the Garden Project reverberated to partisan politics in Washington, D.C. In 1996, House Republicans on the Agriculture Committee complained that $46,000 of taxpayers' money had been used inappropriately to evaluate the Garden Project, since it was taken from an $11 million food-stamp research fund. GOP lawmakers saw this as wasteful spending by the Clinton administration and questionable judgment on the part of Ellen Haas, the USDA undersecretary of Food, Nutrition and Consumer Services who oversaw the funds and was a close friend of Waters's. Republicans were aware that federal funds were being used not to subsidize the Garden Project or to benefit Chez Panisse directly but rather to evaluate the project with the idea of promoting it in other states. USDA officials contended that there was nothing improper about the expenditure because most of the Garden Project participants were on welfare, and it was entirely appropriate to evaluate the program to see if it could work elsewhere. Democrats blamed the flap on Republican leadership that had called on committee chairs to use their staff to uncover damaging information against the Clinton administration. Republicans were particularly interested in embarrassing Haas, a liberal, and in targeting San Francisco, a Democratic stronghold. When Waters was besieged by reporters wanting to know if she was really behind the government's interest in organic vegetables, she replied, "Absolutely. I took [Haas] to the Garden Project a couple years ago. It's a wonderful program. I've seen the transformation that happens when people stick their hands in the earth and feed themselves."[24] "I try to support those gardeners who are growing food and helping themselves to grow and stay out of jail.

We buy many radishes and wild rocket (an arugula-like leafy vegetable), spinach, cabbage, various herbs . . . as much as we can."[25]

The Edible Schoolyard Project

Another way that Alice Waters has put her theory into practice is the Edible Schoolyard, a garden project at Martin Luther King Jr. Middle School, directly inspired by Catherine Sneed's Garden Project. For several years, Waters had driven past the school and was dismayed at the neglected grounds and buildings. She recalls "[I wondered] what it might look like if there were a garden project at the school similar to the one at the jail, and the school grounds were covered by edible landscaping—orchards, grape arbors to sit under, groves of oranges and lemons, and herb and vegetable gardens, all producing food that could actually be used at the school. I was trying to imagine a way to seduce kids into a whole new way of thinking about food." The school had a large, abandoned kitchen and cafeteria that had been replaced by concession stands serving reheated burgers and fast-food snacks. Waters imagined turning the kitchen into a bakery where the children could bake for themselves.

> A good loaf of bread is something that is irresistible to everyone: the way it smells, what it feels like to handle the dough—everything that's involved in baking. You could start teaching about bread from all different angles: students could learn to bake tortillas on the *comal* and loaves of sourdough bread in the brick oven, and learn all about pita bread and pappadums. Children would not only learn how to bake, they could get a valuable lesson in cultural diversity. Most important, they would learn responsibility to each other if they actually had to help feed each other. School would be more digestible in every way.[26]

Professional bakers and gardeners would lend their expertise, alongside parents, teachers, and neighbors. "Children would learn mutual respect from sharing meals; they would learn self-respect from learning how to prepare them; and they would learn respect for the planet from learning how to grow food in an ecologically sound way. I believe those are the results we could expect to see. Why should we settle for less in the education and nourishment of our children?"[27]

In a newspaper interview, Waters complained about the deterioration of the school, prompting a call from its principal. "He wanted to talk about what I'd said, so I invited him to lunch. It turned out we were on the same wavelength. Although we were both worried about the next generation and felt the same urgency about what was going on out there in the world, we were both optimistic about how the schools could help." Waters wanted to do her part to "take responsibility for what Jonathan Kozol has called the 'savage inequalities' of American education—then we could not only turn the situation at King around—we could renovate schools everywhere, so that the kids will know that we really care about them." She believes that children learn by example, and they will not learn to respect themselves, others, or the community in dilapidated schools. "Such schools reflect all too well the carelessness, anarchy, and wrenching unfairness of our society, where the gap between rich and poor just gets wider and wider, and where all too many kids—both rich and poor—are disconnected from civilized and humane ways of living their lives."[28]

Since the family meal is becoming rarer, Waters looks to schools to teach the lessons of the table.

> We must value and respect each other, and we learn best how to do this at the table. . . . But the schools educate our children as if there were no family emergency, on the one hand, and no planetary emergency, on the other. As educators from Socrates onward have recognized, the goal of education is not the mastery of various disciplines, but the mastery of one's self. Being responsible to one's self cannot be separated from being responsible to the planet. I know of no better way to get this lesson across than through a school curriculum in which food takes its place at the core level. From the garden, and the kitchen, and the table, you learn empathy—for each other and for all of creation; you learn compassion; and you learn patience and self-discipline. A curriculum that teaches these lessons gives children an orientation to the future—and it can give them hope.[29]

Waters sees gardening, cooking, serving and eating, and composting as antidotes to rampant consumerism. "Kids today are bombarded with a pop culture which teaches redemption through buying things. School gardens, on the other hand, turn pop culture upside-down: they teach redemption through a deep appreciation for the real, the authentic, and the lasting—for the things that money can't buy: the very things that matter most of all if we are going to lead sane, healthy, and sustainable lives. Kids who learn environmental and nutritional lessons through school gardening—and school cooking, and eating—learn ethics." It takes something pleasurable, and frequent, to draw children away from the incessant allure of consumerism. Eating has the potential to bring enormous pleasure on a daily basis. And pleasure can be tied to ethics. As Waters observes, "I realize that our society is uncomfortable with the notion that education might teach our children how to experience pleasure; but the sensual pleasure of eating beautiful food from the garden brings with it the moral satisfaction of doing the right thing for the planet and for yourself."[30]

Waters has taken issue with the nation's budget priorities: governments spend too little on schools and too much on prisons and cut school costs by replacing teachers with computers. She urged President Bill Clinton to articulate a new national goal of rebuilding schools, "our single most democratic institution."[31] She contends,

> The frightening condition of the worst schools is a horrifying symbol of the kind of nation we have become; a nation where new prisons are cleaner, safer, and more comfortable than old schools. Rebuilding the schools so they are physically inviting, and inspiring—and perhaps even beautiful—is more important than wiring them for computers. We cannot expect computers to function as a kind of substitute for schools. Just as agribusiness, processed food, and supermarkets fail to provide the benefits of real communities—the kinds of communities that are nurtured by small-scale local agriculture, home-cooked family meals, and farmers' markets—the virtual classroom can never replace the real classroom in creating a socially responsible public.[32]

She supports a federally funded, WPA-style employment program to alleviate "the epidemic of inner-city unemployment while functioning as a restoration corps for the schools. If the unemployed were put to work renovating their own neighborhood schools, the students would receive a message of empowerment and hope." She advocates a curriculum "designed to educate both the senses and the conscience—a curriculum based on sustainable agriculture" that would teach children "their moral obligation to be caretakers and stewards of the finite resources of our planet" and "the joy of the table, the pleasure of real work, and the real meaning of community."[33]

Using these kinds of arguments, Waters convinced more than a dozen parents, teachers, and other volunteers from the community to pitch in. Together they raised more than twelve thousand dollars for supplies and cleaned out the abandoned kitchen, which became the project's headquarters. In 1995, King Middle School officials broke ground on the patch of land that became the Edible Schoolyard. In the garden, children built arbors, picked vegetables for lunch, drew landscapes for art classes, and studied insects and plant life for science classes. "Once you've grown food and cooked it, you want to eat it. And you want your friends to eat it. So in about six weeks these kids go from saying 'I don't like salad' to saying 'You've gotta try the arugula.'"[34] "All the things we'd hoped would happen began to happen. If a kid didn't like salad—well, if they grew the salad and prepared it themselves, they ate the salad. They liked to clean up, they liked to set the table, they even liked the hard work in the garden."[35]

Many Edible Schoolyard activities have impressed Waters. On one occasion, five hundred children voted on which flavor of school-made sherbets they liked best: Meyer lemon, tangerine, blood orange, or lime. An adobe oven was built near the garden site for bread and pizza baking. The community came together on the full moon to celebrate the harvest. The school developed a relationship with a local organic farm, Terra Firma, which delivered produce to each class every week. After one group of students prepared a big salad with this produce, they stopped to think about the people who tilled the land, planted the seeds, and harvested the vegetables—and then they stood up and gave the salad a huge standing ovation.[36] Terra Firma is a community supported agriculture (CSA) farm. Such farms enter into contracts with individuals and organizations to deliver fresh produce on a periodic basis. This provides financial security to small-scale organic farmers and helps them avoid advertising costs. Every week the farm delivered seven boxes of produce to the classrooms; opening them was like a wonderful show-and-tell for the students. Sometimes the students prepared the vegetables in the classroom; other times they took them home for their families to prepare. Students also visited the farm.[37]

From her work with children in the Edible Schoolyard, Waters learned that they were hungry for good food and attention. They needed to be cared for and appreciated, but too often they were neglected. "As soon as you give them a little attention, their response is incredible. Even teenagers! Positive reinforcement is so essential to their lives. So many of us are so busy, we don't give them this. The garden can help them: it's a tangible way of showing how actions have consequences—if you plant it and take care of it, it will grow!"[38]

Today, much of the funding for the Edible Schoolyard comes from the Chez Panisse Foundation, which Waters established in 1996 (the restaurant's twenty-fifth anniversary) to support educational and cultural projects that promote sustainable agriculture, strengthen community, and reinforce self-esteem by creating opportunities for people to grow, prepare, and share their food.[39] Waters states, "Having this very essential experience in the garden, in the kitchen and around the table can transform people; it brings families and communities together. I felt there was the potential for reaching a lot of people through the restaurant who would give money to the project." Donations came from over 350 individuals and organizations, making it possible for the foundation to give thousands of dollars to sustainable agricultural

Washington Mall Garden. Alice Waters believes that growing, preparing, and sharing food brings people together and creates community. It also helps improve the eating habits of school children. This garden on the Mall in Washington, D.C., in 2005 was part of her plan to accomplish these goals. Photo by Matt Dunn/*The New York Times*/Redux.

projects.[40] Waters also raised money for the Edible Schoolyard by participating in local benefits. For example, in 1999 she and illustrator David Lance Goines autographed their *Chez Panisse Menu Cookbook* at a book-signing party featuring Chez Panisse hors d'oeuvres and a copy of Goines's Chez Panisse twenty-eighth anniversary poster.[41]

In recognition of her work with the Edible Schoolyard, in 1998 Waters received a federal Excellence in Education award from U.S. Senator Barbara Boxer (D-CA). At a gathering in the school garden, Boxer, noting that she had entered politics the same year Waters opened Chez Panisse (1971), said she would try to secure matching federal funds for the Edible Schoolyard. Clearly overcome with emotion, Waters said with a quavering voice, "I don't feel I have any choice. I have to do this." A reporter wrote,

> She filled the garden with laughs when she called her crusade "The Delicious Revolution," but her effort is as serious as it is ambitious. It's a battle against not

only the literal wasteland that once sat behind King school, an abandoned two-acre lot of broken asphalt and weeds, but also the educational wasteland that neglects basic knowledge about food and the nutritional wasteland of fat-filled, low-nutrition school lunches that sap the health and energy of our youth. . . . Ultimately Waters wants to restore a fully-functioning cafeteria, not just to King, but to all other schools in Berkeley, if not in the nation, supplied at least in part by the food grown by the students at each school.[42]

Later that year, at a ceremony in Washington, D.C., Waters was one of ten citizens honored by Secretary of Education Richard Riley for creative and innovative approaches to education, in recognition for her leadership in establishing the Edible Schoolyard.[43]

School Lunches

A final way in which Alice Waters has implemented her theory of a delicious revolution is by working to improve the quality of school lunches. A 1993 USDA study states that the average school lunch had 20 percent more fat, 50 percent more saturated fat, and 100 percent more sodium than federal dietary guidelines recommended.[44] Ellen Haas, the USDA Undersecretary of Food, Nutrition and Consumer Services, invited Waters to testify at a public hearing on nutrition objectives for school menus in October 1993. In her remarks, Waters noted that it was going to be difficult to change schoolchildren's attitudes about food since they only had half an hour for lunch. This encouraged "thoughtlessly gobbling down some fast food snacks shoved over the counter" and was not enough time for "the sensual, emotional, and social education that comes from sharing and savoring good food." She reiterated her view that eating food "is not just refueling, as though we were so many internal combustion engines needing gas. Food can and should be the medium of exchange for the most intimate and valuable parts of ourselves. And learning about food, diet, and nutrition can be at the center of a truly liberal education."[45]

In her testimony, Waters advocated more community participation in all phases of food preparation for schools lunches. For example, bread baking could be part of the curriculum, and bakers could teach children how to do it. "Such a program not only opens a door into our whole history; it also teaches a sense of responsibility: if students, baking for the whole school, fail to do their job well, at the other end their fellow students will know it. Start with pizza, a food familiar to virtually all the kids in the country; but move on to different kinds of bread. Indeed, couldn't an adventurous, hands-on school lunch program teach children about multiculturalism through exploring diverse tastes? 'Eat a variety of foods' say the guidelines: this is an open invitation to learn more about ourselves."[46]

She contended that adding gardening to the curriculum contributes healthy foodstuffs to school lunches, beautifies the schoolyard, and teaches children about ecology.

> There is scarcely a school in the country that couldn't be improved by a little edible landscaping. And children can learn directly that decisions about agriculture even on such a small scale have ecological consequences. School lunches do not have to be mass-produced and pre-processed. The alternative is not necessarily more expensive. Students can learn from lunch that different foods taste best and cost least when they are eaten in season. I hear over and over that given the choice, kids always choose the familiar and the unhealthy over the unknown and the nutritious. What they want is fries and candy. But what is education for, if not to lead children to make educated choices for themselves based on the knowledge of the very best? You have to awaken their senses and make them want to try new experiences.[47]

She reported that many members of the community are ready to help improve school lunches. "Many chefs, farmers, restaurateurs, and parents understand the dimensions of the problem, but don't know how to help. They're waiting to be asked. Most people seem to feel, instinctively—and I believe, correctly—that good food is a right, not a privilege. Let them be involved with providing it!" She acknowledged that her goals sounded idealistic but noted that in the Bay Area many people were trying very hard to reach them. She was disturbed that children could emerge from public schools without "the most basic requirement for a happy and healthy life: the knowledge of how to nourish themselves responsibly and well."[48]

In 1995, both the USDA and the state of California issued new dietary guidelines, "Dietary Guidelines for Americans" and "The California Daily Food Guide," respectively. At the time, the National School Lunch Program fed more people nationally than McDonald's—4.3 billion free or low-cost lunches annually. Previous guidelines had required each school meal to include specific quantities of food from five specific categories: meat, dairy products, bread, fruit, and vegetables. The revised standards urged an increase in fiber, vegetables, fruits, and grains and a reduction in fat, sodium, and cholesterol. No more than 30 percent of calories in lunches could come from fat, and no more than 10 percent from saturated fat.[49]

In an effort to promote the new guidelines for healthy school lunches, the USDA sponsored seven "chefs' lunches" in schools around the country. One of them took place at Berkeley's Jefferson School, with Alice Waters and eleven other prominent Bay Area chefs feeding 345 five- to nine-year olds. Also in attendance was USDA undersecretary Ellen Haas, who remarked that a better strategy than government-mandated change was the motivation of children through education to make more healthful, low-fat choices. The chefs transformed the sterile cafeteria into an inviting dining room, replete with checked bistro cloths and pots of herbs and pansies. The children were served fresh garden vegetables with vinaigrette, tacos with handmade torti-llas, salsa and beans cooked over an open fire, and sugared strawberries and oranges in tangerine juice. While chefs talked to third-graders about fruits and vegetables and stirred black beans in a cast-iron pot over a fire on the asphalt playground, Waters washed and sliced carrots in the school garden as fast as eager kindergartners could pull them up. A reporter noted: "Despite a reputation for picky standards, the petite critics seemed to give the meal high marks. Although many left untouched the beautiful baby romaine let-tuce and picture-perfect radishes on their plates, the tacos and dessert were clear winners. But is it repeatable, once the Bay Area's top chefs pack up their knives and head home? Says Jefferson principal Marion Altman: 'It comes down to how important people think it is to feed children well.'"[50]

Waters admits that it can be a challenge to get children to try healthy, new foods, especially when they are addicted to salty and sugary snacks. Even though scientific evidence indicates that children universally fear new things to eat, adults should not abrogate their responsibility to expose them to more-nutritious alternatives. Waters notes,

> In many cultures, adults take the time to overcome these fears in their children by introducing them to a varied, changing diet. They do this mostly by sharing meals—meals that have meaning, because they are actually cooked and served by the adults who take primary care of their children, and because they are prepared from ripe, seasonal food. These children are socialized almost automatically: it just happens in the course of things, by osmosis. Children go with their parents to the markets, and they grow up knowing how to feed themselves. I think that when people grew things in their backyards and out on the farm, and then put that produce on the table, that people couldn't help gathering 'round. I believe people always want to sit down if there's good food on the table.[51]

Both parents and teachers need to educate children's palates away from fa-miliar, salty, and sugary foods; otherwise, they will never grow out of these addictions, because their palates are dulled. Waters observes, "It's almost like their palates were out of calibration: I think that when many people taste foods that are outside the range of the salty and sugary things they're used to, they taste very strange to them, and they can't appreciate their real qualities. When kids like this grow up, they will have never learned to be especially curious about good food, and it just won't matter much to them."[52]

Waters also acknowledges the pressure for quick school lunches. But we pay a price for sending a message to children that "eating quickly is something of value. That no mess, no fuss, no preparation time—these are the good things. But we're missing the point when we try to save time by not cooking and shopping for ourselves. If we rush to eat quickly so we can get to the 'worthwhile' stuff, we're cheating ourselves." She notes, "One of the few really and truly worthwhile pleasures in life, it seems to me, is not getting away from work, but in doing work that means something. Tomatoes I grow myself in my backyard have a different value than the ones from the supermarket. They taste better. They mean something to me and I pass on that enthusiasm at the table so that they mean something more to my guests. The pride you feel from doing something like that is exactly the kind of self-esteem I think children should learn to feel."[53]

Waters believes that ultimately, improving school lunches involves more than changing what is on the plate—it is about moral education.

> Just giving them nutritionally-sufficient meals, with plenty of vegetables, won't work. If our only goal is improved nutrition, and we start to give kids such meals at schools, they may well not want to eat them, or care much for them, or about them. But if we started to educate them early, if we involved them physically, and brought all their senses into play, and taught them to name and discriminate among flavors; if children were taught at school, from an early age, how to garden; and if then they were able to eat what they had grown—this could transform the moral education of our children![54]

In 1999, the Berkeley Board of Education voted to adopt many of the school food policies that Waters had been advocating: a garden for each school site, the use of organic foods as much as possible, and relationships with local farms. The Berkeley district was one of four nationwide selected to participate in a USDA program that supported district efforts to build relationships with local farmers by using their fresh produce for meals and snacks. Eleven of Berkeley's sixteen schools already had gardens. Organic food was going to be phased in as grant money became available to pay organic farmers. Organic produce was more costly than nonorganic, but officials hoped to keep costs down by working with local farmers to buy their produce in bulk, and they emphasized that participating farmers would save costs by not having to market their produce or transport it very far. Berkeley's policy also had a provision stating that if a school did not have a full-service kitchen, one would be included when the school was remodeled with bond money.[55] Waters called the school board's decision remarkable. Children would have a beautiful place to eat and time enough to eat and talk, and organic suppliers would get more business. At Chez Panisse, she served only about five hundred people a day; by her estimation, King Middle School alone would need about 350 pounds of asparagus on a day it was served in season.[56]

Waters also set her sights on the more challenging clientele at Berkeley High School. When she was principal for a day there, she asked 150 students what they had eaten for breakfast and lunch that day. Most of them had skipped one of the meals and eaten candy or sodas to tide them over until after school, when they purchased fast food.[57] According to a 2001 USDA report requested by Congress, soft drinks and sweets sold in the nation's schools were a poor lesson in nutrition and contributed to obesity and other health problems. "When children are taught in the classroom about good nutrition . . . but are surrounded by vending machines, snack bars, school stores and a la carte sales . . . they receive the message that good nutrition is merely an academic exercise," the report concluded.[58]

Berkeley High had a cafeteria until 1989, when it had to be closed due to earthquake damage. Since the high school was an open campus, most students walked to local fast-food restaurants and delis for lunch or grabbed a pizza pocket or chips from an on-campus "snack shack." A new cafeteria was slated to open in 2003. In the meantime, to comply with the school district's organic food policy, in 2001 it opened a food court with organic fare from five local restaurants that delivered to campus every day. The restaurants had to be willing to make organic substitutions to their menus. On opening day, for three dollars, students had a choice of vegetable chow mein made with produce from the farmer's market or chicken devoid of growth hormones, among other dishes. The apple juice came from local, pesticide-free orchards. The food was delivered by bicycle messengers in baskets that read, "One Less Car!" Waters rolled in her barbecue pit to prepare organic pork tacos. "'Any high school in the country would kill for this,' said Principal Frank Lynch, who couldn't believe someone so famous was making his lunch."[59]

Waters has been consistent in delivering her message that everyone—from students to school officials to patrons of Chez Panisse—learns through her or his experiences with food. In any event she becomes involved in, she urges people to pay attention to the food and take the time to eat leisurely. When a big conference on nutrition in the schools was being planned in a large Oakland hotel, she asked the hotel caterers what they were serving, with the admonition, "You need to make the right decisions about this. You need to think about how the tables should be, how you are going to feed this group of people, because that's going to change the way they think about nutrition in the schools."[60]

Public concern about a national obesity epidemic have bolstered Waters's school lunch efforts. In July 2004, she persuaded the Berkeley Unified School District, which then educated about ten thousand children, to offer academic credit for a lunch curriculum. Her proposal was backed by a $3.8 million grant from the Chez Panisse Foundation, the first of its kind in the nation. To meet the $5 million price tag to implement the curriculum in all Berkeley schools, supporters of a new obesity center at the renowned Children's Hospital and Research Center in Oakland signed on in an effort to attract grants from the national Centers for Disease Control and Prevention and federal agencies. Berkeley educators were tasked with writing a curriculum based on growing and serving food for school lunches for both students and teachers: measuring a garden plot for math, understanding molecules by watching bread rise, and learning economics by studying sustainable farming practices. According to the district's curriculum director, lunch needed to be reintegrated back into the school day. "Teachers have their own lunchtime, and kids are sent off to make their own choices. Now, in light of the obesity crisis, we're trying to reclaim that time and look at it as learning."[61]

Detractors of Waters's school-lunch agenda raised concerns that her plan was unrealistic, even irresponsible, given a shrinking pool of education dollars in California and pressure on teachers to prepare students for standardized tests. California's classrooms were among the most crowded in the nation, and one million students attended schools with bathrooms that did not work. Fifty-seven school districts had filed reports with the state warning of imminent financial insolvency. How would educators measure learning outcomes? How would components of the new curriculum meet the state's academic content standards, which outline what should be taught at each grade level? Waters left these details to Berkeley educators and was not deterred by detractors. She compared her new curriculum to the introduction of physical education courses in public schools in the early 1900s, when resources were devoted to gymnasiums, track equipment, and hiring teachers because such allocations were regarded as important for students' health and ability to learn. The obesity crisis was a public health concern that needed to be addressed in the schools. As for learning outcomes, Waters accepted the challenge. "Give me any kid. In six weeks, they'll be eating chard. Something changes when children participate in the ritual of eating, the ritual of the land. Food that is economical and nutritious and delicious also gives another outcome, which is a nurtured human being." Based on successes to date, Waters was encouraged to continue with her efforts. By 2004, every school in Berkeley had a garden plot, and the Center for Ecoliteracy had developed Rethinking School Lunch, "a how-to guide for midsize school districts that want to start a farm-to-school program."[62]

This case study of the delicious revolution in restaurants, jails, schools, and farmers' markets has illustrated how a whole new world of civic activity opens up when we see food and meals as integral building blocks of civil society. Some of Alice Waters's civic activities are familiar: testifying at public hearings, lobbying officials, giving speeches to organizations, meeting with high school principals, joining a host of civic associations, raffling off items as fund-raisers, trying to reduce recidivism rates, advocating a WPA-style employment program to refurbish public schools, and creating a foundation.

But others are novel, hidden from view until we examine the role of food in civil society: wheeling a barbecue into a high school to feed students; creating the Farm-Restaurant Project to help local farmers; returning compost to the farm providing produce; employing foragers; supporting farmers' markets especially when it rains; getting to know vendors as people; introducing children to CSA; buying produce for a world-renowned restaurant from jail and school gardens; introducing gardening into school curricula; mobilizing a community (of chefs, farmers, restaurateurs, and parents) willing to improve school lunches; sponsoring chef lunches in schools; persuading the local school district to have a garden at each school, use organic foods, and build relationships with local farmers; getting school children to vote on their favorite sherbets; and measuring success by demand for asparagus and chard. Waters has built relationships among disparate groups of people to promote physical, emotional, social, economic, and ethical well-being, with special attention to the moral education of future citizens.

Part Five

Community Food

Chapter 11

. . . .

Community Food and Belonging in America

I first heard of Alice Waters's delicious revolution at a farmers' market where I had gone to shop and she had come to discuss her philosophy and sell her cookbooks. It is a town square, a commons area, where food and ideas are interchanged, and growing cycles and life cycles are shared. It is a location where urban dwellers connect with farmers in a common love of fresh produce, and both benefit from what the other has to say. It is place to support local farmers and organic produce. There is a street-fair atmosphere, with flowers, musicians, people of all ages, and homemade jams. Shopping at a farmers' market is a countercultural act: both to corporate agriculture's pesticide-laden and genetically modified foods and to the convenience of supermarket shopping. The proliferation of farmers' markets across the country signals that an increasing number of Americans want to connect with food in a more direct, less processed and packaged way. The benefits of fresh-picked flavors, face-to-face exchanges, a community atmosphere, and purchases made in an ecologically defensible way are increasingly worth the effort. Where one shops is a gustatory, economic, social, and political statement.

Public gardens also connect people with larger common purposes. In a burst of patriotism, Americans rolled up their sleeves to toil in victory gardens during World War II. For many jail inmates, gardens provide needed connections in their disconnected worlds. Pride of accomplishment, patience, and sharing produce and flowers with their communities are counterweights to hopelessness, poor impulse control, and low self-esteem. At community gardens, class, race, and economic differences coexist with the common experiences of getting muddy and taking pride in producing nutritious food and revitalizing forsaken patches of land. For children, school gardens open up new worlds of food traditions and healthy eating alternatives. Community and school gardeners share what they produce with local needy groups.

In many communities, festive and ritual foods cement bonds of geographic and cultural groups. Food is a ritualized but not necessarily formal way for people to connect with their heritage, a subtle form of strengthening civil society. The inevitable dislocations of economic and social mobility cause many Americans to ground themselves in familiar foods, while at the same time embracing the unfamiliar foods associated with their new locations.

Community food extends thoughtfulness and generosity beyond immediate acquaintances to more expansive spheres: nation, neighborhood, schools, jails, outdoor markets. They involve common things to discuss: the work of planning and planting, the cycles of growth and death, the tedium but necessity of weeding, alternative forms of pest control, the enjoyment of fresh and delicious food, decisions about the fair sharing of food and distribution of any surplus, and the importance of marking significant moments in the life cycle with ritual meals. Community food is the occasion for these conversations about common purposes. Of course, not all interactions in these settings are community building. At farmers' markets, one finds pickpockets and fraudulent vendors offering supermarket produce as fresh and organic. Some neighbors lobby for much-needed low-income housing instead of beans and peas on lots in their communities. Not all students or inmates think that gardening is exciting or worth the effort. Nevertheless, there are surprisingly few reports of vandalism or theft in community, school, or jail gardens. For the most part, they are oases of cooperation, civic discourse, and common purpose.

Community Bonds

What does it mean to say that food forges communities? Table connections among family and friends are obvious. But what is there about food, meals, and foodways that enables Americans to identify with larger communities: ethnic, racial, religious, neighborhood, local, regional, state, and national? And what does community building have to do with American democracy? The bonds of community, like those of family and friends, are adhesives in civil society.

The term *community* derives from the Latin *communis*, meaning "fellowship, shared relations, or feelings." Community membership is subjective—a personal sense of belonging and responsibility. It is also objective—a legal relationship to a state, formal membership in a religious or civic group, residence in a neighborhood, or parentage of a particular ethnicity or race. Members of a community mutually recognize that they have something in common that is worth preserving—a commonweal, or general welfare.

The dynamics of subjective and objective community membership animate America, whose national fabric has been woven with racial and ethnic fibers. Politics obtains in racial and ethnic group definition, mobilization to participate in the political process, political representation by elected officials, and reaping group policy benefits from the government. Group members want to promote the welfare of their group, along with that of the nation. Throughout American history, this *dual sense of belonging* has been reflected in the "hyphenated-American" terminology used by group members and government officials—Irish-, German-, Italian-, Japanese-, Chinese-, Latin-, African- and the like.

Consider the categories used to denote the African American community. The term *African* was used sporadically during the seventeenth and eighteenth centuries. In the nineteenth century, *colored* gained popularity to refer to those of mixed-race as well as African heritage. The 1890 government census asked blacks to choose among four labels: black, mulatto, quadroon, and octoroon, depending on the degree of white blood in their ancestry. In the twentieth century, many black Americans have shifted, often in one lifetime, from colored, to Negro, to black, to African American. The term *African American* has gained in popularity since 1988, when the Reverend Jesse Jackson urged Americans to use it to refer to blacks. Since that time, the number of blacks using the term has steadily increased. In a 2003 poll, 48 percent of African Americans preferred to use the term, with 35 percent favoring the term *black,* and 17 percent liking both terms. By the turn of the twenty-first century, the number of African-born citizens was growing, thanks to changes in immigration laws, and they and their children were achieving economically at higher levels than native-born blacks. This prompted a discussion in the black community. Should a different term be used to distinguish native-born blacks, who had to overcome the psychological and economic obstacles of slavery's legacy, from immigrant Africans, who stood to benefit from the civil rights struggle in which they did not participate?[1]

Native-born blacks and African-immigrant blacks are engaged in a lively debate. One Ethiopian-born American citizen says that Americans whose ancestors were slaves do not see him as an African American. He wants to be described simply as a universal man, but he knows that the United

States has had a long history of categorizing its people. He is trying to find a way of stitching his twin identities—one Ethiopian, one American—into a whole. With these things in mind, he and some of his Ethiopian friends sat down with some American-born friends "over a meal of savory meats and Ethiopian bread," in an attempt "to start a dialogue about their similarities, their differences and issues of identity at a time of demographic change."[2] This is but one example of the everyday role of food in the ongoing process of forging community identity in America's democracy.

Another transnational example of community bonds and the role of food is the experience of Asian American Pacific Islanders (AAPI) who served in the U.S. armed forces during the Vietnam War. Unlike other racial groups of soldiers, they were a visible minority fighting an enemy of the same race and were victims of the "gook syndrome": the military's dehumanization of the Vietnamese through the use of derogatory terms such as *gook, dink,* or *slant eye* that were often used to refer to any Asian, friend or foe. Some AAPI veterans, fearful of friendly fire, watched each others' backs. Food was used as a weapon by some military personnel, who threw cans of C-rations at barefoot children, "busting their faces with the cans to kill the gooks." Many AAPI veterans, especially those from the Pacific Islands, reported that their identification with the landscape, lifestyle, and foodways of the Vietnamese made it difficult for them to dehumanize the enemy. "Spontaneous moments of connection through food occurred with Vietnamese civilians and villagers, both in town and in the field." Some AAPI veterans "responded positively to Vietnamese food as an affirmation of their own identity and values, even while being exposed to pervasive racial degradation of the Vietnamese by other U.S. personnel."[3]

Food, Region, and Ethnic Belonging

In the fluid social structure of the United States, food has provided people with a sense of belonging. In a nation of mobile immigrants, region and ethnicity have often been intertwined. Cultural geographers note that the first ethnic group to establish itself economically and socially in an area usually creates the cultural norms there; subsequent immigrants regard the already settled group as American. They want to eat American to fit in.[4]

A case in point is the city of Detroit. In the nineteenth century, the Irish, as the most numerous old immigrant group, were regarded as American by the more recently arrived Serbs, who changed their names from Obradović and Dragić to O'Bradovich and O'Dragich. Another example was Michigan's

Upper Peninsula, where immigrants from Cornwall, England, established the work practices in the region's iron and copper mines in the mid-nineteenth century. By the end of the century, the Cornish had become the skilled workers, foremen, and owners of the mines, and the more recently arrived Finns, Italians, Poles, Croats, and Serbs provided the unskilled labor. As the need for unskilled labor declined, the social hierarchy became entrenched, with the Cornish defining much of the cultural life of the community and representing American culture.[5]

A native food of Cornwall, the pasty, came to symbolize the Upper Peninsula. A turnover with a pielike crust filled with a combination of ingredients, it was designed to be carried to work and eaten in the hand. In Cornwall, it was particularly associated with miners; it retained heat and provided a hearty meal-in-one. Before long, Finnish, Italian, and Slavic miners in the Upper Peninsula were asking their wives to prepare the pasty that they saw their Cornish foremen eating. Over time, many local Finns and Italians came to believe that the pasty was *their* own ethnic food, mostly because it had become a family tradition passed down by mothers and grandmothers. The first pasties available outside the home were sold at church sales, events dominated by older women who played a supervisory and authoritative role in monitoring the work of younger women to produce authentic pasties. After the extractive industries abandoned the area, the local economy began a steady decline in the 1920s, from which it never fully recovered. Beginning in the 1960s, as tourism became increasingly important, pasty shops proliferated to provide regional flavor. Legends were told about how hardworking miners warmed pasties on shovels held over candles of mining lamps; or how they were kept warm by hot pasties wrapped in newspapers and tucked under their shirts on cold mornings, keeping the pasties warm as they worked. Locals used this food lore to draw group boundaries and distinguish themselves from outsiders (including ridicule of outsiders' pronunciation "pay-stee" instead of the correct "pass-tee"). In an area of high unemployment, the pasty became a source of regional pride and comfort. Its acceptance by outside tourists validated the culture of the Upper Peninsula.[6]

Region and ethnicity were also interrelated in the case of the use of the crawfish as a Cajun ethnic symbol. At one time, crawfish were so plentiful in the Cajun area of Louisiana that they were the food of low-status poor people, available for the picking in swamps and streams. Twentieth-century newcomers ridiculed Cajuns as backward swamp-dwellers for eating unclean, inedible vermin. The crawfish moved from everyday fare to cultural icon during the 1960s, a result of increased Cajun self-esteem and regional tourism. Crawfish became an expensive food item, appearing on Cajun-power T-shirts and bumper stickers. Throughout southern Louisiana, a crawfish festival was added to the roster of existing food festivals based on rice, yams, sugar, alligators, oysters, frogs, and shrimp. The festival triggered outsiders' interest in crawfish, which in turn helped the crawfish industry, the restaurant industry, and the regional tourist industry.[7]

Ethnicity and location interacted in interesting ways to give disparate peoples a sense of belonging. For example, one explanation for the historic attachment of New York City Jews to Chinese food was that newly arrived Jews could feel cosmopolitan by eating out, and in Chinese restaurants they were safe from anti-Semitism. For their part, the owners of Chinese restaurants welcomed everyone in order to survive financially. Many Chinese came to New York from California in the 1880s, in the wake of Chinese exclusion acts and anti-Chinese riots, and many of them turned to restaurants for their livelihood. While immigrant Jews opened delicatessens for other Jews, and Italians ran restaurants for other Italians, the Chinese welcomed all immigrant families at their restaurants. Indeed, both Jews and Italians often felt more at home in Chinese restaurants than they did in each other's eateries. The urban Jewish culture that formed in New York included such traditional Eastern European elements as an emphasis on family meals, intense dinner-table conversation, and love of an abundant table. The communal character of Chinese restaurant food, with shared dishes, enabled Jews to indulge their love of discussion and debate. They thought that a good meal required companions. Mimi Sheraton describes the sentiments of many New York Jews whose childhood memories included eating Chinese food as part of what it meant to be a New York Jew: "These dishes, with their meltingly tender vegetables and soothing garlic overtones, are for me what Federico Fellini once described as 'the soft and gentle flavors of the past.'"[8]

Sometimes, food and its attendant community identity are locally, as opposed to ethnically, defined. A case in point is Cincinnati chili, which residents since the 1920s have regarded as symbolic of their city. Originated by a Macedonian and served primarily in Greek-owned chili parlors, it consists of spicy chili layered between two bland layers, say of spaghetti or cheese, to tame the flavor for local palates. Many Cincinnatians take civic pride in testing and exchanging chili recipes.[9]

On occasion, food provides an identity that is more foisted on a community than embraced by it. A case in point is the association of Maine with lobster. Many poor and inland Maine residents think that lobster is an inappropriate state emblem imposed by a summer elite who seasonally descend on the coastal area. Although Canada provides about half of the lobster sold in the United States, lobster symbolizes Maine just as maple syrup stands for Vermont (even though Maine has more maple trees than Vermont). Throughout the seventeenth and eighteenth centuries, abundant lobster was a cheap and low-status food in New England. After the Civil War, urban demand for lobster rose dramatically as steam-powered transportation made shipping feasible, and newly wealthy national elites bought prime real estate on the Maine coast for their summer homes. Locals resented these elites. One local who had worked at an elite club in the 1920s told a story about what happened after a local child jumped into the club pool—the pool was drained and refilled. In their social milieu, wealthy summer residents "discovered" Maine and its lobster, and middle-class tourists and consumers soon followed suit. Maine's inland residents resented the power of the coastal economy. When the state legislature adopted a new design for the state license plate—a red lobster on a white background—many residents whited out the lobster. As one local voiced her opposition, "Personally, the decision to use the lobster on the plates is insulting. I mean, the lobster has no reality for most real Mainers. If you wanted to show the typical Maine food, you'd be more accurate with the potato. Or better still, how about macaroni and cheese?"[10]

For American consumers, food is a way to identify vicariously with a place and its image of community. Advertisers sell food by associating it with a place that consumers presumably want to be part of: Vermont means wholesome, authentic, small scale; California evokes easy-going, sophisticated, and innovative; and Texas represents flamboyant individualism. Buying based on these images enables the geographically bound to have a "taste" of what a place is like, even if the product does not originate in that state.[11]

Community Drinks

Drinks are also markers of community identity. Indeed, historically, drinks have been linked to major civilizations and global events: beer was the popular drink at the dawn of civilization in Egypt and Mesopotamia; wine lubricated the cradle of Western thought in Greece and Rome, and its association with Christianity was part of the reason for the Muslim ban on alcohol (ironically the modern word *alcohol* has its origins in distilled drinks in Arabic laboratories); distilled drinks transported well on ships and became valuable economic goods as part of the international slave trade (rum and whiskey were drinks of choice in colonial America); coffee originated in the Arab world and became the drink of reasoned discourse in Western colonial capitals and coffeehouses; tea was consumed in China's immense empire and was spread across the globe by the British (who cultivated it in their Indian colony and saw it dumped into Boston harbor by American colonists); and around the globe, Coca-Cola has symbolized American culture (and is thought to be the world's second most commonly understood term, after *OK*).[12]

In the United States, coffee has signaled different community identities. For years it was associated with bohemian and intellectual subcultures at urban and university-area cafés. Then, beginning in the 1980s, coffeehouses became corporate chains, best exemplified by Starbucks. In the Pacific Northwest, the specialty coffee business exploded: there was one commercial espresso machine for every 750 people in the state of Washington in 1995. Espressos and lattes represented a community of high culture, bookstores, art galleries, and good taste. Coffee provided a cosmopolitan identity as a vicarious form of world travel—to Kenya, Costa Rica, Sumatra, and Java. Some specialty coffee consumers, concerned about the negative ecological and social consequences of coffee's production (fertilizers, herbicides, water contamination, and low standard of living in producing countries), have rallied the ecology community to influence Starbucks's practices.[13]

Specialty teas have helped some Asian American youth to navigate the waters of community identity. A delicious tea called *boba* (a term used interchangeably with tapioca milk tea, pearl tea, bubble tea, and *zhen zhou nai cha*) originated in Taiwan in 1983 and spread across the cities and suburbs of the United States in the 1990s. It is the drink of choice for some Asian American college and high school students who want a comfortable setting to relax, talk, and forge a sense of community. "Much like the cyber café, the boba café presents Asian American youth, particularly high school students with an alternative to social spaces where barriers such as age, financial resources, and distance prevent them from becoming participants." Boba cafés are safer than clubs, where alcohol is served, and the streets, where youth are profiled as gang members. "It is difficult for Asian American youth to just 'hang out' in public urban spaces in groups without arousing suspicion from law enforcement officers. Asian American high school and college-age youth in southern California often complain about profiling and harassment by police officers who stop them because of the import cars [i.e., rice rockets] they drive and the type of clothing they wear, automatically treating them as 'gang members.'" A boba café is an example of a "counter-space," defined by critical race theorists as "a supportive environment wherein [youth or student] experiences are validated and viewed as important knowledge." It is "forged from the transnational exchanges of cuisines, aesthetics, and media," a place where "Asian American youth, from a wide assortment of ethnicities, participate in a hybridized experience."[14]

Festive Foods

In addition to everyday foods and drinks, communities have distinctive festive foods to signal special occasions. American community fund-raising cookbooks contain two types of recipes: frequently consumed family favorites and special occasion festive foods, whose more-expensive ingredients and greater preparation time distinguish them from everyday fare. Festive foods link people to religious and ethnic communities. In cookbooks in Middle America's Great Plains, recipes such as "Bohemian Christmas Balls" and "Lenten Cocoa Cake" are printed with explanations of their significance, use, and in some cases, ethnic origin. Explanations range from the familial ("This was my mother's Christmas candy which we loved") to the historical ("Jan Hagel is a historical cookie. He was a mercenary soldier and this cookie looks like it is covered with buckshots").[15]

For some, the celebration of Chinese New Year is not complete without wonton soup. Mary Uyematsu Kao grew up in a Japanese American family with few family rituals. Thanksgiving was celebrated for a while but stopped when her parents divorced. Her grandmother prepared New Year's food that was not appreciated by Mary and her sister, who, raised by Nisei (second-generation) parents who wanted their children to be "American," were not given Japanese names. She credits the Asian American movement of the 1970s for instilling in her a rebirth of Asian traditions. "Cultural traditions were revived and readapted to give us a sense of pride and identity in where we came from. Potlucks were a mainstay of movement traditions because they embodied a communal spirit of sharing and eating together—basic components of building collective unity and strength." Through her participation in this movement, she met her husband, a first-generation Chinese. "Our married/family life reflects a mixture of movement, ethnic and American traditions in a kind of spontaneous collaboration given the needs of the moment or occasion." He pushed for developing family traditions, including Chinese New Year and the making of wonton soup, which was prompted by their memories of his mother's soup. Although his mother lives three thousand miles away in New York City, he recalls, "[the] warm moist smell of chicken broth that emanated from Ma's kitchen into the dining room is hard to forget." "Making wonton soup is a great family project that can easily become a family ritual because everybody loves to eat it. With all the work it requires, division of labor is a key ingredient." Kao plans to continue this family tradition with her grandchildren, not only because it is enjoyable and maintains group and ethnic identity, but also because it is a collective alternative to "one poor soul in the kitchen who feeds a whole family day-in-and-day-out." Too many food choices that freed women from being kitchen slaves took the cooking out of the meal and have resulted in unhealthy fast food. "What can be learned from the wonton soup model is how everybody can help out to make a meal and how responsibility can be organized to be shared by everyone. One family tradition which has gotten lost in the fast-paced ready-made food era that we live in is the role of children in helping the parent prepare the meals. The most important tradition is when children learn how to cook the family's ethnic specialties, for this is how foodways get passed on."[16]

Chinese New Year's Dinner. Food and foodways are important markers of communi-ties: ethnic, religious, neighborhood, regional, and national. Festive foods are a special way to solidify and honor different community traditions and to provide continuity across generations. This painting by eight-year-old Stephanie Yu shows the family's New Year's dinner. Painting by Stephanie Yu, courtesy of the Chinese American Citizens Alliance.

At festivals, religious observances, and ethnic New Year's celebrations, when different ethnic groups are asked to contribute food, they typically choose to share items that are authentic and distinctive, yet tame enough to appeal to the uninitiated. To spare embarrassment at events meant to generate goodwill, shared foods are often easily handled finger foods such as tacos or miniature Greek pitas (pies), appetizers or snack food instead of celebratory fare. Traditional foodways for public consumption convey ethnicity in a simplified, pleasant, and manageable form.[17] For example, Italian Americans in Clinton, Indiana, use one set of esoteric foods to affirm their own identity, and another set of stereotypical display foods for financial success and sharing with non-Italian Americans. Esoteric dishes are regional Italian specialties that are served at home, shown in cooking demonstrations at Little Italy festivals, and included in a local charity cookbook. They are valued more for their sensual ties to an immigrant past than for their ability to reveal anything about the immigrants to outsiders. Display foods, on the other hand, are chosen to represent Italians to outsiders—pasta dishes with tomato sauce, pizza, and Italian sausage fried with peppers and onions.[18]

Most food festivals are seasonal. Perhaps the most famous seasonal food festival in the United States is Thanksgiving, which joins together the pre-Christian European folk celebration of home harvest with Christian festivals thanking the Virgin Mary for a wholesome food harvest. Drawn from Pilgrim and Puritan celebrations in early seventeenth-century Massachusetts, Thanksgiving became an established institution in the 1700s. New World Puritans chose Thursday for this feast day to distinguish it from the fasting and feasting days of the Catholic Church and the Church of England (typically Fridays, Wednesdays, and Mondays).[19]

Another seasonal New England food festival is the summer clambake. Quakers in Allen's Neck, Massachusetts, have held an annual clambake since 1888. What began as a modest beach outing expanded over the years to include friends, neighbors, and summer tourists. It has become a major community celebration, representing the continuity of tradition. One resident said that she has a wonderful feeling knowing that "on the third Thursday of every August through eternity, [she is] going to have a child there, a grandchild there, or a great-grandchild there, and on, and on, and on." She remarked that the tradition is not a part of other clambakes: no ritual, meaning, or family ties. Those clambakes are just food: you pay your money and you get your food. But her clambake is like a holy day. For these New Englanders, laboring as a group provides a way to get to know one another. Clambakes involve a lot of work: assembling melon-sized rocks and wooden cribs for the fire; collecting rockweed along the shoreline; cleaning clams; bagging fish, sausage, and tripe; husking corn; and baking brown bread and pies. Locals regard the clambake as part of their history, with different legends about its origins: either with indigenous peoples, or early colonists, or at a Quaker meeting a hundred years earlier.[20]

Folklorist Kathy Neustadt writes that something resonates between the directness of the clambake as a way of cooking, without pots and pans, without chefs, and the directness of Quakerism, an unmediated experience of the divine, without priests, texts, or creed. What people most wanted to share about the clambake were stories. In their Quaker community, silence is valued and emotions are rarely expressed directly. Their stories about the clambake reveal not so much nostalgia as gratitude: an appreciation of what came before as the foundation for what is now. Many of their narratives center on the goodness of people, particularly as they are inspired by the clambake. They construct "a vision of the perfect community, laboring together, serving themselves by honoring their neighbors, breaking bread with people who are, in some respects, their enemies." Tensions are infrequent, as generations work together with respect and humor. For the people of Allen's Neck, the clambake is "a symbol of survival, permanence, tradition and immortality—'same as last year'—in the face of change in the world, the mutability of nature, the imperfection of humankind, and the certainty of their own mortality."[21]

A ubiquitous American summer food festival is the picnic. Appearing in the 1830s, it began as a leisure activity of the wealthy and soon spread to other classes. Picnics included rituals of baskets and cutlery sets and of men and women chatting in the lovely and invigorating outdoors. They were viewed as a healthy respite from industrial life. As one proponent wrote in 1869, "The great charm . . . is to eat, to chat, to lie, to sit, to talk, to walk, with something of the unconstraint of primitive life. We find a fascination in carrying back our civilization to the wilderness."[22]

Ceremonial and Ritual Foods

Ceremonial and ritual foods flavor community remembrance and cohesion. For Jews, the seder, a Passover meal celebrating their exodus from captivity in Egypt, consists of symbolic food. Matzo (unleavened bread) represents the hurried departure from bondage. *Karpas* (a green vegetable, parsley, or lettuce) symbolizes new growth but is eaten dipped in salty water as a reminder of the tears of a captive people. *Maror* (bitter herbs such as horseradish or chicory) recalls slavery. *Betza* (a roasted egg) represents the sacrifice offered to God in the temple. *Zeroa* (a knuckle or joint of lamb) symbolizes the paschal sacrifice offered to God on the eve of the exodus. *Haroset* (a paste of dried fruit and nuts) resembles the Nile mud used by the Jews to build the Egyptian pyramids. At the meal, all these food items are distributed and examined for their deeper meaning, serving to educate the young and offer comfort to the elderly.[23]

Across the United States, Christian communities commemorate the birth of Christ with distinctive Christmas foods of many national origins: Mexican tamales, English plum pudding and hard sauce, German roast goose and red cabbage, Norwegian *kransekake* (Christmas wreath cake) and *hjortetakk* (reindeer antler cookie fritters), Swedish Santa Lucia's peppersnaps (Christmas cookies), French *pompe à huile* (Provençal Christmas bread), Portuguese *buddim do bacalhao* (baked salt cod), Italian panettone (Christmas bread), and Irish Christmas beef and soda bread. For Easter ceremonies, Christians decorate eggs and bake breads embedded with whole colored eggs.[24]

For some, meat and poultry are luxuries reserved for special occasions. For instance, as a child writer Shirley Geok-lin Lim ate chicken only on four occasions: Chinese New Year, Ch'ing Ming, the Mid-Autumn Festival, and the Feast of the Hungry Ghost. "And then, as my aunts told us was the practice when they were children, the chickens were divided according to gender, the father receiving the white breast meat, the sons the dark drumsticks, and the daughters the skinny backs, while the women ate the feet and wings." Her aunts warned her not to eat chicken feet until she was married; otherwise she would grow up to run away from her husband. She resisted eating chicken feet until one day she realized how inventive hunger had made the poor masses of ordinary Chinese. They had created a delicious cuisine from scraps and leftovers. She suddenly realized why as a child she was taught to greet her elders politely, "Have you eaten yet?"[25]

Every group's rites of passage—rituals commemorating birth, coming-of-age, marriage, and death—are accompanied by foods laden with symbolic meaning. Immigrants from Eastern Europe welcome new members to the community with the formal presentation of a birth basket of food. Many cultures mark the birth of a child with a common feast: eating meat or fowl and drinking from a communal cup of fermented liquor that is used to anoint the infant's head. This ceremony confers legitimacy—the group's acceptance of the new member as one of its own. The feast ensures that, by partaking of the same foods, eaten from the same dish, the tribe will know and recognize its own.[26]

The Catholic coming-of-age ritual of first communion is celebrated by the Maltese with *timpana* (a succulent macaroni pie of Sicilian origin), spit-roasted meats, and many sweets: cookies, pastries, and cakes. For the bar mitzvah feasts of Ashkenazi Jews, recipes come from the food of the shtetl, the townships established by landowners who employed Jews to manage their vast estates in Eastern Europe. These celebratory feasts include "goose in all its parts—flesh, fat, and chopped liver; sweet and sour fish; noodles or pinch-finger dumplings cooked in chicken or pigeon broth; boiled beef; sugar-sweetened carrots. For dessert, there [is] a *kugel*, a dish of noodles baked with sugar, raisins, and cinnamon; or pancakes; or a spicy gingerbread."[27]

The ritual foods of weddings symbolize new life: seeds, nuts, fruits, and round foods representing fertility. According to food writer Elisabeth Luard, the universal wedding food is a sweet cake. "Sweetness reminds all to speak well of each other—not an inconsiderable task at a wedding feast, notorious for family feuding. . . . Sweet talk—sweetheart, sugarplum, honey-lamb— translates without explanation into every language. Sugar . . . is the element that transforms a meal into a feast." The French celebrate weddings with the *croquembouche,* a tower of cream-stuffed pastry buns secured in place with caramel, and Provençal *soupe de mariage.* Russian newlyweds eat ritual bread and salt. Multicolored eggs are served at Hungarian weddings. Moroccan weddings feature saffron-spiced *tafaya* (lamb cooked with whole eggs, almonds, and raisins) and pancakes with whipped cream and cherries. Chinese wedding banquets follow nutritional rules based on the Taoist principles of yin and yang and include texture foods such as shark's fin, bird's nest, and fish maw. Japanese wedding guests dine on a clear soup, raw fish, grilled food, steamed food, deep-fried foods, foods dressed with vinegar, and cooked salads; they take home journey food—rice products in portable bundles to fortify them on their way home. Indonesian weddings feature rice pilaf colored with turmeric and enriched with coconut. Indian Brahmin Hindu weddings serve stews, rice, dal, breads, curries, pickles, and sweetmeats. Rice throwing at Indian weddings began as a sacrifice to propitiate the gods—a pre-Hindu ritual that has survived to the present.[28]

Funeral and mourning foods express the hope and expectation of rebirth, for example, sesame seeds in Indian burial rites. Many cultures observe the custom of taking food to burial grounds on a certain day—Halloween for Christians; in Eastern cultures, the dead visit the living at the winter solstice. In China and Japan, ancestors share a meal with their earthbound descendants in early spring. Greeks customarily provide mourners with *koliva* (wheat-grain oatmeal finished with raisins, pomegranate seeds, and almonds). At Romanian remembrance services, one year after someone's death, people make graveside offerings of bread and wine, with candles in the bread serving as reminders of resurrection. Many funeral foods are formed in the shape of heavenly objects: circular breads such as pancakes, tortillas, chapatis, bagels, dough fritters, and donuts; or spherical pulses such as chickpeas, peas, and seeds, especially sesame and pomegranate.[29]

The Mexican Day of the Dead (All Souls' Day) features both sweet and savory comestibles: gaily painted sugar skulls, marzipan bones, and All Souls' Day salt fish. *Mole negro de Todos Santos* (Mexican black chili pork for All Saints') is a comfort food for the morning of All Saints' Day, the day after All Souls', left on the back of the stove and reheated on the family's return from the cemetery. *Pan de muerto* (bread of the dead) is egg enriched, circular, and decorated with stylized bones laid like the spokes of a wheel around a bun to represent the skull. It may also take the shape of "small figures of animals or people—*monos*—made in precisely the same shapes as the ancient pottery figurines that were included in the grave furniture of pre-colonial-Christianized times."[30]

Immigrants from around the world brought these food traditions to the United States. They are markers of subjective and objective membership in a community. They signal a sense of belonging that is both savored for community cohesion and shared with outsiders. They link a particular community to the rites of passage of the human condition: commemorating birth, coming of age, marriage, and death with thoughtful and generous sharing of delicious and symbolic food. Foods and drinks link generations in the collective preparation of holiday food, provide a safe haven for youth subject to racial profiling, and give soldiers a reason to resist dehumanizing their enemies. Members of a community mutually recognize that they have something in common that is worth preserving and sharing—a commonweal, or general welfare—at the boba café, the dinner of the Ethiopian-born and the American-born African Americans, the pasty shops of Cornish immigrants, and the New England clambake. Civil society is replenished on a daily basis by the shared fellowship of community food.

Chapter 12

Gardens and Community

The bonds of civil society are reinforced in a variety of garden settings: community, urban, youth, school, and jail. Like tables, gardens are great levelers. They require cooperative effort, produce a tangible common good, and provide familiar topics of conversation. Throughout the course of American history, community and urban gardens have served many civic and civilizing purposes: producing wartime food and patriotism, providing economic relief, revitalizing urban areas, and bridging the old and the new worlds of immigrants. Youth gardens have provided at-risk children with a sense of purpose and community. School gardens have promoted an appreciation of healthy, delicious food and the experience of sharing at the table and broken down gender barriers in food preparation. Jail gardens have enabled the incarcerated to give something back to their communities: the fruits, vegetables, and flowers they have carefully tended.

Community Gardens and Patriotism

During World War I, the United States government encouraged citizens to help the war effort by planting liberty gardens and postwar victory gardens. Five million citizens, rallying to such slogans as "plant for freedom" and "hoe for liberty," grew over $500 million worth of food in 1918.[1] Victory gardening during World War II was orchestrated by the USDA. The peak year for home-front food production was 1943, when some 20 million households, constituting three-fifths of the population, produced more than 40 percent of the vegetables Americans consumed. Also, over four billion jars of food were preserved at home and community canning centers. According to Amy Bentley, along with food rationing, wartime victory gardening and canning functioned as community builders. Promoters of victory gardens tapped into the American mythology of gardens as symbols of abundance, order, progress, and civilization. Gardens even took on religious overtones, connoting an earthly paradise and promoting the virtues of hard work, thriftiness, and moral uprightness. Gardening evoked images of a seemingly simpler preindustrial America, a Jeffersonian agrarianism. USDA officials reminded Americans that Thomas Jefferson, an enthusiastic gardener, said, "But though an old man, I am but a young gardener."[2]

Victory gardening was designed not only to produce much-needed food but also to promote patriotism and community cohesion. Government and media emphasized the "American-ness" of gardening. Some Americans even

Victory Garden. This World War I poster encouraged citizens to raise their own vegetables and to write for free books on gardening, canning, and drying—activities that brought people together in a common patriotic enterprise. The Slow Food movement adopted this poster's image, replacing the text with "Vote for Small Farms & Local Food. Join Slow Food U.S.A." and "Eating is an agricultural act—Wendell Berry." U.S. National Archives and Records Administration (ARC Identifier 512498).

wrote to Franklin and Eleanor Roosevelt, asking them questions about gardening and inviting them to inspect their gardens if they were ever in the neighborhood. As one Baltimore woman described the new civil connections in her victory garden: "It's surprising how many new friends one makes here. People who live across the street but whom you hardly knew come over to chat and compare notes on the progress of their plants." At community picnics, neighbors shared dishes made from vegetables from their gardens. Cities sponsored neighborhood victory garden harvest shows.[3]

It is unclear whether men or women took responsibility for most of the victory gardening. Traditionally, kitchen gardens were women's domain, and fields of crops were men's. One wartime survey indicated that men did most of the work, and wartime publications portrayed men as the dominant gardeners. Ads and articles depicted gardens as battlefields, with men wielding hoes instead of guns and women in supporting and decorative roles as "farmerettes" or gardening in a clean dress and high heels. Calendars featured glamorous "Victory Garden Girls." Most women victory gardeners were portrayed as harvesters rather than growers. Images of women holding overflowing baskets of produce hearkened back to ancient associations of women, fertility, and the earth. But such images conflicted with the reality of the many women who embraced victory gardening as an outgrowth of household gardening or membership in garden clubs. Women both grew food and harvested it. One magazine featured a story of two women neighbors who pooled their resources and started a victory garden that supplied them with delicious fruits and vegetables year round. As one of them described the positive results: "We have a feeling of well-being and health such as we never had before. We are tanned, lean, hard as rocks, more easy-going, inclined to laugh more frequently."[4]

In contrast to government wartime messages that victory gardening, while male-dominant, involved both men and women, canning was portrayed as women's civic responsibility. Within a year of the government's call for canning as a war obligation, the proportion of women who canned food for their family's use rose from 64 to 75 percent. Half of the produce preserved was grown by family members in victory gardens or on farms. Thousands of movie theaters nationwide showed newsreels on home canning, and "Of Course I Can" posters appeared everywhere. Some counties and cities provided community canning centers where women could preserve their produce without having to buy expensive equipment. Many women enjoyed working together in a communal atmosphere, as opposed to the isolation of their own homes. In one newspaper account, a majority of housewives preferred centers because it was so much more pleasant to work with friends than to undertake the long, tedious job of peeling and preparing vegetables at home alone. A community cannery in Washington, D.C., asked that women donate one can or jar out of every ten to local charities. The government promoted this communal, even festive, atmosphere in the belief that a contented home-front army was a productive one.[5]

After World War II, most cities abandoned community gardens in favor of other land uses. There were a few notable exceptions to this trend. Boston's Fenway victory garden, originally planted on seven and a half acres of city property in 1942, was still operative in the late 1990s as some four hundred vegetable and flower gardens, whose gardeners reflected the diversity of the neighborhood's gay and senior-citizen communities. Chicago's Cornell Oasis was also gardened for over fifty years.[6]

Community Gardens, Economic Relief, and Urban Revitalization

Community gardens have also been used by the government for purposes of economic relief and urban revitalization. During the economic depression of the 1890s, about twenty cities provided the poor with garden allotments. For example, Detroit plowed four hundred acres of plots and provided seeds to more than nine hundred families. These poverty-relief programs lasted only about five to ten years, eventually supplanted by real-estate development and city beautification. During the Depression of the mid-1930s, the Works Progress Administration (WPA) sponsored relief gardens on vacant city lots for unemployed and poor people. New York City built five thousand gardens on seven hundred acres. In 1937, the federal government abandoned its relief garden program when the USDA initiated a food-stamp program for farm-surplus products.[7]

In the wake of environmental and antipoverty activism in the early 1970s, local governments and community activists partnered in creating community gardens to combat urban blight, poverty, and unemployment. By the mid-1970s, the beautification model of public gardens was challenged in Philadelphia, Boston, and New York City. In 1974, a horticulturist founded Philadelphia Green to promote reciprocity and self-help between horticulturalists and community gardeners. By 1994, Philadelphia Green had worked with low- and middle-income urban neighborhoods to create more than 2,000 community gardens. In Massachusetts, a 1974 law enabled urban gardeners and farmers to grow food rent free on vacant public land. By 1995, three thousand households had worked in Boston's 120 community garden projects. In the mid-1970s in New York City, a group of landscape professionals formed the Green Guerrillas to assist people who wanted to start gardens on vacant lots; by 1985 they had established over 1,000 gardens.[8]

The federal government got into the act in 1976, when the USDA began an urban gardening program in six cities to help low-income people grow and preserve vegetables. By 1993, that program had grown to include twenty-three cities where 200,000 urban gardeners produced an average of six dollars worth of vegetables for every dollar invested by the USDA. A fifteen-by-fifteen-foot plot, gardened intensively, yielded up to five hundred dollars worth of food over a growing season.[9] Often these programs could not be justified by the value of their agricultural output, since the monetary value of the land was much greater in most alternative urban uses. However, the social and civic benefits were seen as important enough to warrant continued public investment.

The American Community Gardening Association (ACGA) was formed in 1978 to promote community gardens in urban, suburban, and rural America as a tool for political organizing and community development. ACGA estimates that there were between 250 and 500 citywide community gardening programs in the United States in the late 1990s. The community garden movement drew supporters from the civil rights, women's liberation, environmental, and social justice movements. The unifying theme was a belief in the community-building power of gardens. As one advocate observed, community gardens are "the glue that holds a block together until long-term economic and social development can take place."[10]

Urban gardeners have had to make the case for the use of public land for horticulture, as opposed to lucrative real-estate development, much-needed low-income housing, or stress-reducing recreational and pastoral parks. By the 1990s, many urban planners had observed that when neighborhoods declined, so too did their parks, which often became dangerous and run-down places. Parks need people. When H. Patricia Hynes interviewed urban gardeners in Harlem, Chicago, San Francisco, and Philadelphia, she was struck by how often neighborhood activists had transformed abandoned parks into urban gardens, and how they loved the mutual give-and-take of working in gardens. They enjoyed being attached to a place through physical and social engagement. Community gardens created relationships between city dwellers and the soil and instilled an ethic of urban environmentalism that neither parks nor wilderness could provide. Community gardens were intimate: tiny "vest-pocket" sitting gardens, sidewalk tree-pit gardens, and vegetable and flower gardens; they brought the soothing yet enlivening power of nature to the actual neighborhoods where people lived.[11]

Hynes also noticed that the prime movers in the community gardening movement in inner cities were women, primarily women of color. This was the case in the Greening of Harlem, seventeen grassroots gardens built on land reclaimed from abandoned lots, parks, and playgrounds. In 1989, Bernadette Cozart, a city gardener, noticed a group of black and Latino children watching her as she removed pruning tools from her garden cart. She asked if they wanted to help, and they did but were unsure how to use the tools. This prompted her to think: "Their grandmothers grew gardens in Virginia, South Carolina, Alabama, and Puerto Rico; they kept fruit trees and put up food. But these kids didn't know how to use a shovel, loppers, or pruning saw!" So she asked them, "Where's your grandmother from? Tell me about her garden. Did she grow berries and make you pies? What did she put up for the winter?" Cozart used their stories about their grandmothers' gardens and orchards to teach the children about landscaping and gardening. She hired these nine fourteen-year-olds as gardeners to work under her supervision, on condition that they go back to school. Each was given a plot to attend, modeled after Cozart's childhood experience of tending her own school garden. Local residents hired the children to take care of their yards, and Cozart helped her student gardeners open savings accounts. When members of the park association complimented them, Cozart said that it was the only positive feedback that some of the children had ever received. "The gardens were esteem-boosters and stress-busters; they healed kids. A garden is a mini-world; making one and tending one enabled the kids to believe that they could accomplish other things elsewhere."[12]

Cozart began her efforts in Harlem with kitchen gardens—growing cherry tomatoes on fire escapes—to motivate neighborhoods to want larger gardens. She frequently heard parents say that they could not get their children to eat anything green until they grew their own. She organized women's canning projects, beginning with the grandmothers. They sponsored taste tests for the best salsa and chutneys and canned the best ones, which they sold in farmers' markets. They produced watermelon-rind jelly and even planted vineyards to make their own wine. Farmers dropped off materials by the truckload, and Home Depot donated tools. Community gardens were gathering points for plays, birthday parties, weddings, and other community events. Cozart attended one birthday party and noticed that "nothing at all was trampled, people were very careful about the plants, and the kids themselves picked up every piece of trash without being asked at the end." City officials had warned her that her projects would not be taken care of and would be vandalized; however, this was not the case. As one reporter praised Cozart's civic efforts: "There is no better security than a vigilant community, and the kids themselves make great enforcers. In neighborhoods where graffiti is everywhere, the gardens she's started are untouched, even inviting murals and signs are untouched. City park flowers vanish on Mother's day, [but] in one of her tulip gardens, not one flower had been touched at 5 p.m. last Mother's day. She always works with all interested persons in the local community on any project, to ensure the continued support of gardens."[13]

Women were also instrumental in creating Philadelphia's Norris Square Greene Countrie Towne, established in a neighborhood devastated by drugs and crime. Two women were leaders in developing Las Parcelas, a program centerpiece, with its "sixteen family vegetable plots; an orchard planted with peaches, pears, nectarines and grapes; *La Casita* (a small traditional Puerto Rican house built by neighbors); perennial and herb gardens; ornamental grasses; and a patio for cookouts." Most of the work was done by a group of ten women who called themselves *motivos*—ones who are motivated and who want to motivate others. They met weekly to discuss Puerto Rican history, watch films, and enjoy Latino food and music.[14]

In urban areas, neglected vacant lots are associated with significant hazards to community life: criminal behavior, trash, health risks, and frustration and despair among nearby residents. A 1998 study reported that more than one-fifth of all land in American cities was classified as vacant, and that the most universal problem cities faced in using vacant land was managing oddly shaped parcels in undesirable locations. Such parcels, of course, were ideal locations for gardens in areas in need of community building. Across the country, the development of urban community gardens has led to the beautification and greening of many neighborhoods and an enhanced sense of community cooperation. However, the permanence of urban gardens is always in question, given changes in market demand for vacant land (most famously in Manhattan), difficulties in obtaining access to resources, and concerns about legal liability.[15]

Reports from all across the country have documented that community gardening bolsters civil society by fostering collaboration among nearby residents across racial and generational lines. Unlike municipal parks, which have been developed in predominantly white, well-to-do neighborhoods, community gardens are often in racially mixed areas, where community is forged by a common interest in beautification, local food production, personal safety, health, or group projects. Income and educational differences are not barriers to participation. Gardening requires trust: mutually agreed-upon rules about working and reaping the benefits of common labor. Community gardens also provide local food production in areas with substandard grocery stores. As part of community food systems, they improve the quality of a community's diet and foster the social pleasures associated with food production. Since 1975, for example, Detroit's Farm-A-Lot program has used vacant lots to provide inexpensive, fresh produce to low-income communities.[16]

In a study of 178 community gardeners in Newark, New Jersey, respondents, mostly low-income African American women, reported benefits such as healthy food, substantial money saved, and the sense of community, friendship, and reaching out to others that came with community gardening. They noted, "Even people just passing felt like stopping and talking to gardeners," and "Over the garden, we know who our neighbors are."[17] A study of the Philadelphia Urban Gardening Program found that gardeners were more likely than control subjects to regard their neighbors as friendly and to participate in food-distribution projects, neighborhood cleanups, and neighborhood social events. A 1984 study of 197 participants in a master-gardener program found that though the program was intended to disseminate horticultural information, it had a serendipitous effect on community-development knowledge, skills, and experience.[18] A survey of community gardens in upstate New York found that many of them improved social cohesion, especially in low-income and minority neighborhoods.[19]

Denver Urban Gardens (DUG) spawned over seventy gardens in the Denver metropolitan area: places for senior citizens, for residents in a broken neighborhood, and for young and old to get together. Many gardens were in the city's toughest neighborhoods, providing a much needed space for "the sharing of interests, a listening ear, a sense of safety, a place of pride." Community gardeners have assumed collective responsibility for improving their neighborhoods, boosting civic pride in their surroundings, and growing fresh, organic food close to home. DUG gardens host educational programs for over twenty thousand individuals annually.[20]

In Cleveland's Summer Sprout Program, neighbors and community leaders have worked together to reclaim vacant lots, church grounds, and school tracts, and to organize community gardens covering some thirty acres and yielding a harvest worth nearly $1 million annually. At one school, one hundred gardeners planted seeds to harvest food for themselves, with two tons of fresh produce left over to share with needy neighbors at hunger centers. Neighbors at a public housing project put aside their fears of theft and vandalism and sowed seeds in the garden in one of the large commons areas. All around the city, almost two hundred sites are gardened with the assistance of church groups, Master Gardeners, the Cleveland Botanical Garden, juvenile court, Safe Space, Growing Together Organically, and the Women's Pre-Release Center.[21]

As part of the Garden Angel program, community gardeners in Huntsville, Alabama, and Portland, Maine, provide fresh vegetables to elderly and homebound residents, who need social connection as well as food. Most people served by the program love gardening: they had gardened during the Depression and greeted the community gardeners with the question, "How's your garden doing?" Volunteers help elderly clients plant vegetables and make weekly visits to keep their gardens maintained. Gardening keeps the elderly interested in life and others and forges intergenerational friendships. As one forty-year-old Portland participant remarked, "When Mary and I work together, we open up and converse at a different level than we might if we were meeting at an exhibit opening in a gallery or somewhere else. Being a garden angel is about relationships. It's about community building and intergenerational connection." Another garden angel enjoyed working with her eighty-year-old partner. "We've connected in a woman-to-woman way. We haven't gotten into politics yet and maybe we won't, but it's been like neighbor-to-neighbor. It's very comfortable." One eighty-seven-year-old woman in rural Alabama was effusive. "We've laughed and we've talked, and there's hardly been a time we haven't cried. It's been good to keep me busy." She had planted enough in her garden to share with neighbors and credited the program with giving her back her ability to share.[22]

Rural gardens are also locations of community building. In his comprehensive study of African American gardens in the rural South, Richard Westmacott notes that gatherings of family and friends in the yard were symbolic of commitment to family and community. Some of these gatherings were for foodwork, such as hog killing and cane grinding. Produce from the vegetable garden was shared with friends.

> The yard and the shaded, decorated seating areas within it, visible from the road, were gestures of welcome, invitations to stop and visit. Even gardeners who rarely took time to stop and sit down themselves made carefully arranged seats visible to the passer-by. The floral displays in the yard and in containers around the porch and other seating areas were also gestures of welcome. The mention by several gardeners that, in spite of their heavy workload, their parents had grown flowers suggests that the yard was seen as a demonstration that despite other pressures, time was made to create a peaceful, beautiful sanctuary.[23]

The goal of some community gardening ventures is to provide job training for low-income citizens. San Francisco's Neighborhood Green Program prepares residents of the city's poorest neighborhoods for careers in horticulture. Most students have been unemployed or held minimum-wage jobs. They work full time at wages above the minimum wage to learn about horticulture and to spruce up their own neighborhoods. One participant admitted that, before the program, he had not paid much attention to the trees in his neighborhood, but he came to view them with awe. "It's life," he said. "It's opened my eyes to so much. I drive around my neighborhood now and see things in a whole new way. I'm surprised by how much I like gardening." Students learn by doing, renovating playgrounds, parks, and roadway medians. They proudly recount adventures pulling rotting stumps from playgrounds, rebuilding crumbling brick walkways, and nurturing new shrubs and plants. "It's a great feeling, even doing something like cleaning glass out of the sandbox," said another participant. "It makes you proud to plant something and see it grow." The in-class curriculum includes botany, biology, ecology, and irrigation techniques. Students find the program demanding but rewarding: "At the end of the day, it's like, 'Damn! I'm tired'" said one. "But it's rewarding to drive home, see a tree and know what it is."[24]

Immigration and Community Gardens

Newly arrived immigrants, many of whom have been farmers in their native countries, discover that working the soil in their new neighborhoods is a powerful way to connect their past and present. Indeed, the language of immigration is that of gardening: emigrants are "uprooted" from their homeland, migrants are "rootless," and immigrants are "transplanted" people in need of setting down new roots. As an example, in Chicago's community gardens, a Jamaican American man wielded a scythe to prepare his plot to grow callaloo (a spinachlike green vegetable); a Polish American woman had imported seeds from her homeland to grow flowers for the church altar; and Cambodian refugees saw their gardens as symbols of abundance and freedom after persecution and war. A fig tree was ritualistically buried each winter and resurrected each spring by a group of Italian American men, who celebrated the custom with a glass of wine made from grapes they had grown. "We love to garden the food of our country," one said. "It makes it feel like home. It is home."[25]

New York City's community gardens read like an anthropological history of the city's immigrants. The initial gardeners were southerners who had grown up on farms, followed by Caribbean peoples, and then by Latinos. Beginning in 1973, Green Guerillas has worked with thousands of people to turn abandoned lots into some seven hundred community gardens. The organization claims that neighborhoods with community gardens tend to have lower crime rates than those that do not, since gardeners serve as extra eyes and ears on the streets. Community gardens provide safe havens for children, parents, and grandparents in low- and moderate-income neighborhoods, and food for many families in soup kitchens and food distribution centers.[26] Since 1978, New York City's Green Thumb has supported over six hundred member gardens serving twenty thousand city residents. Its gardens are managed by neighborhood residents and offer educational workshops, children's programs, food pantries, and block parties.[27] At one Green Thumb community garden in the Bronx, room was made for each new group of immigrants. In talking with neighbors in the garden, some newcomers realized they were being gouged in rent payments. The garden's community association worked to help them get their landlord to lower the rent.[28] In a 1997 survey of New York City's community gardens, the most commonly reported uses were friends meeting place (78%), neighborhood gatherings (69%), nature education (57%), recycling/composting (54%), parties (42%), board games (23%), and art classes, playground, performance space (22%).[29]

In Sacramento, California, dozens of community gardens sprang up in the 1980s and 1990s, largely to serve the sizable population of Southeast Asian refugees who had immigrated to the area. In a ten-acre community garden, one Hmong refugee grew cabbage, peppers, basil, and onions. The thirty-seven-year-old mother of six had grown up on a farm in Laos and now lived in an apartment. "We want to eat fresh food," she said. "That's why we come here. We don't put chemicals on it. We just put water on it and it grows. It's healthier." Another garden was planted on vacant county land. "It's neat because it has really brought the community together," said one neighbor. Before the garden, she said, "We only knew the people who were right next door. . . . Now you see people walking by and you say, 'Hey Bob, Sue, how are your tomatoes?'" Neighbors said that working in the garden was the best form of neighborhood watch they ever had. Even the developer of a local upscale housing subdivision incorporated a community garden into its plan.[30]

The city of San Jose, California, helped fund an intricate system of community and cultural gardens, created by the local Japanese American, Chinese American, Mexican American, and Filipino American communities. At the Chinese Cultural Garden, home to tai chi classes, one of its founders "was aglow when she described how children in the summer months spend a lot of time in the Chinese Cultural Garden and tell others that it is their park even when they have no Chinese background." She said that she gardened both to relax and to connect with others, adding: "Each part of the garden can have a message which is universal, especially when you go beneath surface appearances." Weekly garden barbecues were held at the Mexican American "Mi Tierra." In the Filipino American garden, seniors mentored high school dropouts, and they cultivated plants to enhance their sexual energy.[31]

In Holyoke, Massachusetts, Nuestras Raices (Our Roots) is a grassroots organization that has revitalized neighborhoods through gardening. In the 1970s, it cleaned up a run-down area of the city and planted an urban garden. About one-third of the local population were Puerto Rican immigrants, many of whom had worked as migrant farmers in the region. Many of these immigrants tended the garden, which provided organically grown fruits and vegetables and gave a sense of hope to a community that felt abandoned by the city's political leaders. By 2001, Nuestras Raices' Centro Agriculo had a café/restaurant, a bilingual library with agricultural and environmental resources, a meeting space for workshops on organic farming techniques, a community kitchen for people from the neighborhood to prepare and can Hispanic foods to bring to market, and a space for residents to run small catering businesses from the center. In its greenhouse, youth and elders work together to cultivate over five thousand seedlings: peppers, tomatoes, eggplants, and native Puerto Rican crops such as *ajices dulces* and *culantro*. The organization manages five large community gardens, with ninety-five families participating, and a youth garden in urban sections of Holyoke. A group of local children have formed Protectores de la Tierra (Protectors of the Earth) to work together to clean up the community, to learn gardening from their elders and teach it to other children, to take field trips, and to receive weekly help with their schoolwork.[32]

Both immigrant and nonimmigrant populations reap a wide range of individual and community benefits from community gardens: greater consumption of fresh vegetables; enhanced psychological and social well-being; cheaper food; the experience of sharing food with neighbors and the needy; decreased vandalism; increased neighborhood involvement in music, theater, and storytelling; and crime reduction. Community gardens continue to grow in popularity: in 1996 there were some six thousand community gardens in the United States; about two-thirds were urban, 16 percent were in public housing, and about 8 percent were school gardens.[33] The nation's largest municipally run urban gardening program was in Seattle, with forty-two sites, five thousand gardeners, and hundreds on the waiting list. In 2000, its

Interbay P-Patch garden donated more than five thousand pounds of organic produce to local food banks.[34]

The civic scope of community gardens is far reaching, as illustrated by the 2001 Seeds of Hope award winners. Seeds of Hope is a program that honors America's top volunteer-run community gardens. Winning gardens were located in eight cities: New York City (where in the aftermath of the September 11 attacks, exhausted city police and firefighters often visited these gardens to regain their strength); Detroit, Michigan (where over three hundred seniors grew food for the hungry and taught youth about community involvement); Portland, Oregon (where low-income children grew food for needy neighbors and a local domestic violence shelter); Chicago, Illinois (where crime disappeared from a former drug haven); Washington, D.C. (where seventy-five students designed and tended the garden on a former vacant lot); Houston, Texas (where at-risk youth used gardening to learn life skills); New Orleans, Louisiana (where children grew vegetables with seniors on a formerly crime-ridden lot); and Cedar Rapids, Iowa (where political refugees from war-torn areas such as Somalia and Sierra Leone transformed the garden from a burned-out, drug-riddled arson site).[35]

Youth Gardens

Many local governments and nonprofit agencies have established youth gardens to provide at-risk children with a sense of purpose and community. Nineteenth-century centers for troubled children typically included a common garden to grow plants for residents' meals. For example, the Children's Aid Society in Ohio's Cuyahoga County has had a gardening program since its inception in 1832. Originally established to supply the center's kitchen with food, by the 1990s the garden provided therapeutic activities for the children, who sold their produce to the kitchen. Garden plots afforded the children a sense of ownership, control, responsibility, and generosity in sharing produce and bouquets of flowers. High-energy children had a focus. Teachers reported fewer discipline problems during gardening season. Experiencing the life cycles of plants and insects and the change of seasons gave the children a much-needed sense of predictability in their lives. The garden occasioned connections with their kin: "Grandmother grew peonies," "Daddy enjoyed tending tomatoes."[36]

Boston's Food Project has brought together thousands of youths and adults to grow organic vegetables for homeless shelters and farmers' markets. According to a project director, the program not only keeps kids busy and off the streets during the summer, it also teaches them leadership, investment in their community, and community service. Each summer sixty Boston teens work on a twenty-one-acre farm. As one youth described what he learned, "On this farm we create a better life for the living. In order to do that effectively we have to have a friendly, caring, peaceful environment, that way as the plants grow, we grow, we learn, we produce." Participants sell their produce at farmers' markets, prepare lunches at shelters and soup kitchens, and host community lunches. Young people work in the kitchen alongside well-known Boston chefs, who teach them culinary skills. Their meals feed nearly one hundred people, including community members, neighbors, media, funders, staff, policy makers, and business leaders. These lunches were described by a program director as "an opportunity to build community through food and the youth are encouraged to practice conversation skills with their guests."[37]

Berkeley Youth Alternatives, a nonprofit community-based organization, runs two programs for teens: a youth-employment landscape program and the Garden Patch, created on a half-acre lot with an abandoned railroad right-of-way. Many teen gardeners, who had previously eaten up to three meals a day at fast-food restaurants, have discovered a whole new world of food. Indeed, arugula, a spicy lettuce, has become a badge of maturity for experienced gardeners to pick and eat in front of newcomers. The teens have toured Chez Panisse, where they ate arugula pizza. The Garden Patch provides arugula and radishes to the restaurant. Both the landscape crews and the youth gardeners work with younger children in after-school programs. The Garden Patch is a community focal point where teens are the center of attention. Passersby comment on their gardens and give advice. At the Harvest Faire, teen gardeners proudly show the fruits of their labor to the community. They enjoy teamwork, having a safe place to go after school and on weekends, and relating to adults on their own terms at the farmers' market where they sell their produce. The Garden Patch serves as a neighborhood commons: locals of all ages meet, interact, and discuss cultural traditions at risk of extinction. The grandparents of many of these teens had cultivated gardens before migrating from the South during World War II. Due to a shortage of housing in the East Bay area in the 1940s, many of the teens' parents grew up in public housing without gardens. Professional communities also contribute to these programs, with students from the University of California at Berkeley's planning and business schools helping with program administration and market strategies for produce.[38]

Children pitch in at the Peace Garden, a large plot in a predominantly

Hispanic neighborhood of Denver. A project of Denver Urban Gardens (DUG), it includes an Aztec ball court, places for dances, graffiti art, murals, and memorial tiles for youths killed by gang violence. In the view of a DUG coordinator, "For many youngsters involved in the garden, creating and maintaining compost piles has provided a rare sense of order in their lives. The children soon grow to delight in tending their heaping piles of compost. They learned to use 'trash' to create fertile soil. They came to appreciate the slow process of nurturing and caring for something, and taking pride in completing a task."[39]

School Gardens

Children are also the center of attention at school gardens. The first school garden in the United States opened in Boston in 1891. Throughout the early twentieth century, proponents of the nature-study movement set up children's garden programs in many cities. Their goal was to replace book learning with observational learning and hands-on experimentation. Advocates also saw gardening as a way to address concerns about new child-labor laws and mandatory school attendance. Child labor in gardens and the sale of their produce were considered more acceptable than child labor in factories. Manuals on children's gardening mentioned precision and efficiency through drill-like activities. Gardening promoted the work ethic, and it was considered an especially useful means to teach good social behavior to immigrants, delinquents, and the infirm. Civic and women's organizations often provided the initial funding and volunteer labor for these programs. The U.S. Bureau of Education established a Division of Home and School Gardening, which promoted children's gardens nationally from 1914 to 1920. Most programs were extracurricular and occurred during nonschool hours. Eventually, the school-garden movement and the Bureau of Education focused on home gardens because of limited space on school grounds and a concern for neighborhood beautification.[40]

Interest in school gardens resurfaced nationwide in the 1970s and 1980s in the wake of the environmental movement, with California leading the way. In 1995, the California state superintendent of public instruction launched the Garden in Every School initiative, with the rationale that "students who participate in school garden projects also discover fresh food and make healthier food choices, and develop a deeper appreciation for the environment, the community, and each other." Students would increase their consumption of healthy fruits and vegetables if they came from their own gardens. Furthermore, "school garden projects nurture community spirit, common purpose, and cultural appreciation by building bridges among students, school staff, families, local businesses, and organizations."[41]

Between 1995 and 2000, the number of school gardens in California doubled, to around two thousand (out of eight thousand total schools). Most gardens are in elementary and middle schools, with just over one hundred in high schools. Elementary school gardens take advantage of young children's curiosity about insects, dirt, tools, and growing things. At one elementary school in Berkeley, when the garden coordinator asked kindergartners at the beginning of each year where their food came from, they replied, "From a truck," "From the freezer," and "From underneath Safeway." These children quickly learned differently after playing in the garden, where they became fascinated with roly-poly bugs, ladybugs sleeping on sunflowers, and the joy of digging with their miniature shovels.[42]

Reaching middle and high school students is a greater challenge. For preteens and teens, getting dirt on expensive sneakers is not cool, and insects have lost their allure. Teachers use gardens to demonstrate principles of science, math, nutrition, language arts, and history. In San Francisco Bay–area high schools, chemistry students have applied the periodic table to their cultivation of sunflowers, cucumbers, and peppers. "Nitrogen, potassium, and phosphorus," repeated one student walking from the garden to her next class. "They keep plants alive." Environmental-science students work in the gardens each spring, thinking about pest management without pesticides, plant physiology, and the ecology of composting. Students learn about migration and habitats by building a habitat for monarch butterflies that migrate over their school. First-time teen gardeners at a San Francisco high school became protective of the plants they nurtured daily on the school roof. "It's like this is our family and we've got to take care of them," said a fifteen-year-old.[43]

One purpose of school gardens is to foster cooperative approaches to counter the competitive pressures of the classroom. This possible outcome is the hope of David Hawkins, a garden manager of the Edible Schoolyard at Berkeley's Martin Luther King Jr. Middle School. At the end of each garden class, students gather in a straw-bale circle and talk about the day's experiences. One day, a boy admitted that he had not worked hard, and students snickered. Hawkins told them that sometimes people did not work hard on a particular day, but that every week in the garden was a new week—the boy could start fresh anytime he chose. "For a moment the boy sat reflecting, perhaps a little confused. Then to my surprise, he came across the circle to shake my hand, smiling broadly. One of the wonderful things about the garden is that students have the chance of starting over and experiencing success. Unlike their academic classes, they are not hampered by their lack of experience or previous learning."[44]

Hawkins contrasts the schools' concept-based model of learning with the experiential learning "by osmosis" of gardening and cooking—"young people were just there with their bodies alongside the adults who transmitted the skills and sensibilities." He notes that adolescents crave respectful relationships with adults, and the garden is a wonderful context for healthy interaction. When a reporter asked one boy who had participated in a summer garden program what he considered the best thing about being in the garden, the boy replied, "It was the way the adults treated us." The boy had summed up what was also most important about the Edible Schoolyard to Hawkins, who remarked: "It is easy to fail to recognize how much adolescents need us because of all the hype and fears about youth culture. If we abandon our youth, the consumer culture will not."[45]

Hawkins thinks that one of the best ways to find out what students are learning is to eavesdrop when they give tours to visitors. It turns out that many who seem only marginally interested in the garden have actually learned a lot. He remembers one boy who came every day to a summer program but would not do any gardening.

> He hung out with the others who were making and planting their own beds, but despite all the cajolery and encouragement he did not plant a single thing. Toward the end of the summer it seemed that the garden had failed to appeal to him. One day his mother came down to thank the staff. Her son had been transformed she said. He no longer watched television and played video games all evening. Instead he wove long stories recounting everything that had happened in the garden and described in detail the plants and every little bit of information anyone mentioned about them. The garden, she said, had totally captured his imagination.[46]

The Edible Schoolyard's kitchen manager, Esther Cook, wants to change the way students perceive food, from isolated, quick-action fuel to something shared at meals with conversation and community. "I live near Oakland High School, where I see kids having a liter of Coke and a bag of Doritos for breakfast. They're getting food at a gas station. Everything is so lonely in that scenario for me." Remembering her childhood growing up on a large family farm in New England, she starts each school year "teaching students to be part of a group and to enjoy meals and conversation in a communal setting." Some students have not yet learned how to pass food at the table. She focuses on "how to take care of yourself and how to take care of others, how to feel that you have enough, that you can be generous and not locked into a life because of your background, or your neighborhood, or what your parents do." Cook observes, "There has to be a level of equity."[47]

When students grind grain into flour, churn butter, and press tortillas, Cook finds that their sense of instant gratification is challenged. She has also used food as a window to new cultures. For example, students studying India have made chapati, whole-wheat flat bread, as they learned about concepts of Indian culture such as wholeness, the sacredness of food, and the absence of waste. "The introduction of *ghee* (clarified butter) and its many uses, not only as food, but as lamp oil, a religious offering, and lotion for softening skin, prompted a discussion on the roles of food in different cultures." Students have also baked bread honoring the spirit of a departed friend or relative for a Day of the Dead altar. Cook describes the significance of this ritual: "The altar had many daily visitors as students stopped in to see what had been added the previous day, or to show a friend the remembrance that they had written. In a school where nearly every student has experienced a personal loss through death (many due to violence), this lesson provided a structured and safe process to deal with these enormous issues. It also had the added benefit of tapping into the expertise and enthusiasm of the Mexican students as we sought their guidance and knowledge." Students read cookbooks to identify and sample staple foods from around the world and to relate them to geography and climate. Cook is convinced that children benefit from sensory learning whose memories remain long after formal lessons are forgotten.[48]

In the Edible Schoolyard's kitchen classroom, about three hundred students a week—boys and girls—work together to transform the garden's harvest into sit-down meals. Classes begin with a lecture/demonstration, followed by "food preparation, setting the table (always with a table cloth and flowers), sharing of food and conversation, and class clean-up." Students practice the principles of ecology: reuse, recycle, and compost. The kitchen goals are "to foster an appreciation of organic produce which is locally grown and eaten in season through experiential learning and using the senses; to teach basic kitchen skills; to gather at the table to savor the beauty of our work and to enjoy conversation; and to create a sense of community through reconnecting with the earth and caring for our environment."[49]

Even Mr. Rogers got into the act. During the taping of *Mr. Rogers' Neighborhood* at the Edible Schoolyard garden in 1999, he observed, "I'm hoping

Edible Schoolyard Kitchen. At the kitchen of the Edible Schoolyard at the Martin Luther King Jr. Middle School in Berkeley, California, students prepare the organic food that they have grown and harvested. They also set the table and share meals and conversation. Courtesy of The Edible Schoolyard, Martin Luther King Jr. Middle School, Berkeley, California.

to show children, and we have many children from the inner city who watch, that they can grow what they eat. This is a very healthy enterprise. It teaches respect for the land, and it shows what fun these children have."[50]

In Santa Fe, New Mexico, a restaurant owner launched Cooking with Kids to help children take control of their diets by making their own food that reflects their cultural heritage. At an elementary school garden and orchard, students bake bread and *empañaditas* (turnovers stuffed with vegetables and meat) in their own *horno* (outdoor oven). The local school system has altered its school lunch program to include more locally grown and locally made foods in close partnership with the students and their families.[51]

When a bus garage was demolished next to a junior high school in New York City, teachers and administrators worked with a nonprofit organization to develop a garden on the site. Through volunteer workdays and fundraising, they designed and developed the garden, where they held regular science, language, math, and art classes. "Students, staff and volunteers designed and built a compost-heated greenhouse, a fish and turtle pond, a solar-powered waterfall, murals, grape arbors, tree mounds with evergreen and fruit trees, intensive organic vegetable beds, herb gardens, organic lawns, and bird and butterfly habitats. The project has become a model of community and student design, and is used for city-wide teacher workshops."[52]

The San Francisco League of Urban Gardeners (SLUG) has incorporated school gardens into a comprehensive program of coordinating over one hundred community gardens at public buildings, senior and community centers, and schools throughout the city. Its school programs include field trips, in-class presentations, and technical assistance for in-school gardens for thousands of city school children. Over ten thousand visitors a year tour its public demonstration garden, Garden for the Environment. SLUG helps low-income communities develop small businesses, such as Urban Herbals, which produce organic jams and vinegar with ingredients grown by SLUG youth and local farmers. Urban Herbals has successfully trained young adults in sales throughout San Francisco Bay–area stores. SLUG's youth programs offer employment, education, and personal support to low-income youth and young adults. Its Youth in Gardening Internship, Woodside Landscape Internship, Green Team, and Horticulture and Landscape programs take place in public-housing communities, Juvenile Hall, and Golden Gate Park.[53]

In the 1990s, San Antonio, Texas, was dubbed the "Youth Garden Capital of America." The school district, in partnership with a master-gardener program, set out to establish eight new gardens every fall in inner-city schools. By 1995, over ten thousand students were involved in school gardens, and three hundred community volunteers contribute more than 21,000 hours of community service each year gardening with the children. One veteran master gardener has logged some 600 hours of community service a year teaching children herbology, nutrition, and social studies through gardening. The Brains and Grains Garden produces six types of grain to introduce children to ancient civilizations. The Dietcise Garden includes a nutritional and medicinal guide to vegetables. And the Melting Pot Garden grows foods from San Antonio's Hispanic, Native American, Asian, and African American communities, along with a study unit on the cultural and geographic origins of garden vegetables.[54]

At North Hollywood High School in California, one student saw gardening as a welcome respite from the pressures of school. "You get a different energy here," she said of the school garden. "In other parts of campus, out in the schoolyard, there's a lot of pressure and negative vibes, but here it's peaceful." She planned to garden when she had children, even if she lived in an urban area. "There's very few places in the city where you can grow stuff," she commented. She was enrolled in a naturalist academy funded by a state grant and founded by one of the high school's teachers. Upon completion of the four-year horticultural program, students receive an additional title of "naturalist" on their diplomas. The teacher hoped to expand the program to include a community garden for nearby residents, who would grow organic food and donate half the produce to local charities. A committee of residents would set up the rules for use of the garden. He saw gardening as a bridge between local residents and students, who could learn life lessons from the adults.[55]

Although school gardens encourage stewardship among students, parents, and the neighboring community, they present challenges to teachers, who face increased pressure to cover a set curriculum and prepare students for standardized tests. Some teachers view gardens as simply more work. Controlling thirty children outside the classroom requires new rules. There are also problems regarding funding, vandalism, and resource cutbacks in arts, sports, and music. Why should gardens take precedence over these other important subjects? Proponents agree that three elements are crucial to the success of school gardens: administrative support, integration of garden activities into the standard curriculum, and funding independent of the school district's budget. In 2002, the National Gardening Organization's Web site had a directory of 1,400 schoolyard gardens, curriculum and fundraising ideas, and information on its grant program.[56]

Of course, gardening is not uniformly attractive to all children. As Karen Payne, program director of the American Community Gardening Association, observes, some kids love to garden and others cannot stand it—just like adults. From her work with From the Roots Up, a mentorship program for new community gardens, she has learned that significant social and cultural meanings are attached to gardening and agriculture, which have an impact on people's working the soil. Differences are related to a child's race, culture, and class—as well as to children's individual personalities and experiences. Age also makes a difference: Many preschool and elementary school children think the garden is fun. During middle school, clothes, status, and pressures of conformity overpower the fun of getting dirty. Some teens do not want to get their expensive sneakers dirty, and they think that gardening is stupid: low status, low tech, low paying, and irrelevant. Gardening also goes against the dominant cultural values of speed, efficiency, and convenience. Payne observes that in this age of technology and speed, it is important to offer students compelling reasons to value traditional practices such as gardening and cooking.[57]

Some parents think that a gardening curriculum takes time away from academic subjects, and others complain that gardening is exactly the kind of backbreaking toil they hope their children will escape by getting an education. Given the history of slavery, sharecropping, and farm labor in the United States, some African American parents resist mandatory school garden programs. One day, Payne saw a white teacher instruct an African American boy who hated gardening to pull weeds. Just then, two girls walked by and taunted him: "Slave." Payne emphasizes the importance of directly confronting the painful legacies of slavery and other oppressive forms of farm labor as part of children's education. At the same time, she observes that countless African American youth who at first hated dirt eventually became proud of what they grew and appreciated the positive aspects of their agricultural past. Her views were seconded by the founder of Strong Roots, a gardening program primarily for African American youth, who sought to reconnect African Americans with their lost agricultural heritage: growing nutritional, traditional food crops, such as sweet potatoes, peanuts, and many types of greens; honoring and connecting with ancestors and elders who offer a positive perspective on agricultural knowledge; and owning land as a method of economic power and self-sufficiency.[58]

Jail Gardens

A sense of community and new kinds of civic ties are also created in jail gardens. San Francisco County Jail's Horticulture Project is one of the best known in the country. When counselor Catherine Sneed began the project, some jail administrators warned her that the prisoners would hurt her or try to escape. These fears turned out to be unwarranted. Since 1982, thousands of men and women have worked on the ten-acre farm, harvesting tens of thousands of crates of potatoes, corn, spinach, beets, Russian kale, mustard greens, beans, herbs, and flowers—much of it donated to the homeless and to AIDS patients. It is not uncommon for inmates to have previously eaten at the same soup kitchens that use the jail garden's produce. Many inmates have said that they are motivated to help others ("It gives you motivation. Every time we're picking something and putting it into a crate, we know where it's going and that it's gonna help somebody") and to provide restitution to society ("We took a lot out of our community and this is a way of giving back to our community by growing produce for them. We grow the best and give the best to the people"). Others speak of a self-transformation enabling them to connect with others in new ways. As one greenhouse worker remarked,

"What I am doing is feeding myself with love of plants. I never knew I had these feelings inside of me, now I do. Being here, working in the greenhouse is gonna help people. You gotta work with people you never seen before and don't know how they think."[59]

As mentioned earlier, Sneed was dismayed at how many of her students went back on the streets when they left jail—most had no other place to go. So she worked with the owners of a commercial bakery in Bayview Hunter's Point, a low-income neighborhood where many of the county jail inmates resided, to set up a program for horticulture students leaving the county jail. At the half-acre Garden Project, which opened in 1991, students divide their twenty-hour workweek between community-service projects and working in the market garden. Together, the garden and the bakery symbolize Sneed's long-term vision of partnership between income-generating gardens, orchards, and tree nurseries, on the one side, and local businesses, restaurants, and markets, on the other. Within a year, a crew of ten from the Garden Project had formed the Tree Corps, a nonprofit organization established by Sneed and the sheriff's department to contract with the City of San Francisco to plant trees in low-income neighborhoods. One woman who had been in the Tree Corps from its inception said that the program had changed her life: getting her off the street selling drugs, enabling her to pay for Catholic school tuition for her granddaughter—something she did not do for her own children—and motivating her to work as a drug counselor when she became too old to plant trees.[60]

San Francisco jail officials have noted the positive results from garden projects. Lieutenant Robert Limacher, who oversaw the day-to-day operations at the jail and its garden in 1994, was initially skeptical about the garden, but eventually recognized differences between students in the garden project and other inmates: "They don't have the institutionalized jail mind," he said. "They develop more self-awareness and are more willing to hold themselves accountable for what they did and what they don't want to repeat." Most county jail inmates have been incarcerated for misdemeanor offenses, usually drug related. Limacher thought that horticulture was the most humanistic of the jail's programs, more so than Alcoholics Anonymous, drug recovery efforts, and cultural group sessions. He praised the project's many salutary effects on inmates: getting outside in the fresh air everyday, being trusted by the garden staff, learning powerful metaphors (such as "organic gardening is like a chemical-free body and a cleaning of the mind"), and experiencing "the clean feeling of self-respect" derived from donating their produce to the needy, as opposed to providing free labor to the jails. Sheriff Michael

Hennessey was convinced that the garden programs motivate people, build their self-esteem, and save them from turning back to crime on the streets. The jail manager observed that the Horticulture Project had an immediate effect on new inmates. "People come in here with their hands in their pockets, looking down, full of attitude." Once they start working in the garden, "they're clear-eyed, they're saying hello every morning to the staff and the counselors and to each other. It's really very amazing."[61]

A few years after the Garden Project began, Sheriff Hennessey ordered a study to see what effect, if any, the program had on recidivism rates. For three years the jail tracked three hundred former inmates. Within four months of their release, 29 percent of all those released had been arrested again, but only 6 percent of Garden Project workers had. After two years, the numbers were 55 percent for the general jail population and 24 percent for garden program participants.[62] After four years, the recidivism rate for the Garden Project was only 27 percent, as compared to a two-thirds recidivism rate for the California prison population.[63]

Another positive civic effect of the Garden Project is building bridges between the police and ex-convicts in the community. When the police department opened up a new station right next to the Garden Project, the precinct captain recalled when Sneed and her gardeners came to a community meeting.

> One by one they got up and spoke about how proud they were of what they did in the garden and how they were being nurtured as they nurtured the plants and pulling out the bad weeds in themselves while weeding the garden. The audience was practically in tears. This was a brand new station and the grounds were just a mess. So they got to work here. And the guys are always bringing in flowers and vegetables for us. The interaction is just tremendous. There were guys who were very uncomfortable around police, and the officers thought of them as bad people. Instead, now we see the best coming out of human nature here.[64]

A reporter who visited the police station was stunned by the sight of an ex-bank robber with years of incarceration behind him, carefully weeding a garden he and other former inmates had planted at the police station and being cheerfully hailed by police as they climbed into their patrol cars. Every Halloween, a team of ex-cons and police officers visit schools in low-income neighborhoods and give away twenty thousand pumpkins—half of them grown by participants. Sneed notes that the children jump up and down and hug the police, in spite of their having grown up mistrusting them. She loves seeing "the cops and the crooks and [everyone] working side by side, throwing pumpkins like footballs to each other" and jokes that the cycle of crime could be stopped with pumpkins.[65]

Sneed is convinced that gardening produces positive changes among the inmates and their communities. "They didn't fight with each other, they were cooperative, every morning they were ready to go. They were into it—which is not usually the case with people in prison."[66] When they plant trees, it bolsters neighborhood cohesion: "People know that this tree in the ground means that their uncle, or brother, or sister has a job and so they protect the tree, whereas before they often cut it down." Gardening even sparks a love of learning among inmates. "They want to be able to read the bean packets, to know why the beans are growing. You should see me teach a roomful of women in jail for prostitution the concept of asexual plant reproduction."[67]

Sneed also regards the gardens as a corrective to the poor eating habits of inmates. In growing food for others, inmates begin to learn, often for the first time, about their own health. Over the years, she has asked them about their eating practices at the time they were arrested. When the poor get money, they often take their children to McDonald's as a source of pride. She sees more and more people who are not eating or cooking food at home. Having talked with thousands of prisoners over the years, she has concluded that their eating habits contribute to their drug use. They do not eat fresh vegetables, and the corner store is a liquor store. "When my mother was feeding fourteen children, she'd make huge pots of chili, beans and rice, string beans with a little ham, potatoes. Unfortunately, African Americans aren't getting this vegetable-based diet anymore. There's a connection between communities with high crime, violence and drug addiction and the people's diets."[68]

Another civic aspect of Sneed's garden programs is mending the tattered relations between inmates and neighborhood seniors, many of whom have been crime victims. She invites seniors to pick vegetables from the inmates' gardens and watch "the same people who might have been on the corner trying to take their purses, or knock them out and rob them. They see that the same people are now giving back and trying to help. That changes something for them. The prisoners begin to see and feel badly about what they have done to support their habit. The garden does that, growing this food does that. The garden also offers a place for parents. Most people who are in jail or prison are parents."[69]

Other jail garden projects report similarly positive contributions to a sense of community. In Illinois, some two hundred inmates of the Cook County Sheriff's Office prerelease center tend a jail garden as part of a program to rehabilitate nonviolent drug offenders while providing food for Chicago's poor and homeless. The garden was first planted in 1993 under the guidance of the University of Illinois Extension Urban Gardening Program, whose staff provided weekly technical assistance to the gardeners. According to a program official, the fact that the garden feeds hungry people motivates many of the inmates. "I've had some of the gardeners say to me that the main reason they're involved in this project is because they are helping hungry children. They tell me they'll put up with the bugs and the hard work as long as they're helping the babies and the kids."[70]

The coordinator of the horticultural program at the Patuxent Institution in Jessup, Maryland, observes that many inmates have substance abuse problems, have suffered from physical or sexual abuse, or have a long history of poor impulse control or anger management. "Most of them have such a warped perception of what a human connection is, and I think they get a great opportunity (by gardening) to really appreciate and respect themselves and other human beings." They give back to the community by working on community beautification projects in Baltimore, raising tree seedlings for the Department of Natural Resources, and donating plants to nursing homes and schools.[71]

Even one of the nation's largest and most desolate jail complexes—New York's Rikers Island—had its Greenhouse Project, which was run by the Horticultural Society of New York. Between 1993 and 1999, some 265 prisoners tended grapevines and herb gardens on a one-and-one-half-acre plot. They planted one garden solely to attract birds and butterflies. Inmates praised the ease they felt in the greenhouse and the sense of purpose their work gave them. "It makes you feel like you're more free," said a twenty-one-year old from the Bronx. "You can't be upset when you come in here. . . . You can't help but smile."[72] Elsewhere in New York, in 1999, the Medina County Jail became the third county jail in the state to plant flower and vegetable gardens. To launch the project, a local attorney donated his time and tractor, and a farm neighbor provided fertilizer.[73]

At the maximum-security prison in Graterford, Pennsylvania, nearly every inch of available soil is cultivated with flowers and vegetables. Each evening about three hundred inmates tend their gardens instead of playing cards or watching television. In response to a proposal from one of the inmates, a master gardener from Pennsylvania State gathered volunteers and materials to start the program in 1991.[74]

One inmate at the Chittenden County Correctional Center in Vermont initially scoffed at a garden project as "women's work." Within a year, he and six other inmates had tilled three and one-half acres, producing vegetables for the facility's prison, other penal institutions around the state, and a senior citizen's apartment building. One elderly person sent a note of appreciation to one of the gardening inmates, who responded that it was the first time he had ever received a thank-you note from anyone. A Burlington-based group, Gardens for All, convinced the Department of Corrections that fresh produce and a marketable skill would be good for inmates, and the University of Vermont lent the land for the project. An unexpected bonus has been the changed attitudes of the participants—a sense of accomplishment, pride, achievement, and positive self-image. This, according to the prison superintendent, is the most important contribution any prison program can make. "Self-concept, in my opinion, is the biggest single factor governing whether someone can make it on the 'outside' or not." One inmate, released in the middle of a growing season, asked, and was allowed, to stay in the program through the summer. Another man, initially so tense in the presence of strangers that he could barely speak, relaxed over time from the constant exposure in a positive setting to strangers who shared a common interest: passersby who were interested in the garden's progress. Shortly after his release from prison, he testified before the state legislature on Vietnam veterans' rights.[75]

By the 1990s, prison gardens had become widespread. In 1990, researchers contacted fifty-five prison authorities in forty-one states. The survey revealed that 75 percent of the facilities had either vocational or correctional horticultural industries, 19 percent had formal or informal horticultural therapy programs, and only 6 percent had no horticultural programs.[76] Master gardeners trained through the U.S. Cooperative Extension Service have been instrumental in bringing horticultural activities to prisons. In 1992, 374 of them were working in twenty-one states at prisons, nursing homes, hospitals, rehabilitation centers, and other special service facilities.[77]

Gardens, like tables, are important sites for building civil society through food connections. Many different kinds of people connect civilly with one another in meaningful, and often new and surprising, ways: victory garden homemakers canning with neighbors, urban gardeners talking with neighbors for the first time, immigrants bridging two worlds in their gardens, children discovering delicious food and table rituals at school gardens, disaffected young gardeners being thanked for the first time in their lives, and inmates donating the fruits of their labor to give back to their communities.

Chapter 13

· ·

Farmers' Markets

At first glance, farmers' markets may seem far afield of the civilizing connections of mealtime conversations and community gardens. But they have played a central role in the history of civil society. Public market places were found in all ancient civilizations, bustling centers of food, commerce, ideas, and politics. The agora was the center of economic and political life in ancient Greek cities. In Athens, the agora was cleared in the early sixth century BC in order to be lined with public buildings for officials and the governing council. In the early years of the Republic, the Roman forum teemed with food stalls, brothels, temples, and the Senate House. In the second century BC, food stores were replaced with business centers and law courts. During the Roman Empire, the forum became a ceremonial showplace for emperors' temples and monuments to successful military campaigns.

Farmers' Markets in America

At one time, nearly every American city had at least one public market, as evidenced by the ubiquitous Market Street in most downtowns. For example, Baltimore's first public market was built in 1763 with funds raised through a lottery.[1] Like the agora and the forum, early public markets in America doubled as community centers, replete with public meeting rooms, military armories, seats of town government, and fire watchtowers, with the market bell serving as a fire alarm. The first government building in Chicago contained a market house on the first floor and a Common Council meeting place on the second. In 1794, Richmond, Virginia, constructed a brick market building with arcades on the first floor and stalls and a large hall on the second floor for dances, city council meetings, and theatrical events. As cities grew in size and population, municipal officials created public market systems to meet demand for food, with a large central market and numerous smaller venues scattered throughout neighborhoods. In 1918, the municipal market system in New Orleans contained twenty-three neighborhood markets, satellites to the French Market at Jackson Square; Baltimore had eleven, New York nine, and Pittsburgh six. Shortly thereafter, market halls began to decline as city governments redirected market-rent revenues from repair and maintenance toward other municipal obligations. Facilities deteriorated and became unsafe. A new, private class of grocers emerged, discouraging further government funding of public markets. They were better managers than their predecessors, who were often chosen more for reasons of political patronage than ability to run businesses. Beginning in the 1940s, independent food retailers were increasingly replaced by chain supermarkets, which relied on large corporations for food production and distribution and could afford to comply with strict food-safety and handling laws.[2]

After the Second World War, cities grew by paving over surrounding farmlands. In the 1960s, the open-space preservation movement emerged to put the brakes on this practice. Advocates increasingly realized the need to preserve some land for agricultural and horticultural production. Farmers' markets became a critical component in the strategy of making farming near cities profitable again, which in turn would protect open space from sprawling suburban development. Local farmers needed face-to-face contact with consumers to learn their preferences and remain economically viable. The strategy appeared to work. The National Farmers' Market Directory reported a 79 percent increase in the number of farmers' markets in the United States between 1994 and 2002, with some 3,100 in operation in 2002. According to the USDA, those who benefited most from farmers' markets were small farm operators: those with less than $250,000 in annual receipts who worked and managed their own operations, or 94 percent of all farms. The USDA praised the community benefits of farmers' markets: providing fresh, nutritious foods for those in urban areas where such goods were scarce and promoting nutrition education, wholesome eating habits, and better food preparation. A USDA study of farmers' markets in 2000 found that they were economically significant and viable: nineteen thousand farmers reported selling their produce *only* at farmers' markets, and 82 percent of markets were self-sustaining (their market income was sufficient to pay all costs associated with the operation of the market, not including grant or in-kind support). Farmers' markets also played a vital community role helping those in need: 58 percent of markets participated in Women, Infants, and Children (WIC) coupons, food stamps, and state and local nutrition programs, and 25 percent of markets assisted in the distribution of food to needy families. The federal government has recently begun to subsidize the use of farmers' markets by the poor and the elderly. In 1992, the USDA provided additional coupons to WIC recipients to purchase fresh fruit and vegetables at participating farmers' markets. In 2002, the USDA funded state pilot programs that distributed coupons to low-income seniors to use for eligible foods at farmers markets, roadside stands, and CSA programs. These programs reduced barriers to seniors' access by driving them to these venues and arranging for local growers to take their produce directly to senior housing.[3]

Producers, Consumers, and Community Supported Agriculture

Farmers who sold their produce at farmers' markets also participated in CSA ventures, whereby groups of people agreed to pay farmers in advance for periodic delivery of their produce. This movement was started by a group of women in Japan in the late 1960s and was brought to New England in 1982. *Teikei* means "to tie together" in Japanese; when applied to community-supported agriculture it connotes "food with a farmer's face." Between 1985 and 1997, some six hundred CSA projects were begun in North America. Sometimes volunteer participation on the farm is required, as members become partners in planning crops and experiencing the vicissitudes of nature. CSAs trim costs by allowing farmers to concentrate on growing rather than marketing. Relying on volunteer labor and consumers who paid in advance, participating farmers earn about 50 percent more than they would if they sold wholesale. And they pass these savings on to the shareholders. A 1996 study by economists at the University of Massachusetts found that the food delivered for a $450 share would have cost up to $1,150 in a conventional grocery store, a local food market, or an organic food market. CSAs afford greater income security than did farmers' markets, where farmers had to pay fees and sold virtually nothing on rainy days. However, there are disadvantages for consumers: they are often required to donate volunteer time, the contents are sometimes paltry, and deliveries are not always convenient. But for one New York man, CSAs are worth the effort: "At first it is a chore. Then it is a challenge. Then it is a new circle of friends. I work at the farm about 10 weekends a year. Sharing the vulnerability of the seasons, the connection with the earth, the weeding, the harvest—it sounds weird, but it is powerful, healing stuff."[4]

In spite of the fees and unpredictability of fair-weather clients, farmers' markets still save farmers money by lowering their distribution and marketing costs. Also, first-time entrepreneurs can take advantage of a viable location and proximity to more-experienced vendors, facilitating upward mobility for immigrants who have few economic resources and are intimidated by formal requirements. This is particularly true for immigrants from Latin American, Asian, and African communities that have long-standing market and street-trading traditions. Farmers' markets legitimize street vending by offering a legal, safe, and supportive environment for business.⁵ For example, in 1995 some Vietnamese immigrants in Dallas asked the city for permission to hold a weekly market in a large, vacant, city-owned lot. City planners were sympathetic to the idea and drafted plans, studies, regulations, and grant applications. After a year of bureaucratic foot-dragging, the Vietnamese merchants finally gave up and moved out of Dallas. Urban sociologist Jane Jacobs thinks that this was a silly fiasco, especially since people from Southeast Asia are among the world's greatest experts on how to organize, set up, and run stall markets. In her view, all the city had to do was grant permission with two provisos: that it be open to all merchants of legal goods in the community, and that the market take responsibility for satisfactorily cleaning up after itself.⁶

For consumers, farmers' markets provide a venue to support local agriculture and to purchase organic and seasonal produce. Since trust is essential, consumers need to be protected from fraudulent vendors. At certified farmers' markets in California, growers are given a reprieve from state laws if they meet certain qualifications regarding the size of their operation, the organic nature of their produce, and the promise that it is indeed their produce. Market managers are supposed to check vendors' certificates, but at many markets such supervision is uneven. One vendor in Milpitas, California, told a reporter that at every market usually two or three vendors did not grow what they sold. The explosive growth of farmers' markets across California— from one hundred to three hundred in just a decade—has been predicated on consumer trust that customers are buying fresh, seasonal, and local produce. Farmers' markets associations struggle to keep up with the new challenges of certifying the integrity of products and accommodating the long waiting lists of vendors wanting to join. For most counties, pursuing fraudulent vendors is not a high priority.⁷

In other parts of the country, farmers' markets are more casual. For example, in Hastings, Nebraska, vendors, whose number fluctuates with the cycles of the seasons and the availability of produce, set up shop in a parking lot of an old store. They agree to simple ground rules: chip in to buy some advertising, honor the 8:30 starting time for the changing of money, and set your own prices, but don't disrupt the market by getting too far out of line. According to the market organizer, an organic-gardening enthusiast, many shoppers return every week to get fresh produce. "They get to know each other and the vendors, so the Saturday morning market becomes a community-building event."[8]

Civic Connections

In addition to economic benefits, shoppers and vendors at farmers' markets also value the civic connections found in earlier times at the central market, the agora, and the forum. An example is Angel Garcia, a vendor in the

Berkeley Farmers' Market. Farmers' markets hearken back to the days of the Greek agora and the Roman forum, centers of economic and political life. Citizens converse over food and vote with their wallets to support organic food, local farmers, sustainable agriculture, and recycling. It was at a farmers' market in Berkeley that I first heard Alice Waters discuss her delicious revolution. Photo by Alexander Friedman and Lee Friedman.

Fresno-Clovis area of central California. He appreciates how the market has forged important connections with his family, his employees, other vendors, and his customers. The camaraderie and community of the market has made it easier to get up at 2:30 every Saturday morning, with his family and field-workers in tow. He employs five people to help him with the fieldwork, and they all take turns selling at the market. "I want them to come here and to see how people react to the quality of the produce. That way they learn both ends of the business." His wife and children also pitch in on the farm and at the market. In the beginning he planted mostly cotton and field corn, which remain his major crops. But he has always liked watermelons, so he started growing them, along with vegetables. He remembers the days when farmers sold their produce from trucks by the roadside. "My kids loved carrying our watermelons to customers' cars," he recalls.[9]

The market owner describes Garcia as the type of farmer who keeps farm-ers' markets in business. "Angel understands that the key ingredient in mak-ing the market a success is committed growers who show up every day, week after week, even when they don't make money every day." Garcia has never missed a market because of the weather, even during periods of the Central Valley's dense and dangerous Tule fog (when only a couple of vendors would show up), and when the temperature dipped to 13 degrees in 1991 ("We put our stuff out on the table and within an hour it was all frozen solid"). Gar-cia is appreciated by long-time customers, who think of vendors as their friends: "I feel you make friends at the market after years of doing business with them"; "Most of all I enjoy the friendliness of the vendors." For his part, Garcia refers to his clients as friends he knows by name: "We have so many friends up here that we know by name. I wish I could know the names of all the people who have been coming here for years. I recognize the faces, but I don't know their names. Everyone wants to be recognized. I think if I knew everybody's name that comes to our stand, it would make them feel a lot better, feel important." Of course, taking the trouble to learn customers' names makes good business sense. But Garcia also has a civic motivation: a belief that people feel better about themselves when others give them the courtesy of a conversation in which they are addressed by name.[10]

In urban areas, regulars at farmers' markets typically represent many races, ethnicities, and income levels, and the market provides an occasion for civil exchanges across these social barriers. Take the case of Chicago. In the mid-1990s, the ethnic composition of vendors at Chicago's Maxwell Street Market was 40 percent Latino, 35 percent African American, 15 percent white, with the remainder Asian and mixed heritage. Customers had been coming to the market for an average of twenty-one years; half visited every Sunday, and another 25 percent shopped once or twice a month. Many customers were two- and three-generation family groups. On an average Sunday, twenty thousand customers visited the market.[11]

Some farmers' markets make a concerted effort to serve the needs of low-income communities that often feel politically dispossessed. For example, in California three-quarters of all farmers' markets accept food stamps; at some, up to half of the sales are transacted with them.[12] The oldest continuous farmers' market in the state (since 1944) is the Alemany Farmers' Market, located in San Francisco between a subsidized housing project and a freeway interchange. During the week, it is a patch of pavement and weeds, but on Saturdays it is transformed into a thriving multiethnic neighborhood, with the feeling of a town square. The stalls are made of wood, metal, and cement and decorated with murals. Across town at the United Nations Plaza, another farmers' market is populated by low-income residents using food stamps. One customer noted, "A lot of locals come here, and you'll see them getting on buses with bags full of stuff. There aren't a lot of markets in the Tenderloin. It's good for the community." High-quality items such as organic mushrooms are available at reasonable prices. When asked why farmers' markets were popping up all over the Bay Area, one organic farmer replied, "I would speculate that in some ways it's a rejection of mass commercial culture. It's a way of supporting local agriculture and creating a sense of contact, a relationship, between the product, the vendor and the customer. It's also kind of a hangout." Indeed, two vendors who met at the Alemany Market, when one was a vendor and the other his customer, are now married and selling the organic mushrooms. Other San Francisco markets are more upscale, such as the one in the Ferry Building, where family farmers and artisanal foodmakers sell fruits, vegetables, cheeses, and breads not found in local supermarkets.[13]

Many California farmers' markets are explicitly designed as community gathering spots. The Main Street Market in Santa Monica features live music in a family setting with patio coffee and pastry. The market in Hollywood hosts street musicians as well as local nonprofit community organizations. It is part of an economic revitalization effort to create a free, public attraction on Hollywood Boulevard. In addition to produce, the Westwood Farmers' Market sells tamales and Jamaican barbecue, accompanied by a jazz band and a crafts market. It is sponsored by the Westwood Community Alliance and was the brainchild of two UCLA graduate students who wanted to revitalize Westwood Village. The Encino Farmers' Market is sponsored by an organization providing services and programs for the elderly.[14]

Farmers' markets are often vibrant bazaars with lively interchanges among peoples and foods of many cultures. In "Giving Good Weight," John McPhee paints a picture of Brooklyn's Greenmarket in the 1970s. The space was leased from the Brooklyn Academy of Music, which charged seventy-five dollars a week. The block was fenced and graveled, once occupied by condemned buildings, spent bars, and liquor stores. "The people, in their throngs, are the most varied we see—or that anyone is likely to see in one place west of Suez. . . . Greeks. Italians. Russians. Finns. Haitians. Puerto Ricans. Nubians. Muslim women in veils of shocking pink. Sunnis in total black. Women in hiking shorts, with babies in their backpacks. Young Connecticut-looking pants-suit women. There are country Jamaicans, in loose dresses, bandannas tight around their heads."[15]

McPhee's description of Alvina Frey combines the themes of immigration, community, food, and farms. At the Greenmarket, she attracted crowds, even though customers did not know anything about her, except perhaps her farm's New Jersey address painted on her truck. But they could easily sense "a consistent standard, a kind of personal signature, in the colors and textures before her." For McPhee, she represented both the universality of food and the particularity of a human in relation to food. In contrast to the anonymity of supermarkets and corporate consumerism, she made her mark and had standards. She told him that what the small farmer offered was fresher, more select material. "The small farmer throws away the bad stuff. If my produce is better than some people's, I'll charge more for it. Some of the other guys say I'm Fifth Avenue. I don't care." She took her time to educate people about quality and freshness: don't be impressed by fat cucumbers; the long thin ones have fewer seeds. Check the freshness of an ear of corn by the color and consistency of its stem.[16]

People probably sensed that Frey embodied what the Greenmarket was all about: the nexus between land, farm, food, and community. It turned out that she worked on a family farm that was on its way to being subdivided and sold until she found the Greenmarket as an outlet for her produce. Her grandmother was born on a farm in Saxony in the 1860s and emigrated as an adult to New Jersey. She purchased fifty-five acres, cleared the land, dug a well, and constructed a barn. When her husband went to work as a loom mechanic in the Patterson mills, he took her tomatoes, corn, beans, potatoes, and beets to the Island Market and sold them there. Frey was grateful to the customers of the Greenmarket for saving her family farm, and they in turn showed their appreciation of her. An elderly woman from the neighborhood brought her orange juice every week. People took pictures of her and invited her for coffee. One distinguished-looking man once brought her a hard-boiled egg in clear gelatin. Frey graciously remarked: "Some kind of French dish. You don't like it, but you have to eat it." She received weekly reports from a man who had purchased a gourd from her. Following her directions, he had cut holes in it and hung it from his twentieth-story window, and a bird came to live in it. At the market there was reciprocity and interdependence between vendors and locals: locals enabled Frey to keep her farm and expanded her horizons beyond her produce stand in Mahwah, New Jersey; vendors brought fresh and delicious food to a run-down area of Brooklyn. Frey remarked, "I love the city—meeting different people, learning that all the things you learn about the city are not true. I see more people in the two markets I come to—Brooklyn and Fifty-ninth Street—than I do in several weeks in Mahwah at the stand. I wouldn't quit this for nothing in the world. The people are wonderful, and the market means a lot to them. They don't want anything to screw it up so we won't come in anymore."[17]

A testimony to the civil connections at farmers' markets was expressed poignantly by Cynthia Bronte, a vendor specializing in sweet basil and pesto sauces. She was selling her wares at the Santa Monica farmers' market in July 2003, when a driver lost control of his car and sped through the market, killing ten people and injuring dozens before stopping just a few feet from her booth. The dead came from many backgrounds: a thirty-five-year-old Mexican immigrant and office cleaner; an Iranian immigrant and her seven-month-old grandson; a married couple who had just moved to Los Angeles from New York; a seventy-eight-year-old Lithuanian immigrant; a three-year-old girl; a fifty-five-year-old homeless man from Louisiana; and a forty-seven-year-old woman who volunteered with the nearby nonprofit group After-School All Stars. Haunted by the horror and carnage, Bronte took some comfort in the fact that the tragedy was an accident, not an act of malice. "One of the things that's so great about that farmers' market is it's a real community. You know the women, then you see them pregnant, then you meet their babies. That's why I'm so happy it wasn't an act of malice. It would have been worse if someone was trying to destroy all that."[18]

Regional and Sensual Connections

Farmers' markets are meaningful to people not only for forging interpersonal and community connections but also for preserving regional foodways that are sources of pride and distinction. Around the country, farmers markets are often the only place where one can find traditional foods grown and sold by farmers with a deep appreciation for the product's integrity. Deborah Madison, a chef, cookbook author, and member of Santa Fe, New Mexico's Slow Food convivium, argues that "outside of these markets, you just about have to know a farmer personally if you want foods with integrity. Along with those comparatively few restaurants that make serving regional food their mission, it is the farmers' markets that give us the surest clue about what is unique to any region of this large country, the United States." She gives several examples of regional variations in the produce at farmers' markets: Madison, Wisconsin, features fresh-cracked hickory nuts; in Birmingham, Alabama, okra is sorted by size, depending on whether it is going to be fried, stewed, or pickled; large, sweet muscadine grapes are found in the South, but not the Southwest; fragrant Meyer lemons are unique to California; and Santa Fe is the only place to find New Mexico's native chiles.[19]

Madison describes the Santa Fe Farmers' Market as an intensely social place where farmers and shoppers exchange conversation as well as food and money. It started with a handful of farmers, mostly Hispanic, who sold carrots, onions, peas, chokecherry jelly, and some dried chiles. It has grown to include more than one hundred vendors from northern New Mexico. "Anyone suspected of selling corn from a cousin up in Colorado had better be prepared to defend himself against a fierce market manager and other angry farmers!" Chile peppers were thought to have been introduced to Santa Fe in 1598 by a conquistador who brought them from Mexico. Madison writes that over the course of four hundred years, chiles have become northern New Mexico's most emotionally significant food. They differ from the hybrid chiles developed by the state university and grown in the southern part of the state. Those are shipped around the country and the world, for example, to season German sausages. In northern New Mexico, seeds are passed down from generation to generation, with varietal names reflecting the places where they are grown: Española, Velarde, Dixon, and Chimayo. The largest field of native chiles is three acres; most are cultivated in patches and gardens and stay in their neighboring communities. Whole chiles are tied into strings, or *ristras,* and hung to dry under the eaves of houses. In Santa Fe, one *ristra* always stays in the kitchen to supply chiles for cooking; others are used for decoration, providing a feeling of connection with the traditions of the region.[20]

The sensual lure of farmers' markets attracts both everyday cooks and chefs interested in improvisational cooking. Food writer Molly O'Neill savors walking through San Francisco's Ferry Plaza Farmer's Market. "A farmers' market is a delightful counterpoint to modern life, a little patch of green in an asphalt city, an oasis of sight and touch and smell in a climate-controlled, vacuum-sealed world." She enjoys the slow pace, meandering through the market, taking in the smell of fresh-cut basil and mint. Reason and the senses operate in tandem. "Even as the pace quickens and the shoppers move in accordance with mental lists, the senses remain in charge." O'Neill thinks that direct contact is the lure of farmers' markets: "direct contact with the growers, with the produce, and, if one is lucky, with one's appetite. This leads to a certain kind of improvisational cooking—simple and straightforward—that is characteristic of the cooks who minted California cuisine and who can be counted on to be at Ferry Plaza on a Saturday morning: to pinch the peaches and sniff the apricots and talk, as people do when their senses are engaged, with respect (and not a little awe) for the bounty of the Bay Area."[21] A chef at a San Jose restaurant touts the variety of produce at farmers' markets as an inspiration for his cooking. "It keeps your menu from being what I call commercial gray product. At the market you discover apples you never knew about, plums, peaches—ooh, when the peaches come in, the variety, the colors! Farmers' markets keep the inspiration in cooking."[22]

Farmers' markets allow people to satisfy their need for direct contact with delicious and sensuous food, with the farmers who grow it, and with other hungry and curious eaters and cooks. They perpetuate regional food traditions, provide a seasonal and ecological alternative to mass-produced fare, and facilitate civil exchanges about delicious food, meals, foodways, and family farms and histories. They continue the civic tradition that began in the agora and the forum.

Conclusion

· ·

The concept of civil society has a respected place in Western political thought. Like other contested concepts in this tradition (after all, the essence of the Western tradition is to contest ideas), it has had many meanings. However, some consistent themes can be discerned. For most theorists, with the notable exception of Marx, who objected to its ruling-class function, civil society has been viewed as a space that brings out the best—the virtuous—in people. For libertarians, this is achieved by scaling back the reach of government and allowing individuals to express themselves freely, especially in the market-place. This book takes a different approach, since it emphasizes social relations, rather than the individual, and it calls for government curbs on work hours to make more time for foodwork and foodways. It also departs from a libertarian conception of civil society in its focus on gendered foodwork. Convincing people to value foodwork will not be effective unless and until its gendered underpinnings are made manifest.

Most civil-society theorists want to bolster social relations, but only those that are civil. Of course, the meaning of "civil" is contested. There is general agreement that social bonds between people based on hatred and destruction, such as those of white supremacists or terrorists, are not civil. However, it remains a matter of debate whether people who bond for purposes that are offensive to some (such as pushing cultural boundaries related to drug use, obscenity, satire, or profanity) are bolstering civil society. In the tripartite division of human organization into state, economy, and society, civil society is not the same thing as society. It is a subset of social relations that promotes a common good and purposes larger than individual gain. Individuals forfeit the right to say or do whatever they please. They take the thoughts and feelings of others into account—to use the most common metaphors—to create the reservoir of goodwill and to weave the social fabric that enable good things to happen. When civil relations replenish the reservoir and repair the tattered fabric, they reconnect people, energizing them to engage constructively in their inevitable disagreements about important matters. Proponents of civil society try to create conditions that enable expression of our better selves and that encourage virtuous behavior such as generosity and thoughtfulness.

This book has demonstrated how the preparation and consumption of food are integral and neglected facets of civil society and, ultimately, democracy. On a daily basis, they can bring out the best in people by prompting them to think about the common good and larger purposes. Foodwork requires thoughtfulness and generosity on a daily basis. It is commendable to belong to civic groups that promote larger purposes, but rarely are citizens reminded of these larger concerns three times a day, as they are by the call of hunger pangs to think about meals, foodwork, and foodways. For most people most of the time, eating is not a solitary act, devoid of social meanings or relations. To the contrary, depending on the circumstances, it can involve many layers of meaning—physical, social, emotional, economic, and political.

One must look into the household to find these activities, a place most civil-society theorists have excluded from their purview. In the household people learn how to use diplomatic speech, to be thoughtful and generous, and to act in a civilized fashion. Civility must be taught, and the expectation is that women will be the teachers. They are also expected to plan and cook the meals. As long as foodwork is gendered, civil-society theorists will continue to devalue and marginalize it. What lessons have we learned about degendering foodwork and convincing everyone to engage in it?

Household Foodwork

Household foodwork takes time, which most people agree is in increasingly short supply. One way for working families to get more time for meals is for breadwinners to work fewer, or more flexible, hours. Two models provide alternatives for contemporary Americans: the practices of our own agrarian past and the shorter work schedules of Europeans. The first model works for breadwinners with jobs that can be performed in part or entirely from the home, the second model for the rest of the workforce. It is in the interest of most working families who want family mealtime to lobby for shorter workdays. In the meantime, flexible work hours help.

Households with children vary enormously. Some preschoolers are in full-time or part-time day care. Some parents are home when their children return from school. Other parents rely on after-school day care; still others split shifts in child care. Solutions to finding time for foodwork will be as varied as these households are. There will never be one way to find time. But certain family food times seem more likely than others: weekday dinners and weekend meals.

Invisible foodwork needs to be acknowledged so that meal providers are not worn down by deficits in the economy of gratitude. Meal providers must educate meal consumers about the importance of pitching in to help and expressing gratitude. It is hard for some mothers to ask their sons or husbands for help in the kitchen. Some women enjoy the kitchen as their domain of competence, and they thwart efforts by others to tread on their territory. Some parents are hesitant to ask their overscheduled children to add foodwork to the daily demands of homework, sports, and other extracurricular activities. Many children have their own time crunch. But there is no reason to abrogate the responsibility to teach others about the importance of gratitude.

Commercial foods will always be a convenient shortcut for harried working parents. These foods have their pluses and minuses. On the positive side, less meal preparation time means potentially more time for conversation. Ethnically different kinds of food can be savored. They are cheap, plentiful, and convenient. On the negative side, there is usually a relationship between price and quality: cheap convenience food is often laden with unhealthy fats and salts, exacerbating the obesity crisis. Many families cannot afford higher-priced and healthier "gourmet" take-out items. Home-cooked meals are usually healthier and often cheaper, especially soups and stews. And food preparation can be an occasion of quality conversation. Indeed, many children are more forthcoming about their concerns when they are doing a project with their parents that does not involve direct eye contact. They clam up during the third-degree "What did you do at school today?" but open up while preparing vegetables.

Only in Australia do recent immigrant groups comprise a higher proportion of the population than in the United States. Newly arrived immigrants tend to be attached to their native foodways, especially as sources of comfort to ease the disruption of relocation. They are eager to pass on home-country food traditions to their children born in the United States. These children, and sometimes their parents as well, are torn between attachment to home country and desire to fit into the new country by eating American. Household foodwork in America almost always has an ethnic-tradition layer superimposed on generic household food decisions. Traditional food gives people a sense of attachment, belonging, and loyalty, but it can also be a source of tension as generations assimilate in different ways.

Finally, America's fast-paced culture puts impossible demands on anyone wanting to savor a leisurely meal with extended conversation. Why bother with elaborate, time-consuming food preparation, when time-pressed family members screech up to the table, refuel, and speed away to lessons, practices, and meetings? The Slow Food movement is asking the right questions. How important is it for families to take time for meals given competing pressures for children to excel in so many areas? Psychologists warn that children can be overprogrammed and overscheduled. They need down time, and mealtime can be such a time, provided it too is not a command performance. At a minimum, cell phones and televisions can be turned off during dinner.

Table Conversation

Conversation is an art best learned through an apprenticeship with skilled conversationalists. Table time is precious time to teach, practice, and hone this art. Of course, equally good, and even better, venues exist for conversation. Some people prefer to eat first and talk later, when they are sated and relaxed. Many children, uncomfortable speaking at the table, are talkative in the car with their parents. Roommates have late-night discussions in their apartments. Loved ones talk on the phone for hours. Everyone seems to have a cell phone. So why the focus on food preparation, meals, and the table?

People gather around a table, come together for a frequent and universal need, and make an effort at positive group dynamics. These physical ways of connecting can set the stage for other forms of connection, especially sharing ideas, opinions, and interests. Table activities are nonhierarchical, but they require the rules of table manners. Rules provide order and structure and define appropriate practices, including speech, at the table. Table rules are not as formal and detailed as parliamentary procedures used at official meetings, but they mirror them. Manners help to channel strongly held and disparate beliefs and points of view, for the benefit of the common good. Of course, manners, like all rules, can be arbitrary, stifling, and exclusionary. Learning to change unfair rules is just as important as observing fair ones. Once people learn that table manners are conventions, varying by household, class, and social group, they understand that they can be changed. Table rules and conversations need authorities, not authoritarians.

Most table rituals are both comforting and civilizing. Lighting candles sheds light on table exchanges. Sharing bread puts the same thing in everyone's hands. Convivants enjoy the same aromas when they pass platters of food. Waiting for everyone to be served before eating signals respect. Expressing thanks for the food honors a common good, God, or the cook.

Mealtimes tend to be casual story times. Since meals are frequently prepared and consumed with the same group of people, interchanges are usually informal, low keyed, involving whatever is on someone's mind, as opposed to formal, high-performance affairs. Stories are shared about the events of everyone's day, not as intimately as two loved ones talking on the phone, yet not severely scrutinized either. People connect but gear their remarks to group dynamics. Across generations, thought is given to appropriate ways to talk about controversial topics or upsetting events of the day.

Food preparation and sharing at the table require paying attention to the needs of others in front of them, as opposed to hearing them on the phone or sending them instant messages on the computer. Body language speaks volumes, if you are there to see and hear it. It allows for midcourse correction of a potentially disastrous course of conversation.

Mind-Body Dualism

Food is pleasurable, and people go to great lengths to share pleasure at the table. Unfortunately, in the Western philosophical tradition, pleasure has been suspect, as a source of sin, indulgence, and loss of control. First food pleasures come from women's bodies, which have been equally suspect for the same reasons. Much effort will be required to swim against these currents and make the case for pleasure at the table, and for men as well as women to prepare food. The French and the Italian approaches to food are preferable to those of most philosophers, who have perpetuated the mind-body split and devalued the sense of taste.

Meals need to be seen as products of mind-body unity: desire and planning, impulse and science. Mushrooms can be added to a dish on a whim, but they had better not be poisonous. A peach may start out delicious, but without careful planning it can be rotten before it is served. Meals perpetuate trust, a vital feature of civilization and civil society.

Appetites can be sated in healthy and delicious ways. Too often, appetites are viewed as something to control, whether through domestic science, the diet industry, or most destructively, eating disorders. Deadened palates, bland food, and starvation diets do not help people connect with one another in civilizing ways. Civil people welcome and celebrate different tastes as pathways to understanding cultural variations in people.

Like sight and hearing, taste is an important gateway to knowledge. It is often disparaged as providing transient, subjective, and unreliable information in comparison to the more lasting, objective, and reliable information of sight and hearing. Tastes create and bring back memories, add zest to life, and are the subjects of endless comparisons. Flavors let people belong and explore. Wars have been fought over spices and trade routes. Tastes matter a lot to all of us.

The Delicious Revolution

The delicious revolution insists that good food is delicious, not just healthy. Alice Waters has shown that delicious food can be grown in many settings: organic farms that sell fruits and vegetables to restaurants and to farmers' markets, jail gardens that donate food to soup kitchens, school gardens that provide children's school lunches, and community gardens that feed the neighborhood. Of course, some parts of the United States do not lend themselves to such food production year round. But since the 1970s, the number of organic farms, jail gardens, school gardens, and community gardens has steadily increased, all across the country. Delicious food promotes important civil connections.

Delicious food is not just for the rich. Chez Panisse *is* an expensive restaurant, but it is not the only place to find delicious food. Fresh ingredients are key. Cooking with fresh ingredients poses a problem for harried working people who do not have time for frequent trips to the produce market, let alone to till their own organic garden. The hope is that increased consumer demand for fresh, organic produce will drive down its cost and increase its availability, both in supermarkets and at farmers' markets. Of course, farmers' markets are increasingly popular with men, women, and children.

It is revolutionary to put sensual pleasure—tasting that perfect peach—at the center of a philosophy to change the way Americans eat. Most critiques of U.S. food production and consumption are based on ecological and health grounds. The pleasure of a good meal with companions, enlivened by robust conversation, unites people in common purpose in a way that reading statistics about ecology and nutrition does not. *Knowing* what is good for you, or society, or the planet, is one thing. *Doing* something about it on a daily basis, in a pleasurable way, is quite another. Revolutions are abstractions that need to be put into practice.

Waters puts her revolution into practice in restaurants, farms, jails, schools, and public hearings. The civilizing functions of preparing food and sharing meals do not occur only at the family table. Indeed, as families have *less* time to spend performing these activities, it is important, for children's sake, that they occur in schools. Public schools serve the public purpose of educating future citizens. They are an appropriate setting for promoting civility, conversation, and community through food production and consumption. School gardens make an especially important contribution for sharing across race and class lines. And they break down the gender barriers of foodwork.

Jail gardens connect inmates with society in beneficial ways. Jails serve two public purposes: to punish and to rehabilitate. Punishment has always been easier to accomplish than rehabilitation. Preliminary evidence suggests lower recidivism rates for inmates who participate in jail garden projects, where they learn impulse control. Inmates in such programs feel more connected with society by creating things of value to share with the poor and the sick in their community. Often they want to give back to the communities they have damaged through their crimes. They feel supported by new circles of acquaintances: restaurant owners and shoppers at farmers' markets who purchase their produce. Rehabilitation requires impulse-control skills, connection with communities outside the world of crime, and job skills such as gardening.

Community Food

Community food can be just as important as family food in forging civilizing connections among people. Of course, it can do quite the opposite if outsiders are excluded. By definition, communities have members and nonmembers. For the most part, however, communities in the United States are eager to share their food with nonmembers. Perhaps this is so because food is an easily shared part of every culture—it does not require extensive knowledge of a community's language, history, rituals, religion, or other belief systems. When a nonmember expresses a desire to eat a community member's food, it is a form of curiosity and courtesy. Conversation ensues: What is this ingredient? How spicy do you like your sauce? How are you supposed to eat this? Nonmembers usually respond to the food with respect, even if they do not particularly care for the taste of it. And the conversation can expand into areas of the community's history, language, and culture.

In the United States, one finds significant ethnic and regional food differences. Food travelers venture in and out of ethnic enclaves and across the country's vast geographical distances. Americans are as proud of their country's food (typically, some combination of apple pie, hot dogs, hamburgers, pizza, beer, and Coca-Cola) as they are of their community food traditions. Eating American is a constant work in progress. Americans want to belong to their ethnic group, region, and country. One important way to do this is through food.

Festive, ceremonial, and ritual foods unite members and welcome non-members in many communities. When Jews invite non-Jews to seders, it leads to conversations about Jewish history and beliefs. At Chinese New Year parties, non-Chinese participants learn about the significance of different delicacies. Anglos enjoy tamales at Latino Christmas celebrations, as they learn more about Latino history and culture. At weddings, guests compare ethnic differences and similarities in sweet cakes and candies. Food prompts conversation within and across communities.

Enjoying community food is not always a simple matter of showing up at a party. Food from community gardens requires much hard work, socially and physically. Neighbors agree to rules about supplies, tilling, weeding, watering, insect control, and sharing the fruits of everyone's labor. They get to know one another, share their food traditions, and reduce neighborhood blight. They have conversations across race, class, and generational lines.

For many immigrants, gardens ease the transition from life in their home countries to their new life in the United States. Many immigrants are farmers with a limited knowledge of the English language. A lot of communication takes place as neighbors from different immigrant groups watch crops grow and share produce and traditional recipes. When they sell their goods at farmers' markets, they broaden their community ties and sense of belonging.

The United States is not the only place where food preparation and meal sharing has a civilizing impact on disparate communities. The European Union also recognizes the role that food plays as a cohesive force in the face of social divisions, especially intolerance and discrimination. As representatives from European countries work to integrate the European Union, they are well aware of their history of disparaging one another with food epithets (e.g., potato-eaters, krauts, and frogs). Nonetheless, in 2003 the Council of Europe embarked on a three-year project to broaden conceptual frameworks used to address these problems, including an exploration of the idea that food could be used to promote tolerance and diversity. At an initial meeting, representatives debated whether the experience of diverse food cultures could enhance respect for intercultural relations in everyday life but agreed that the act of sharing a meal could further intercultural understanding.[1]

People in different countries and cultures seem to agree that something important happens at the table, something beyond the biological necessity of eating. We enjoy connecting with others, sharing, and giving of ourselves for a common purpose. If civility can happen at the table, why can't it occur in the neighborhood, the nation, and the world? If we can make rules that work at the table, why can't we make them for the human family writ large? Every culture has its table rules. In what ways, if any, should children participate? What language and behavior is courteous and what is offensive? Who gets to talk, and for how long? How is gratitude properly expressed to the cook and the host? How heated should disagreements become? People look for subtle clues in the delicate art of crafting expectations and boundaries of the acceptable and the unacceptable, the civil and the uncivil. Commonly agreed-upon rules create a support structure for the enjoyment of good food, lively conversation, and warm conviviality. It is good practice for democracy's rule making, idea sharing, reciprocity, and generation of goodwill.

Food-related negotiations also animate geographic regions, ethnic enclaves, festivals, rituals, community gardens, youth and school gardens, jail gardens, and farmers' markets. These food communities connect people with larger purposes: solidifying ethnic and regional identity, honoring religious traditions, giving back to the community, promoting local farming, eating more healthfully, forging stronger relations with neighbors, removing blight from vacant lots, and teaching children about the environment. Many pockets of cross-cultural and cross-generational civility are made possible by the universality of food and the pleasures of delicious food.

It is appropriate to end at the table, with what has been called the most consequential meal in American history. Washington, Jefferson, Hamilton, and Madison were faced with the difficult decision of where to locate the new nation's capital. Prevailing wisdom was to find the midpoint on a north-south axis. Madison led the fight in the House for a Potomac River location, cleverly reminding Washington that the precise geographic midpoint was Mount Vernon (Washington's home), so the mouth of the Potomac was preferable. Eventually a private bargain was struck over dinner in Jefferson's apartment. Hamilton agreed to deliver enough votes from northern states for the Potomac location in exchange for Madison's pledge to permit the passage of a bill favored by Hamilton. As historian Joseph Ellis notes, although multiple behind-the-scenes bargaining sessions were taking place at the same time, "the notion that an apparently intractable political controversy could be resolved by friendly conversation over port and cigars has always possessed an irresistible narrative charm."[2]

Notes

Introduction

1. In addition to the works cited later in this discussion, see, for example, Chambers and Kymlicka, *Alternative Conceptions of Civil Society*; Dionne, *Community Works*; Eberly, *Essential Civil Society Reader*; Edwards, Foley, and Diani, *Beyond Tocqueville*; Ehrenberg, *Civil Society*; Fullinwider, *Civil Society*; Novak, *To Empower People*; O'Connell, *Civil Society*; and Post and Rosenblum, *Civil Society and Government*.
2. Edwards, *Civil Society*, 11, 61.
3. Walzer, "Idea of Civil Society," 124, 142.
4. Carter, *Civility*, 58, 292, 62.
5. Cahoone, "Civic Meetings, Cultural Meanings," 42.
6. Ibid.; and Schmidt, "Is Civility a Virtue?" 23, 27, 29.
7. Seligman, *Idea of Civil Society*.
8. Schmidt, "Is Civility a Virtue?" 29–30.
9. Dewey, *Public and Its Problems*, 211, 218–19.
10. Boisvert, "Clock Time/Stomach Time."
11. Habermas, *Structural Transformation*; and Chambers, "Critical Theory of Civil Society."
12. Edwards, *Civil Society*, 38–39.
13. Edwards and Foley, "Civil Society and Social Capital."
14. Bourdieu, "Forms of Capital"; Coleman, "Social Capital in the Creation of Human Capital"; and Robert Putnam, *Bowling Alone*.
15. Bobbio, "Gramsci."
16. Edwards, *Civil Society*, 49; and Carter, *Civility*.
17. Dean, "Including Women," 379.
18. Pateman, *Sexual Contract*, 102.
19. Pateman, "Feminist Critiques," 132.
20. Phillips, "Does Feminism Need a Conception?"
21. Elshtain, "Democracy on Trial," 103.

22. Wolfe, *Whose Keeper?* 20.
23. For examples of the social-capital interpretation, see Baron, Field, and Schuller, *Social Capital*; Caiazza and Putnam, *Women's Status and Social Capital*; Fine, *Social Capital versus Social Theory*; O'Neill and Gidengil, *Gender and Social Capital*; and Putnam, *Bowling Alone*. For examples of the civic-engagement understanding, see Burns, Schlozman, and Verba, *Private Roots of Public Action*; Macedo et al., *Democracy at Risk*; Milner, *Civic Literacy*; Sirianni and Friedland, *Civic Innovation in America*; Skocpol and Fiorina, *Civic Engagement in American Democracy*; and Verba, Schlozman, and Brady, *Voice and Equality*.
24. Schudson, *Good Citizen*.
25. Ellis, *Coffee-House*.
26. For European manners, see Aresty, *Best Behavior*. For manners in the United States, see Kasson, *Rudeness and Civility*.
27. Kathlene, "Power and Influence."
28. Kathlene, "Alternative Views of Crime."
29. Tannen, *Conversational Style*.
30. Blum-Kulka, *Dinner Talk*.
31. DeVault, *Feeding the Family*; and Fishman, "Interaction."
32. Gamson, *Talking Politics*.
33. Eliasoph, *Avoiding Politics*.
34. Walsh, *Talking about Politics*.
35. Skocpol, "Advocates without Members."
36. Putnam, *Bowling Alone*, 102.
37. Edwards, *Civil Society*; and Newton, "Social Capital and Democracy."
38. Eilperin, *Fight Club Politics*.
39. Visser, *Rituals of Dinner*, 39–40.
40. Dinkin, *Voting in Provincial America*.
41. Putnam, *Bowling Alone*, 98–101.
42. Bennhold, "Love of Leisure."
43. Putnam, *Bowling Alone*, 222, 234–43.
44. Ibid., 173–77.

Chapter 1. The Time Crunch

1. Cowan, *More Work for Mother*, 17–18.
2. Ibid., 20, 38, 47.
3. Hochschild, *Second Shift*, 2; and U.S. Bureau of the Census, *Statistical Abstract*.
4. Presser, *Toward a 24-Hour Economy*.
5. Schor, *Overworked American*.
6. Jacobs and Gerson, *Time Divide*, 8.
7. Williams, *Unbending Gender*.

8. Strasser, *Never Done*, 48.
9. Vanek, "Time Spent in Housework."
10. Cowan, *More Work for Mother*, 79–80.
11. Ibid., 81–85.
12. Hochschild, *Second Shift*, 3–4.
13. Galinsky, Bond, and Friedman, *Changing Workforce*, 55, 48.
14. Ibid., 50, 52–53.
15. Ehrenreich, "Maid to Order," 89–91.
16. Ehrenreich and Hochschild, "Introduction," 10–11.
17. See, for example, Oakley, *Sociology of Housework*; and Pleck, *Working Wives/Working Husbands*.
18. Walker and Woods, *Time Use*.
19. DeVault, *Feeding the Family*, 55–56.
20. Ibid., 56–57.
21. Ibid., 149, 151.
22. Ibid., 151, 101–2.
23. Ibid., 105, 140–41.
24. Jacobs and Gerson, *Time Divide*.
25. Schor, *Overworked American*.
26. Reich, *Future of Success*, 248–49.
27. Warner, *Perfect Madness*.
28. De Graaf, *Take Back Your Time*.
29. Honoré, *In Praise of Slowness*, 86–87.

Chapter 2. Domesticity: Meals, Obligation, and Gratitude

1. Matthews, *Just a Housewife*; and Kerber, *Women of the Republic*.
2. Matthews, *Just a Housewife*.
3. Ibid.
4. Williams, *Unbending Gender*, 4, 204.
5. Carrington, *No Place like Home*.
6. Finch, *Married to the Job*.
7. Carrington, *No Place like Home*.
8. DeVault, *Feeding the Family*, 203–4.
9. See, for example, Charles and Kerr, *Women, Food and Families*; DeVault, *Feeding the Family*; Luxton, *More than a Labour of Love*; and Murcott, "It's a Pleasure."
10. Goode, Theophano, and Curtis, "Framework for the Analysis," 66–88.
11. U.S. Bureau of the Census, "America's Families and Living Arrangements."
12. U.S. Department of Agriculture, "Food Consumption, Prices, and Expenditures."
13. U.S. Department of Agriculture, "Food Service Trends."

14. Lukanuski, "Place at the Counter," 115. She cites the following studies: Strongman and Hughes, "Eating Style and Body Weight"; Krantz, "Naturalistic Study"; Davis, Murphy, and Neuhaus, "Living Arrangements"; and Latane and Bidwell, "Sex and Affiliation in Cafeterias."

15. Bell and Valentine, *Consuming Geographies*, 65. They cite Graham, "Let's Eat!"

16. Carrington, *No Place like Home*, 63–65.

17. Kruger, "Get Fat, Don't Die!"

18. U.S. Department of Agriculture, "Food Consumption, Prices, and Expenditures."

19. DeVault, *Feeding the Family*, 169–73.

20. Ibid., 178–79.

21. Stack, *All Our Kin*, 31–32.

22. Bell and Valentine, *Consuming Geographies*, 67.

23. Mauss, *Gift*.

24. Stack, *All Our Kin*, 32.

25. Ibid., 34, 38.

26. DeVault, *Feeding the Family*, 194.

27. Hochschild, *Second Shift*, 18, 206.

28. Ibid., 15–16.

29. Ibid., 203, 157.

30. Berry, "Pleasures of Eating," 125.

31. Kavasch, "My Grandmother's Hands," 104.

32. Pogrebin, "Mother I Hardly Knew You," 83.

33. Babayan, "The Cook, the Maid and the Lady," 115.

34. Coss, "My Mother/Her Kitchen," 13–14.

35. E. R. Shapiro, "On Becoming a Cuban Jewish Cook."

36. Randall, "What My Tongue Knows."

37. Pillsbury, *From Boarding House to Bistro*.

38. Levenstein, *Revolution at the Table*, 185.

39. Ritzer, *McDonaldization of Society*; and McDonald's Web site, http://www.mcdonalds.com.

40. DeVault, *Feeding the Family*, 123.

41. McCarthy and Straus, "Tastes of America 1992."

42. Martinac, "Fast, Free Delivery," 163.

43. Pilcher, *¡Que vivan los Tamales!*

44. Gabaccia, *We Are What We Eat*, 71.

45. Jerome, "Frozen (TV) Dinners."

46. Finkelstein, *Dining Out*, 5–8.

Chapter 3. American Food

1. Hess and Hess, *Taste of America*, 22–23.

2. Ibid., 24–25, 29–31.

3. Ibid., 25–26.
4. Gabaccia, *We Are What We Eat,* 28–29.
5. Benjamin Franklin, *On the Art of Eating* (American Philosophical Society, 1958), quoted in Hess and Hess, *Taste of America*, 28–29.
6. Gabaccia, *We Are What We Eat,* 29–30.
7. Hess and Hess, *Taste of America,* 26.
8. Ibid., 71–72.
9. Gabaccia, *We Are What We Eat,* 30–32.
10. Ibid., 18.
11. Ibid., 25–26.
12. Ibid., 26–27.
13. Ibid., 33–34.
14. Ibid., 37.
15. Levenstein, *Revolution at the Table,* 233 (where he cites Jenks and Lauck, *Immigration Problem,* 667) and 101 (where he cites Sombart, *No Socialism in America,* 106).
16. Levenstein, *Revolution at the Table,* 169–70, 107.
17. Ibid., 169–70.
18. Ibid., 145–46.
19. Hess and Hess, *Taste of America,* 27.
20. Kalcik, "Ethnic Foodways in America," 38.
21. Brenner, *American Appetite,* 99–100.
22. Witt, *Black Hunger,* 6, 82.
23. Gabaccia, *We Are What We Eat,* 176.
24. Kalcik, "Ethnic Foodways in America," 38–39.
25. Ibid., 40.
26. Spiro, "Acculturation of American Ethnic Groups."
27. Passin and Bennett, "Social Process and Dietary Change," 113.
28. Douglas, "Deciphering a Meal," 36, 41.
29. Powdermaker, "Feasts in New Ireland," 236.
30. Kalcik, "Ethnic Foodways in America," 48–49.
31. Pesquera, "Work and Family."
32. Finz, "Slow Food Nation."
33. Petrini, *Slow Food,* xxiii–xxiv.
34. Slow Food Web site at http://www.slowfood.com.
35. Unterman, "Savoring Slow Food."
36. Holzschuher, "Not So Fast."
37. Unterman, "Savoring Slow Food."
38. Ibid.
39. Laudan, "Plea for Culinary Modernism," 36–37.
40. Ibid., 38–39, 42.
41. Ibid., 42–43.
42. Schlosser, *Fast Food Nation,* 244.

43. Nestle, *Food Politics*, 373.

44. Kingsolver, *Animal, Vegetable, Miracle*, 16.

45. Pollan, *Omnivore's Dilemma*, 300–301, 3.

46. Ibid., 302–3.

Chapter 4. Conversation and Manners

1. Adorno et al., *Authoritarian Personality*.

2. Simpson, "Cult of 'Conversation'"; Edwards, *Civil Society*, 70; and Schudson, "Why Conversation," 307.

3. Schudson, "Why Conversation," 301.

4. Quoted in Miller, *Conversation*, 305 and xi.

5. Ibid., 5, 20–21, 296–97, 308.

6. Ibid., 45–46.

7. Peter Burke, *Art of Conversation*, 47.

8. Miller, *Conversation*, 47, 68–70.

9. Ibid., quoting Montaigne (1), Fielding (15–16, 19), Swift (4), and Johnson (28).

10. Ibid.; and Gibian, *Oliver Wendell Holmes*.

11. Tannen, *Argument Culture*.

12. Locke, *Why We Don't Talk*, 57.

13. Zeldin, *Conversation*. Quotes are from 14, 36–37, and 93–94.

14. Shepherd, *Art of Civilized Conversation*, 4.

15. Visser, *Rituals of Dinner*, 83, 22–23.

16. Elias, *Civilizing Process*; and Cahoone, "Civic Meetings, Cultural Meanings," 42–43.

17. Calhoun, "Virtue of Civility," 257; and Schmidt, "Is Civility a Virtue?" 17.

18. Kasson, *Rudeness and Civility*.

19. Martin, *Star-Spangled Manners*, 42.

20. Ibid.

21. Rosenblum, *Membership and Morals*, 351.

22. Kennedy, "Case against Civility."

23. DeMott, "Seduced by Civility."

24. Calhoun, "Virtue of Civility," 254.

25. Buss, "Appearing Respectful," 798.

26. Schambra, "Progressive Assault of Civic Community," 320.

27. Kerber, *Women of the Republic*, 283.

28. Matthews, *Just a Housewife*.

29. Black, *Social Feminism*.

30. Matthews, *Just a Housewife*, 142.

31. Beauvoir, *Second Sex*, 480; and Ruddick, *Maternal Thinking*.

32. Visser, *Rituals of Dinner*, 1–3.

33. Ibid., 59–60.

34. Ibid., 62–68.
35. Ibid., 66–68.
36. Elias, *Civilizing Process*, 60–61; and Visser, *Rituals of Dinner*, 58–59.
37. Visser, *Rituals of Dinner*, 69, 70.
38. Ibid., 70–73.
39. Ibid., 60–61.
40. Kasson, *Rudeness and Civility*, 59–62.
41. Visser, *Rituals of Dinner*, 75–76.
42. Martin, *Star-Spangled Manners*, 25, 197–98.
43. Visser, *Rituals of Dinner*, 41–51.
44. Ibid., 47–52.
45. Ibid., 54–55, 82.

Chapter 5. Table Rituals

1. Visser, *Rituals of Dinner*, 19–20.
2. Bossard and Boll, *Ritual in Family Living*.
3. Fiese et al., "Review of 50 Years of Research."
4. Visser, *Rituals of Dinner*, 92, 97–98.
5. Ibid., 23, 25, 87.
6. Ibid., 145–46.
7. Ibid., 23.
8. Sheraton, *From My Mother's Kitchen*.
9. Visser, *Rituals of Dinner*, 35–36.
10. Ibid., 123, 149, 151–52.
11. Ibid., 273–74.
12. Ibid., 126, 127.
13. Ibid., 57, 189–90, 190–92.
14. Ibid., 91.
15. Ibid., 87.
16. Mauss, *Gift*, 81–82.
17. Visser, *Rituals of Dinner*, 53–54.
18. Joannes, "Social Function of Banquets," 33.
19. Toussaint-Samat, *History of Food*. 475.
20. Visser, *Rituals of Dinner*, 87.
21. Ibid., 84–85, 87, 89.
22. Hughes, "Soul, Black Women, and Food," 277.
23. Williams-Forson, "Suckin' the Chicken Bones Dry," 186.
24. Toussaint-Samat, *History of Food*, 213.
25. Visser, *Rituals of Dinner*, 2–3.
26. Toussaint-Samat, *History of Food*, 229, 231.
27. Ibid., 230–31.
28. Barbotin, *Humanity of Man*, 327–28.

29. Symons, *History of Cooks and Cooking,* 257.
30. Root and De Rochemont, *Eating in America,* 32–33, 38, 51, 61, 138.
31. Ibid., 132–33.
32. Ibid., 136–38, 225.
33. Ibid., 225–27.
34. Ibid., 245, 461, 481–82; and Beard, *Beard on Bread.*
35. Barolini, "Appetite Lost, Appetite Found," 229.
36. Visser, *Rituals of Dinner,* 262–63.
37. Ibid., 263–64.
38. Ibid., 146–47.
39. Ibid., 129.
40. Ibid., 129–30, 267–68, esp. 267.
41. Ibid., 268–69.
42. Ibid., 269–71.
43. Robert Burford, quoted in Batterberry and Batterberry, *On the Town,* 46.
44. Brenner, *American Appetite,* 262.
45. Visser, *Rituals of Dinner,* 266–71.
46. Mauss, *Gift,* 83.
47. Goffman, *Behavior in Public Places.*
48. Visser, *Rituals of Dinner,* 49.
49. Christopher, *Come to the Table,* 59–60.
50. Ibid., 66.

Chapter 6. Generations at the Table

1. DeVault, *Feeding the Family,* 53–54.
2. Ibid., 54, 49.
3. Ibid., 189.
4. Ibid., 49.
5. Christopher, *Come to the Table,* 65.
6. Hughes, "Soul, Black Women, and Food," 273.
7. Christopher, *Come to the Table,* 43–44.
8. Ibid., 56–57.
9. DeVault, *Feeding the Family,* 49–50.
10. Lareau, "Invisible Inequality," 763.
11. Christopher, *Come to the Table,* 1–3.
12. Ibid., 38.
13. Ibid., 39–40, 47.
14. Ibid., 58.
15. Katrak, "Food and Belonging," 267–68.
16. Barolini, "Appetite Lost, Appetite Found," 228–29.
17. Ibid., 233–35.
18. Minnich, "There Are No Recipes," 147.

19. Wade-Gayles, "Laying on Hands through Cooking," 98–99.
20. Ibid., 100–102.
21. Dash, "Rice Culture," 22.
22. Christopher, *Come to the Table*, 44–45.
23. Visser, *Rituals of Dinner*, 55. She cites the findings of Charles and Kerr, *Women, Food and Families*.
24. Hymowitz, "Quality Time Is Authority Time."
25. Salamon, "It's Always Saturday on TV."
26. "White House Conference on Teenagers."
27. Cited in "White House Conference on Teenagers."
28. Cited in "White House Conference on Teenagers."
29. Hymowitz, "Quality Time Is Authority Time."
30. Ruddick, *Maternal Thinking*, 121, 122–23, 123. She cites Murdoch, *Sovereignty of Good*, 43.
31. DeVault, *Feeding the Family*, 116.
32. Ibid., 116–17.
33. Ibid., 115.

Chapter 7. The Human Psyche and Mind-Body Dualism

1. Oliver, "Nourishing the Speaking Subject."
2. Chodorow, *Reproduction of Mothering*, 218.
3. Quandt, "Infant and Child Nutrition."
4. Ibid., 1444–45.
5. Ibid., 1446–47.
6. Ibid., 1447.
7. Ibid., 1448–49.
8. Ibid., 1450.
9. Counihan, *Anthropology of Food and Body*, 134–35.
10. Ibid., 135–50.
11. Ibid., 153, 18.
12. Ibid., 153.
13. Holmberg, *Nomads of the Long Bow*; and Hallowell, "Social Function of Anxiety."
14. Richards, *Hunger and Work*; and Richards, *Land, Labour and Diet*.
15. Curtin, "Food/Body/Person."
16. Ibid., 5–6.
17. Symons, *History of Cooks and Cooking*, 35–36.
18. Ibid., 36–37.
19. Ibid., 37–38.
20. Plato, *Symposium*, 320, 322.
21. Ibid., 322–23.
22. Augustine, *Confessions*, 238.

23. Ruether, "Misogynism and Virginal Feminism."
24. Descartes, *Discourse on Method,* 21.
25. Bordo, "Anorexia Nervosa," 246n25.
26. Counihan, *Anthropology of Food and Body,* 180–81.
27. Blume, "Sin Be Damned."
28. Counihan, *Anthropology of Food and Body,* 183–84.
29. Symons, *History of Cooks and Cooking,* 127.
30. Ibid., 111–13.
31. Draper, "Human Nutritional Adaptation," 1473–74.
32. Ibid., 1474.
33. Ehrenreich and English, *Witches, Midwives and Nurses,* 13–14, 19.
34. Visser, *Rituals of Dinner,* 277–78.
35. Ibid., 139–40.
36. Beardsworth and Keil, *Sociology on the Menu,* 150–51.
37. Visser, *Rituals of Dinner,* 140.
38. Beardsworth and Keil, *Sociology on the Menu,* 152–59.
39. Ibid., 162.
40. Fischler, "Food, Self, and Identity."

Chapter 8. Appetite and Taste

1. Korsmeyer, *Making Sense of Taste.* See Lévi-Strauss, *The Raw and the Cooked*; Goody, *Cooking, Cuisine and Class*; and Farb and Armelagos, *Consuming Passions.*
2. Bordo, "Hunger as Ideology."
3. Shapiro, *Perfection Salad,* 4–5.
4. Ibid., 7, 191.
5. Ibid., 191–92.
6. Ibid., 198–99.
7. Ibid., 203–4.
8. Ibid., 215–16.
9. Brumberg, *Fasting Girls.*
10. Ibid., 249–55.
11. Manton, *Fed Up,* 108.
12. Brumberg, *Fasting Girls,* 255–57, 265–66.
13. Bordo, "Anorexia Nervosa," 231–33.
14. See, for example, Chernin, *Obsession* and *Hungry Self*; Orbach, *Fat Is a Feminist Issue*; and Roth, *Feeding the Hungry Heart, Breaking Free from Compulsive Eating,* and *When Food Is Love.*
15. Manton, *Fed Up,* 117–24.
16. Heldke, "Foodmaking as a Thoughtful Practice," 203, 206.
17. Ibid., 216–19. See Dewey, *Experience and Nature.*
18. Berry, "Pleasures of Eating," 131.

19. Korsmeyer, *Making Sense of Taste*, 3.
20. Ibid., 13–26.
21. Ibid., 26–27.
22. Ibid., 31–33.
23. Ibid., 41–42, 2, 67, 68.
24. Ibid., 3–4.
25. Ibid., 69–71.
26. Brillat-Savarin, *Physiology of Taste*, 13–14.
27. Ibid., 47–48, 52, 54–55.
28. Korsmeyer, *Making Sense of Taste*, 72–74.
29. Ibid., 87–88.
30. Ibid., 88.
31. Capaldi, "Introduction," 6.
32. Rozin, "Sociocultural Influences," 242, 235, 245–46.
33. Goody, *Cooking, Cuisine and Class*, chap. 4.

Chapter 9. Alice Waters's Delicious Revolution

1. For accounts of Waters and her delicious revolution, see, for example, McNamee, *Alice Waters and Chez Panisse*; and A. Waters, *Art of Simple Food*.
2. Sundelson, "After Quiche, What?"
3. A. Waters, "Farm-Restaurant Connection," 120.
4. A. Waters, "Ethics of Eating."
5. Ibid.
6. Ibid.
7. Ibid.
8. Ibid.
9. A. Waters, "Making Food the Educational Priority."
10. Reardon, *M. F. K. Fisher*, 213.
11. Alice Waters, personal interview, March 19, 2001.
12. Ibid.
13. Ibid.
14. Reardon, *M. F. K. Fisher*, 19–20.
15. A. Waters, *Chez Panisse Menu Cookbook*, x–xi.
16. Reardon, *M. F. K. Fisher*, 21.
17. A. Waters, "Farm-Restaurant Connection," 122.
18. Ibid., 113.
19. *Merriam-Webster's Collegiate Dictionary*, 10th ed.
20. Alice Waters, quoted in Chriss, "Chez Panisse Founder."
21. Alice Waters, quoted in Brenner, *American Appetite*, 131.
22. A. Waters, "Farm-Restaurant Connection," 115.
23. Ibid.

24. A. Waters, "Ethics of Eating."
25. Winn, "Delicious Revolution."
26. Ibid.
27. Ibid.
28. Ibid.
29. Quoted in A. Waters, "Ethics of Eating, Part Two."
30. Quoted in A. Waters, "Garden, the Table, and Educational Equality."
31. Ibid.
32. A. Waters, "Ethics of Eating, Part Two."
33. Alice Waters, personal interview, March 19, 2001.
34. Alice Waters, quoted in Winn, "Delicious Revolution," 27.
35. Alice Waters, personal interview, March 19, 2001.
36. Ibid.
37. A. Waters, *Chez Panisse Menu Cookbook,* 3.
38. Alice Waters, personal interview, March 19, 2001.

Chapter 10. Putting the Delicious Revolution into Practice

1. A. Waters, "Farm-Restaurant Connection," 113–15.
2. Ibid., 115–17.
3. Ibid., 117–18.
4. Ibid.
5. Ibid., 119.
6. Ibid., 118–19.
7. Pendleton, "Pure Alice."
8. Ibid.
9. A. Waters, "Farm-Restaurant Connection," 121.
10. A. Waters, "Biography."
11. A. Waters, "Ethics of Eating"; "Ethics of Eating: Part Two"; and "Waters to Speak at Strybing."
12. Morse, "What If They Don't Go Home?"
13. Wood, "Beach Party."
14. Garchik, "Personals."
15. Ritchie, "American Piazza," 76.
16. David Armstrong, "Food Fight"; and Abate, "Trade Debate."
17. "Ditty's Saturday Market."
18. "Alice Waters Speaks."
19. Steger, "Hillary and Chelsea Do Dinner."
20. A. Waters, "Making Food the Educational Priority."
21. Ibid.
22. Alice Waters, quoted in Garcia, "Jail Sentences Reduced."
23. Alice Waters, personal interview, March 19, 2001.
24. Alice Waters, quoted in Sandalow, "Republicans."
25. Alice Waters, quoted in Brazil, "D.C. Dogfight Nips Garden Project."

26. A. Waters, "Making Food the Educational Priority."
27. Ibid.
28. A. Waters, "Garden, the Table, and Educational Equality."
29. Ibid.
30. Ibid.
31. Ibid.
32. Ibid.
33. Ibid.
34. Alice Waters, quoted in Finnamore, "Food for Thought," 53, 56.
35. Alice Waters, quoted in Pendleton, "Pure Alice," 13.
36. A. Waters, "Ethics of Eating: Part Two."
37. A. Waters, "StarChefs Interview with Alice Waters."
38. Ibid.
39. "Chez Panisse Foundation."
40. Riddle, "Edible Schoolyard," 100–102.
41. "Berkeley Project Boosted by Cookbook."
42. Burress, "Tribute."
43. "Waters Receives National Honor."
44. Fletcher, "Chefs' School Lunches."
45. A. Waters, remarks at a public hearing.
46. Ibid.
47. Ibid.
48. Ibid.
49. Krieger, "School Lunch Revolution."
50. Fletcher, "Chefs' School Lunches."
51. A. Waters, "Making Food the Educational Priority."
52. Ibid.
53. Ibid.
54. Ibid.
55. Hoover, "Berkeley School Lunches"; May, "Lunch Going Organic"; and Palmer, "Trading Tater Tots."
56. Alice Waters, interview with Gorney.
57. Ibid.
58. Associated Press, "Report Pans School Vending."
59. May, "Souped Up School Food."
60. Alice Waters, personal interview, March 19, 2001.
61. Severson, "Food Joins Academic Menu."
62. Ibid.

Chapter 11. Community Food and Belonging in America

1. Swarns, "African-American."
2. Ibid.
3. Kiang and Loo, "Food in Racial Experiences."

4. Zelinsky, *Cultural Geography*; and Gastil, *Cultural Regions*.
5. Lockwood and Lockwood, "Pasties in Michigan's Upper Peninsula."
6. Ibid.
7. Gutierrez, "Social and Symbolic Uses"; and Gutierrez, "Cajuns and Crawfish."
8. Tuchman and Levine, "New York Jews and Chinese Food." They cite Sheraton, "Jewish Yen for Chinese," 71.
9. Lloyd, "Cincinnati Chili Culinary Complex."
10. Lewis, "Maine Lobster as Regional Icon."
11. De Wit, "Food-Place Associations."
12. Standage, *History of the World*.
13. Frenkel, "Pound of Kenya."
14. De Guzman, "Beyond 'Living La Vida Boba.'"
15. Ireland, "Compiled Cookbook as Foodways Autobiography."
16. Kao, "Ma's Killer Won-Ton Soup."
17. Kaplan, Hoover, and Moore, "Introduction."
18. Magliocco, "Playing With Food."
19. Neustadt, *Clambake*.
20. Ibid., 162, 172.
21. Ibid., 175, 178–81.
22. From "Picnic Excursions," *Appleton's* (1869), cited in Hern, "Picknicking."
23. Luard, *Sacred Food*, 233.
24. Pilcher, *¡Que vivan los Tamales!* 161; Luard, *Sacred Food*, 74–105, 187.
25. Lim, "Boiled Chicken Feet."
26. Luard, *Sacred Food*, 70, 106.
27. Ibid., 113, 115.
28. Ibid., 146–47, 159, 170, 176.
29. Ibid., 186–87, 170, 189–90.
30. Ibid., 199, 201.

Chapter 12. Gardens and Community

1. Hynes, *Patch of Eden*, xi.
2. Bentley, *Eating for Victory*, 114–16.
3. Ibid., 120–23.
4. Ibid., 125–29.
5. Ibid., 131–35.
6. Hynes, *Patch of Eden*, x–xi.
7. Ibid.
8. Ibid., xii–xiii.
9. Ibid., xiii–xiv.
10. Ibid., xiv.

11. Ibid., xiv–xvi.
12. Ibid., 3–6.
13. Patterson, "Greening of Harlem."
14. Hynes, *Patch of Eden,* 73–79.
15. Schukoske, "Community Development through Gardening."
16. Ibid.
17. Hynes, *Patch of Eden,* 90–91; and Patel, "Gardening's Socioeconomic Impacts."
18. Grieshop, "Serendipity and Community Development."
19. Donna Armstrong, "Survey of Community Gardens."
20. http://www.dug.org.
21. "Seeds of Hope."
22. Ferriss, "Garden Variety Angels"; Hicks, "Harvesting Care"; and Casa Assurance System for the Aging, "Miss Bessie's GardenAngel."
23. Westmacott, *African-American Gardens,* 112.
24. Squatriglia, "Growing Gains."
25. Bjornson, "Immigrant Gardens."
26. http://www.greenguerillas.org.
27. http://www.greenthumbnyc.org.
28. Keller, "Gardening Changes a Community."
29. Nemore, "Rooted in Community."
30. Vellinga, "Gardens Nurture a Sense of Community."
31. Dotter, "Cultivating People-Plant Relationships."
32. http://www.neustras-raices.org.
33. American Community Gardening Association, *National Community Gardening Survey.*
34. Atkin, "He Has Down-to-Earth Recipe."
35. "Community Garden Bulletins."
36. "Seeds of Hope."
37. The Food Project, Boston, http://www.thefoodproject.org.
38. Lawson and McNally, "Putting Teens at the Center."
39. Elliot, "Compost."
40. Lawson, "Planner in the Garden."
41. "Garden-Enhanced Nutrition Education."
42. E. Bell, "Sprouting Minds."
43. Ibid.
44. Hawkins, "Developing the Edible Schoolyard."
45. Ibid.
46. Ibid.
47. Bahar, "Many Lessons Are Taught."
48. Cook, "Kitchen Classroom."
49. Cook, "On Any Given Day."

50. Burt, "Students, Vegetables, Sunshine."
51. Kiefer and Kemple, *Digging Deeper,* 122.
52. Ibid., 118.
53. http://www.slug-sf.org.
54. Kiefer and Kemple, *Digging Deeper,* 8.
55. Berbeo, "Hands-On Assignment."
56. Rich, "Cultivating School Grounds."
57. Payne, "Listening with Respect."
58. Ibid.
59. Hynes, *Patch of Eden,* 57–59.
60. Ibid., 59–65.
61. Ibid., 41, 46–47, 48–49.
62. Garcia, "Jail Sentences Reduced."
63. http://www.gardenproject.org (2002).
64. Wanning, "Profile: Catherine Sneed."
65. Rathbone, "Tough Guys Do Garden."
66. Wanning, "Profile."
67. Scott, "Catherine Sneed."
68. Wanning, "Profile"; and Sneed, "Garden Project."
69. Sneed, "Garden Project."
70. University of Illinois Extension, "Cook County Sheriff's Garden."
71. Fesperman, "Blooming behind Bars."
72. Gardiner, "Gardens Offer a Respite."
73. Dease, "Garden Program Budding."
74. Pruyne, "Gardening."
75. Tonge, "Garden."
76. Rice and Remy, "Evaluating Horticultural Therapy."
77. Flagler, "Master Gardeners and Horticultural Therapy."

Chapter 13. Farmers' Markets

1. Holcomb, "Baltimore Municipal Markets."
2. Spitzer and Baum, *Public Markets and Community Revitalization.*
3. Ibid.; and the USDA farmers' markets Web site, http://www.ams.usda.gov/farmersmarkets/facts.html.
4. O'Neill, "Sharing in the Harvest."
5. Spitzer and Baum, *Public Markets and Community Revitalization.*
6. Jacobs, "Market Nurturing Run Amok."
7. Sine, "Farmer's Doubters."
8. Raun, "Vendors Bring Summer's Bounty."
9. Young, "Grower Profile."
10. Ibid.

11. Eastwood, "Demise of an Urban Market."

12. Smith, "State Welfare Payments."

13. Morse, "Tale of 2 Farmers' Markets."

14. http://www.farmernet.com/TheMarkets.

15. McPhee, "Giving Good Weight," 6–7.

16. Ibid., 68–69.

17. Ibid., 69–70.

18. Sterngold, "Crash Witness Shocked."

19. Madison, "Native Chiles in Santa Fe."

20. Ibid.

21. O'Neill, "Food."

22. C. Waters, "Market Value."

Conclusion

1. Goldstein, "Beyond Table Talk."

2. Ellis, *His Excellency George Washington,* 207.

Bibliography

Abate, Tom. "Trade Debate Echoes Business, Consumer Concerns." *San Francisco Chronicle,* November 25, 1999.

Adorno, Theodor W., Else Frenkel-Brunswik, D. J. Levinson, and R. Nevitt Sanford. *The Authoritarian Personality.* New York: Harper, 1950.

"Alice Waters Speaks on Garden Project." *San Francisco Chronicle,* July 17, 1996.

American Community Gardening Association. *National Community Gardening Survey: 1996.* Philadelphia: American Community Gardening Association, 1998.

Aresty, Esther B. *The Best Behavior: The Course of Good Manners—from Antiquity to the Present—as Seen through Courtesy and Etiquette Books.* New York: Simon and Schuster, 1970.

Armstrong, David. "Food Fight." *San Francisco Examiner,* March 6, 1998.

Armstrong, Donna. "A Survey of Community Gardens in Upstate New York: Implications for Health Promotion and Community Development." *Health and Place* 6, no. 4 (2000): 319–27.

Associated Press. "Report Pans School Vending." *San Francisco Chronicle,* February 7, 2001.

Atkin, Ross. "He Has Down-to-Earth Recipe for Gardening Success." *Christian Science Monitor,* October 10, 2001.

Augustine. *The Confessions of St. Augustine.* Translated by Rex Warner. New York: New American Library, 1963.

Avakian, Arlene Voski, ed. *Through the Kitchen Window: Women Explore the Intimate Meanings of Food and Cooking.* Boston: Beacon, 1997.

Babayan, Caroline. "The Cook, the Maid and the Lady." In Avakian, *Through the Kitchen Window,* 112–16.

Bahar, Zillah. "Many Lessons Are Taught at the Edible Schoolyard." *San Francisco Chronicle,* August 18, 1999.

Barbotin, Edmond. *The Humanity of Man.* New York: Orbis, 1975.

Barolini, Helen. "Appetite Lost, Appetite Found." In Avakian, *Through the Kitchen Window,* 228–37.

Baron, Stephen, John Field, and Tom Schuller, eds. *Social Capital: Critical Perspectives.* New York: Oxford University Press, 2000.

Batterberry, Michael, and Ariane Batterberry. *On the Town in New York: From 1776 to the Present.* New York: Charles Scribner's Sons, 1973.

Beard, James. *Beard on Bread.* New York: Alfred A. Knopf, 1973.

Beardsworth, Alan, and Teresa Keil. *Sociology on the Menu: An Invitation to the Study of Food and Society.* London: Routledge, 1997.

Beauvoir, Simone de. *The Second Sex.* Translated and edited by H. M. Parshley. New York: Vintage, 1974.

Bell, David, and Gill Valentine. *Consuming Geographies: We Are Where We Eat.* New York: Routledge, 1997.

Bell, Elizabeth. "Sprouting Minds: School Gardens Popular Again as a Platform for Learning." *San Francisco Chronicle,* April 11, 2000.

Bennhold, Katrin. "Love of Leisure, and Europe's Reasons." *New York Times,* July 29, 2004.

Bentley, Amy. *Eating for Victory: Food Rationing and the Politics of Domesticity.* Urbana: University of Illinois Press, 1998.

Berbeo, Dominic. "Hands-On Assignment." *Daily News of Los Angeles,* January 14, 2000.

"Berkeley Project Boosted by Cookbook." *San Francisco Chronicle,* September 8, 1999.

Berry, Wendell. "The Pleasures of Eating." In *Our Sustainable Table,* edited by Robert Clark, 125–31. San Francisco: North Point Press, 1990.

Bjornson, Margaret Ross. "Immigrant Gardens: Seeds of Home in Times of Change." In *People-Plant Interactions in Urban Areas: Proceedings of a Research and Education Symposium,* edited by Pat Williams and Jayne Zajicek, 123–26. College Station: Texas A&M University Department of Horticultural Sciences, 1996.

Black, Naomi. *Social Feminism.* Ithaca, N.Y.: Cornell University Press, 1989.

Blum-Kulka, Shoshana. *Dinner Talk: Cultural Patterns of Sociability and Socialization in Family Discourse.* Mahwah, N.J.: Lawrence Erlbaum, 1997.

Blume, Mary. "Sin Be Damned, French Say; Let's Eat." *New York Times,* March 6, 2003.

Bobbio, Norberto. "Gramsci and the Concept of Civil Society." In *Civil Society and the State: New European Perspectives,* edited by John Keane, 73–100. New York: Verso, 1988.

Boisvert, Raymond D. "Clock Time/Stomach Time." *Gastronomica: The Journal of Food and Culture* 6, no. 2 (Spring 2006): 40–46.

Bordo, Susan. "Anorexia Nervosa: Psychopathology as the Crystallization of Culture." In Counihan and Van Esterik, *Food and Culture,* 226–50.

———. "Hunger as Ideology." In Scapp and Seitz, *Eating Culture,* 11–35.

Bossard, James H. S., and Eleanor S. Boll. *Ritual in Family Living: A Contemporary Study.* Philadelphia: University of Pennsylvania Press, 1950.

Bourdieu, Pierre. "The Forms of Capital." In *Handbook of Theory and Research for the Sociology of Education*, edited by John Richardson, 241–58. New York: Greenwood Press, 1986.

Brazil, Eric. "D.C. Dogfight Nips Garden Project." *San Francisco Examiner*, May 31, 1996.

Brenner, Leslie. *American Appetite: The Coming of Age of a Cuisine*. New York: Avon, 1999.

Brillat-Savarin, Jean-Anthelme. *The Physiology of Taste*. 1825. Translated by Anne Drayton. London: Penguin, 1994.

Brown, Linda Keller, and Kay Mussell, eds. *Ethnic and Regional Foodways in the United States: The Performance of Group Identity*. Knoxville: University of Tennessee Press, 1984.

Brumberg, Joan Jacobs. *Fasting Girls: The History of Anorexia Nervosa*. New York: Plume/Penguin, 1989.

Burke, Peter. *The Art of Conversation*. Cambridge: Polity Press, 1995.

Burns, Nancy, Kay Lehman Schlozman, and Sidney Verba. *The Private Roots of Public Action: Gender, Equality, and Political Participation*. Cambridge, Mass.: Harvard University Press, 2001.

Burress, Charles. "Tribute to a 'Delicious Revolution' in Berkeley." *San Francisco Chronicle*, August 4, 1998.

Burt, Cecily. "Students, Vegetables, Sunshine Welcome Mr. Rogers to Berkeley." *Oakland Tribune*, October 15, 1999.

Buss, Sarah. "Appearing Respectful: The Moral Significance of Manners." *Ethics* 109, no. 4 (July 1999): 795–826.

Cahoone, Lawrence. "Civic Meetings, Cultural Meanings." In *Civility*, edited by Leroy S. Rouner, 40–64. Notre Dame, Ind.: University of Notre Dame Press, 2000.

Caiazza, Amy, and Robert D. Putnam. *Women's Status and Social Capital across the States*. Washington, D.C.: Institute for Women's Policy Research, 2002.

Calhoun, Cheshire. "The Virtue of Civility." *Philosophy and Public Affairs* 29, no. 3 (Summer 2000): 251–75.

Capaldi, Elizabeth. "Introduction." In *Why We Eat What We Eat: The Psychology of Eating*, edited by Elizabeth Capaldi, 3–9. Washington, D.C.: American Psychological Association, 1996.

Carrington, Christopher. *No Place like Home: Relationships and Family Life among Lesbians and Gay Men*. Chicago: University of Chicago Press, 1999.

Carter, Stephen L. *Civility: Manners, Morals and the Etiquette of Democracy*. New York: Harper, 1998.

Casa Assurance System for the Aging (CASA). "Miss Bessie's GardenAngel." http://www.casagarden.com (accessed 2002).

Chambers, Simone. "A Critical Theory of Civil Society." In Chambers and Kymlicka, *Alternative Conceptions of Civil Society*, 90–110.

Chambers, Simone, and Will Kymlicka, eds. *Alternative Conceptions of Civil Society*. Princeton, N.J.: Princeton University Press, 2002.

Charles, Nickie, and Marion Kerr. *Women, Food and Families*. Manchester, U.K.: Manchester University Press, 1988.

Chernin, Kim. *The Hungry Self: Women, Eating, and Identity*. New York: Harper and Row, 1985.

———. *The Obsession: Reflections on the Tyranny of Slenderness*. New York: Harper and Row, 1981.

"Chez Panisse Foundation Statement of Purpose." http://www.chezpanisse.com/cpfoundation.

Chodorow, Nancy. *The Reproduction of Mothering: Psychoanalysis and the Sociology of Gender*. Berkeley: University of California Press, 1978.

Chriss, Catherine. "Chez Panisse Founder Alice Waters Popularized California Cuisine." *Oakland Tribune*, December 21, 1999.

Christopher, Doris. *Come to the Table: A Celebration of Family Life*. New York: Warner Books, 1999.

Coleman, James. "Social Capital in the Creation of Human Capital." *American Journal of Sociology* 94 (1988 Supplement): S95–S120.

"Community Garden Bulletins." Urban Agricultural Notes, *City Farmer*, January 8, 2002.

Cook, Esther. "The Kitchen Classroom." The Edible Schoolyard, Berkeley, Calif. http://www.edibleschoolyard.org.

———. "On Any Given Day." The Edible Schoolyard, Berkeley, Calif. http://www.edibleschoolyard.org.

Cortez, Constance. *Carmen Lomas Garza*. Los Angeles: UCLA Chicano Studies and University of Minnesota Press, 2009.

Coss, Clare. "My Mother/Her Kitchen." In Avakian, *Through the Kitchen Window*, 13–16.

Counihan, Carole M. *The Anthropology of Food and Body: Gender, Meaning, and Power*. New York: Routledge, 1999.

Counihan, Carole M., and Penny Van Esterik, eds. *Food and Culture: A Reader*. New York: Routledge, 1997.

Cowan, Ruth Schwartz. *More Work for Mother: The Ironies of Household Technology from the Open Hearth to the Microwave*. New York: Basic Books, 1983.

Curtin, Deane W. "Food/Body/Person." In *Cooking, Eating, Thinking: Transformative Philosophies of Food*, edited by Deane W. Curtin and Lisa M. Heldke, 3–22. Bloomington: Indiana University Press, 1992.

Dash, Julie. "Rice Culture." In Avakian, *Through the Kitchen Window*, 19–23.

Davis, Maradee A., Suzanne Murphy, and John N. Neuhaus. "Living Arrangements and Eating Behaviors of Older Adults in the United States." *Journal of Gerontology* 43, no. 3 (May 1988): 896–98.

Dean, Jodi. "Including Women: The Consequences and Side Effects of Feminist Critiques of Civil Society." *Philosophy and Social Criticism* 18, nos. 3–4 (1992): 379–99.

Dease, Melissa. "Garden Program Budding: County Inmates to Grow Flowers, Vegetables," *Medina (Ohio) County Gazette*, November 16, 1999.

De Graaf, John, ed. *Take Back Your Time: Fighting Overwork and Time Poverty in America*. San Francisco: Berrett-Koehler, 2003.

De Guzman, Jean-Paul R. "Beyond 'Living La Vida Boba'": Social Space and Transnational, Hybrid Asian American Youth Culture." *Amerasia Journal* 32, no. 2 (2006): 89–102.

De Mott, Benjamin. "Seduced by Civility: Political Manners and the Crisis of Democratic Values." *Nation*, December 9, 1996, 11–19.

Descartes, René. *Discourse on Method*. 1637. Translated by Laurence J. Lafleur. Indianapolis: Bobbs-Merrill, 1950.

DeVault, Marjorie L. *Feeding the Family: The Social Organization of Caring as Gendered Work*. Chicago: University of Chicago Press, 1991.

Dewey, John. *Experience and Nature*. New York: Dover, 1958.

——. *The Public and Its Problems*. Athens: Ohio University Press, 1954.

De Wit, Cary W. "Food-Place Associations on American Product Labels." In Shortridge and Shortridge, *Taste of American Place*, 101–10.

Dinkin, Robert J. *Voting in Provincial America: A Study of Elections in the Thirteen Colonies, 1689–1776*. Westport, Conn: Greenwood Press, 1977.

Dionne, E. J., Jr., ed. *Community Works: The Revival of Civil Society in America*. Washington, D.C.: Brookings Institution Press, 1998.

"Ditty's Saturday Market: The Garden Project." http://www.saturdaymarket.com/garden (accessed June 1996).

Dotter, John. "Cultivating People-Plant Relationships in Community and Cultural Heritage Gardens: San Jose, California (1977–1992)." In Flagler and Poincelot, *People-Plant Relationships*, 153–70.

Douglas, Mary. "Deciphering a Meal." In Counihan and Van Esterik, *Food and Culture*, 36–54.

Draper, H. H. "Human Nutritional Adaptation: Biological and Cultural Aspects." In *The Cambridge World History of Food*, vol. 2, edited by Kenneth F. Kiple and Kriemhild Conee Ornelas, 1466–75. Cambridge: Cambridge University Press, 2000.

Eastwood, Carolyn. "The Demise of an Urban Market: Does It Matter? Who Cares?" Paper presented at the meeting of the Central States Anthropological Society, March 1995. http://www.openair.org/cyjour/demise.html.

Eberly, Don, ed. *The Essential Civil Society Reader: Classic Essays in the American Civil Society Debate*. Lanham, Md.: Rowman and Littlefield, 2000.

Edwards, Bob, and Michael W. Foley. "Civil Society and Social Capital: A Primer." In Edwards, Foley, and Diani, *Beyond Tocqueville*, 1–14.

Edwards, Bob, Michael W. Foley, and Mario Diani, eds. *Beyond Tocqueville: Civil Society and the Social Capital Debate in Comparative Perspective*. Hanover, N.H.: University Press of New England, 2001.

Edwards, Michael. *Civil Society.* Cambridge: Polity Press, 2004.

Ehrenberg, John. *Civil Society: The Critical History of an Idea.* New York: New York University Press, 1999.

Ehrenreich, Barbara. "Maid to Order." In *Global Woman: Nannies, Maids and Sex Workers in the New Economy,* edited by Barbara Ehrenreich and Arlie Russell Hochschild, 85–103. New York: Henry Holt, 2002.

Ehrenreich, Barbara, and Deirdre English. *Witches, Midwives and Nurses: A History of Women Healers.* Old Westbury, N.Y.: Feminist Press, 1973.

Ehrenreich, Barbara, and Arlie Russell Hochschild. "Introduction." In *Global Woman: Nannies, Maids and Sex Workers in the New Economy,* edited by Barbara Ehrenreich and Arlie Russell Hochschild, 1–13. New York: Henry Holt, 2002.

Eilperin, Juliet. *Fight Club Politics: How Partisanship Is Poisoning the U.S. House of Representatives.* New York: Rowman and Littlefield, 2006.

Elias, Norbert. *The Civilizing Process: Sociogenetic and Psychogenetic Investigations.* Rev. ed. Oxford: Blackwell, 2000.

Eliasoph, Nina. *Avoiding Politics: How Americans Produce Apathy in Everyday Life.* New York: Cambridge University Press, 1998.

Elliot, Judy. "Compost as a Microcosm of Community." In Kiefer and Kemple, *Digging Deeper,* 29.

Ellis, Joseph J. *His Excellency George Washington.* New York: Knopf, 2005.

Ellis, Markman. *The Coffee-House: A Cultural History.* London: Phoenix, 2004.

Elshtain, Jean Bethke. "Democracy on Trial: The Role of Civil Society in Sustaining Democratic Values." In *The Essential Civil Society Reader: The Classic Essays,* edited by Don E. Eberly, 101–22. Lanham, Md.: Rowman and Littlefield, 2000.

Farb, Peter, and George Armelagos. *Consuming Passions: The Anthropology of Eating.* Boston: Houghton Mifflin, 1980.

Ferriss, Lloyd. "Garden Variety Angels." *Portland Press Herald,* June 8, 2001.

Fesperman, Dan. "Blooming behind Bars." *San Francisco Chronicle,* May 15, 2000.

Fiese, Barbara H., Thomas J. Tomcho, Michael Douglas, Kimberly Josephs, Scott Poltrock, and Tim Baker. "A Review of 50 Years of Research on Naturally Occurring Family Routines and Rituals: Cause for Celebration?" *Journal of Family Psychology* 16, no. 4 (December 2002): 381–90.

Finch, Janet. *Married to the Job.* New York: Harper Collins, 1983.

Fine, Ben. *Social Capital versus Social Theory: Political Economy and Social Science at the Turn of the Century.* London: Routledge, 2001.

Finkelstein, Joanne. *Dining Out: A Sociology of Modern Manners.* Cambridge: Polity Press, 1989.

Finnamore, Suzanne. "Food for Thought." Article provided by Alice Waters's office. December 2000, pp. 53, 56.

Finz, Stacy. "Slow Food Nation Comes to San Francisco." *San Francisco Chronicle,* June 30, 2008.

Fischler, Claude. "Food, Self, and Identity." *Social Science Information* 27, no. 2 (1988): 275–92.

Fishman, Pamela M. "Interaction: The Work Women Do." *Social Problems* 25, no. 4 (April 1978): 397–406.

Flagler, Joel. "Master Gardeners and Horticultural Therapy." *HortTechnology* 2, no. 2 (1992): 249–50.

Flagler, Joel, and Raymond P. Poincelot, eds. *People-Plant Relationships: Setting Research Priorities.* Binghamton, N.Y.: Haworth Press, 1994.

Fletcher, Janet. "Chefs' School Lunches." *San Francisco Chronicle,* May 10, 1995.

Frenkel, Stephen. "A Pound of Kenya, Please, or a Single Short Skinny Mocha." In Shortridge and Shortridge, *Taste of American Place,* 57–64.

Fullinwider, Robert K., ed. *Civil Society: Democracy and Civil Renewal.* Lanham, Md.: Rowman and Littlefield, 1999.

Gabaccia, Donna R. *We Are What We Eat: Ethnic Food and the Making of Americans.* Cambridge, Mass.: Harvard University Press, 1998.

Galinsky, Ellen, James Bond, and Dana Friedman. *The Changing Workforce: Highlights of a National Study.* New York: Families and Work Institute, 1993.

Gamson, William A. *Talking Politics.* New York: Cambridge University Press, 1992.

Garchik, Leah. "Personals." *San Francisco Chronicle,* November 20, 1997.

Garcia, Ken. "Jail Sentences Reduced to Thyme Served: Unique Gardening Program for Inmates." *San Francisco Chronicle,* April 17, 1999.

"Garden-Enhanced Nutrition Education, Garden Resources." Report from the California Department of Education. http://www.cde.ca.gov/nsd.

Gardiner, Beth. "Gardens Offer a Respite at Jail." *Today's Homeowner,* March 8, 1999. http://www.todayshomeowner.com.

Gastil, Raymond D. *Cultural Regions of the United States.* Seattle: University of Washington Press, 1975.

Gibian, Peter. *Oliver Wendell Holmes and the Culture of Conversation.* Cambridge: Cambridge University Press, 2001.

Goffman, Erving. *Behavior in Public Places.* New York: Free Press, 1963.

Goldstein, Darra. "Beyond Table Talk." *Gastronomica: The Journal of Food and Culture* 3, no. 1 (Winter 2003): iii–iv.

Goode, Judith, Janet Theophano, and Karen Curtis. "A Framework for the Analysis of Continuity and Change in Shared Sociocultural Rules for Food Use: The Italian-American Pattern." In Brown and Mussell, *Ethnic and Regional Foodways,* 66–88.

Goody, Jack. *Cooking, Cuisine and Class: A Study in Comparative Sociology.* Cambridge: Cambridge University Press, 1982.

Graham, A. "'Let's Eat!' Commitment and Communion in Co-Operative Households." *Western Folklore* 40, no. 1 (1981): 55–63.

Grieshop, J. I. "Serendipity and Community Development: A Study of Unplanned

Community Development Consequences in a Community Service Program." *Journal of Community Development and Society* 15, no. 2 (1984): 87–103.

Gutierrez, C. Paige. "Cajuns and Crawfish." In Shortridge and Shortridge, *Taste of American Place,* 139–44.

———. "The Social and Symbolic Uses of Ethnic/Regional Foodways: Cajuns and Crawfish in South Louisiana." In Brown and Mussell, *Ethnic and Regional Foodways,* 169–82.

Habermas, Jürgen. *The Structural Transformation of the Public Sphere.* Cambridge, Mass.: MIT Press, 1989.

Hallowell, A.I. "The Social Function of Anxiety in a Primitive Society." *American Sociological Review* 6 (1941): 869–81.

Hawkins, David. "Developing the Edible Schoolyard." The Edible Schoolyard, Berkeley, Calif. http://www.edibleschoolyard.org.

Heldke, Lisa M. "Foodmaking as a Thoughtful Practice." In *Cooking, Eating, Thinking: Transformative Philosophies of Food,* edited by Deane W. Curtin and Lisa M. Heldke, 203–29. Bloomington: Indiana University Press, 1992.

Hern, Mary Ellen. "Picknicking in the Northeastern United States, 1840–1900." *Winterthur Portfolio* 24, nos. 2–3 (1989): 139–52.

Hess, John L., and Karen Hess. *The Taste of America.* 1972. Urbana: University of Illinois Press, 2000.

Hicks, Tai. "Harvesting Care: CASA Community Garden Provides Fresh Vegetables to Elderly and Homebound." *Huntsville (Ala.) Times,* July 2, 2001.

Hochschild, Arlie Russell, with Anne Machung. *The Second Shift.* New York: Avon Books, 1989.

Holcomb, Eric L. "Baltimore Municipal Markets." Openair-Market Net. http://www.openair.org/cyjour/baltmars.html.

Holmberg, Allan R. *Nomads of the Long Bow: The Siriono of Eastern Bolivia.* Institute of Social Anthropology, Smithsonian Institution. Washington, D.C.: U.S. Government Printing Office, 1950.

Holzschuher, Louisa. "Not So Fast." *Oakland Tribune,* August 4, 1999.

Honoré, Carl. *In Praise of Slowness: Challenging the Cult of Speed.* New York: Harper Collins, 2004.

Hoover, Ken. "Berkeley School Lunches Are First in Nation to Go Organic." *San Francisco Chronicle,* August 19, 1999.

Hughes, Marvalene H. "Soul, Black Women, and Food." In Counihan and Van Esterik, *Food and Culture,* 272–80.

Hymowitz, Kay S. "Quality Time Is Authority Time." *New York Times,* May 13, 2000.

Hynes, H. Patricia. *A Patch of Eden: America's Inner-City Gardens.* White River Junction, Vt.: Chelsea Green, 1996.

Ireland, Lynne. "The Compiled Cookbook as Foodways Autobiography." In Shortridge and Shortridge, *Taste of American Place,* 111–17.

Jacobs, Jane. "Market Nurturing Run Amok." Openair-Market Net, October 1995. http://www.openair.org/cyjour/jacobs.html.

Jacobs, Jerry A., and Kathleen Gerson. *The Time Divide: Work, Family and Gender Inequality.* Cambridge, Mass.: Harvard University Press, 2004.

Jenks, Jeremiah W., and W. Jett Lauck. *The Immigration Problem.* New York: Funk and Wagnalls, 1926.

Jerome, Norge W. "Frozen (TV) Dinners: The Staple Emergency Meals of a Changing Modern Society." In *Food in Perspective,* edited by Alexander Fenton and Trefor M. Owen, 145–56. Edinburgh: John Donald, 1981.

Joannes, Francis. "The Social Function of Banquets in the Earliest Civilizations." In *Food: A Culinary History from Antiquity to the Present,* edited by Jean-Louis Flandrin and Massimo Montanari, English ed. by Albert Sonnenfeld, 32–37. New York: Penguin, 2000.

Kalcik, Susan. "Ethnic Foodways in America: Symbol and the Performance of Identity." In Brown and Mussell, *Ethnic and Regional Foodways,* 37–65.

Kao, Mary Uyematsu. "Ma's Killer Won-Ton Soup." *Amerasia Journal* 32, no. 2 (2006): 109–14.

Kaplan, Anne R., Marjorie A. Hoover, and Willard B. Moore. "Introduction: On Ethnic Foodways." In Shortridge and Shortridge, *Taste of American Place,* 121–34.

Kasson, John F. *Rudeness and Civility: Manners in Nineteenth-Century Urban America.* New York: Hill and Wang, 1990.

Kathlene, Lyn. "Alternative Views of Crime: Legislative Policymaking in Gendered Terms." *Journal of Politics* 57 (1995): 696–723.

———. "Power and Influence in State Legislative Policymaking: The Interaction of Gender and Position in Committee Hearing Debates." *American Political Science Review* 99, no. 3 (1994): 560–76.

Katrak, Ketu H. "Food and Belonging: At 'Home' in 'Alien Kitchens.'" In Avakian, *Through the Kitchen Window,* 263–75.

Kavasch, E. Barrie. "My Grandmother's Hands." In Avakian, *Through the Kitchen Window,* 104–8.

Keller, Terry. "Gardening Changes a Community." In Flagler and Poincelot, *People-Plant Relationships,* 177–83.

Kennedy, Randall. "The Case against Civility." *American Prospect* 9, no. 41 (November 1988): 84–90.

Kerber, Linda K. *Women of the Republic: Intellect and Ideology in Revolutionary America.* Chapel Hill: University of North Carolina Press, 1980.

Kiang, Peter Nien-chu, and Chalsa M. Loo. "Food in Racial Experiences of Asian American Pacific Islander Vietnam Veterans." *Amerasia Journal* 32, no. 2 (2006): 7–20.

Kiefer, Joseph, and Martin Kemple, eds. *Digging Deeper: Integrating Youth Gardens into Schools and Communities.* Montpelier, Vt.: Common Roots Press, 1998.

Kingsolver, Barbara. *Animal, Vegetable, Miracle: A Year of Food Life.* New York: Harper Collins, 2007.

Korsmeyer, Carolyn. *Making Sense of Taste: Food and Philosophy.* Ithaca, N.Y.: Cornell University Press, 1999.

Krantz, David S. "A Naturalistic Study of Social Influences on Meal Size among Moderately Obese and Nonobese Subjects." *Psychosomatic Medicine* 41, no. 1 (February 1979): 19–27.

Krieger, Lisa M. "School Lunch Revolution." *San Francisco Examiner,* September 22, 1996.

Kruger, Steven F. "'Get Fat, Don't Die!': Eating and AIDS in Gay Men's Culture." In Scapp and Seitz, *Eating Culture,* 36–59.

Lareau, Annette. "Invisible Inequality: Social Class and Childrearing in Black Families and White Families." *American Sociological Review* 67, no. 5 (October 2002): 747–76.

Latane, Bibb, and Liane D. Bidwell. "Sex and Affiliation in Cafeterias." *Personality and Social Psychology Bulletin* 3, no. 4 (1977): 571–74.

Laudan, Rachel. "A Plea for Culinary Modernism: Why We Should Love New, Fast, Processed Food." *Gastronomica: The Journal of Food and Culture* (February 2001): 36–44.

Lawson, Laura. "The Planner in the Garden: The Relationship between Planning and Urban Garden Programs, 1890s to 1990s." Paper presented at the conference of the Society for American City and Regional Planning History, November 1999.

Lawson, Laura, and Marcia McNally. "Putting Teens at the Center: Maximizing Public Utility of Urban Space through Youth Involvement in Planning and Employment." *Children's Environments* 12, no. 2 (1995): 209–21.

Levenstein, Harvey A. *Revolution at the Table: The Transformation of the American Diet.* New York: Oxford University Press, 1988.

Lévi-Strauss, Claude. *The Raw and the Cooked.* Translated by John and Doreen Weightman. New York: Harper and Row, 1969.

Lewis, George H. "The Maine Lobster as Regional Icon: Competing Images over Time and Social Class." In Shortridge and Shortridge, *Taste of American Place,* 65–84.

Lim, Shirley Geok-lin. "Boiled Chicken Feet and Hundred-Year-Old Eggs: Poor Chinese Feasting." In Avakian, *Through the Kitchen Window,* 217–25.

Lloyd, Timothy C. "The Cincinnati Chili Culinary Complex." In Shortridge and Shortridge, *Taste of American Place,* 45–56.

Locke, John L. *Why We Don't Talk to Each Other Anymore: The De-voicing of Society.* New York: Touchstone, 1998.

Lockwood, Yvonne R., and William G. Lockwood. "Pasties in Michigan's Upper Peninsula: Foodways, Interethnic Relations, and Regionalism." In Shortridge and Shortridge, *Taste of American Place,* 21–36.

Luard, Elisabeth. *Sacred Food: Cooking for Spiritual Nourishment.* Chicago: Chicago Review Press, 2001.

Lukanuski, Mary. "A Place at the Counter: The Onus of Oneness." In Scapp and Seitz, *Eating Culture*, 112–20.

Luxton, Meg. *More than a Labour of Love: Three Generations of Women's Work in the Home.* Toronto: Woman's Press, 1980.

Macedo, Stephen, et al. *Democracy at Risk: How Political Choices Undermine Citizen Participation and What We Can Do about It.* Washington, D.C.: Brookings Institution Press, 2005.

Madison, Deborah. "Native Chiles in Santa Fe." In *Slow Food: Collected Thoughts on Taste, Tradition, and the Honest Pleasure of Food,* edited by Carlo Petrini, 108–11. White River Junction, Vt.: Chelsea Green, 2001.

Magliocco, Sabina. "Playing with Food: The Negotiation of Identity in the Ethnic Display Event by Italian Americans in Clinton, Indiana." In Shortridge and Shortridge, *Taste of American Place,* 145–62.

Manton, Catherine. *Fed Up: Women and Food in America.* Westport, Conn.: Bergin and Garvey, 1999.

Martin, Judith. *Star-Spangled Manners: In Which Miss Manners Defends American Etiquette (for a Change).* New York: Norton, 2003.

Martinac, Paula. "Fast, Free Delivery." In Avakian, *Through the Kitchen Window,* 162–68.

Matthews, Glenna. *"Just a Housewife": The Rise and Fall of Domesticity in America.* New York: Oxford, 1987.

Mauss, Marcel. *The Gift: The Form and Reason for Exchange in Archaic Societies.* 1950. Translated by W. D. Halls. New York: Norton, 1990.

May, Meredith. "Lunch Going Organic." *San Francisco Chronicle,* August 17, 1999.

———. "Souped Up School Food." *San Francisco Chronicle,* February 7, 2001.

McCarthy, B., and K. Straus. "Tastes of America 1992: Who in America Eats Out? Why Do They? What Are They Eating?" *Restaurants and Institutions* 102, no. 29 (December 1992): 24–44.

McNamee, Thomas. *Alice Waters and Chez Panisse: The Romantic, Impractical, Often Eccentric, Ultimately Brilliant Making of a Food Revolution.* New York: Penguin, 2007.

McPhee, John. "Giving Good Weight." In *Giving Good Weight,* 3–73. New York: Farrar, Straus and Giroux, 1979.

Miller, Stephen. *Conversation: A History of a Declining Art.* New Haven, Conn.: Yale University Press, 2006.

Milner, Henry. *Civic Literacy: How Informed Citizens Make Democracy Work.* Hanover, N.H.: University Press of New England, 2002.

Minnich, Elizabeth Kamarach. "But Really, There Are No Recipes . . ." In Avakian, *Through the Kitchen Window,* 134–47.

Morse, Rob. "A Tale of 2 Farmers' Markets." *San Francisco Chronicle,* April 25, 2003.

———. "What If They Don't Go Home?" *San Francisco Examiner,* June 22, 1997.

Murcott, Anne. "'It's a Pleasure to Cook for Him': Food, Mealtimes and Gender in Some South Wales Households." In *The Public and the Private,* edited by Eva Garmarnikow, David H. J. Morgan, Jane Purvis, and Daphne Taylorson, 78–90. London: Heinemann, 1983.

Murdoch, Iris. *The Sovereignty of Good.* New York: Schocken, 1971.

Nemore, Carole. "Rooted in Community: Community Gardens in New York." A report to the New York State Senate, 1997. http://www.cityfarmer.org.

Nestle, Marion. *Food Politics: How the Food Industry Influences Nutrition and Health.* Berkeley: University of California Press, 2002.

Neustadt, Kathy. *Clambake: A History and Celebration of an American Tradition.* Amherst: University of Massachusetts Press, 1992.

Novak, Robert, ed. *To Empower People: From State to Civil Society.* Washington D.C.: American Enterprise Institute Press, 1996.

Newton, Kenneth. "Social Capital and Democracy." In *Beyond Tocqueville: Civil Society and the Social Capital Debate in Comparative Perspective,* edited by Bob Edwards, Michael W. Foley, and Mario Diani, 225–34. Hanover, N.H.: University Press of New England, 2001.

Oakley, Ann. *The Sociology of Housework.* New York: Pantheon Books, 1974.

O'Connell, Brian. *Civil Society: The Underpinnings of American Democracy.* Hanover, N.H.: University Press of New England, 1999.

Oliver, Kelly. "Nourishing the Speaking Subject: A Psychoanalytic Approach to Abominable Food and Women." In *Cooking, Eating, Thinking: Transformative Philosophies of Food,* edited by Deane W. Curtin and Lisa M. Heldke, 68–84. Bloomington: Indiana University Press, 1992.

O'Neill, Brenda, and Elisabeth Gidengil, eds. *Gender and Social Capital.* New York: Routledge, 2006.

O'Neill, Molly. "Food: Market Value." *New York Times,* June 9, 1996.

———. "Sharing in the Harvest: Urban Living Off the Land." *New York Times,* July 9, 1997.

Orbach, Susie. *Fat Is a Feminist Issue.* New York: Paddington, 1978.

Palmer, Jonna. "Trading Tater Tots for Salad at Lunch." *Oakland Tribune,* August 18, 1999.

Passin, Herbert, and John W. Bennett. "Social Process and Dietary Change." In *The Problem of Changing Food Habits,* Bulletin of the National Research Council no. 108. Washington, D.C.: National Research Council, 1943.

Patel, Ishwarbhai C. "Gardening's Socioeconomic Impacts." *Journal of Extension* (Winter 1991): 7–8.

Pateman, Carole. "Feminist Critiques of the Public/Private Dichotomy." In *The Disorder of Women: Democracy, Feminism and Political Theory,* edited by Carole Pateman, 118–40. Stanford, Calif.: Stanford University Press, 1989.

———. *The Sexual Contract.* Stanford, Calif.: Stanford University Press, 1988.

Patterson, Michael O. "Greening of Harlem." *City Farmer,* 1996. http://www.cityfarmer.org.

Payne, Karen. "Listening with Respect: Issues of Class and Race in Working the Land." In Kiefer and Kemple, *Digging Deeper,* 40–41.

Pendleton, Julie. "Pure Alice." *Alta Bates Connection* 3, no. 5 (Spring 1988): 10–14.

Pesquera, Beatrice. "Work and Family: A Comparative Analysis of Professional, Clerical and Blue Collar Chicana Workers." Ph.D. diss., Department of Sociology, University of California, Berkeley, 1986.

Petrini, Carlo. *Slow Food: The Case for Taste.* New York: Columbia University Press, 2001.

Phillips, Anne. "Does Feminism Need a Conception of Civil Society?" In Chambers and Kymlicka, *Alternative Conceptions of Civil Society,* 71–89.

"Picnic Excursions." *Appleton's* (1869).

Pilcher, Jeffrey M. *¡Que vivan los Tamales! Food and the Making of Mexican Identity.* Albuquerque: University of New Mexico Press, 1998.

Pillsbury, Richard. *From Boarding House to Bistro: The American Restaurant Then and Now.* Boston: Unwin Hyman, 1990.

Plato. *The Symposium.* In *The Republic and Other Works,* translated by B. Jowett, 317–65. New York: Doubleday, 1960.

Pleck, Joseph H. *Working Wives/Working Husbands.* Beverly Hills, Calif.: Sage, 1985.

Pogrebin, Letty Cottin. "Mother I Hardly Knew You." In Avakian, *Through the Kitchen Window,* 83–88.

Pollan, Michael. *The Omnivore's Dilemma: A Natural History of Four Meals.* New York: Penguin, 2006.

Post, Robert C., and Nancy L. Rosenblum, eds. *Civil Society and Government.* Princeton, N.J.: Princeton University Press, 2001.

Powdermaker, Hortense. "Feasts in New Ireland: The Social Functions of Eating." *American Anthropologist* 34, no. 2 (April–June 1932): 236–47.

Presser, Harriet. *Toward a 24-Hour Economy.* New York: Russell Sage Foundation, 2003.

Pruyne, R. "Gardening for the Health of It." *Pennsylvania State Agriculture* (Fall–Winter 1994): 34–40.

Putnam, Robert. *Bowling Alone: The Collapse and Revival of American Community.* New York: Simon and Schuster, 2000.

Quandt, Sara A. "Infant and Child Nutrition." In *The Cambridge World History of Food,* vol. 2, edited by Kenneth F. Kiple and Kriemhild Conee Ornelas, 1444–53. Cambridge: Cambridge University Press, 2000.

Randall, Margaret. "What My Tongue Knows." In Avakian, *Through the Kitchen Window,* 83–88.

Rathbone, Diana. "Tough Guys Do Garden: Former Inmates Weed Out the Bad in Their Lives." *San Francisco Chronicle,* July 18, 2001.

Raun, Andy. "Vendors Bring Summer's Bounty to Dinner Table." *Hastings (Neb.) Tribune,* August 21, 1995.

Reardon, Joan. *M. F. K. Fisher, Julia Child and Alice Waters: Celebrating the Pleasures of the Table.* New York: Harmony Books, 1994.

Reich, Robert B. *The Future of Success: Working and Living in the New Economy*. New York: Vintage, 2002.

Rice, Jay Stone, and Linda L. Remy. "Evaluating Horticultural Therapy: The Ecological Context of Urban Jail Inmates." In Flagler and Poincelot, *People-Plant Relationships*, 203–24.

Rich, Deborah K. "Cultivating School Grounds: Elementary School Garden a Good Place for Kids to Put Down Roots." *San Francisco Chronicle*, May 8, 2002.

Richards, Audrey. *Hunger and Work in a Savage Tribe*. Glencoe, N.Y.: Free Press, 1948.

———. *Land, Labour and Diet among the Bemba of Northern Rhodesia*. London: Oxford University Press, 1939.

Riddle, Dean. "The Edible Schoolyard." Article provided by Alice Waters's office, pp. 98–104.

Ritchie, Tori. "American Piazza." *San Francisco Magazine* (June 1999): 74–81.

Ritzer, George. *The McDonaldization of Society*. Newbury Park, Calif.: Pine Forge Press, 1993.

Root, Waverly, and Richard de Rochemont. *Eating in America: A History*. 1976. New York: Random House, 2001.

Rosenblum, Nancy. *Membership and Morals: The Personal Uses of Pluralism in America*. Princeton, N.J.: Princeton University Press, 1998.

Roth, Geneen. *Breaking Free from Compulsive Eating*. New York: Signet, 1984.

———. *Feeding the Hungry Heart*. New York: Signet, 1982.

———. *When Food Is Love*. New York: Plume, 1991.

Rozin, Paul. "Sociocultural Influences on Human Food Selection." In *Why We Eat What We Eat*, edited by Elizabeth Capaldi, 233–63. Washington, D.C.: American Psychological Association, 1996.

Ruddick, Sara. *Maternal Thinking: Toward a Politics of Peace*. Boston: Beacon Press, 1989.

Ruether, Rosemary Radford. "Misogynism and Virginal Feminism in the Fathers of the Church." In *Woman in Western Thought*, edited by Martha Lee Osborne, 62–65. New York: Random House, 1979.

Salamon, Julie. "It's Always Saturday on TV." *New York Times*, February 2, 2001.

Sandalow, Marc. "Republicans Rooting Around in S.F. Garden Project," *San Francisco Chronicle*, May 31, 1996.

Scapp, Ron, and Brian Seitz, eds. *Eating Culture*. Albany: State University of New York Press, 1998.

Schambra, William A. "The Progressive Assault of Civic Community." In *The Essential Civil Society Reader: Classic Essays in the American Civil Society Debate*, edited by Don Eberly, 317–52. Lanham, Md.: Rowman and Littlefield, 2000.

Schlosser, Eric. *Fast Food Nation: The Dark Side of the All-American Meal*. New York: Harper Collins, 2002.

Schmidt, James. "Is Civility a Virtue?" In *Civility*, edited by Leroy S. Rouner, 17–39. Notre Dame, Ind.: University of Notre Dame Press, 2000.

Schor, Juliet. *The Overworked American: The Unexpected Decline of Leisure.* New York: Basic Books, 1992.

Schudson, Michael. *The Good Citizen: A History of American Civil Life.* Cambridge, Mass.: Harvard University Press, 1999.

———. "Why Conversation Is Not the Soul of Democracy." *Critical Studies in Mass Communication* 14 (1997): 297–309.

Schukoske, Jane E. "Community Development through Gardening: State and Local Policies Transforming Urban Open Space." *Journal of Legislation and Public Policy* 3, no. 2 (Spring 2000): 351–92.

Scott, Benjamin K. "Catherine Sneed to Present 1996 Linnemann Memorial Lecture," April 1996. http://www.coloradocollege.edu.

"Seeds of Hope . . . Harvest of Pride! A Resource for Community Vegetable Gardeners by Cultivating Our Community." Ohio State University Extension's Urban Gardening Program in Cuyahoga County. http://www.communitygarden.org/links/index.

Seligman, Adam B. *The Idea of Civil Society.* Princeton, N.J.: Princeton University Press, 1992.

Severson, Kim. "Food Joins Academic Menu in Berkeley School District." *San Francisco Chronicle,* August 29, 2004.

Shapiro, Ester Rebeca. "On Becoming a Cuban Jewish Cook: A Memoir with Recipes." In Avakian, *Through the Kitchen Window,* 169–82.

Shapiro, Laura. *Perfection Salad: Women and Cooking at the Turn of the Century.* New York: Random House, 2001.

Shepherd, Margaret. *The Art of Civilized Conversation: A Guide to Expressing Yourself with Style and Grace.* New York: Broadway Books, 2005.

Sheraton, Mimi. *From My Mother's Kitchen: Recipes and Reminiscences.* New York: Harper and Row, 1979.

———. "A Jewish Yen for Chinese." *New York Times Magazine,* September 23, 1990, 71.

Shortridge, Barbara G., and James R. Shortridge, eds. *The Taste of American Place: A Reader on Regional and Ethnic Foods.* New York: Rowman and Littlefield, 1998.

Simpson, David. "The Cult of 'Conversation.'" *Raritan* 16 (1997): 75–85.

Sine, Richard. "Farmer's Doubters." *Metro,* June 22–26, 1996.

Sirianni, Carmen, and Lewis Friedland. *Civic Innovation in America: Community Empowerment, Public Policy and the Movement for Civic Renewal.* Berkeley: University of California Press, 2001.

Skocpol, Theda. "Advocates without Members: The Recent Transformation of American Civil Life." In Skocpol and Fiorina, *Civic Engagement in American Democracy,* 461–509.

Skocpol, Theda, and Morris P. Fiorina, eds. *Civic Engagement in American Democracy.* Washington, D.C.: Brookings Institution Press, 1999.

Slow Food. http://www.slowfood.com.

Smith, Rebecca. "State Welfare Payments Going Electronic Route." *San Francisco Chronicle*, August 18, 1999.

Sneed, Catherine. "The Garden Project." *Whole Earth Magazine*, Winter 1998. http://www.wholearthmag.com.

Sombart, Werner. *Why Is There No Socialism in America?* 1906. Translated by Patricia M. Hocking and P. T. Husbands. White Plains, N.Y.: M. E. Sharpe, 1976.

Spiro, Melford E. "The Acculturation of American Ethnic Groups." *American Anthropologist* 57, no. 6 (December 1955): 1240–51.

Spitzer, Theodore Morrow, and Hilary Baum. *Public Markets and Community Revitalization*. Chapter 1, 1994. http://www.openair.org/cyjour/rvitone.html.

Squatriglia, Chuck. "Growing Gains." *San Francisco Chronicle*, March 11, 2002.

Stack, Carol. *All Our Kin*. 1974. New York: Basic Books, 1997.

Standage, Tom. *A History of the World in Six Glasses*. New York: Walker, 2005.

Steger, Pat. "Hillary and Chelsea Do Dinner." *San Francisco Chronicle*, November 26, 1997.

Sterngold, James. "Crash Witness Shocked, but Not Angry." *San Francisco Chronicle*, July 18, 2003.

Strasser, Susan. *Never Done: A History of American Housework*. New York: Pantheon Books, 1982.

Strongman, K. T., and R. N. Hughes. "Eating Style and Body Weight." *New Zealand Psychologist* 9, no. 2 (November 1980): 68–69, 84.

Sundelson, David. "After Quiche, What?" *Nation* 235, no. 9 (September 25, 1982): 277–78.

Swarns, Rachel L. "'African-American' Becomes a Term for Debate." *New York Times*, August 29, 2004.

Symons, Michael. *A History of Cooks and Cooking*. Urbana: University of Illinois Press, 2000.

Tannen, Deborah. *The Argument Culture: Moving from Debate to Dialogue*. New York: Random House, 1998.

———. *Conversational Style: Analyzing Talk among Friends*. Norwood, N.J.: Ablex, 1984.

Tonge, Peter. "Garden Gives Prison Inmates a Bridge to Outside World." *Christian Science Monitor*, July 3, 1980.

Toussaint-Samat, Maguelonne. *A History of Food*. 1987. Translated by Anthea Bell. Cambridge, Mass: Blackwell, 1994.

Tuchman, Gaye, and Harry Gene Levine. "New York Jews and Chinese Food: The Social Construction of an Ethnic Pattern." In Shortridge and Shortridge, *Taste of American Place*, 163–84.

United States Bureau of the Census. "America's Families and Living Arrangements: 2003 Population Characteristics." November 2004. http://www.census.gov/prod/2004pubs/p20–553.pdf.

———. *Statistical Abstract of the United States*. Washington, D.C.: U.S. Government Printing Office, 2002.

United States Department of Agriculture. Economic Research Service. "Food Consumption, Prices, and Expenditures, 1970–97." http://ers.usda.gov/publications/sb965/sb965e.

———. Economic Research Service. "Food Service Trends." *National Food Review,* 1987 Yearbook, 10–15.

———. "Facts about Farmers' Markets." http://www.ams.usda.gov/farmersmarkets/facts.html.

University of Illinois Extension. "Cook County Sheriff's Garden: A Patch of Paradise." 2000. http://www.urbanext.uiuc.edu.

Unterman, Patricia. "Savoring Slow Food." *San Francisco Chronicle,* December 31, 2000.

Vanek, Joann. "Time Spent in Housework." *Scientific American* 231 (1974): 116–20.

Vellinga, Mary Lynne. "Gardens Nurture a Sense of Community." *Sacramento Bee,* October 25, 1999.

Verba, Sidney, Kay Lehman Schlozman, and Henry Brady. *Voice and Equality: Civic Voluntarism in American Politics.* Cambridge, Mass.: Harvard University Press, 1995.

Visser, Margaret. *The Rituals of Dinner: The Origins, Evolution, Eccentricities and Meaning of Table Manners.* New York: Penguin, 1991.

Wade-Gayles, Gloria. "'Laying on Hands' through Cooking: Black Women's Majesty and Mystery in Their Own Kitchens." In Avakian, *Through the Kitchen Window,* 95–103.

Walker, Kathryn E., and Margaret E. Woods. *Time Use: A Measure of Household Production of Family Goods and Services.* Washington, D.C.: Center for the Family, American Home Economics Association, 1976.

Walsh, Katherine Cramer. *Talking about Politics: Informal Groups and Social Identity in American Life.* Chicago: University of Chicago Press, 2004.

Walzer, Michael. "The Idea of Civil Society: A Path to Social Reconstruction." In *Community Works: The Revival of Civil Society in America,* edited by E. J. Dionne Jr., 123–43. Washington, D.C.: Brookings Institution Press, 1998.

Wanning, Esther. "Profile: Catherine Sneed, Breaking the Cycle of Crime." *Bay Area Naturally,* Fall–Winter 2001. http://www.gardenproject.org.

Warner, Judith. *Perfect Madness: Motherhood in the Age of Anxiety.* New York: Riverhead Books, 2005.

Waters, Alice. *The Art of Simple Food: Notes, Lessons and Recipes from a Delicious Revolution.* New York: Clarkson Potter, 2007.

———. "Biography." Provided by her office, March 2001.

———. *Chez Panisse Menu Cookbook.* New York: Random House, 1982.

———. "The Ethics of Eating." Address Delivered at Mills College Commencement, Oakland, California, May 22, 1994.

———. "The Ethics of Eating, Part Two." Remarks presented at the 16th Annual Ecological Farming Conference, Asilomar, California, January 25, 1996.

———. "The Farm-Restaurant Connection." In *Our Sustainable Table,* edited by Robert Clark, 113–22. San Francisco: North Point Press, 1990.

———. "The Garden, the Table, and Educational Equality." Remarks presented at "A Garden in Every School: A Conference Promoting the Integration of Garden-Based Education, Cooking and Nutrition, and Sustainable Agriculture Awareness in Schools," Martin Luther King Jr. School, Berkeley, Calif., March 14, 1997.

———. Interview with Cynthia Gorney, *Forum,* KQED radio, San Francisco, August 20, 1999.

———. "Making Food the Educational Priority." Remarks for the American Institute of Wine and Food Conference "Children's Education: Feeding Our Future," no date (ca. 1996).

———. Remarks at a public hearing on nutrition objectives for school menus. United States Department of Agriculture, Los Angeles, October 27, 1993.

———. "StarChefs Interview with Alice Waters," 1997. http://www.starchefs.com/Awaters/inteview.html.

Waters, Christina. "Market Value." *Metro,* May 9–15, 1996.

"Waters Receives National Honor for 'Edible Schoolyard.'" *San Francisco Chronicle,* December 18, 1998.

"Waters to Speak at Strybing." *San Francisco Chronicle,* April 21, 1999.

Westmacott, Richard. *African-American Gardens and Yards in the Rural South.* Knoxville: University of Tennessee Press, 1998.

"The White House Conference on Teenagers: Raising Responsible and Resourceful Youth." Office of the Press Secretary, the White House, Washington, D.C., May 2, 2000. http://www.pub.whitehouse.gov.

Williams, Joan. *Unbending Gender: Why Family and Work Conflict and What to Do about It.* New York: Oxford University Press, 2000.

Williams-Forson, Psyche A. "'Suckin' the Chicken Bones Dry': African American Women, Fried Chicken, and the Power of a National Narrative." In *Cooking Lessons: The Politics of Gender and Food,* edited by Sherrie A. Inness, 169–91. New York: Rowman and Littlefield, 2001.

Winn, Steven. "A Delicious Revolution." *Modern Maturity* (July–August 2000): 27–29.

Witt, Doris. *Black Hunger: Food and the Politics of U.S. Identity.* New York: Oxford University Press, 1999.

Wolfe, Alan. *Whose Keeper? Social Science and Moral Obligation.* Berkeley: University of California Press, 1989.

Wood, Jim. "Beach Party Is Sure Sign Spring Is Here." *San Francisco Examiner,* April 3, 1996.

Young, Sharon. "Grower Profile: Angel Garcia." In *Abundant Harvest.* Fresno, Calif.: Sixth Street Press. http://www.openair.org/cyjour/abprof.html.

Zeldin, Theodore. *Conversation: How Talk Can Change Our Lives.* Mahwah, N.J.: HiddenSpring, 2000.

Zelinsky, Wilbur. *The Cultural Geography of the United States.* Englewood Cliffs, N.J.: Prentice Hall, 1973.

Index

....

13, 79–83; conversible world, 83–85, 99;
courtesy of, 14, 20–21, 79–80, 82, 99,
260; critics of, 83, 85; cult of, 83; cynical
chic, 9; dinner, 1, 8–9, 28, 96, 111–28, 218;
democratic, 14, 83, 88; emotional risk,
88; empirical studies of, 8–11; gender
differences, 9, 16, 84–85; group solidarity, 10; heterogeneous, 83; homogeneous,
83; imagination, 86; interaction work, 9;
intimate, 79, 85–86; legendary style, 9;
listening, 3, 8, 87, 93, 128–29, 235; parlors,
111; political evaporation, 10; problem-
solving, 83; public momism, 10; raillery,
84; rules of, 90, 95, 111–15, 241; schools,
244–46; scripted, 55; skills, 13–14, 19,
87–88, 174, 241, 244; sociable, 83–87; table,
11, 13, 18–21, 93, 113–14, 270–71, 275; voting
qualification, 14
conviviality: Alice Waters and, 189; coffee-
house, 8; conversation, 79, 86; gastronomy and, 167; Italian, 149; Slow Cities and
Slow Food, 38–39, 70; at table, 175
Cook, Esther, 244–45
cookbooks: Chez Panisse, 177–78, 203;
colonial, 58, 60–61, 108; Elizabeth David,
183; family, 51, 88, 175; Fanny Farmer, 71;
fundraising, 221, 223; James Beard, 110;
popularity of, 17; school 245
Cook County, Illinois, 262
cooking: classes, 17, 47, 223; compassion,
188; consumerism, 200; coordinative, 34;
family chore, 27, 33; family memories,
119, 130; gender, 32–35, 51–52, 67, 121, 140,
222; improvisational, 264–65; science
and, 92, 156–58; spiritual experience, 123;
technology, 27, 30, 60–62, 149; thoughtful
practice, 134, 146, 161; toxins 151–53
Cornish Americans, 217, 227
Cortez, Constance, 124
cosmopolitanism, 218, 220
Coss, Clare, 51
Counihan, Carole M., 140–41, 147–48
courtesy, 1, 14, 79, 82, 89, 91, 95, 187
Cowan, Ruth Schwartz, 26, 30–31
crawfish, 217–18, 290
cuisine: African American, 61, 62; concept
of, 161–62, 170; Middle Atlantic Quaker
and Dutch, 60–61; Native American,
57–60, 72, 108; New England, 57–61,

109, 219, 223, 227, 244, 257; Southern, 59,
61–62; Southwestern, 62–63
Cunningham, Marion, 71
Curtin, Deane W., 142
Curtis, Karen, 279n10

Dallas, Texas, 126, 258
Dash, Julie, 125
Da Vinci, Leonardo, 105
Davis, Maradee A., 280n14
Dean, Jodi, 7, 277n17
Dease, Melissa, 292n73
De Graaf, John, 279n28
De Guzman, Jean-Paul R., 290
delicious revolution: as revolution, 183–84;
Chez Panisse, 181–82, 191–96; children,
187–88; concept of, 2, 174–76; conversations, 189; delicious food, 178–81; family
meals, 188; jail gardens, 196–99; land,
184–86; local ingredients, 186; organic
ingredients, 185–86; responses to, 177–78;
school gardens, 199–204; school lunches,
204–10; seasonal food, 186
democracy: civility, 1–3, 20, 91; civil society,
2, 5–6, 11; concept of, 93; conversation, 1,
83, 93; deliberative, 6, 93; household 15,
20, 92; manners, 99; moral dispositions,
91; table, 14, 86, 112
Democrats, 198
DeMott, Benjamin, 91
Denmark, 37, 38, 113–14
Denver Urban Gardeners (DUG), 235, 242
De Rochemont, Richard, 284n30
Descartes, René, 145, 160, 165
Des Moines, Iowa, 120
DeTocqueville, Alexis, 5, 85
Detroit, 216, 231, 235, 240
DeVault, Marjorie L., 9, 33–34, 44, 46, 48,
54, 117, 119, 129
Dewey, John, 6, 162–63
De Wit, Cary W., 290
Diani, Mario, 277n1
Dickens, Charles, 85
Diderot, 5
diets: children's, 158, 206, 208, 246; dietary
guidelines, 204–5; dietary preferences, 16,
146; diet industry, 75, 158–61, 170, 271
dining rooms, 75, 102, 111, 113–14, 121, 125,
206, 221

JANET A. FLAMMANG is a professor and the chair of the department of Political Science at Santa Clara University. She is the author of *Women's Political Voice: How Women Are Transforming the Practice and Study of Politics,* co-author of *American Politics in a Changing World,* and the editor of *Political Women: Current Roles in State and Local Government.*

The University of Illinois Press
is a founding member of the
Association of American University Presses.
· ·

Composed in 10.5/13 Adobe Minion Pro
with Avenir LT Std display
at the University of Illinois Press
Designed by Kelly Gray
Manufactured by Sheridan Books, Inc.

University of Illinois Press
1325 South Oak Street
Champaign, IL 61820-6903
www.press.uillinois.edu

DA FEB 4 2011